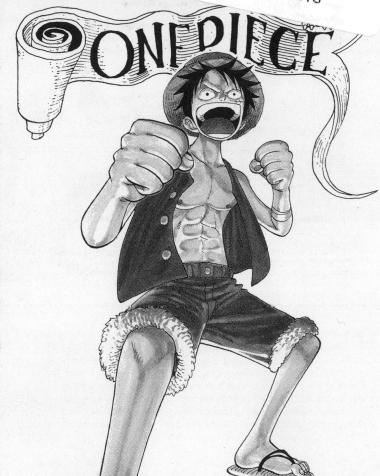

ONE PIECE

Vol. 18
ACE ARRIVES

STORY AND ART BY
EIICHIRO ODA

THE STORY OF ONE PIECE

Volume 18

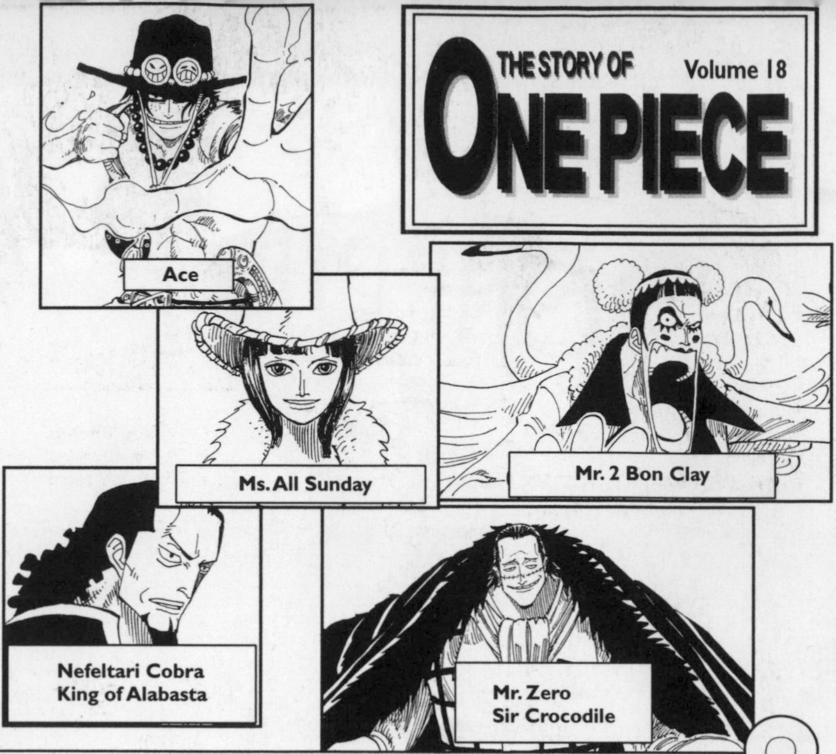
Ace
Ms. All Sunday
Mr. 2 Bon Clay
Nefeltari Cobra
King of Alabasta
Mr. Zero
Sir Crocodile

Monkey D. Luffy started out as just a kid with a dream—and that dream was to become the greatest pirate in history! Stirred by the tales of pirate "Red-Haired" Shanks, Luffy vowed to become a pirate himself. That was before the enchanted Devil Fruit gave Luffy the power to stretch like rubber, at the cost of being unable to swim—a serious handicap for an aspiring sea dog. Undeterred, Luffy set out to sea and recruited some crewmates: master swordsman Zolo, treasure-hunting thief Nami, lying sharpshooter Usopp, the high-kicking chef Sanji, and the latest addition Tony Tony Chopper—the walkin' talkin' man-reindeer doctor.

En route to Alabasta to help Princess Vivi save her kingdom, Luffy and crew have discovered a prehistoric island of giants and an island locked in perpetual winter. Now, having defeated the evil King Wapol and liberated Drum Island, they set sail once more, joined by the new ship's doctor, Chopper. The crew of the *Merry Go* is in a festive mood, but little do they suspect what dangers lie in store for them in the desert kingdom of Alabasta...

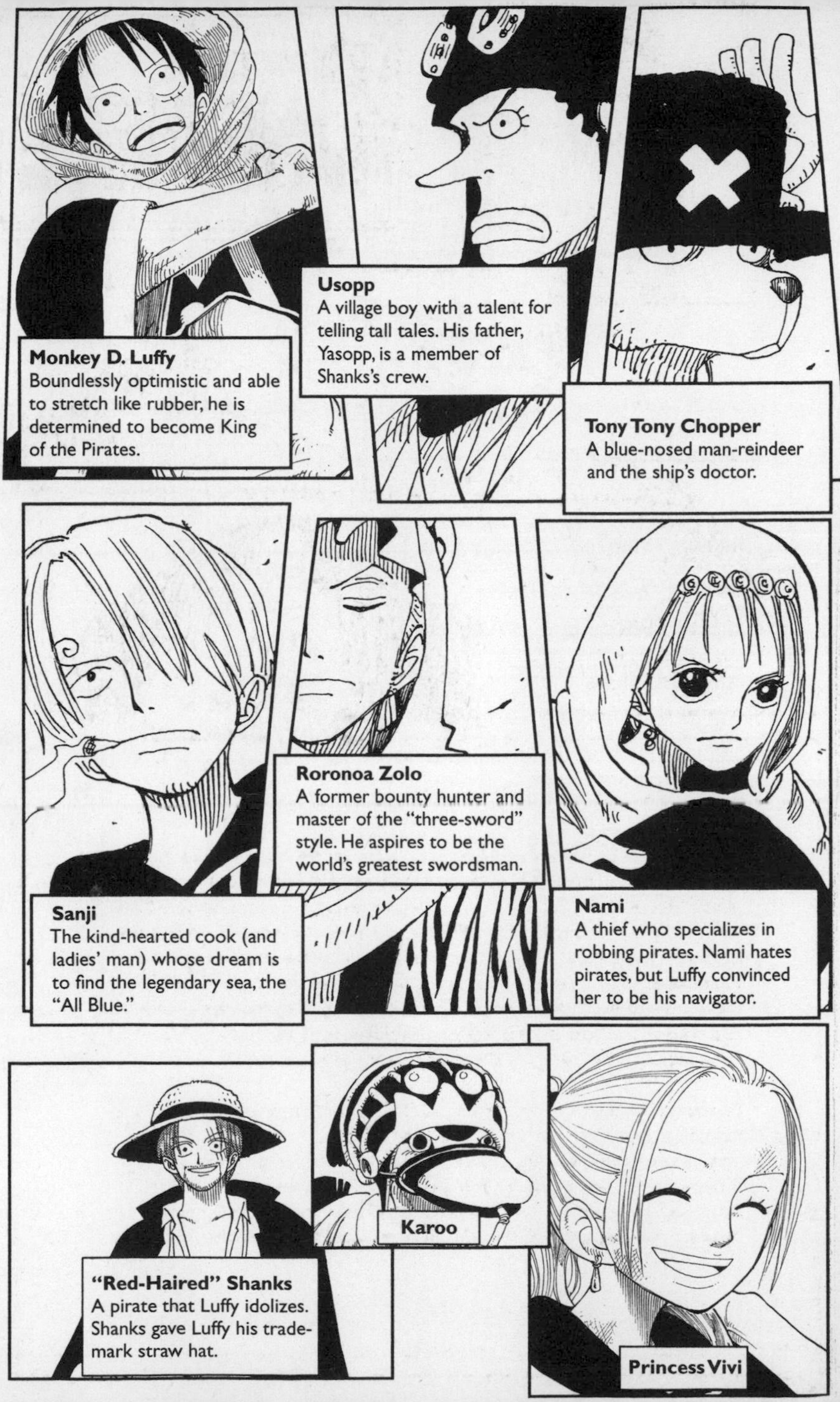
Tony Tony Chopper
A blue-nosed man-reindeer and the ship's doctor.
Usopp
A village boy with a talent for telling tall tales. His father, Yasopp, is a member of Shanks's crew.
Monkey D. Luffy
Boundlessly optimistic and able to stretch like rubber, he is determined to become King of the Pirates.
Nami
A thief who specializes in robbing pirates. Nami hates pirates, but Luffy convinced her to be his navigator.
Roronoa Zolo
A former bounty hunter and master of the "three-sword" style. He aspires to be the world's greatest swordsman.
Sanji
The kind-hearted cook (and ladies' man) whose dream is to find the legendary sea, the "All Blue."
Princess Vivi
Karoo
"Red-Haired" Shanks
A pirate that Luffy idolizes. Shanks gave Luffy his trademark straw hat.

BAROQUE WORKS

ONE PIECE

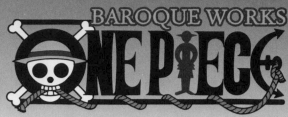

Vol. 18
Ace Arrives

CONTENTS

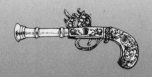

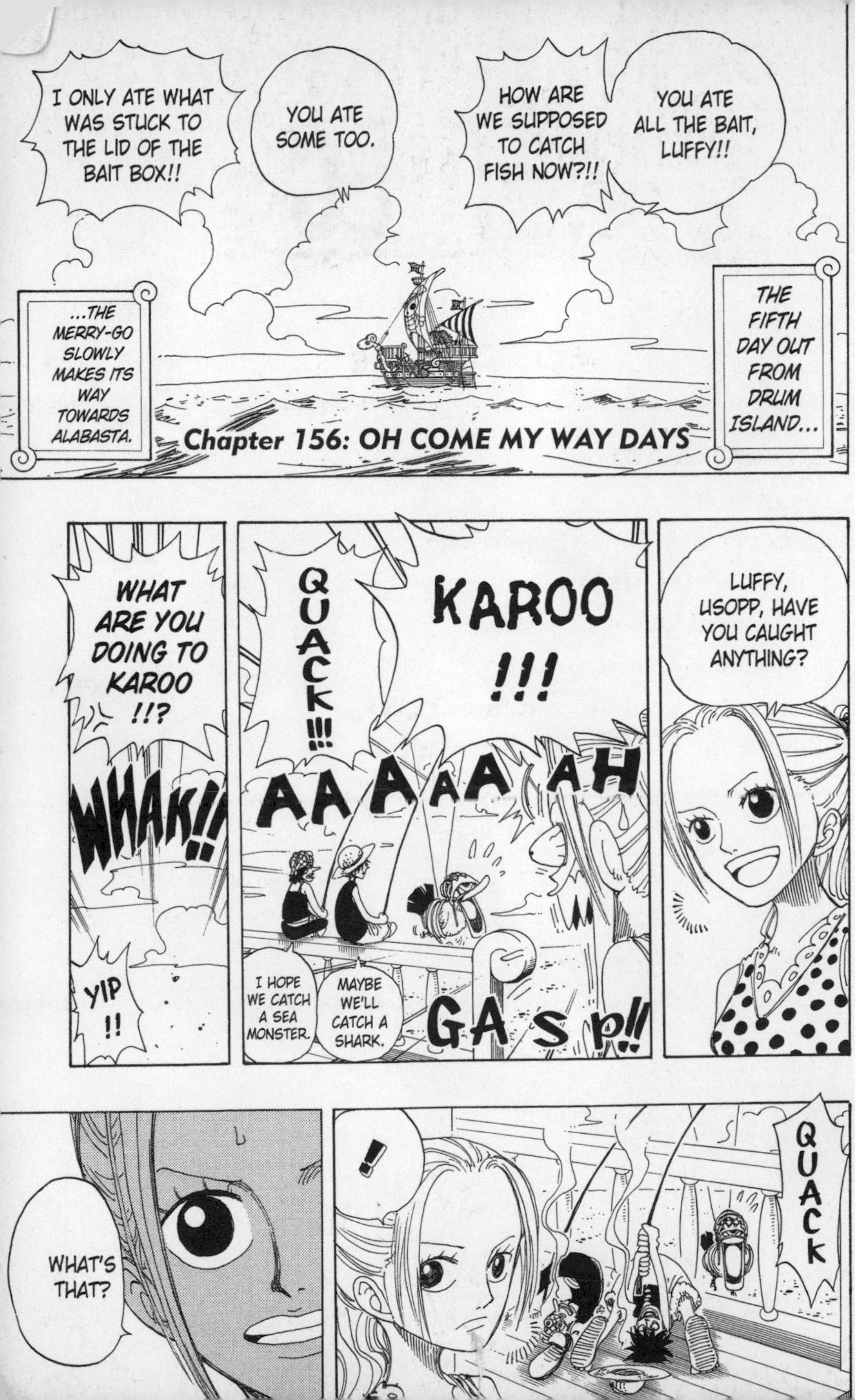
YOU ATE ALL THE BAIT, LUFFY!!
HOW ARE WE SUPPOSED TO CATCH FISH NOW?!!
YOU ATE SOME TOO.
I ONLY ATE WHAT WAS STUCK TO THE LID OF THE BAIT BOX!!
THE FIFTH DAY OUT FROM DRUM ISLAND...
...THE MERRY-GO SLOWLY MAKES ITS WAY TOWARDS ALABASTA.
Chapter 156: OH COME MY WAY DAYS
LUFFY, USOPP, HAVE YOU CAUGHT ANYTHING?
KAROO!!!
QUACK!!!
AAAAAH
MAYBE WE'LL CATCH A SHARK.
I HOPE WE CATCH A SEA MONSTER.
GASp!!
WHAT ARE YOU DOING TO KAROO!!?
WHAK!!
YIP!!
!
QUACK
WHAT'S THAT?

OH COME MY WAY DAYS

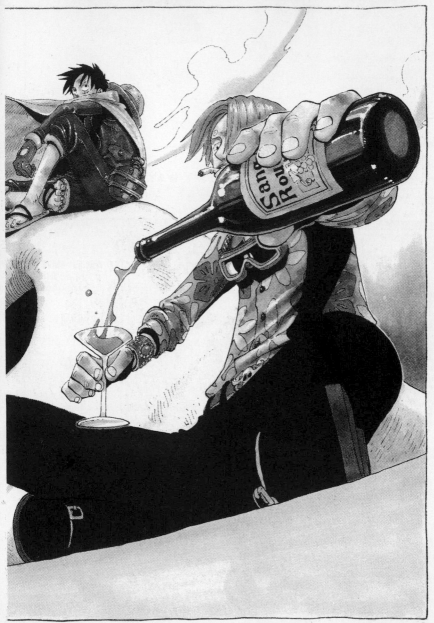

Chapter 156:

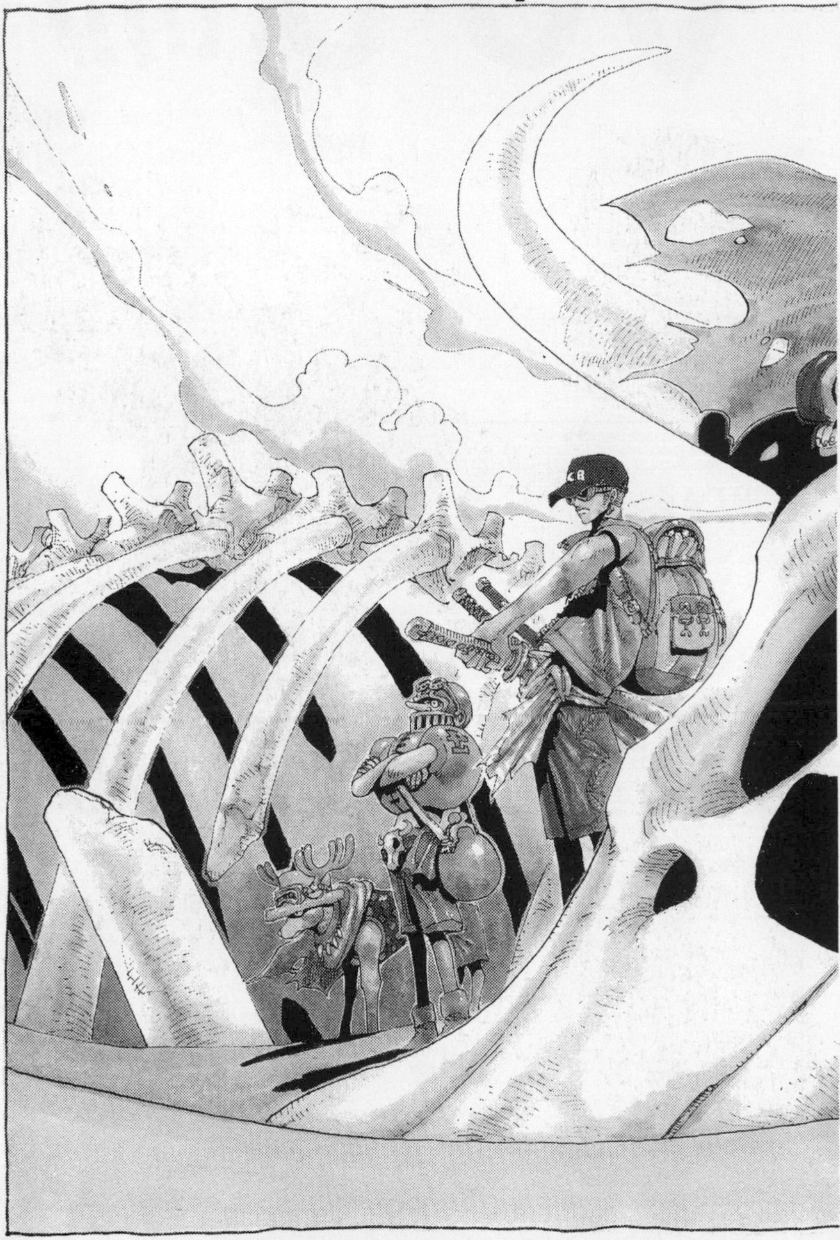
KB

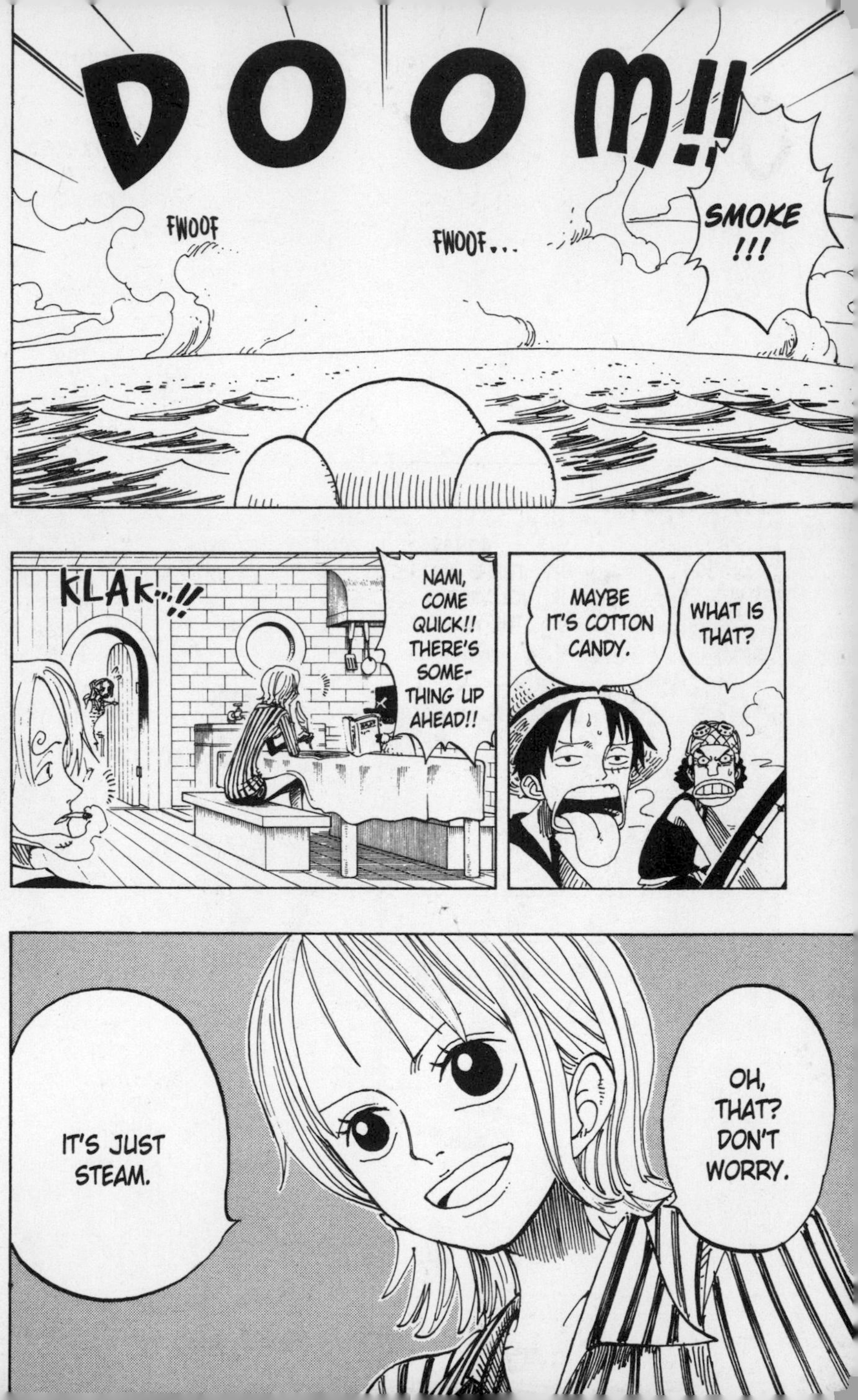
DOOM!!
SMOKE !!!
FWOOF...
FWOOF
WHAT IS THAT?
MAYBE IT'S COTTON CANDY.
NAMI, COME QUICK!! THERE'S SOME-THING UP AHEAD!!
KLAK..!!
OH, THAT? DON'T WORRY.
IT'S JUST STEAM.

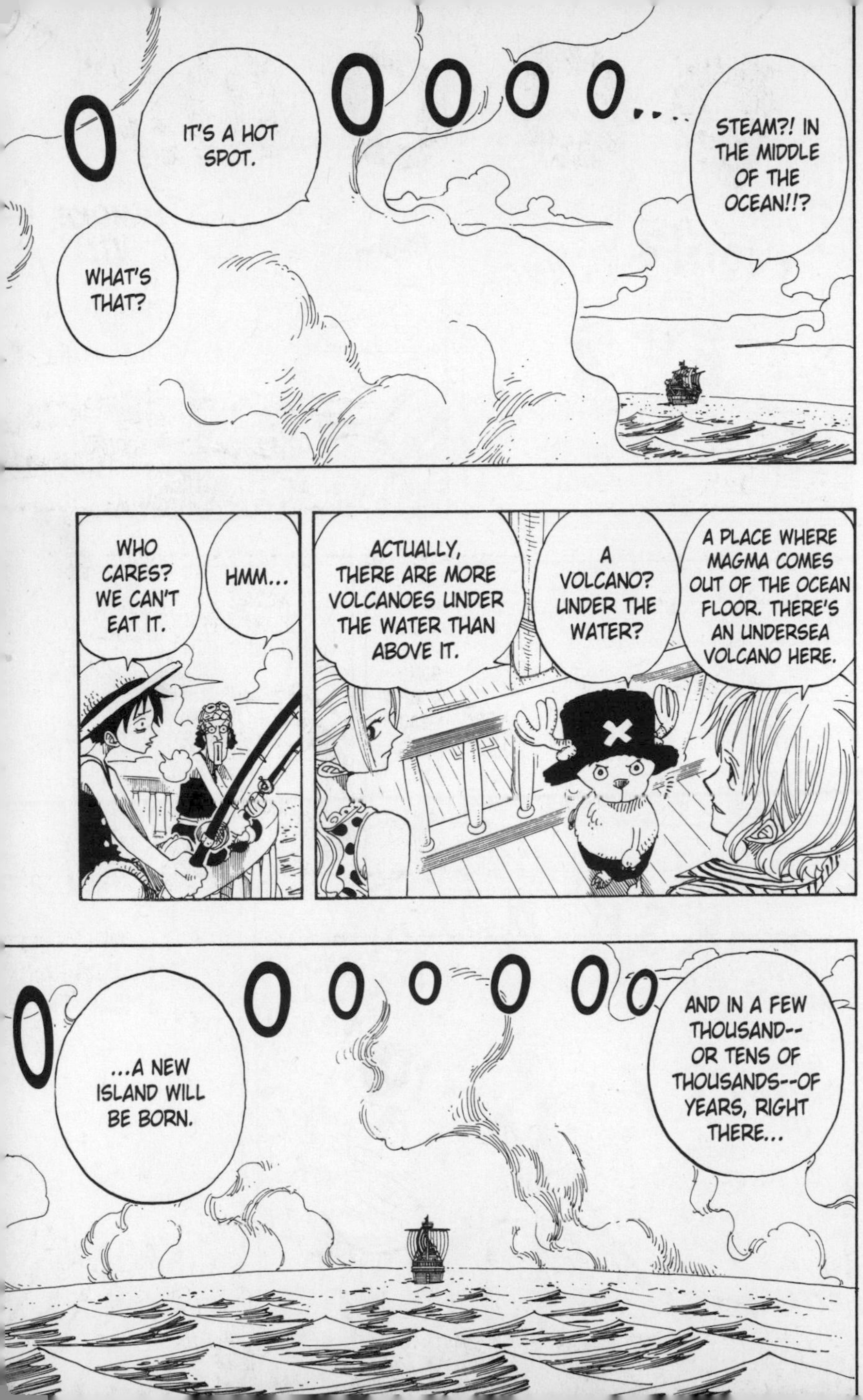
OOOOO...
STEAM?! IN THE MIDDLE OF THE OCEAN!!?
IT'S A HOT SPOT.
WHAT'S THAT?
A PLACE WHERE MAGMA COMES OUT OF THE OCEAN FLOOR. THERE'S AN UNDERSEA VOLCANO HERE.
A VOLCANO? UNDER THE WATER?
ACTUALLY, THERE ARE MORE VOLCANOES UNDER THE WATER THAN ABOVE IT.
HMM...
WHO CARES? WE CAN'T EAT IT.
OOOOOOO
AND IN A FEW THOUSAND-- OR TENS OF THOUSANDS--OF YEARS, RIGHT THERE...
...A NEW ISLAND WILL BE BORN.

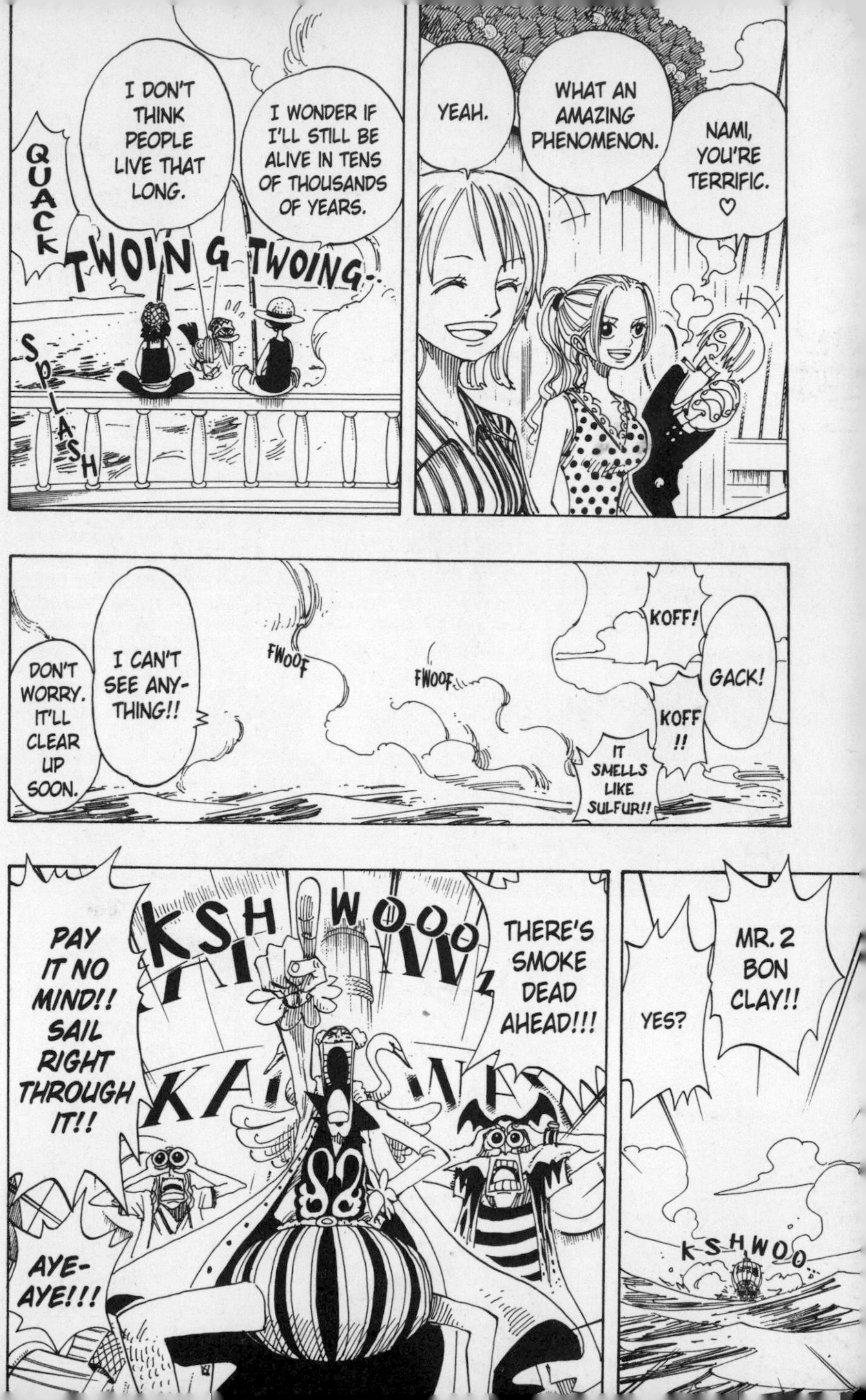
NAMI, YOU'RE TERRIFIC. ♡
WHAT AN AMAZING PHENOMENON.
YEAH.
I WONDER IF I'LL STILL BE ALIVE IN TENS OF THOUSANDS OF YEARS.
I DON'T THINK PEOPLE LIVE THAT LONG.
QUACK
TWOING TWOING
SPLASH
GACK!
KOFF!
KOFF !!
IT SMELLS LIKE SULFUR!!
FWOOF
FWOOF
I CAN'T SEE ANYTHING!!
DON'T WORRY. IT'LL CLEAR UP SOON.
MR. 2 BON CLAY!!
YES?
KSHWOO
THERE'S SMOKE DEAD AHEAD!!!
KSHWOOO
PAY IT NO MIND!! SAIL RIGHT THROUGH IT!!
AYE-AYE!!!

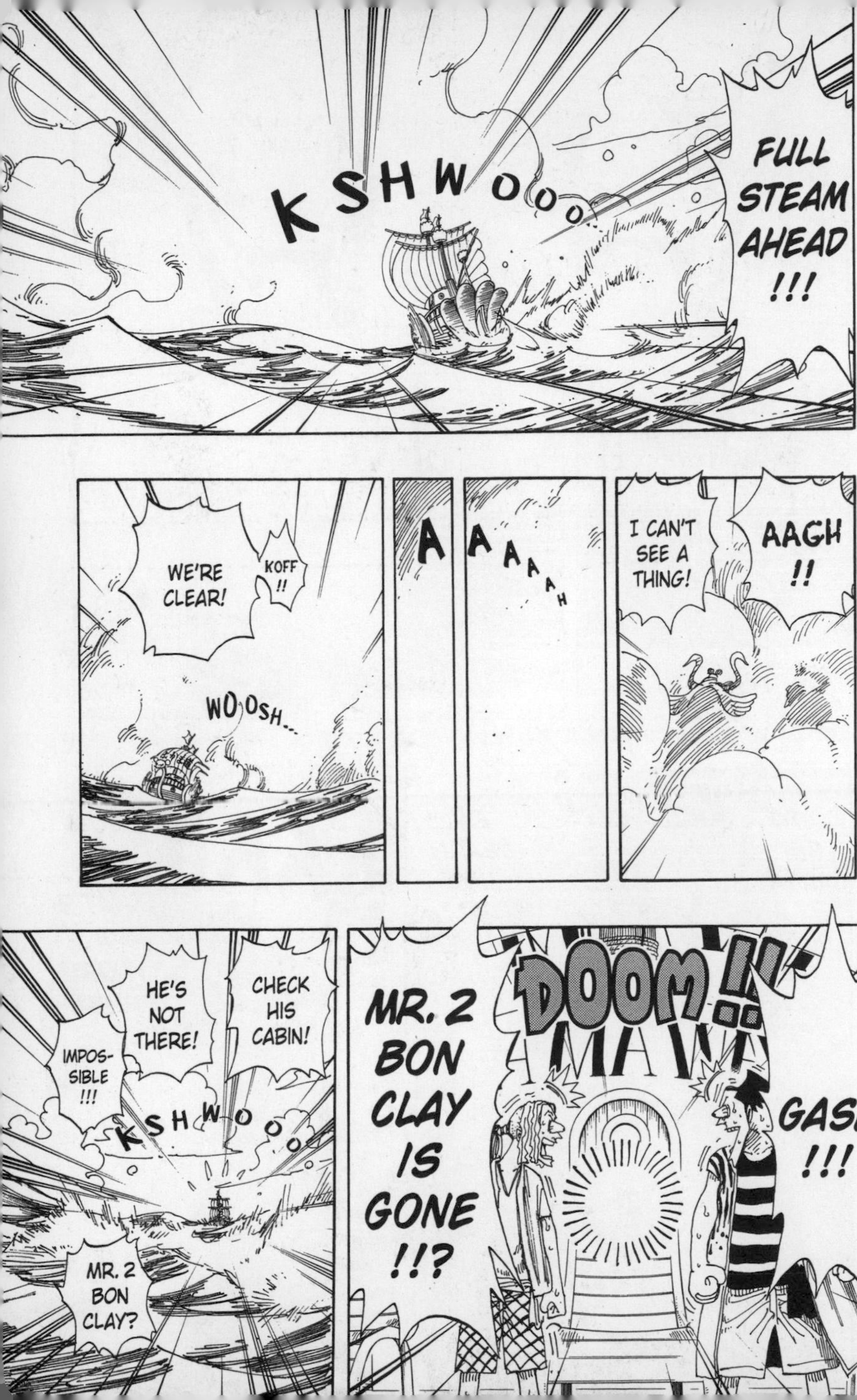
FULL STEAM AHEAD !!!
KSHWOOO..
AAGH !!
I CAN'T SEE A THING!
AAAAAH
KOFF !!
WE'RE CLEAR!
WOOSH...
GASP !!!
DOOM !!
MR. 2 BON CLAY IS GONE !!?
CHECK HIS CABIN!
HE'S NOT THERE!
IMPOS-SIBLE !!!
KSHWOOO
MR. 2 BON CLAY?

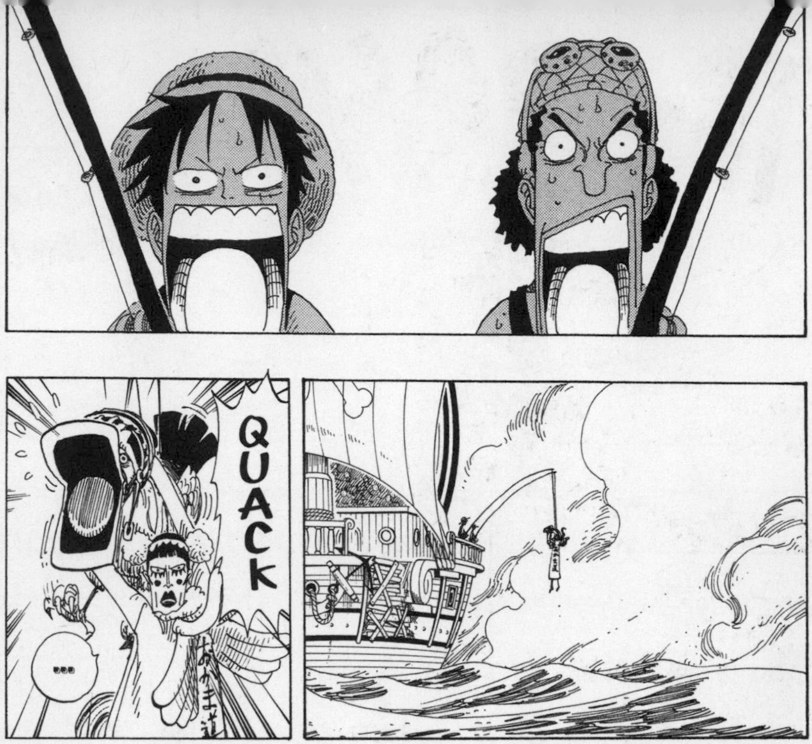
QUACK
...

*TEXT ON JACKET SAYS "OH COME MY WAY" - Ed.

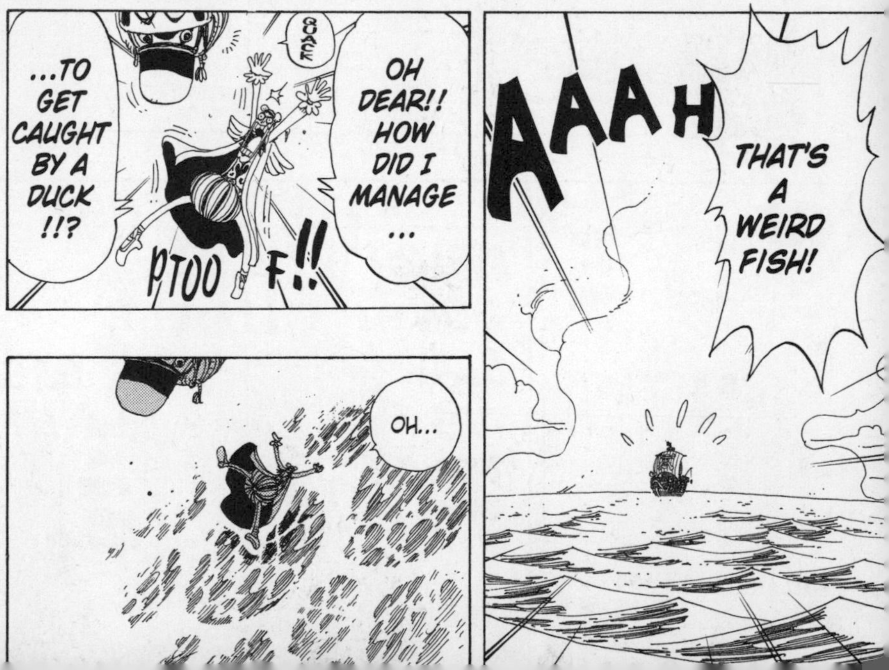
AAAH
THAT'S A WEIRD FISH!
QUACK
OH DEAR!! HOW DID I MANAGE ...
...TO GET CAUGHT BY A DUCK !!?
PTOOF!!
OH...

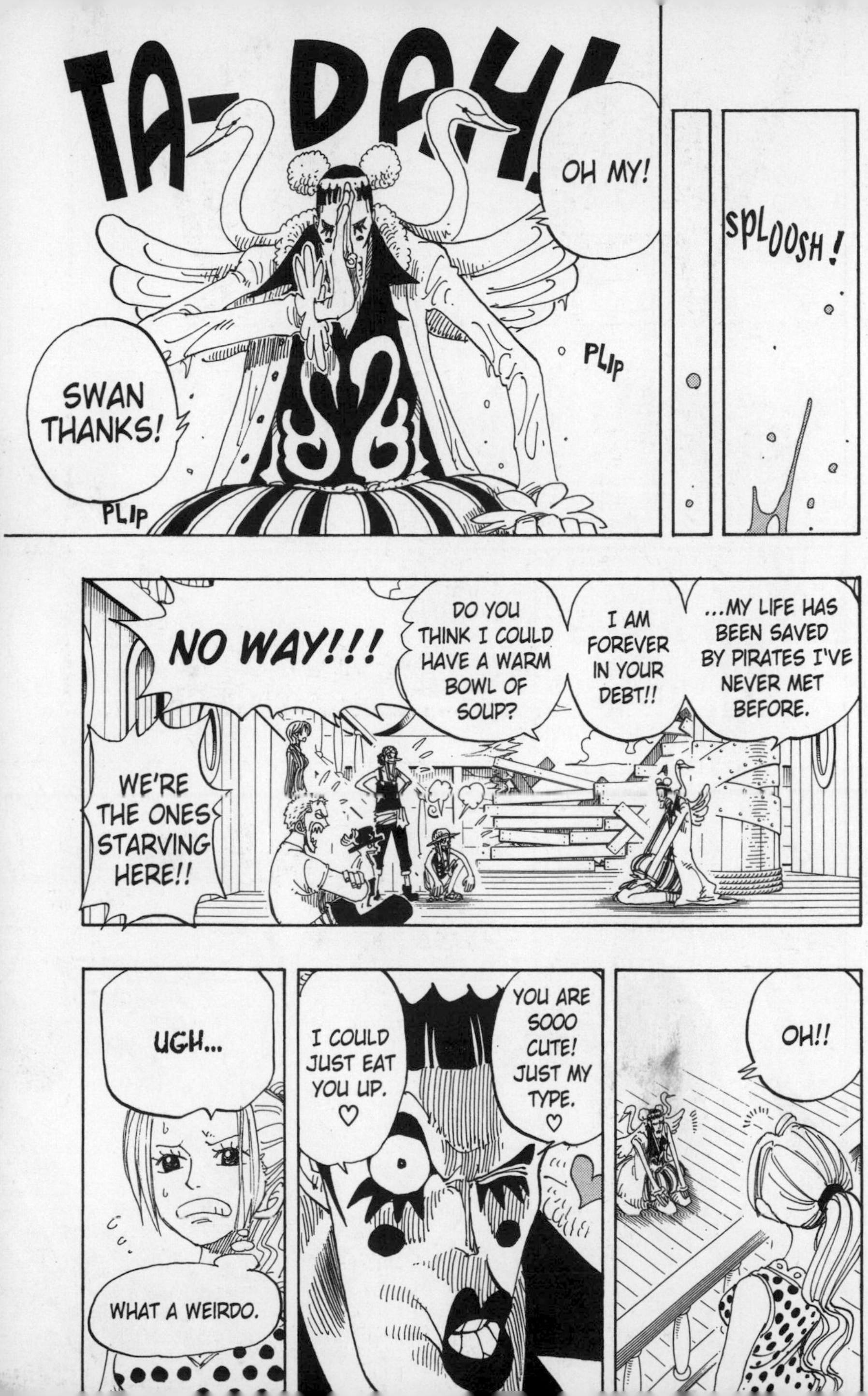

SPLOOSH!
OH MY!
TA-DAH!
PLIP
SWAN THANKS!
PLIP
...MY LIFE HAS BEEN SAVED BY PIRATES I'VE NEVER MET BEFORE.
I AM FOREVER IN YOUR DEBT!!
DO YOU THINK I COULD HAVE A WARM BOWL OF SOUP?
NO WAY!!!
WE'RE THE ONES STARVING HERE!!
OH!!
YOU ARE SOOO CUTE! JUST MY TYPE. ♡
I COULD JUST EAT YOU UP. ♡
UGH...
WHAT A WEIRDO.

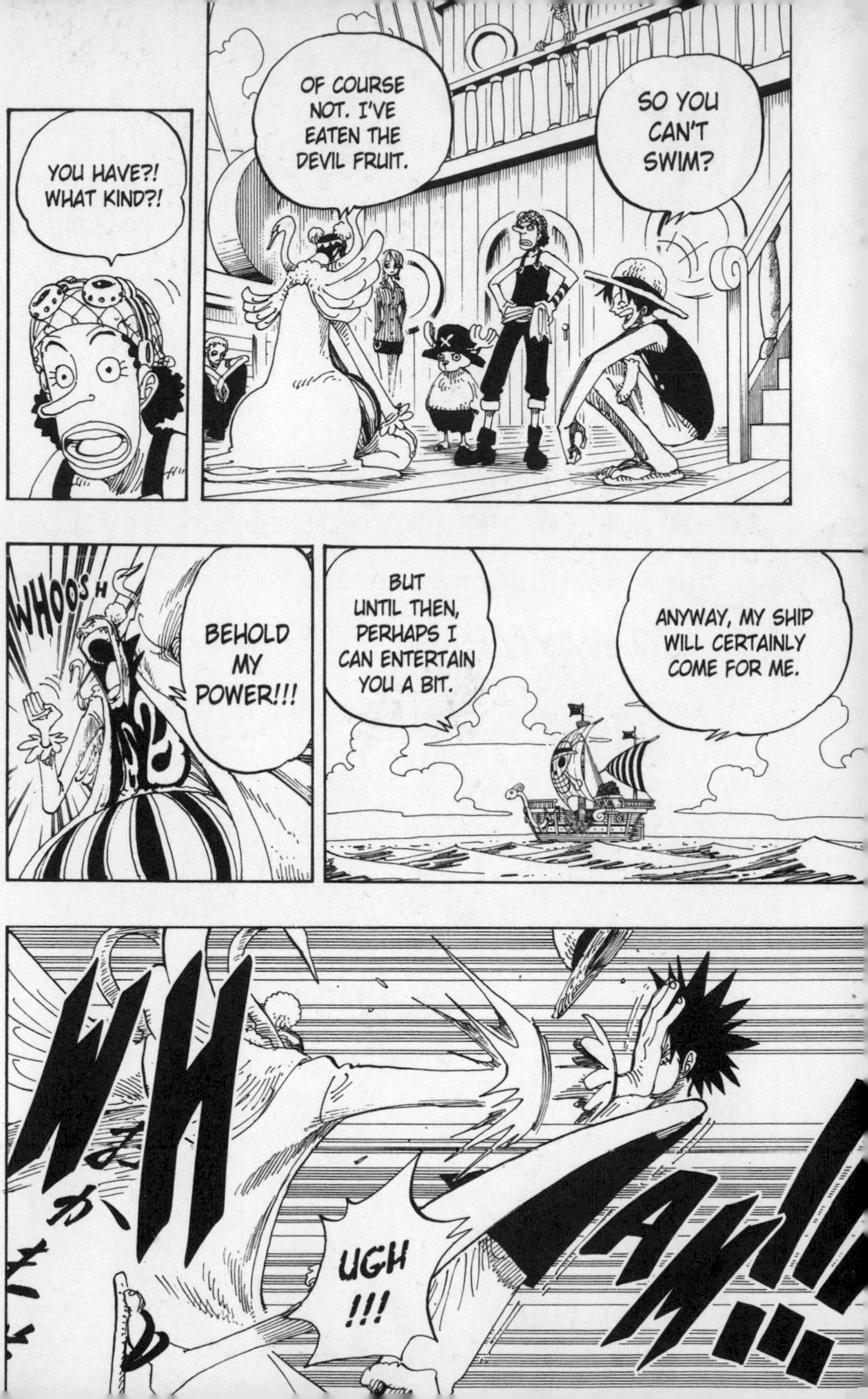
SO YOU CAN'T SWIM?
OF COURSE NOT. I'VE EATEN THE DEVIL FRUIT.
YOU HAVE?! WHAT KIND?!
ANYWAY, MY SHIP WILL CERTAINLY COME FOR ME.
BUT UNTIL THEN, PERHAPS I CAN ENTERTAIN YOU A BIT.
BEHOLD MY POWER!!!
WHOOSH
WHAM!!!
UGH !!!

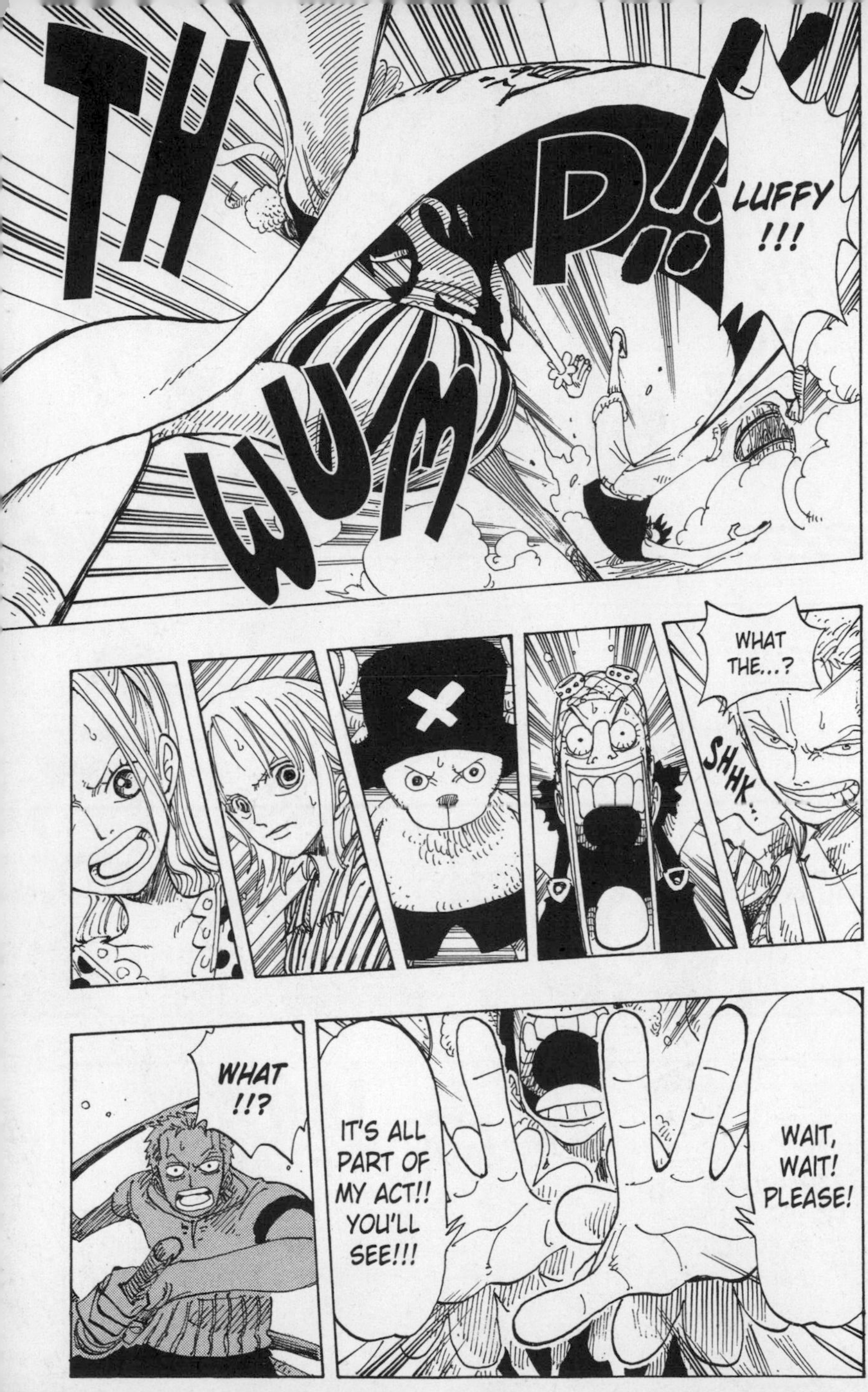
LUFFY !!!
THWUMP!!
WHAT THE...?
SHHK...
WAIT, WAIT! PLEASE!
IT'S ALL PART OF MY ACT!! YOU'LL SEE!!!
WHAT !!?

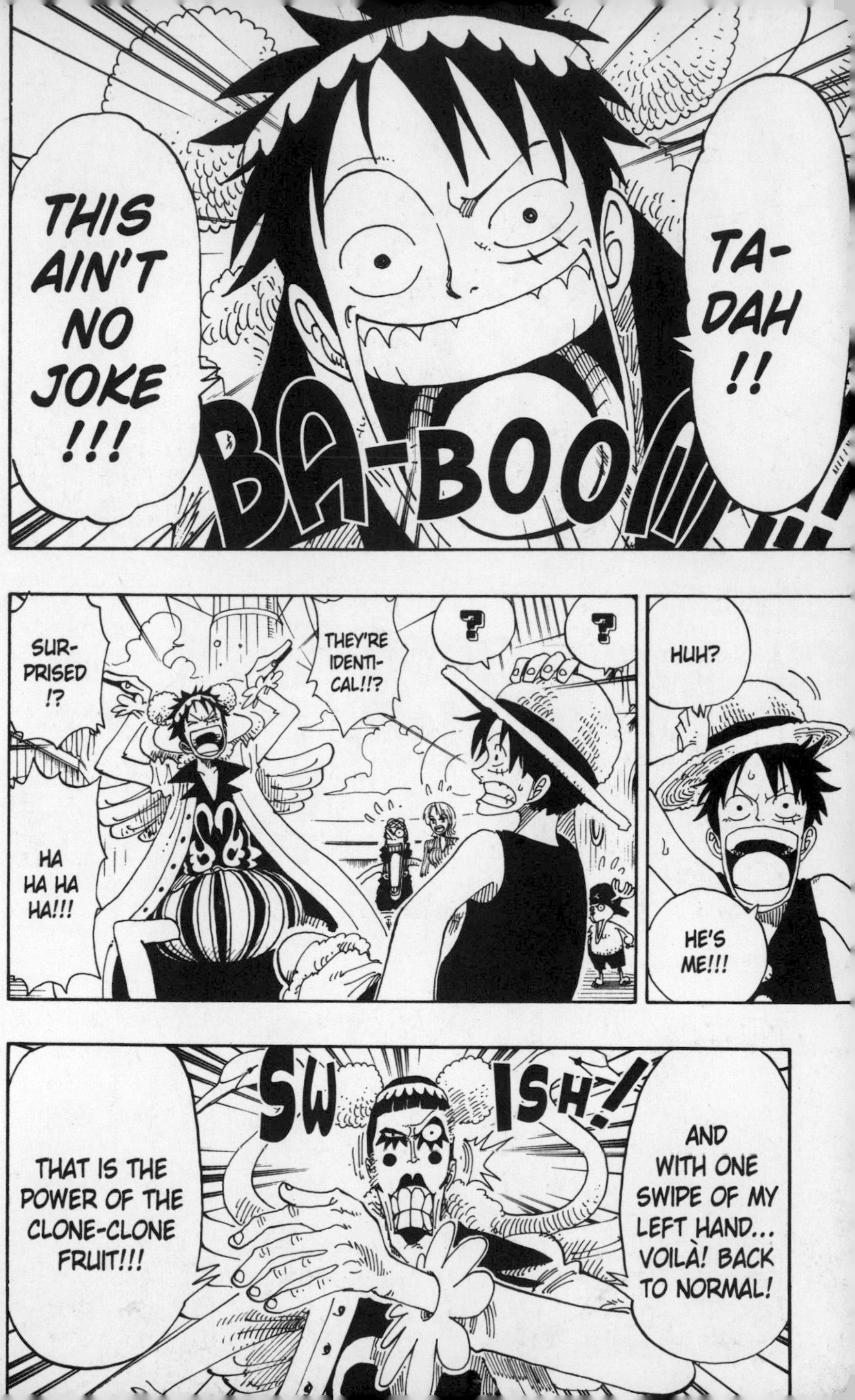
TA-DAH!!
BA-BOO
THIS AIN'T NO JOKE!!!
HUH?
HE'S ME!!!
?
?
THEY'RE IDENTI-CAL!!?
SUR-PRISED!?
HA HA HA HA!!!
AND WITH ONE SWIPE OF MY LEFT HAND... VOILÀ! BACK TO NORMAL!
SWISH!
THAT IS THE POWER OF THE CLONE-CLONE FRUIT!!!

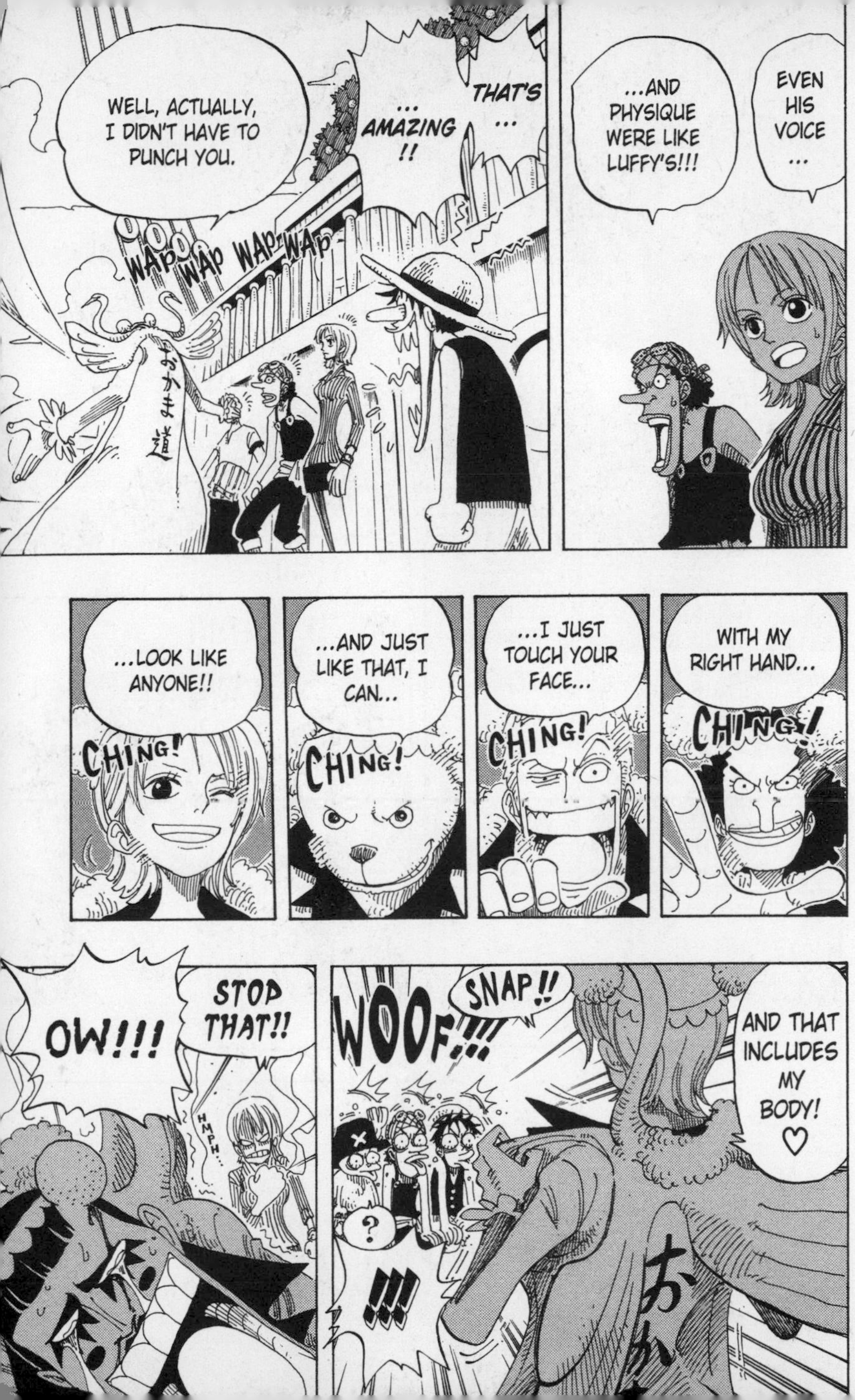
EVEN HIS VOICE ...
...AND PHYSIQUE WERE LIKE LUFFY'S!!!
THAT'S ...
... AMAZING !!
WELL, ACTUALLY, I DIDN'T HAVE TO PUNCH YOU.
WAp WAp WAp WAp
おかま道
WITH MY RIGHT HAND...
CHING!
...I JUST TOUCH YOUR FACE...
CHING!
...AND JUST LIKE THAT, I CAN...
CHING!
...LOOK LIKE ANYONE!!
CHING!
AND THAT INCLUDES MY BODY! ♡
SNAP!!
WOOF!!!
?
!!!
STOP THAT!!
OW!!!
HMPH...

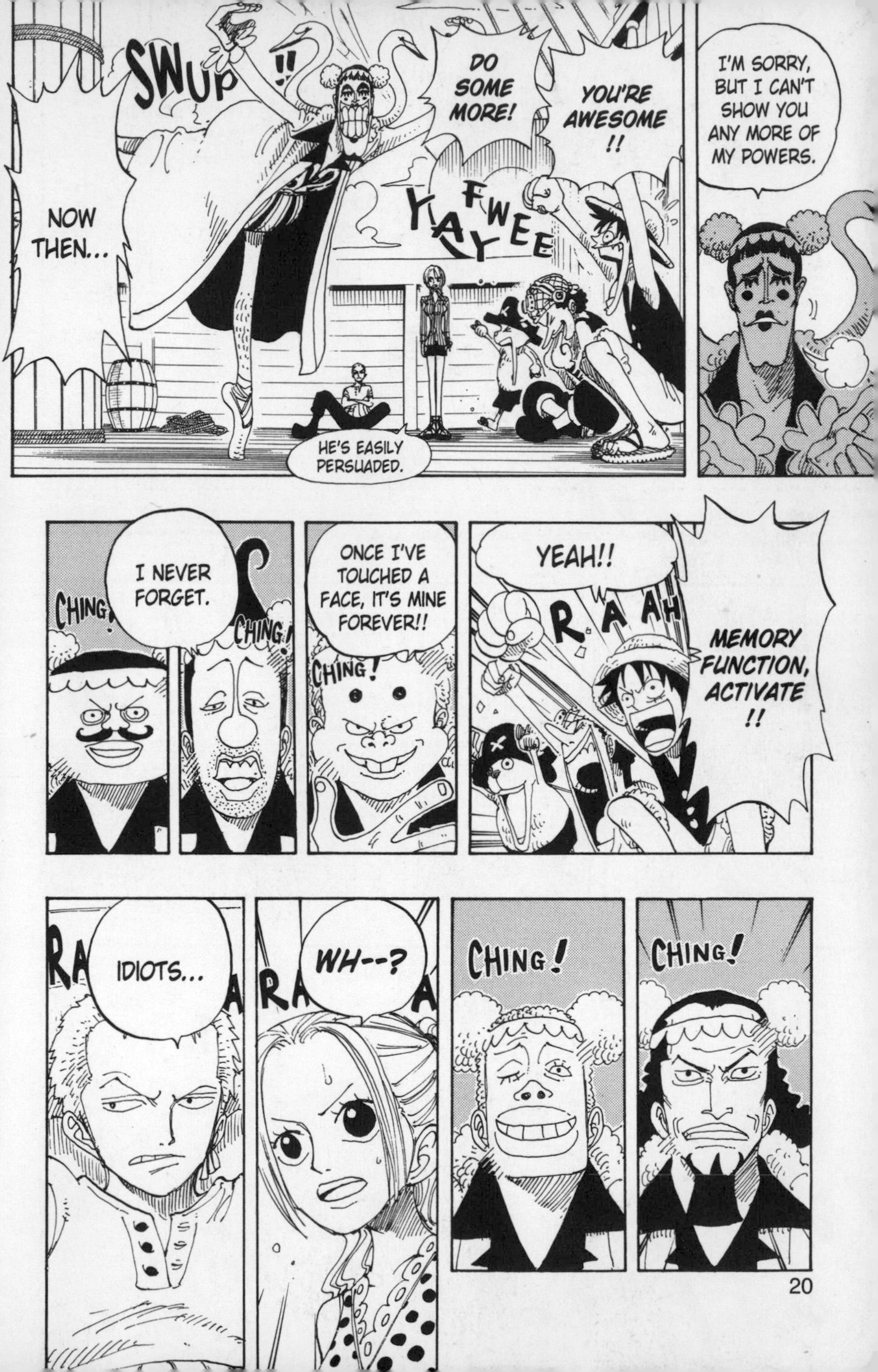
I'M SORRY, BUT I CAN'T SHOW YOU ANY MORE OF MY POWERS.
YOU'RE AWESOME!!
DO SOME MORE!
SWUP!!
FWEE
YAY
NOW THEN...
HE'S EASILY PERSUADED.
YEAH!!
MEMORY FUNCTION, ACTIVATE!!
RAAH
ONCE I'VE TOUCHED A FACE, IT'S MINE FOREVER!!
CHING!
CHING!
I NEVER FORGET.
CHING!
CHING!
CHING!
WH--?
RA
A
IDIOTS...
RA
A

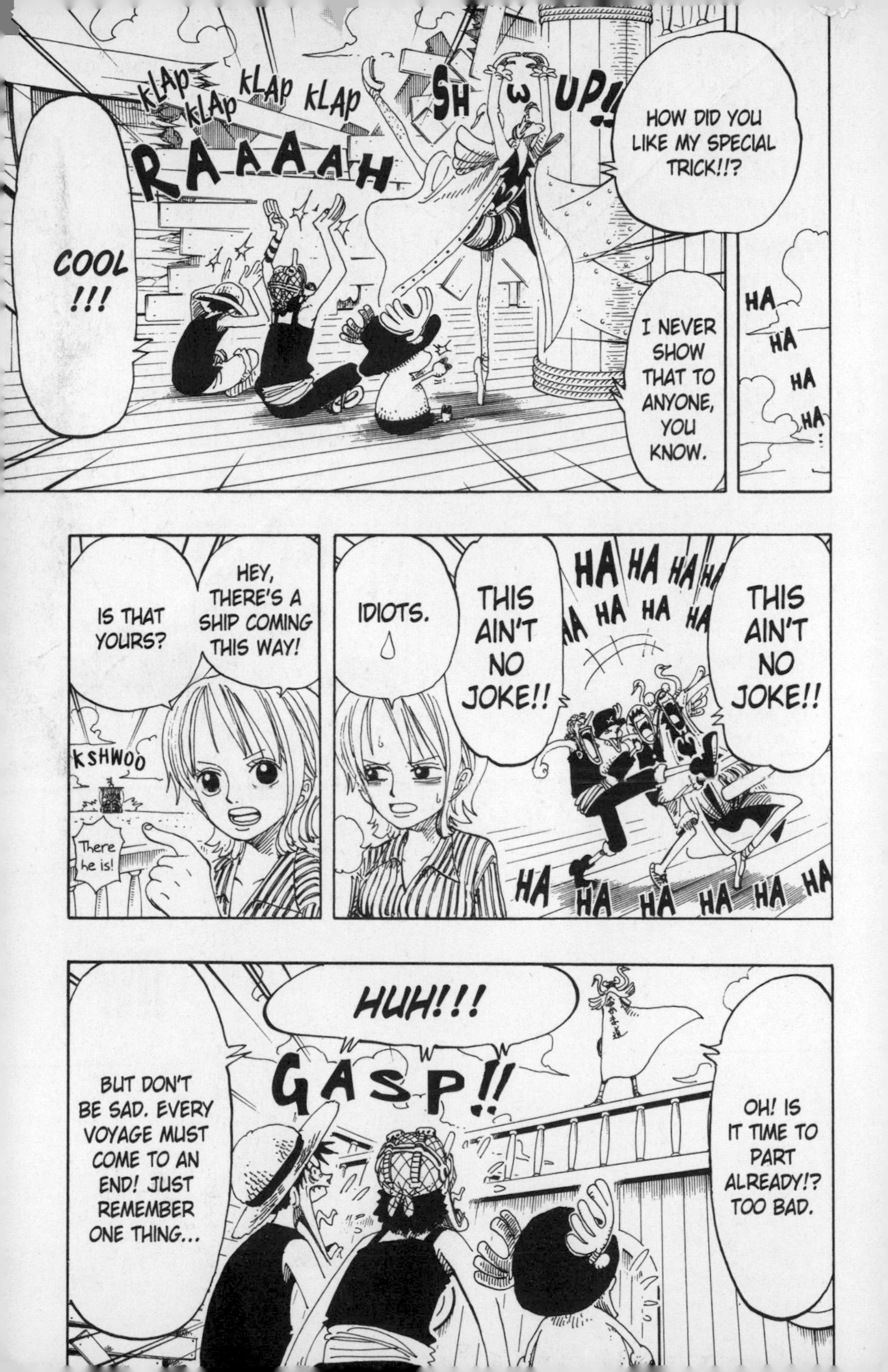
HA
HA
HA
HA
HOW DID YOU LIKE MY SPECIAL TRICK!!?
SHUP!!
I NEVER SHOW THAT TO ANYONE, YOU KNOW.
KLAP KLAP KLAP KLAP
RAAAAH
COOL!!!
THIS AIN'T NO JOKE!!
HA HA HA HA
HA HA HA HA
THIS AIN'T NO JOKE!!
HA HA HA HA HA HA
IDIOTS.
HEY, THERE'S A SHIP COMING THIS WAY!
IS THAT YOURS?
KSHWOO
There he is!
OH! IS IT TIME TO PART ALREADY!? TOO BAD.
HUH!!!
GASP!!
BUT DON'T BE SAD. EVERY VOYAGE MUST COME TO AN END! JUST REMEMBER ONE THING...

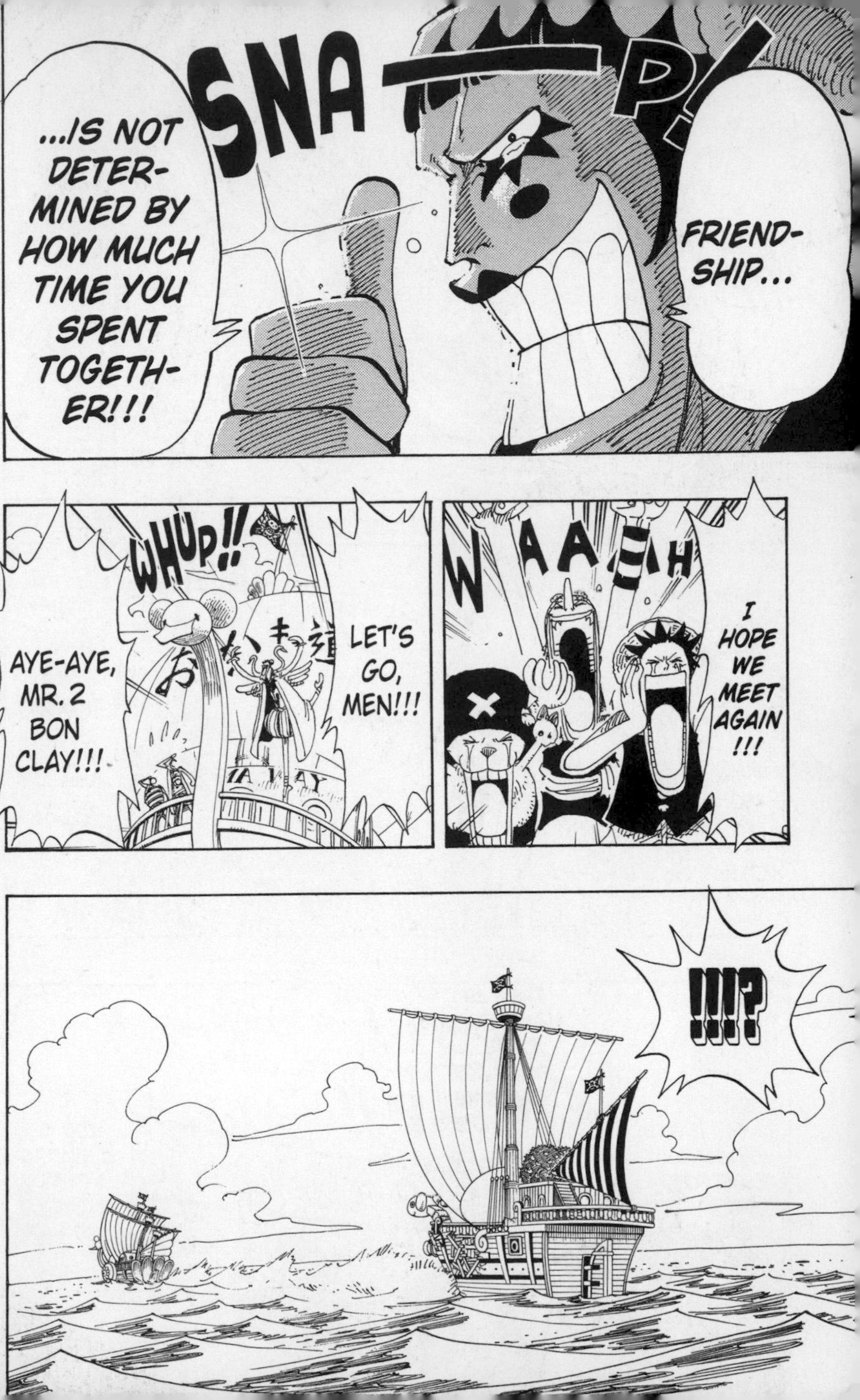
SNA—P!
FRIEND-SHIP...
...IS NOT DETER-MINED BY HOW MUCH TIME YOU SPENT TOGETH-ER!!!
WAAAH
I HOPE WE MEET AGAIN!!!
WHUP!!
LET'S GO, MEN!!!
AYE-AYE, MR. 2 BON CLAY!!!
!!!?

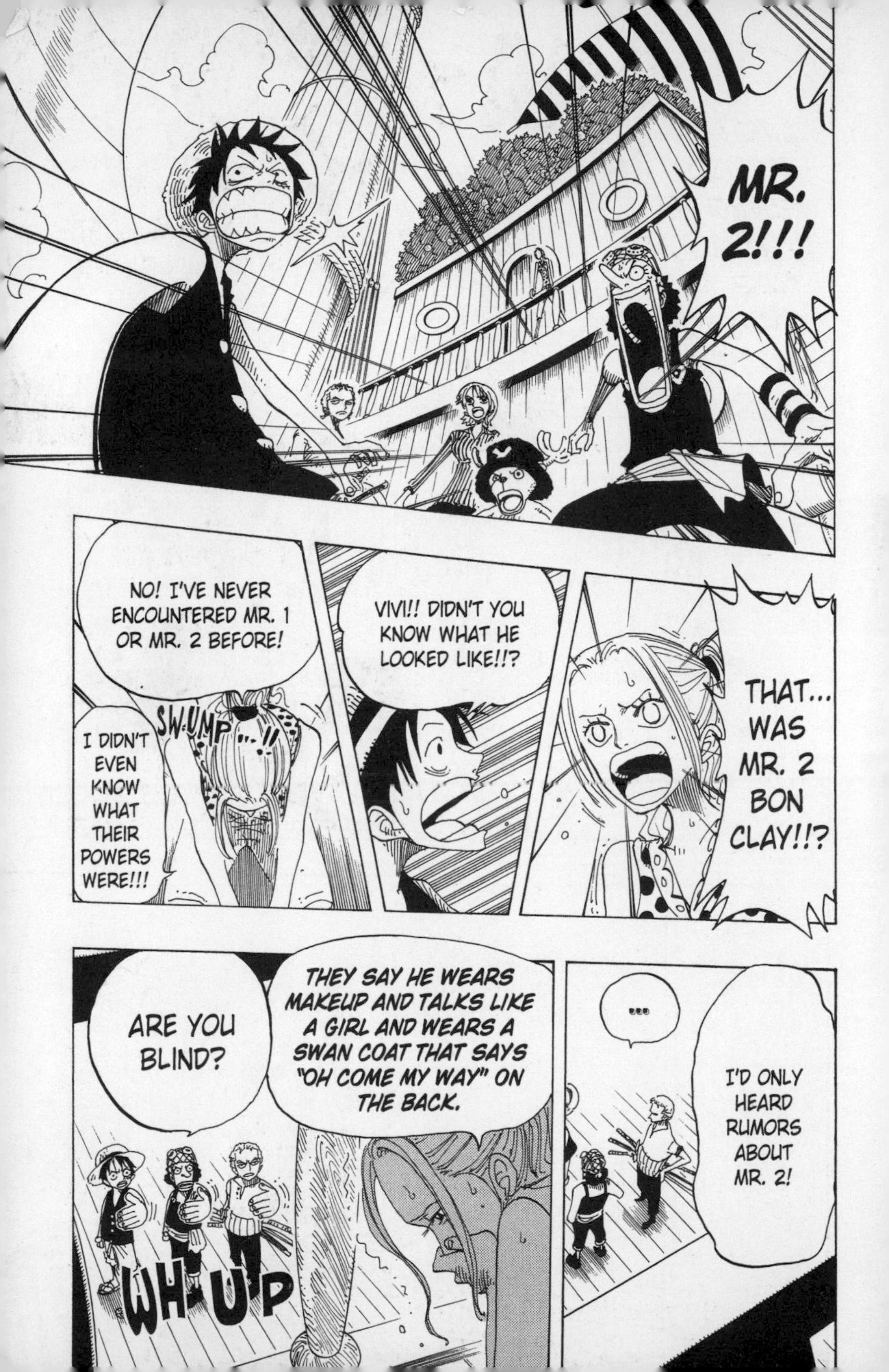
MR. 2!!!
THAT... WAS MR. 2 BON CLAY!!?
VIVI!! DIDN'T YOU KNOW WHAT HE LOOKED LIKE!!?
NO! I'VE NEVER ENCOUNTERED MR. 1 OR MR. 2 BEFORE!
SWUMP
I DIDN'T EVEN KNOW WHAT THEIR POWERS WERE!!!
...
I'D ONLY HEARD RUMORS ABOUT MR. 2!
THEY SAY HE WEARS MAKEUP AND TALKS LIKE A GIRL AND WEARS A SWAN COAT THAT SAYS "OH COME MY WAY" ON THE BACK.
ARE YOU BLIND?
WHUP

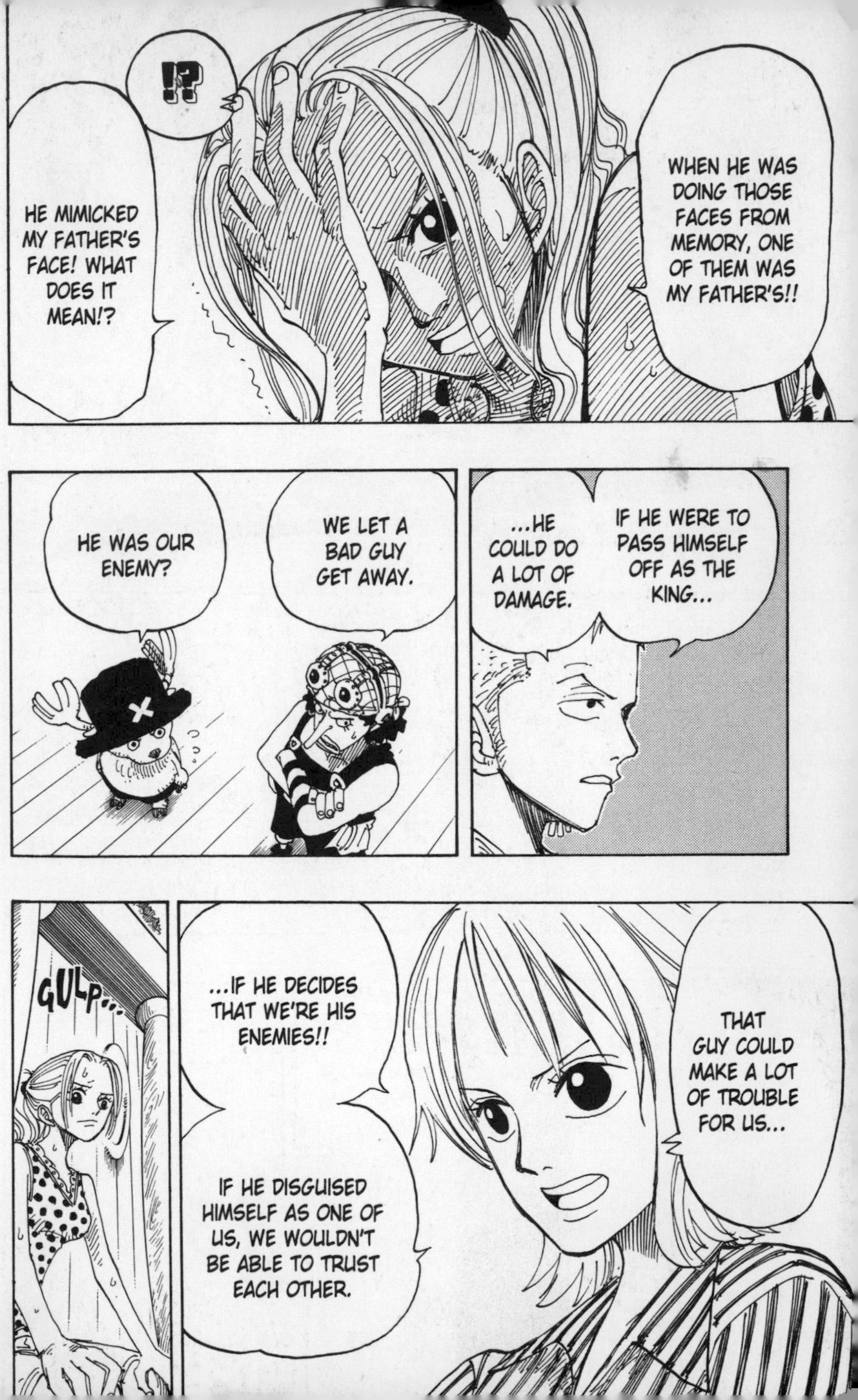
WHEN HE WAS DOING THOSE FACES FROM MEMORY, ONE OF THEM WAS MY FATHER'S!!
!?
HE MIMICKED MY FATHER'S FACE! WHAT DOES IT MEAN!?
IF HE WERE TO PASS HIMSELF OFF AS THE KING...
...HE COULD DO A LOT OF DAMAGE.
WE LET A BAD GUY GET AWAY.
HE WAS OUR ENEMY?
THAT GUY COULD MAKE A LOT OF TROUBLE FOR US...
...IF HE DECIDES THAT WE'RE HIS ENEMIES!!
IF HE DISGUISED HIMSELF AS ONE OF US, WE WOULDN'T BE ABLE TO TRUST EACH OTHER.
GULP...

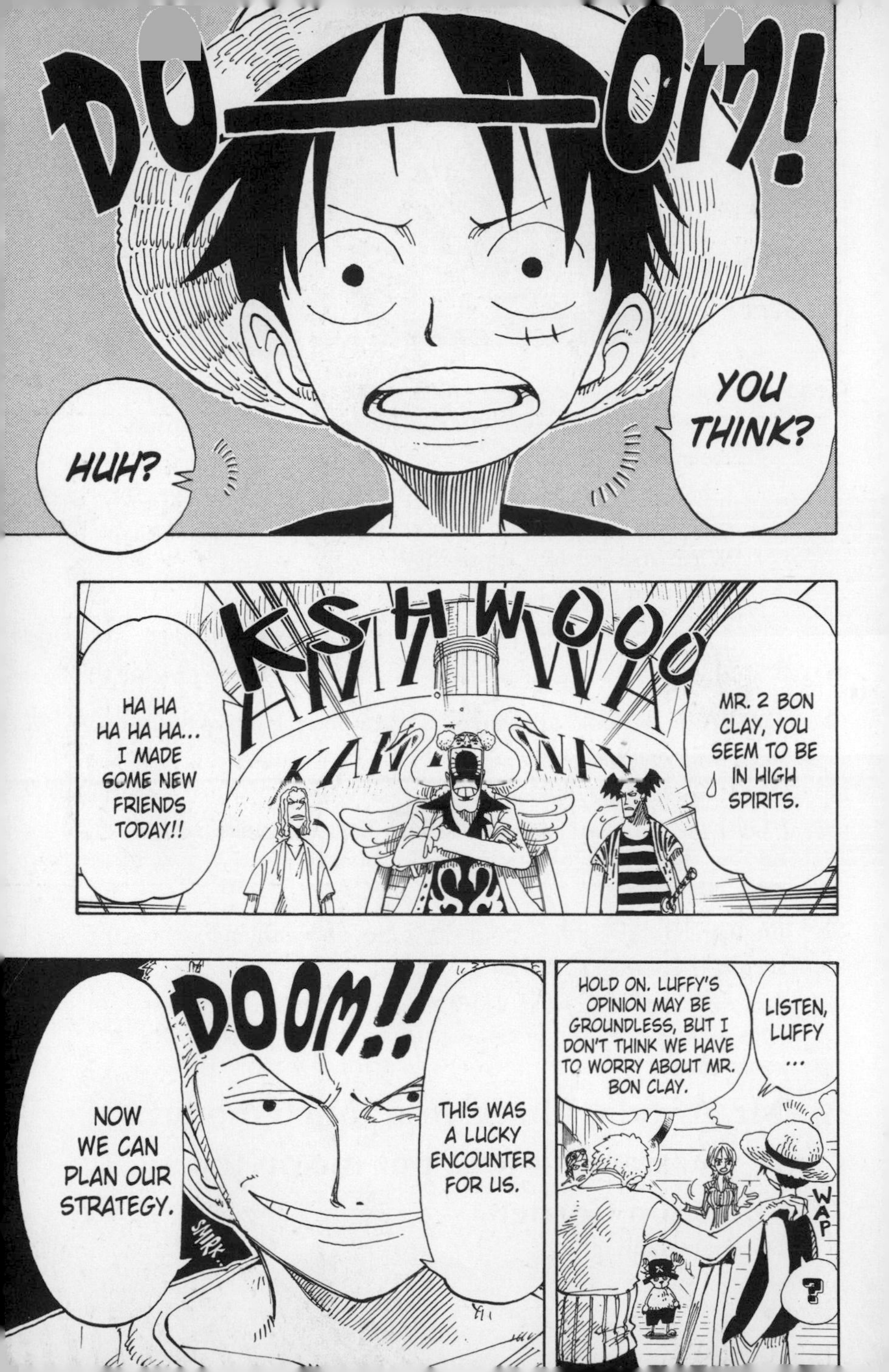
DOOM!
YOU THINK?
HUH?
KSHWOOO
MR. 2 BON CLAY, YOU SEEM TO BE IN HIGH SPIRITS.
HA HA HA HA HA... I MADE SOME NEW FRIENDS TODAY!!
LISTEN, LUFFY ...
HOLD ON. LUFFY'S OPINION MAY BE GROUNDLESS, BUT I DON'T THINK WE HAVE TO WORRY ABOUT MR. BON CLAY.
WAP
?
DOOM!!
THIS WAS A LUCKY ENCOUNTER FOR US.
NOW WE CAN PLAN OUR STRATEGY.
SMIRK...

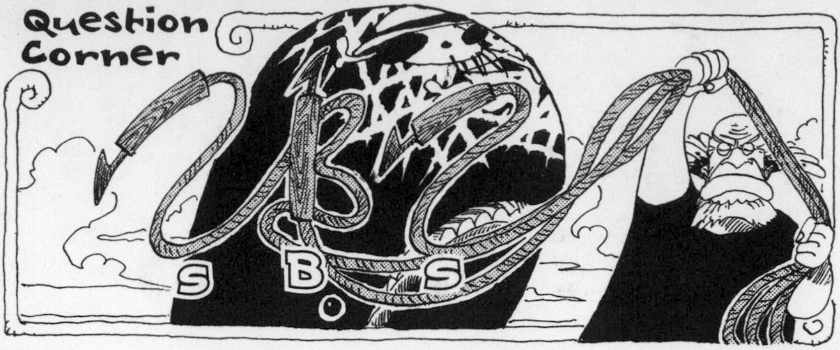
Question Corner
S B S

Reader: You there, the one trying to start the Question Corner without permission!!! Have you no consideration for Oda Sensei's feelings!!? Geez!!!
Oh. Sorry, Oda Sensei. Just say: "Please say, Let's begin the Question Corner today without any hassles!" Okay?
What? Are you sure about this?
Fine, then I'll do it.

Let's begin the Question Corner!

Oda: Hey, I didn't say anything.

Q: Oda Sensei, get hold of yourself. Pardon me for saying this, but…your window to the world is open!!!! It's embarrassing. ♡

A: Oh! Darn. My fly's open.
Phew. I don't ever want that to happen again, so I'd better just take my pants off. [Swuff swuff…] All right, let's continue.

Q: Dr. Kureha always talks about the secret of youth, but what is the secret? I've gotten so old lately.

A: Gotten old? You're only 13! Anyway, the secret is--be happy!! Dr. Kureha is probably going to be around for a long time.

Q: **Mr. Afroda, I have your lunch money. If you want it back, put me on the Question Corner.**
Budomint Tanisugi

A: You!!?

Chapter 157:
ACE ARRIVES

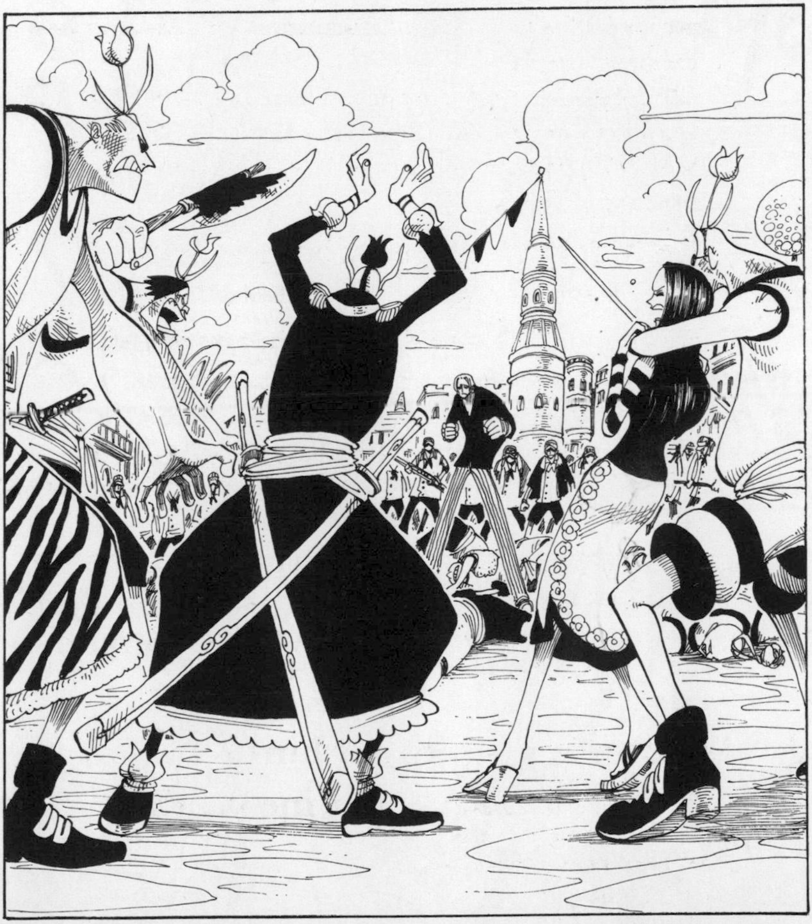

DJANGO'S DANCE HEAVEN, VOL. 24: "THE HOSTAGE GIRL"

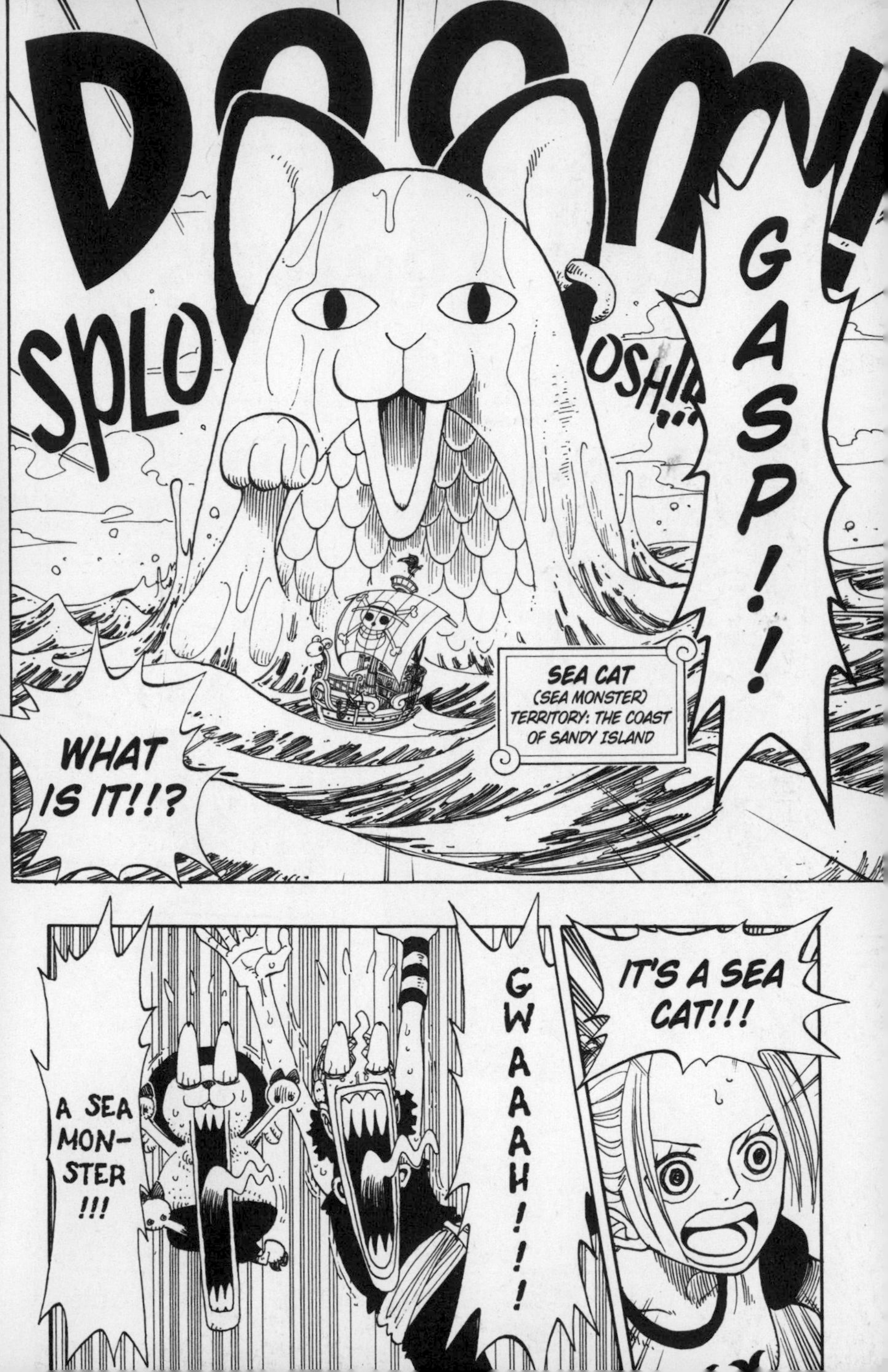
DOOM!!
SPLO
OSH!!...
GASP!!
SEA CAT
(SEA MONSTER)
TERRITORY: THE COAST OF SANDY ISLAND
WHAT IS IT!!?
IT'S A SEA CAT!!!
GWAAAAH!!!
A SEA MON-STER!!!

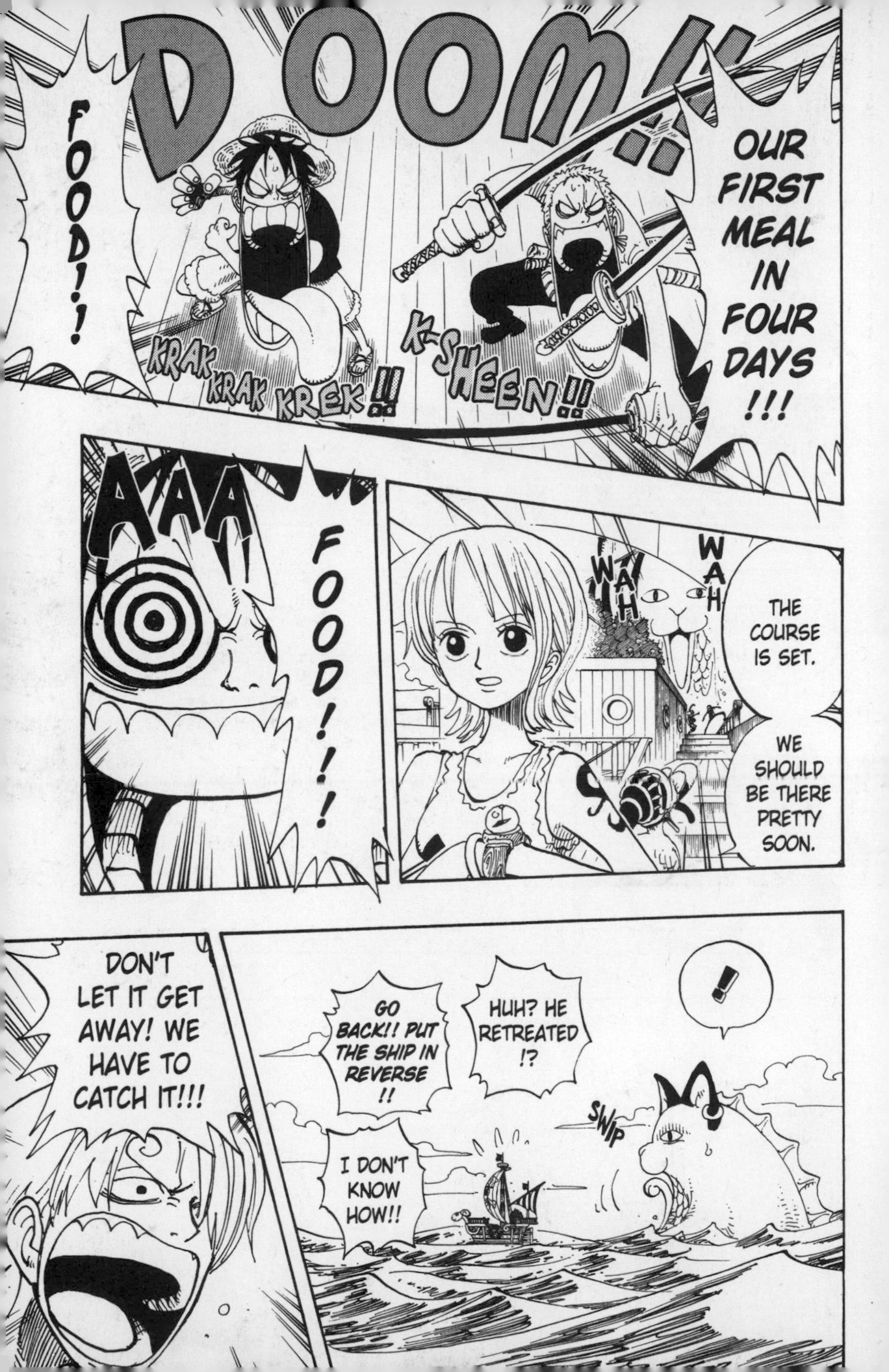
DOOM!!
OUR FIRST MEAL IN FOUR DAYS!!!
FOOD!!!
K-SHEEN!!
KRAK KRAK KREK!!
WAH WAH
THE COURSE IS SET.
WE SHOULD BE THERE PRETTY SOON.
AAA
FOOOD!!!
!
HUH? HE RETREATED!?
GO BACK!! PUT THE SHIP IN REVERSE!!
SWIP
I DON'T KNOW HOW!!
DON'T LET IT GET AWAY! WE HAVE TO CATCH IT!!!

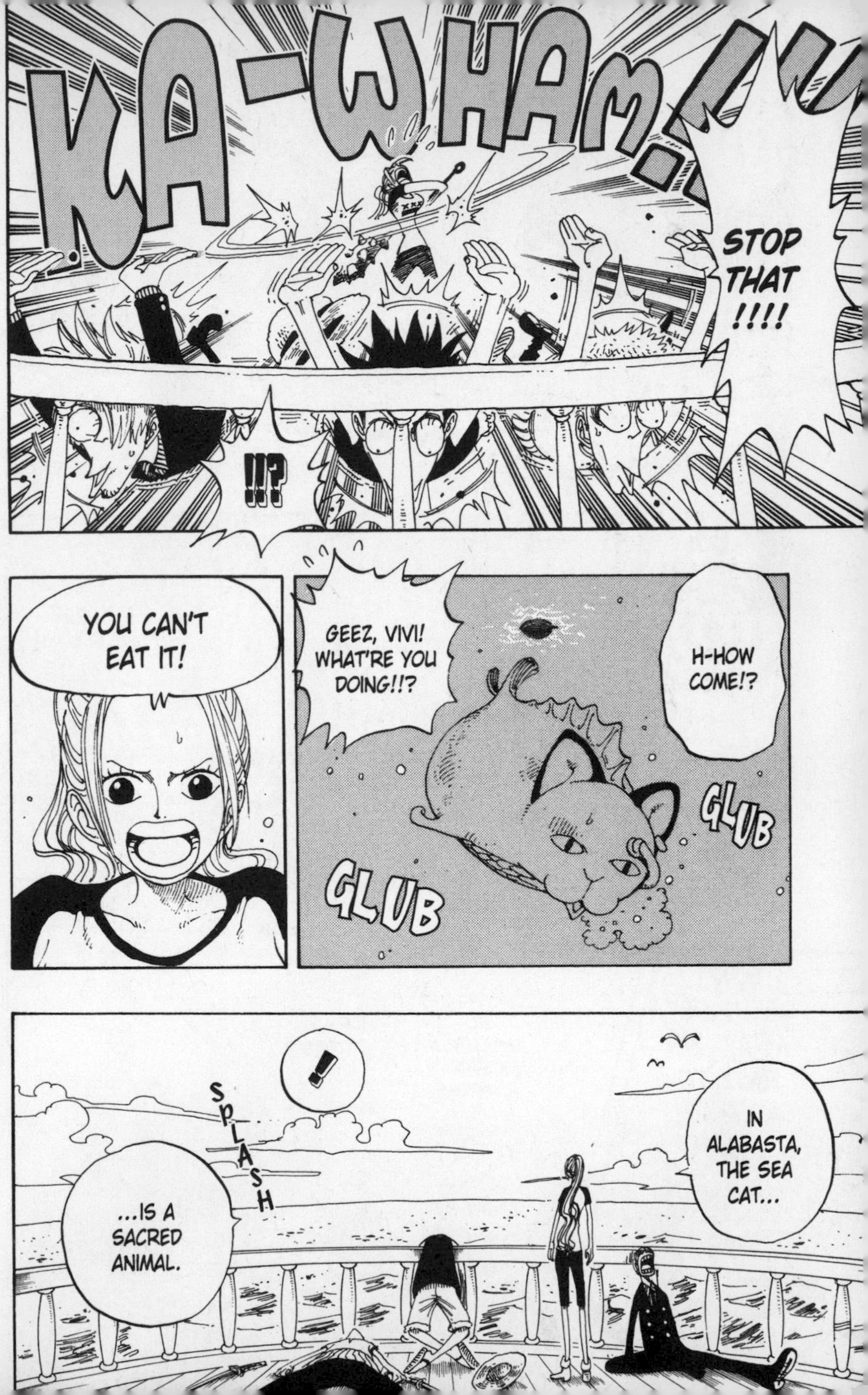

KA-WHAM!!
STOP THAT!!!!
!!?
H-HOW COME!?
GEEZ, VIVI! WHAT'RE YOU DOING!!?
GLUB
GLUB
YOU CAN'T EAT IT!
!
IN ALABASTA, THE SEA CAT...
SPLASH
...IS A SACRED ANIMAL.

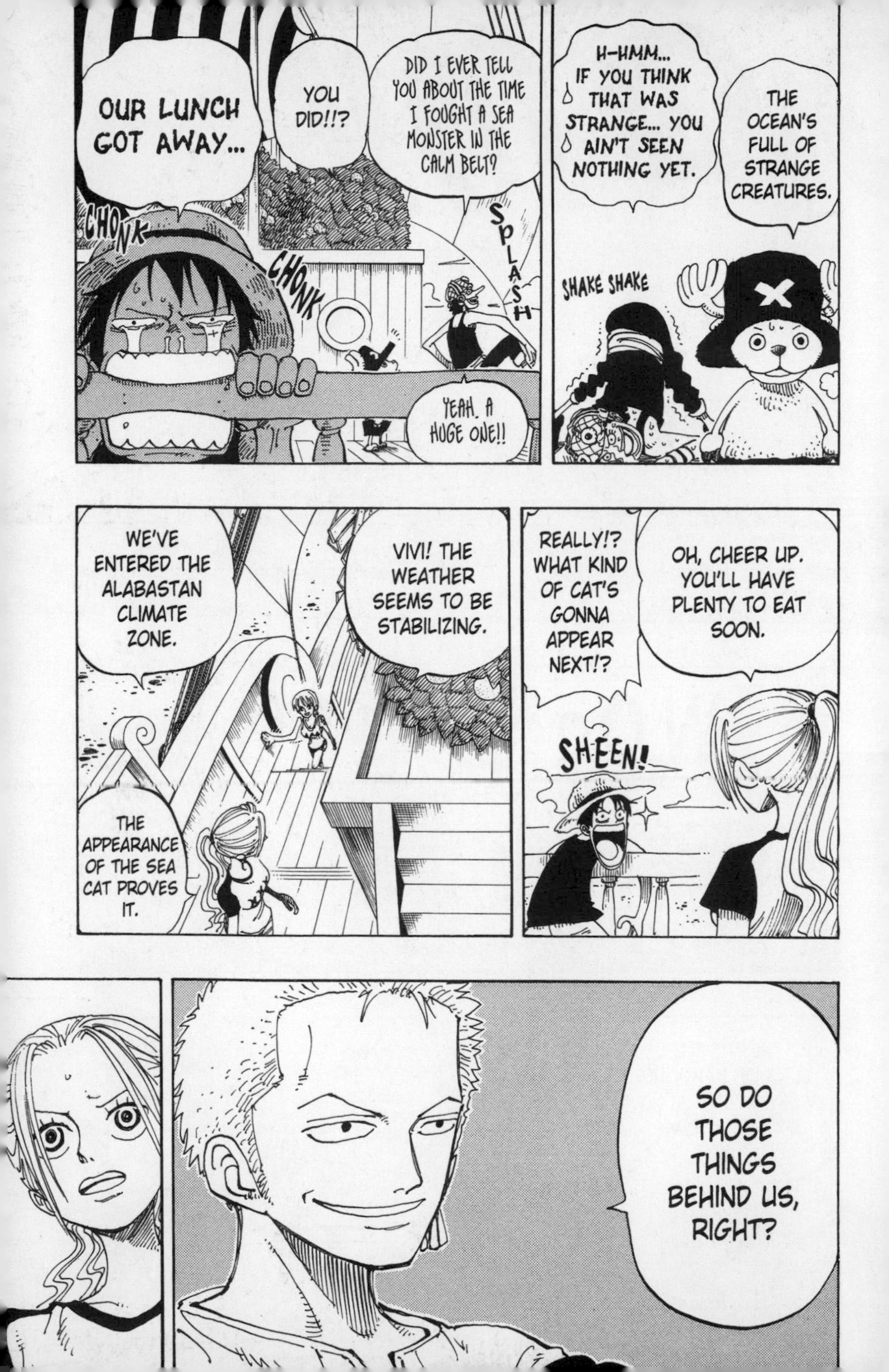
THE OCEAN'S FULL OF STRANGE CREATURES.
H-HMM... IF YOU THINK THAT WAS STRANGE... YOU AIN'T SEEN NOTHING YET.
SHAKE SHAKE
DID I EVER TELL YOU ABOUT THE TIME I FOUGHT A SEA MONSTER IN THE CALM BELT?
SPLASH
YOU DID!!?
YEAH. A HUGE ONE!!
OUR LUNCH GOT AWAY...
CHONK
CHONK
OH, CHEER UP. YOU'LL HAVE PLENTY TO EAT SOON.
REALLY!? WHAT KIND OF CAT'S GONNA APPEAR NEXT!?
SHEEN!
VIVI! THE WEATHER SEEMS TO BE STABILIZING.
WE'VE ENTERED THE ALABASTAN CLIMATE ZONE.
THE APPEARANCE OF THE SEA CAT PROVES IT.
SO DO THOSE THINGS BEHIND US, RIGHT?

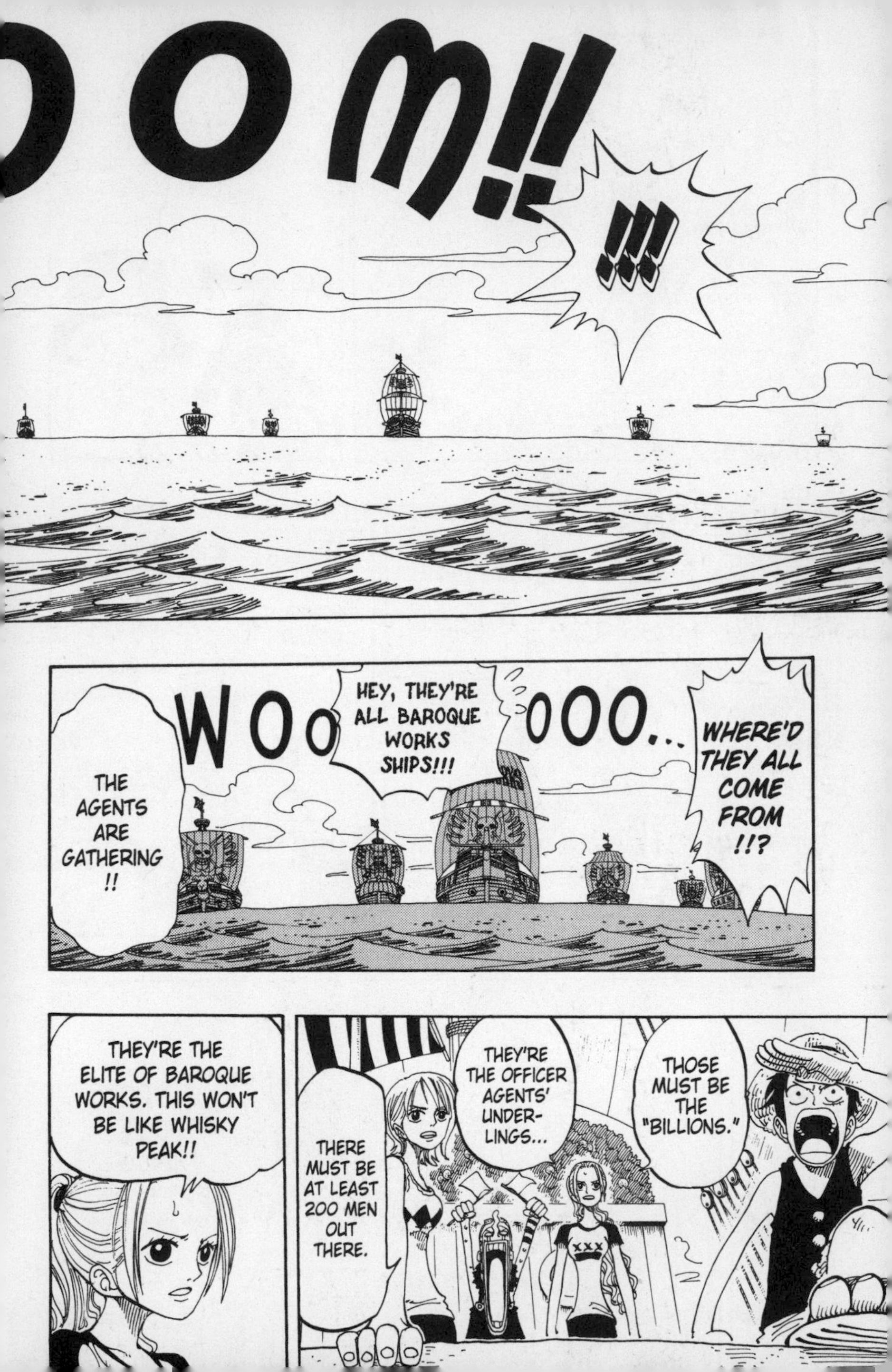

OOM!!
!!!
WHERE'D THEY ALL COME FROM!!?
WOOOOO...
HEY, THEY'RE ALL BAROQUE WORKS SHIPS!!!
THE AGENTS ARE GATHERING!!
THOSE MUST BE THE "BILLIONS."
THEY'RE THE OFFICER AGENTS' UNDER-LINGS...
THERE MUST BE AT LEAST 200 MEN OUT THERE.
THEY'RE THE ELITE OF BAROQUE WORKS. THIS WON'T BE LIKE WHISKY PEAK!!

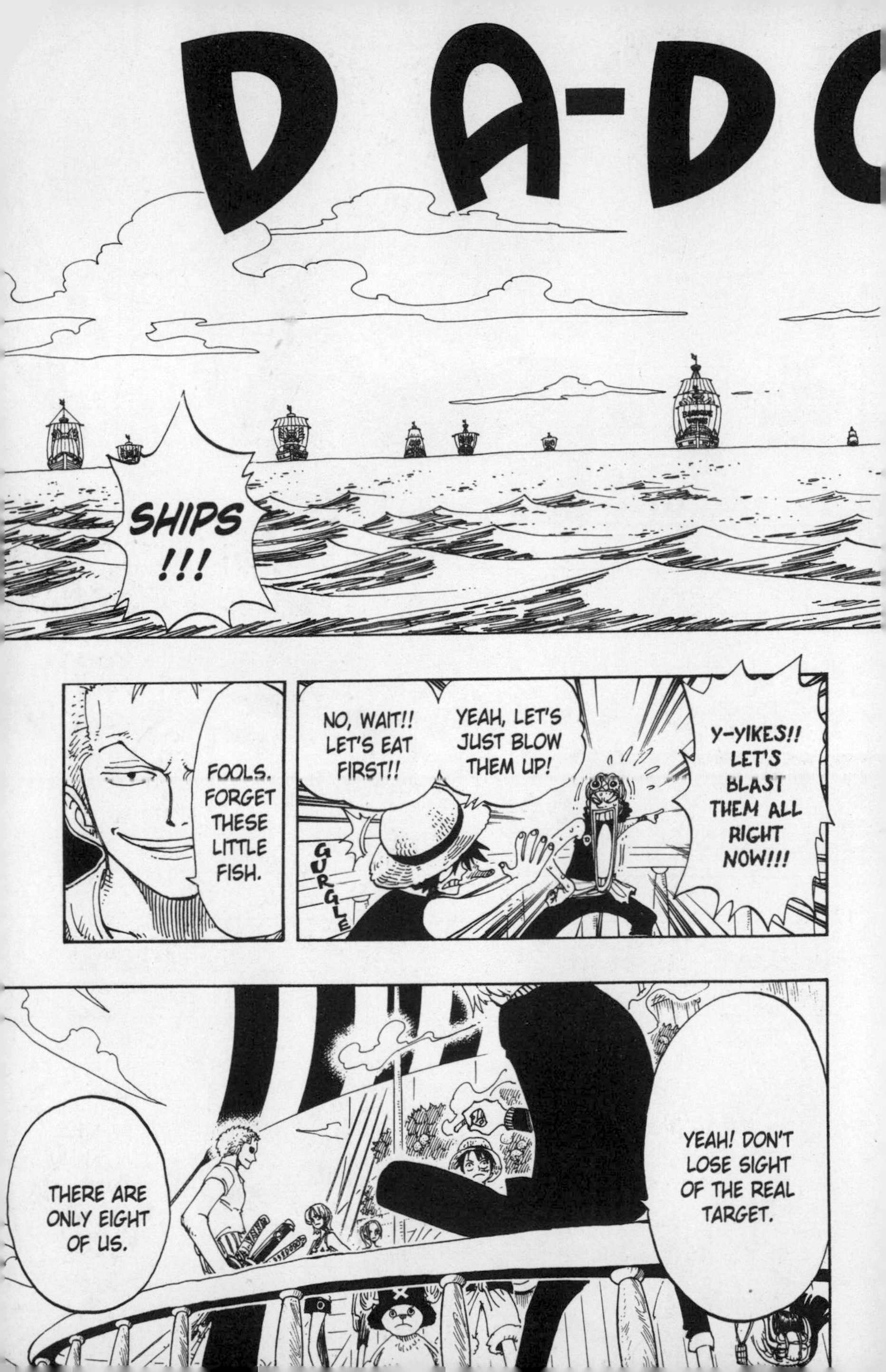
DA-D
SHIPS !!!
Y-YIKES!! LET'S BLAST THEM ALL RIGHT NOW!!!
YEAH, LET'S JUST BLOW THEM UP!
NO, WAIT!! LET'S EAT FIRST!!
GURGLE
FOOLS. FORGET THESE LITTLE FISH.
YEAH! DON'T LOSE SIGHT OF THE REAL TARGET.
THERE ARE ONLY EIGHT OF US.

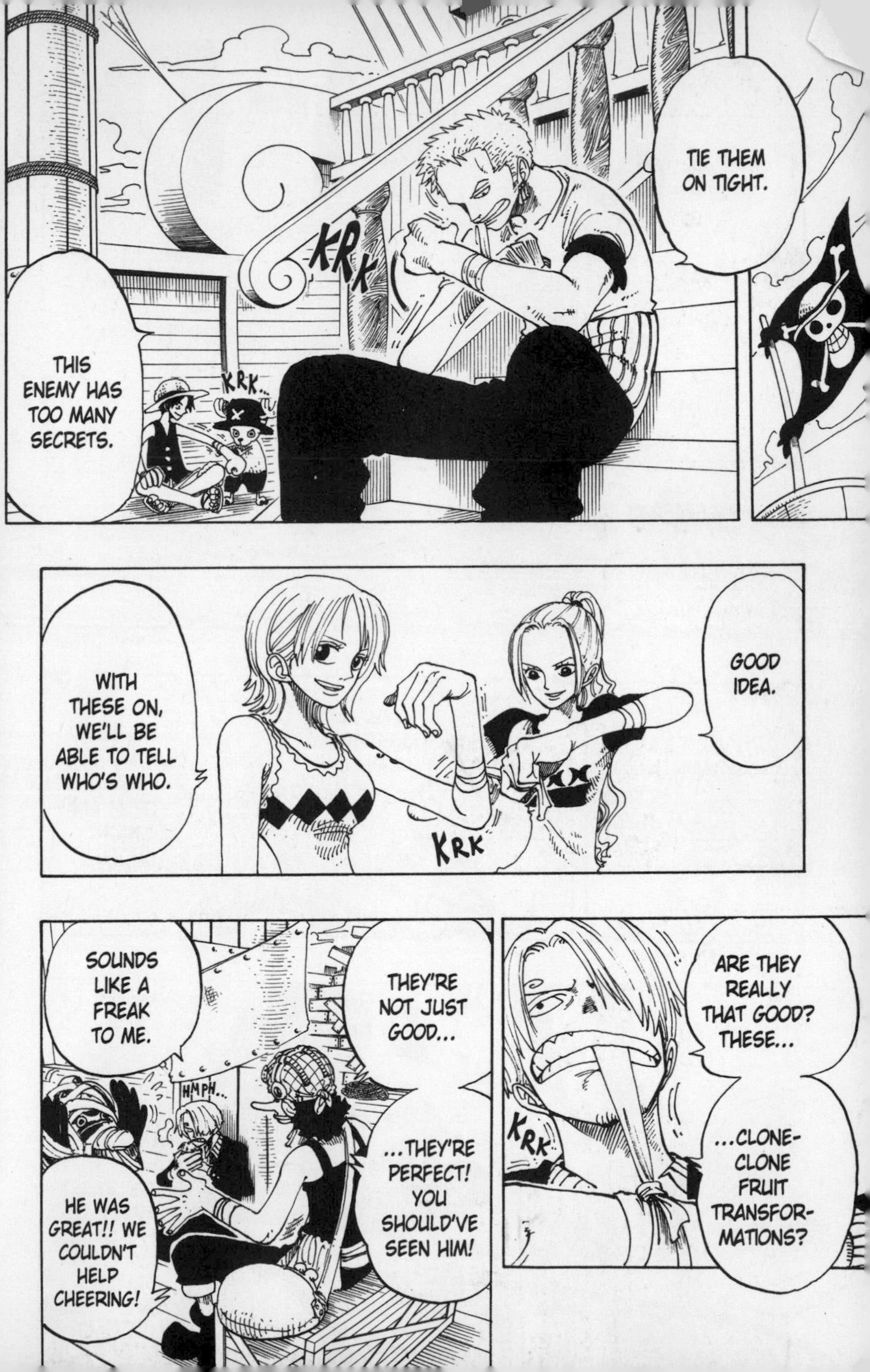
TIE THEM ON TIGHT.
KRK
THIS ENEMY HAS TOO MANY SECRETS.
KRK..
GOOD IDEA.
WITH THESE ON, WE'LL BE ABLE TO TELL WHO'S WHO.
KRK
ARE THEY REALLY THAT GOOD? THESE...
...CLONE-CLONE FRUIT TRANSFORMATIONS?
KRK
THEY'RE NOT JUST GOOD...
SOUNDS LIKE A FREAK TO ME.
HMPH...
...THEY'RE PERFECT! YOU SHOULD'VE SEEN HIM!
HE WAS GREAT!! WE COULDN'T HELP CHEERING!

READ THIS WAY

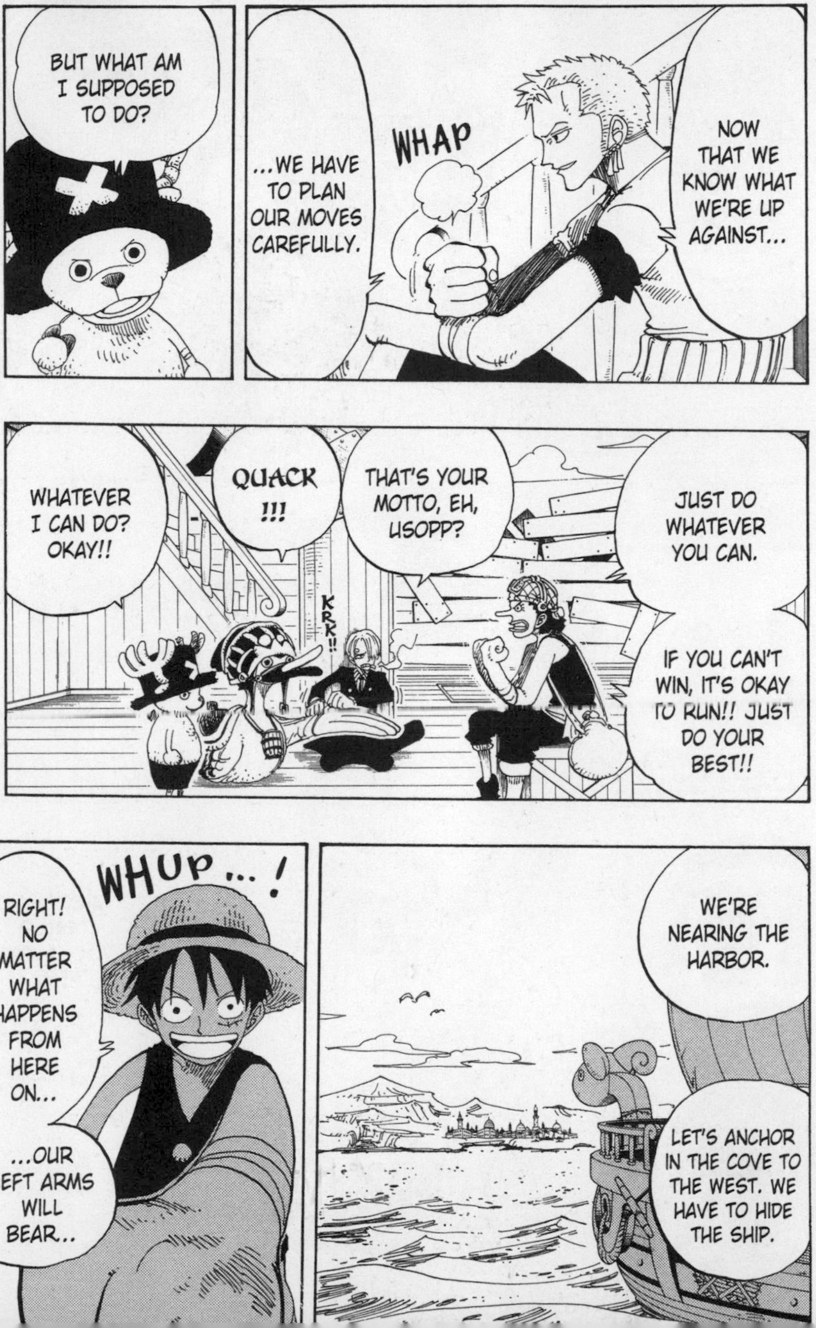
NOW THAT WE KNOW WHAT WE'RE UP AGAINST...
WHAP
...WE HAVE TO PLAN OUR MOVES CAREFULLY.
BUT WHAT AM I SUPPOSED TO DO?
JUST DO WHATEVER YOU CAN.
IF YOU CAN'T WIN, IT'S OKAY TO RUN!! JUST DO YOUR BEST!!
THAT'S YOUR MOTTO, EH, USOPP?
KRK!!
QUACK !!!
WHATEVER I CAN DO? OKAY!!
WE'RE NEARING THE HARBOR.
LET'S ANCHOR IN THE COVE TO THE WEST. WE HAVE TO HIDE THE SHIP.
WHUP...!
RIGHT! NO MATTER WHAT HAPPENS FROM HERE ON...
...OUR LEFT ARMS WILL BEAR..

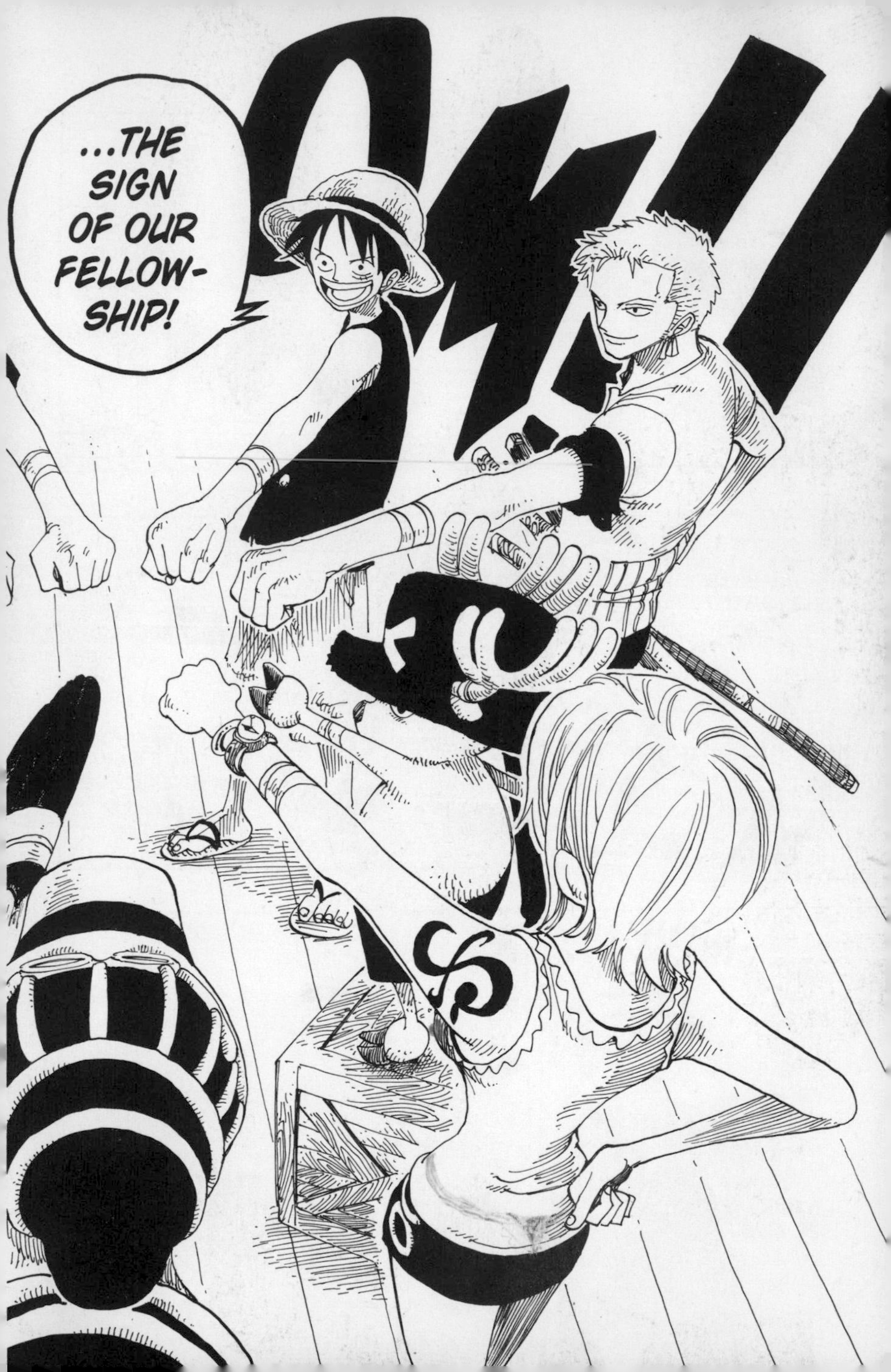
...THE SIGN OF OUR FELLOW-SHIP!

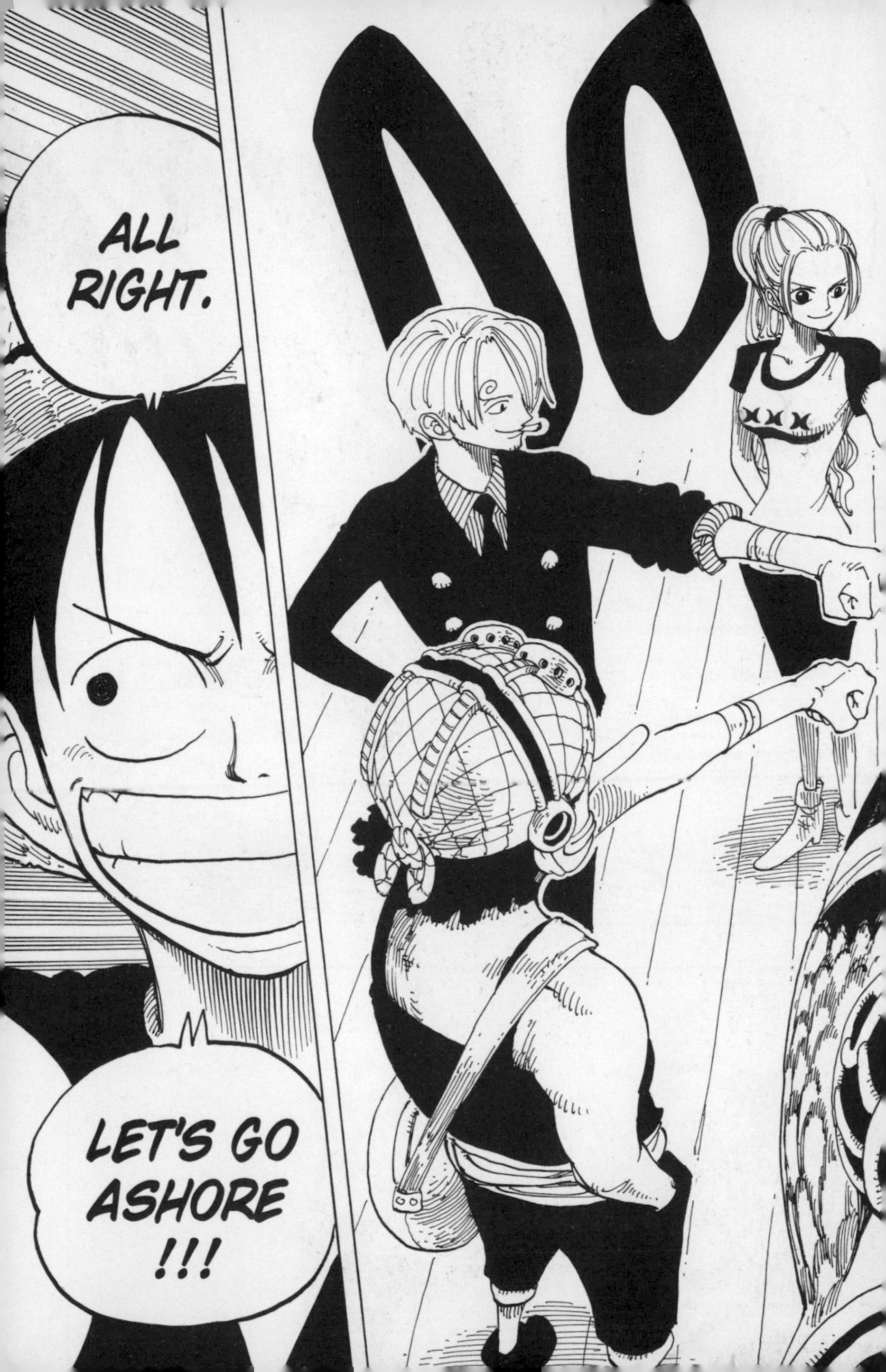
DO
ALL RIGHT.
LET'S GO ASHORE !!!

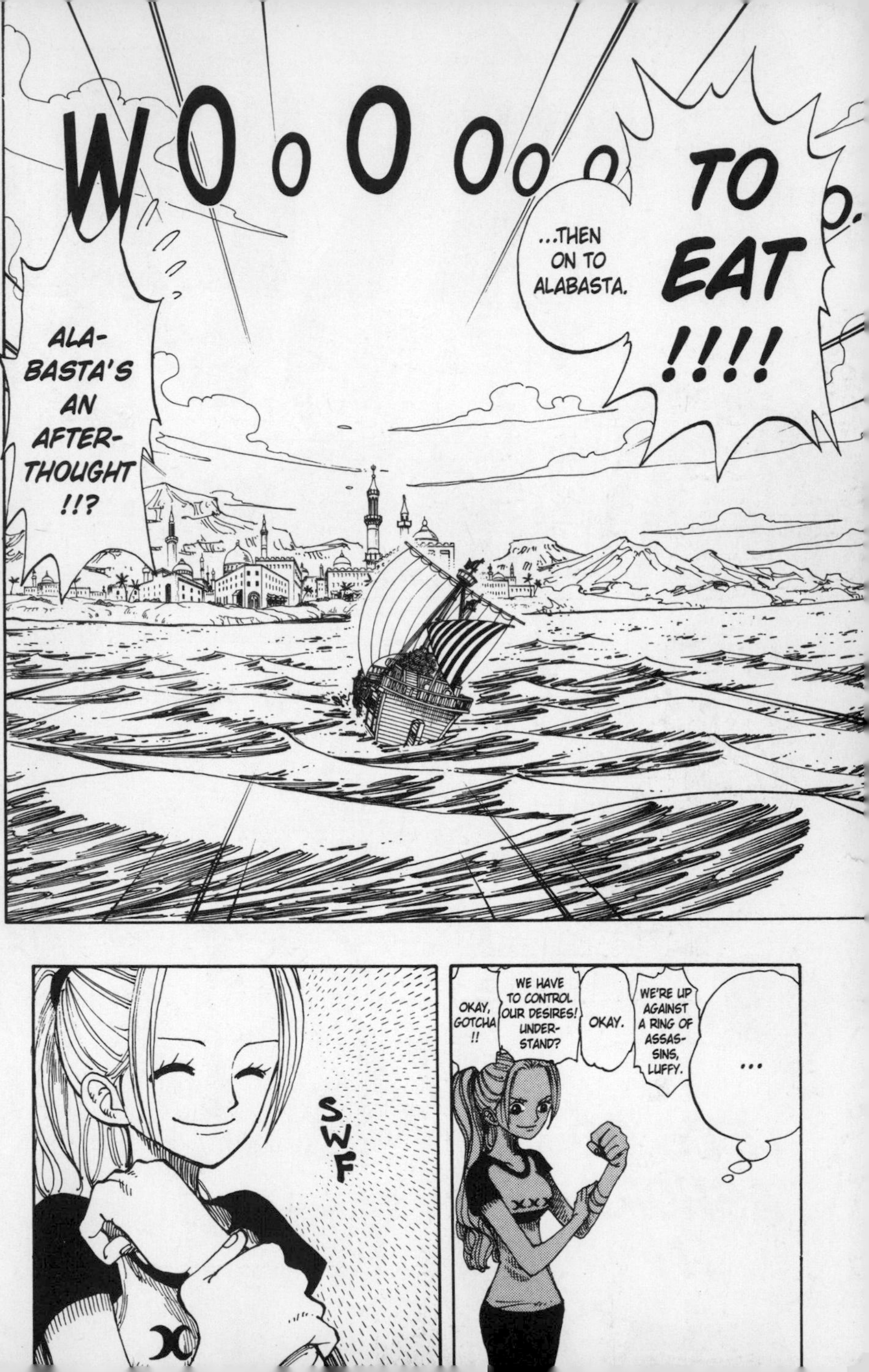
TO EAT !!!!
...THEN ON TO ALABASTA.
WOoOoOoOoOo.
ALA-BASTA'S AN AFTER-THOUGHT !!?
...
WE'RE UP AGAINST A RING OF ASSAS-SINS, LUFFY.
OKAY.
WE HAVE TO CONTROL OUR DESIRES! UNDER-STAND?
OKAY, GOTCHA !!
SWF

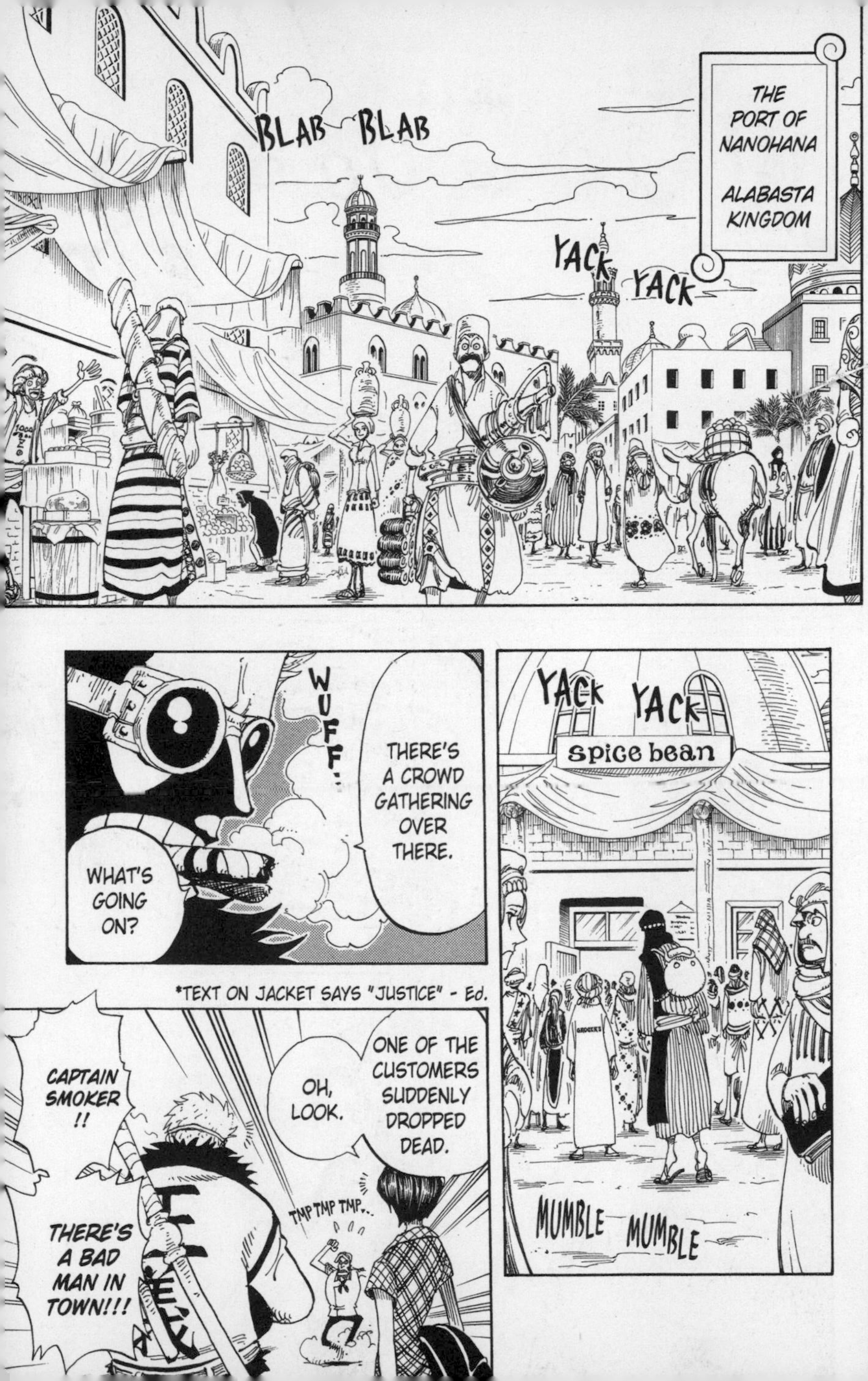
THE PORT OF NANOHANA
ALABASTA KINGDOM
YACK YACK
BLAB BLAB
YACK YACK
spice bean
MUMBLE MUMBLE
WUFF
THERE'S A CROWD GATHERING OVER THERE.
WHAT'S GOING ON?
*TEXT ON JACKET SAYS "JUSTICE" - Ed.
ONE OF THE CUSTOMERS SUDDENLY DROPPED DEAD.
OH, LOOK.
TMP TMP TMP...
CAPTAIN SMOKER!!
THERE'S A BAD MAN IN TOWN!!!

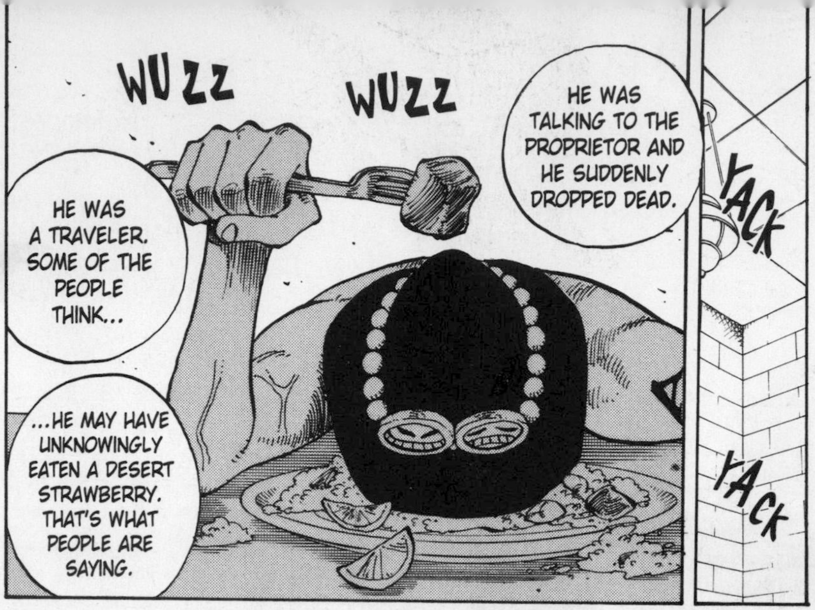
YACK
HE WAS TALKING TO THE PROPRIETOR AND HE SUDDENLY DROPPED DEAD.
WUZZ
WUZZ
HE WAS A TRAVELER. SOME OF THE PEOPLE THINK...
YACK
...HE MAY HAVE UNKNOWINGLY EATEN A DESERT STRAWBERRY. THAT'S WHAT PEOPLE ARE SAYING.

* SYMBOL ON HIS BACK IS AN ANCIENT BUDDHIST SYMBOL, NOT A SWASTIKA - Ed.

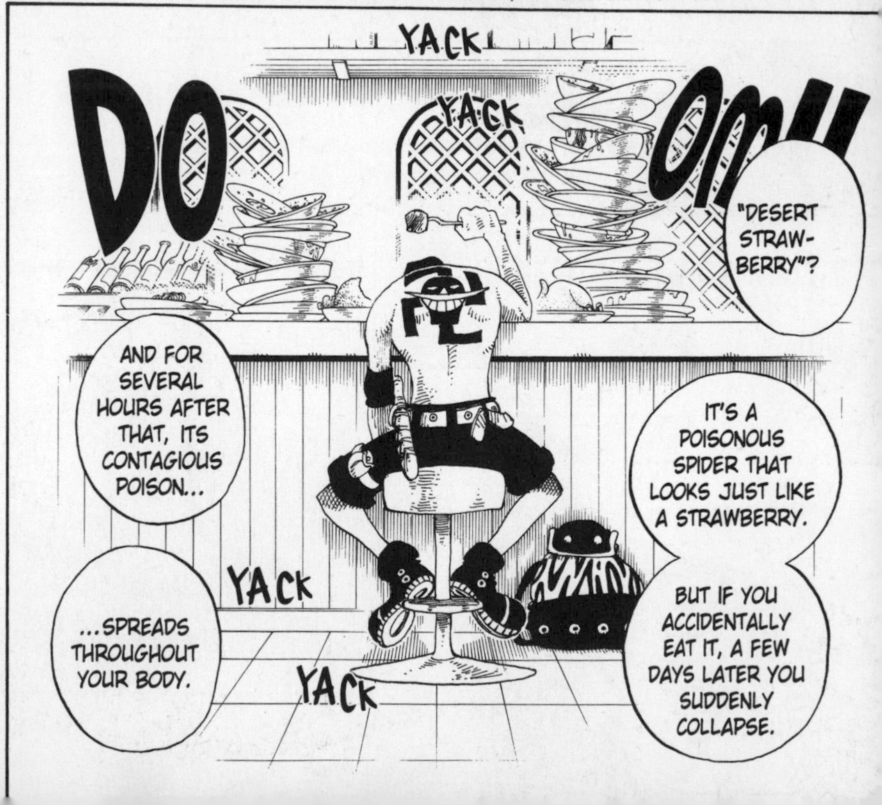
YACK
OM!!
YACK
DO
"DESERT STRAW-BERRY"?
IT'S A POISONOUS SPIDER THAT LOOKS JUST LIKE A STRAWBERRY.
BUT IF YOU ACCIDENTALLY EAT IT, A FEW DAYS LATER YOU SUDDENLY COLLAPSE.
AND FOR SEVERAL HOURS AFTER THAT, ITS CONTAGIOUS POISON...
YACK
...SPREADS THROUGHOUT YOUR BODY.
YACK

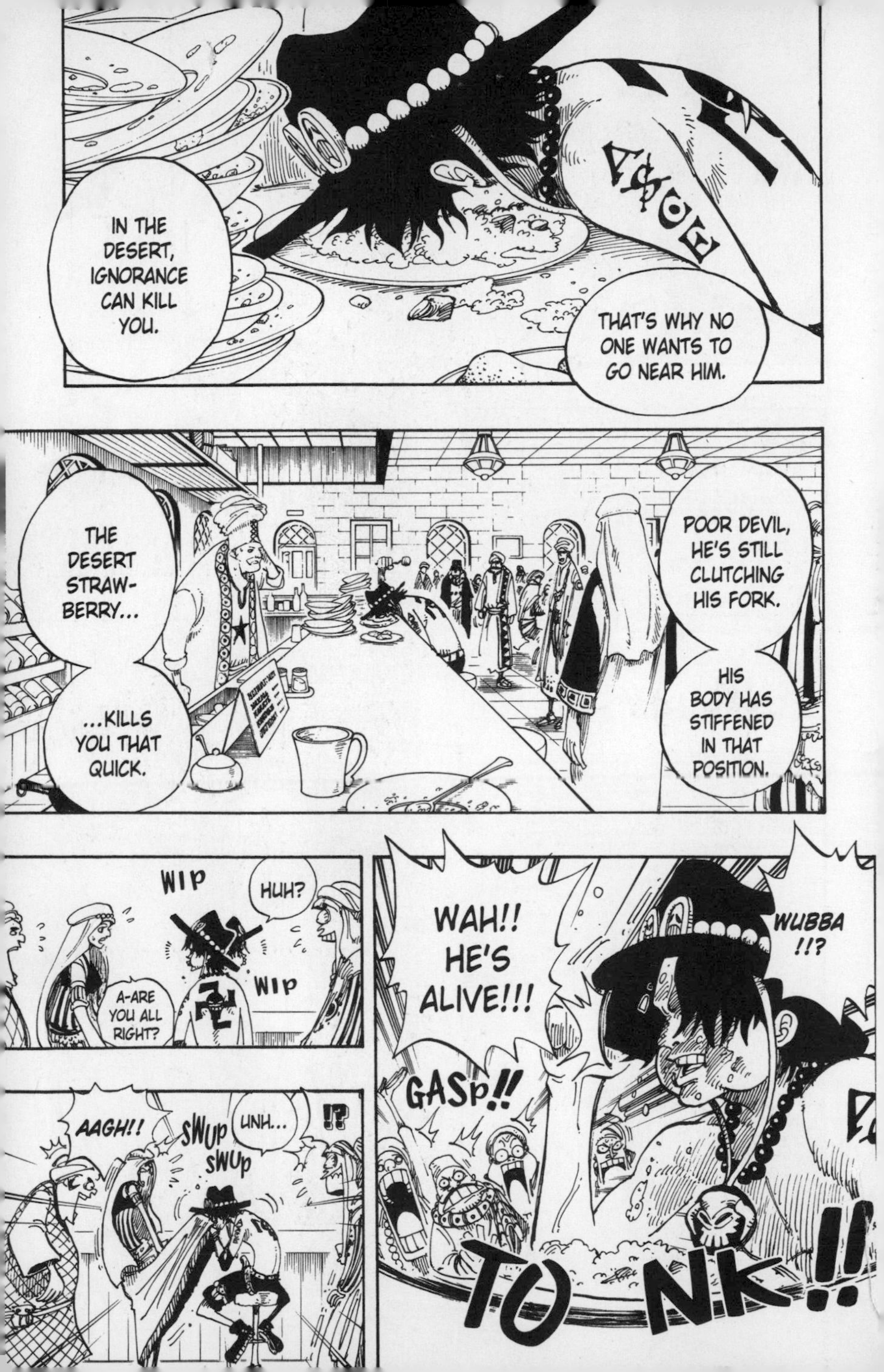
THAT'S WHY NO ONE WANTS TO GO NEAR HIM.
IN THE DESERT, IGNORANCE CAN KILL YOU.
POOR DEVIL, HE'S STILL CLUTCHING HIS FORK.
HIS BODY HAS STIFFENED IN THAT POSITION.
THE DESERT STRAW-BERRY...
...KILLS YOU THAT QUICK.
WUBBA!!?
WAH!! HE'S ALIVE!!!
GASP!!
TONK!!
HUH?
WIP
WIP
A-ARE YOU ALL RIGHT?
!?
UNH...
SWUP SWUP
AAGH!!

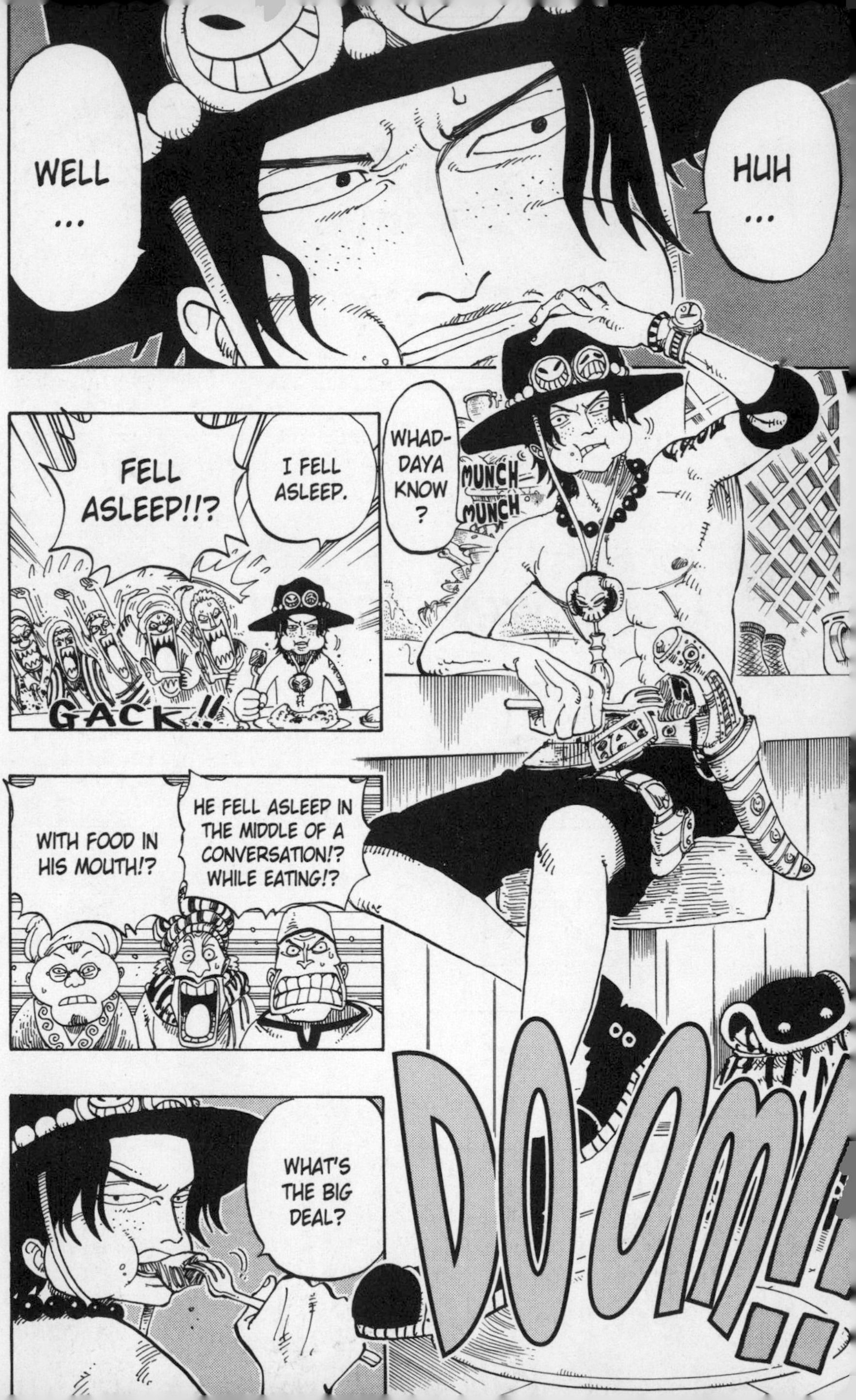
HUH ...
WELL ...
WHAD-DAYA KNOW?
MUNCH MUNCH
DOOM
I FELL ASLEEP.
FELL ASLEEP!!?
GACK!!
HE FELL ASLEEP IN THE MIDDLE OF A CONVERSATION!? WHILE EATING!?
WITH FOOD IN HIS MOUTH!?
WHAT'S THE BIG DEAL?

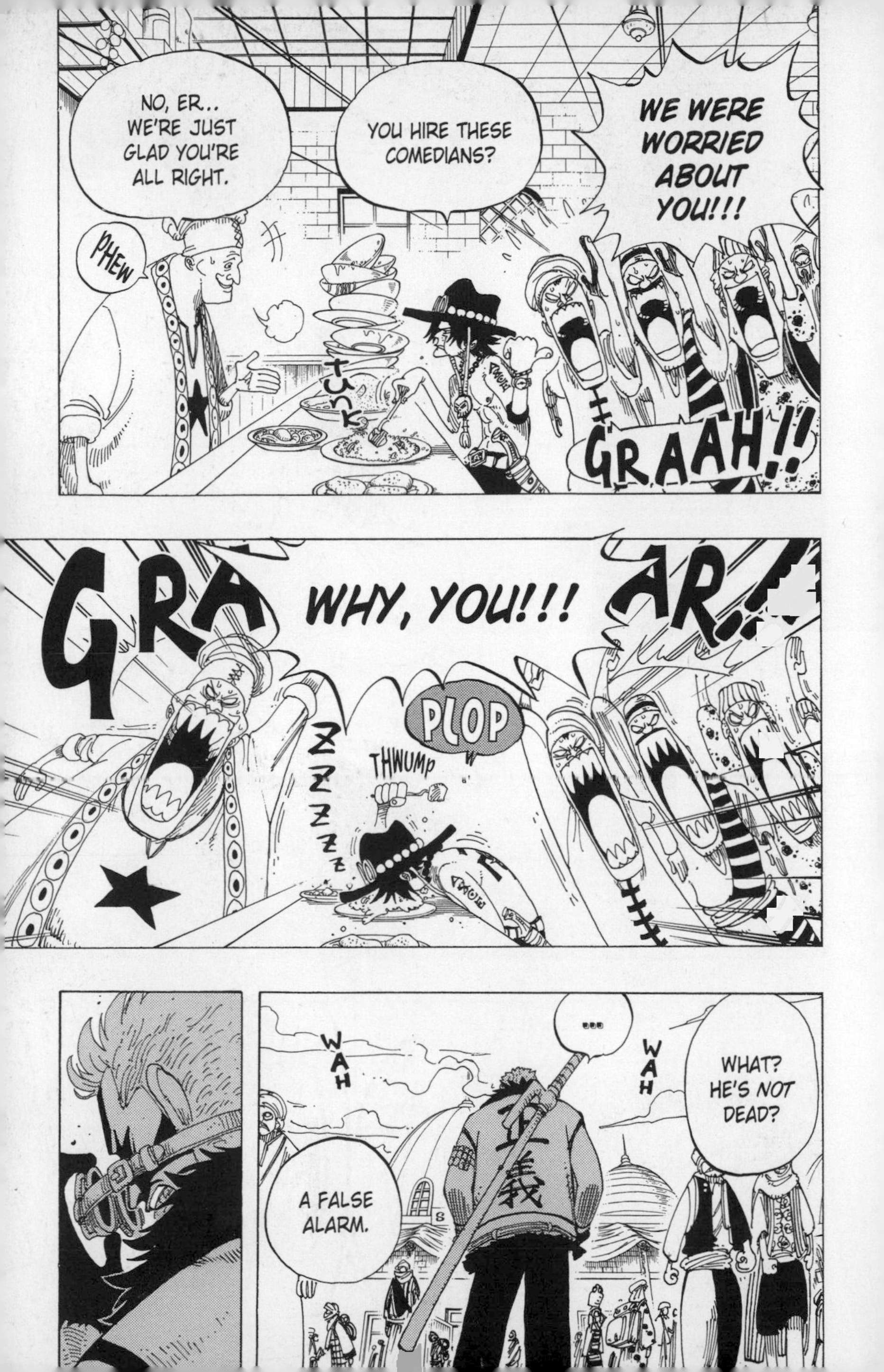
WE WERE WORRIED ABOUT YOU!!!
YOU HIRE THESE COMEDIANS?
NO, ER... WE'RE JUST GLAD YOU'RE ALL RIGHT.
PHEW
TUNK
GRAAH!!
GRA
WHY, YOU!!!
AR..!
PLOP
THWUMP
ZZZZZZ
WHAT? HE'S *NOT* DEAD?
WAH
...
WAH
A FALSE ALARM.

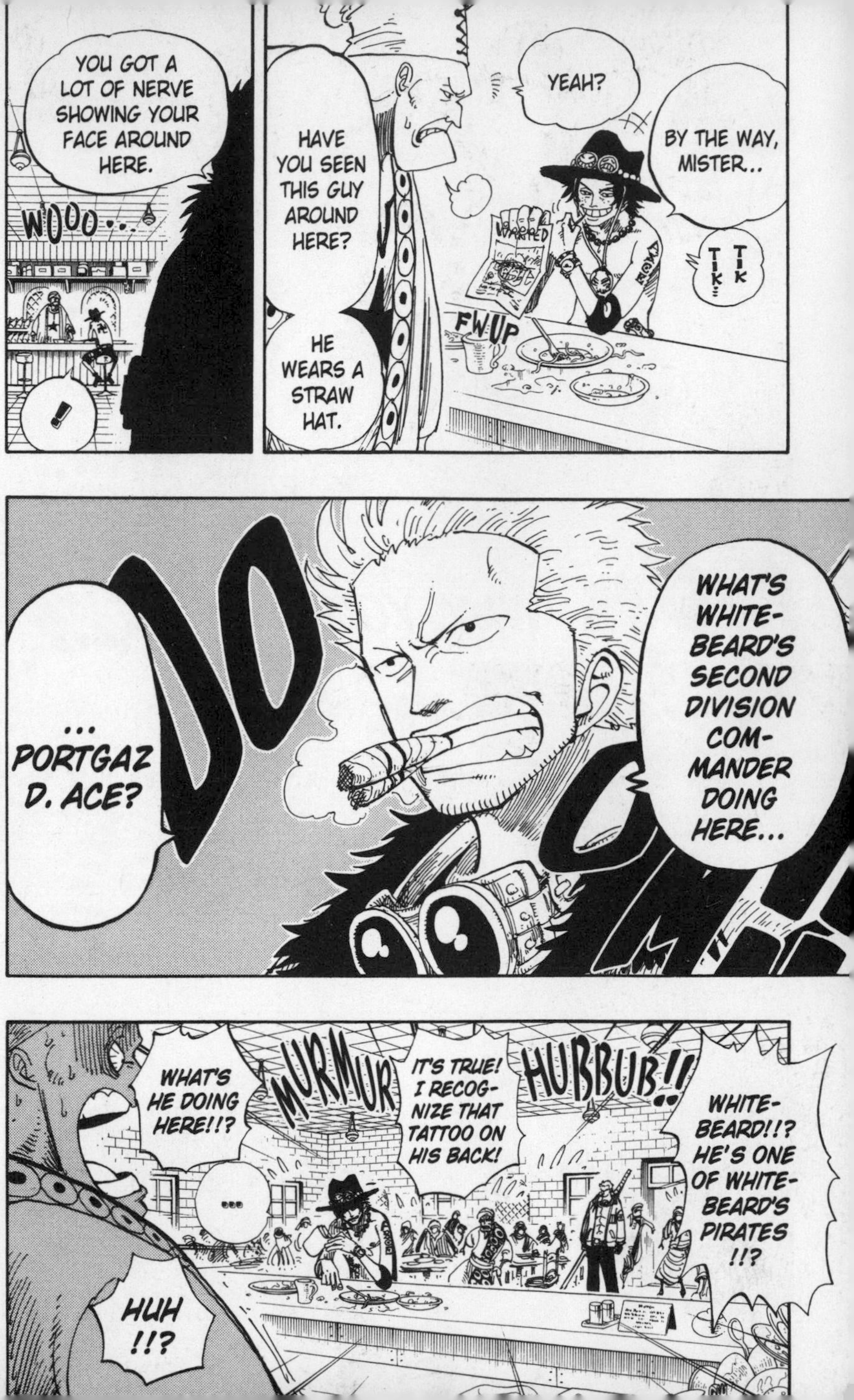
BY THE WAY, MISTER...
YEAH?
TIK TIK...
WANTED
HAVE YOU SEEN THIS GUY AROUND HERE?
FWUP
HE WEARS A STRAW HAT.
YOU GOT A LOT OF NERVE SHOWING YOUR FACE AROUND HERE.
WOOO...
!
WHAT'S WHITE-BEARD'S SECOND DIVISION COM-MANDER DOING HERE...
... PORTGAZ D. ACE?
WHITE-BEARD!!? HE'S ONE OF WHITE-BEARD'S PIRATES!!?
HUBBUB!!
IT'S TRUE! I RECOG-NIZE THAT TATTOO ON HIS BACK!
MURMUR
WHAT'S HE DOING HERE!!?
...
HUH!!?

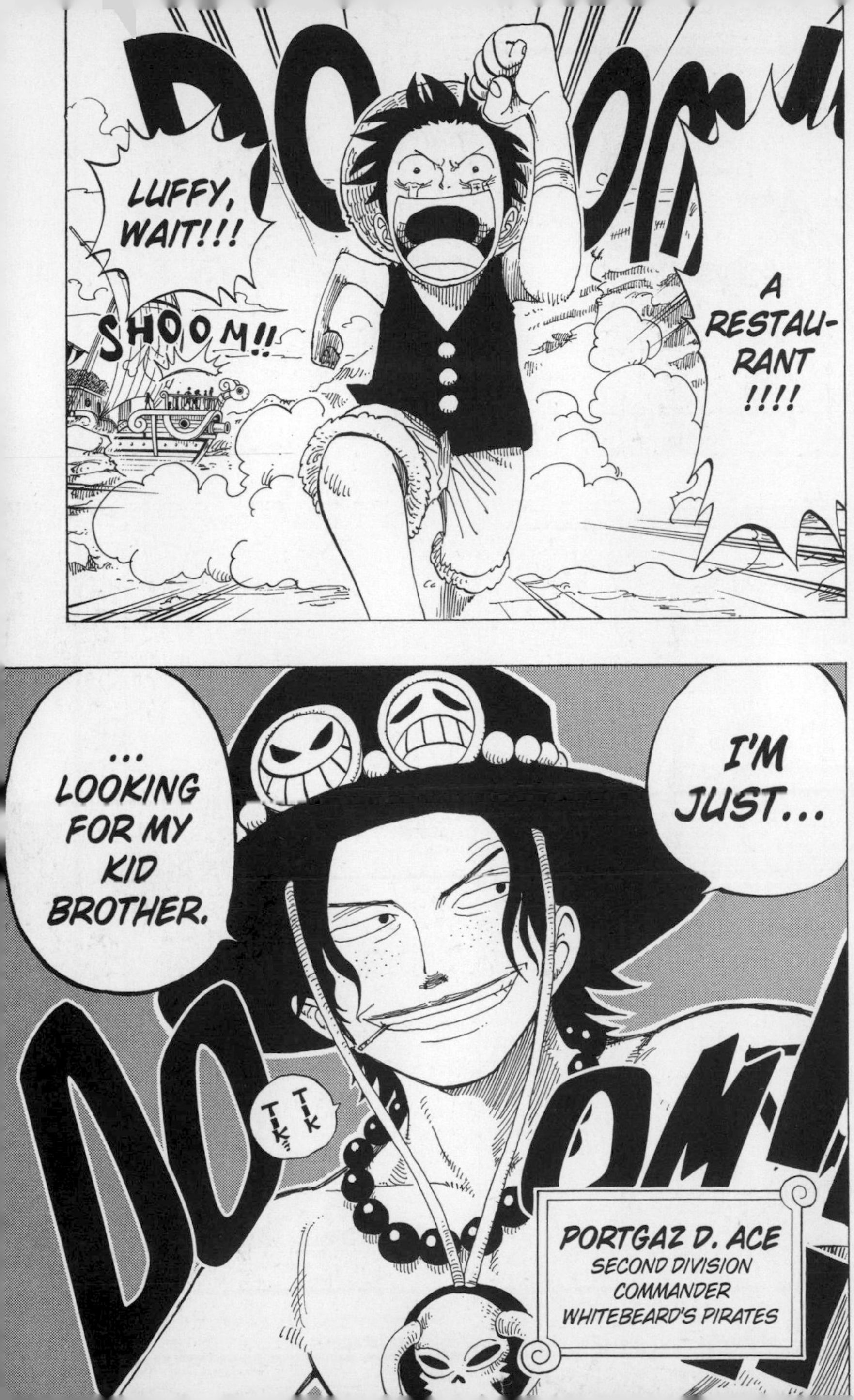
A RESTAU-RANT!!!!
DOOM
LUFFY, WAIT!!!
SHOOM!!
I'M JUST...
...LOOKING FOR MY KID BROTHER.
TIK TIK
DOOM
PORTGAZ D. ACE
SECOND DIVISION COMMANDER
WHITEBEARD'S PIRATES

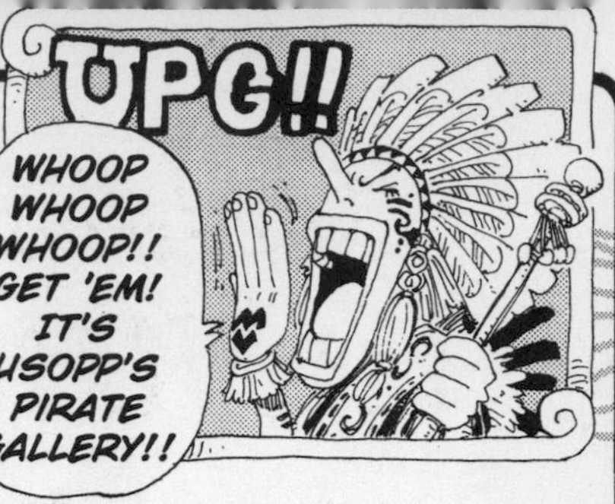
UPG!!
WHOOP WHOOP WHOOP!! GET 'EM! IT'S USOPP'S PIRATE GALLERY!!

WE'RE GONNA WIN NEXT YEAR'S DANCE CONTEST!!

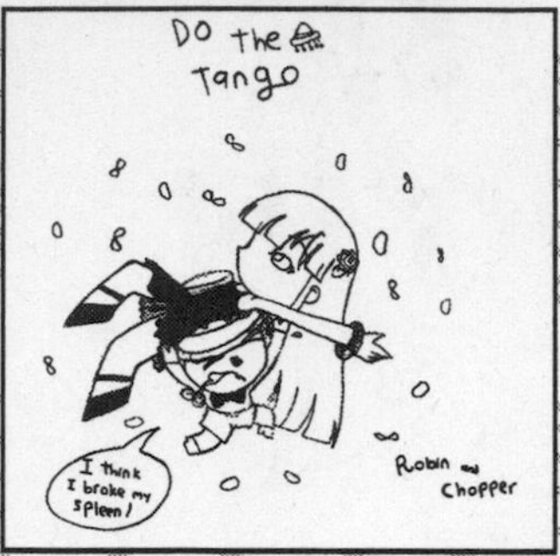
Do the Tango
I think I broke my spleen!
Robin and Chopper

DOYIN, 14

ARRRGH!! FEED ME!!!

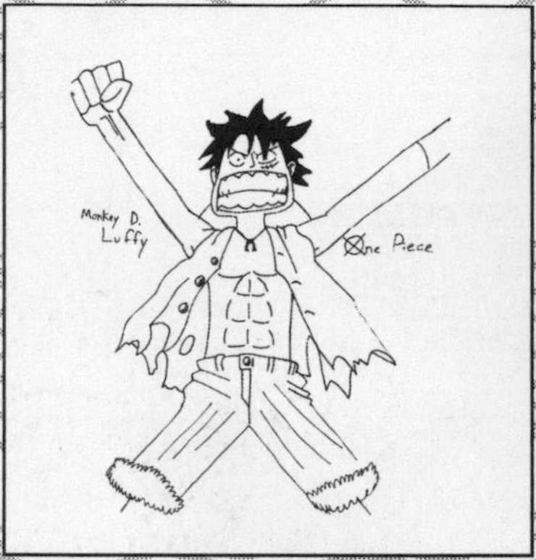
Monkey D. Luffy
One Piece

CHRIS C.

I GOT YOUR BACK!

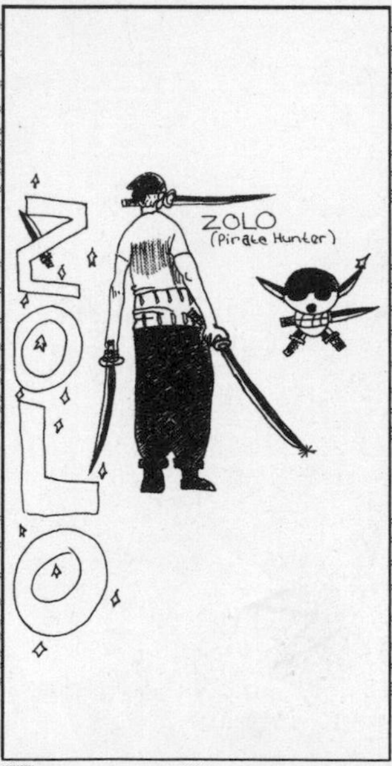
ZOLO
ZOLO
(Pirate Hunter)

TIFFANY, 13

I'M AFTER YOU, STRAW HATS!!

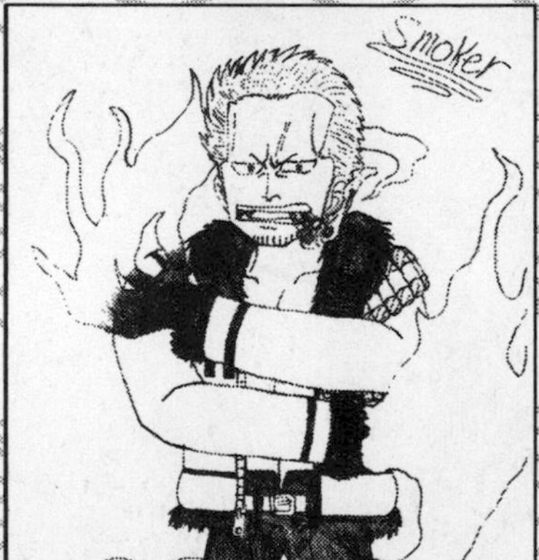
Smoker

KAYLEIGH

SUBMIT YOUR FAN ART TO:
SHONEN JUMP C/O VIZ MEDIA, LLC P.O. BOX 77010 SAN FRANCISCO, CA 94107
*REMEMBER TO INCLUDE YOUR NAME, AGE AND PARENT RELEASE FORM!!

USOPP'S COMMENTS WERE TRANSMITTED THROUGH THE U.S. SHONEN JUMP TEAM -EDITOR

Chapter 158:
LANDING IN ALABASTA

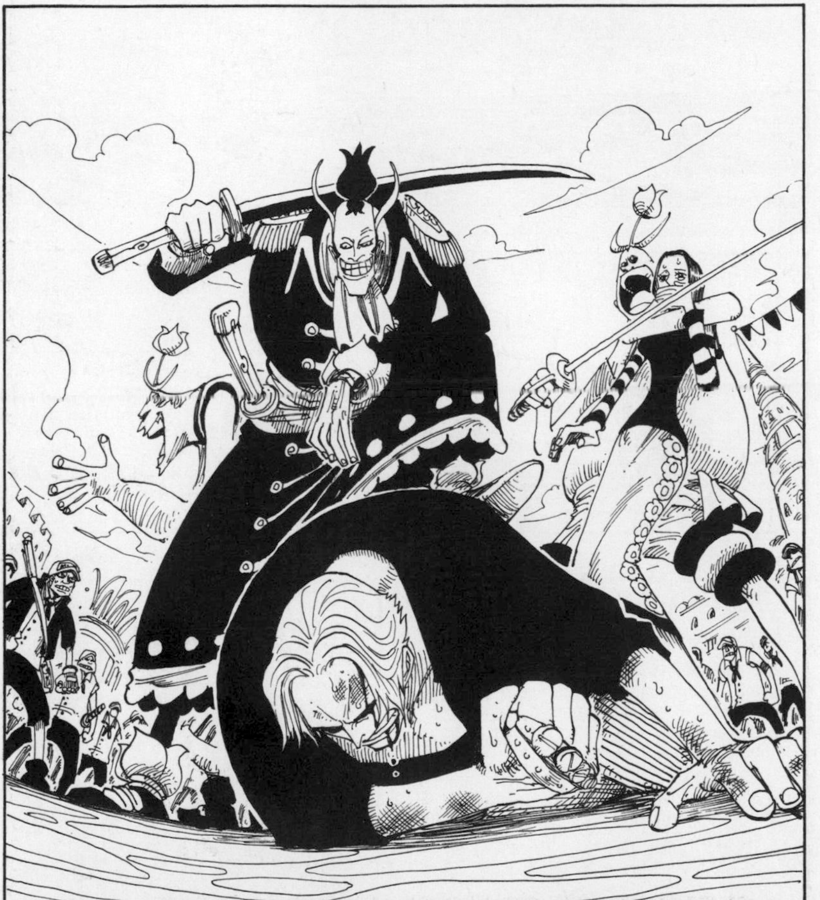

DJANGO'S DANCE PARADISE, VOL. 25:
"THE WEAK FANG OF JUSTICE"

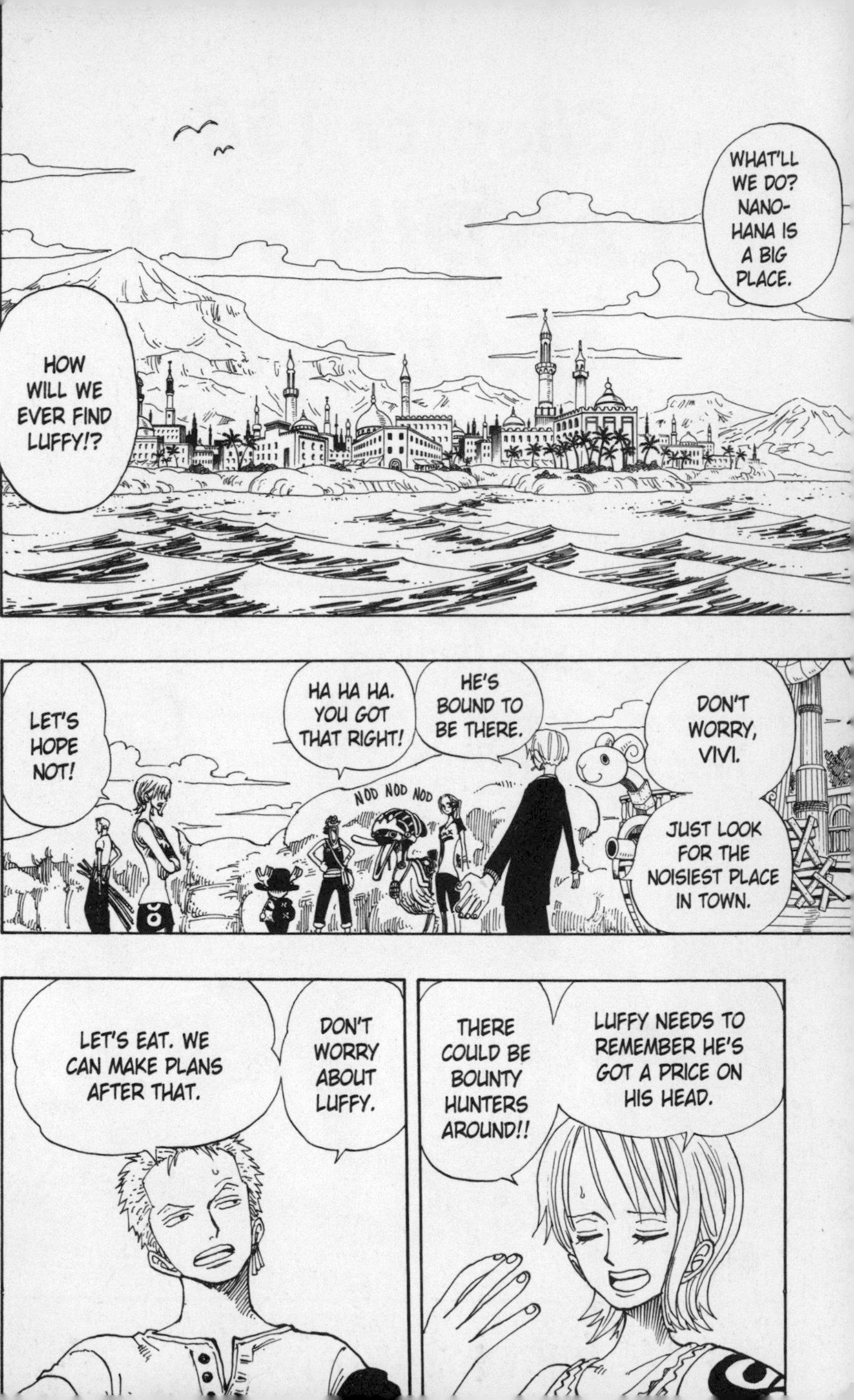
WHAT'LL WE DO? NANO-HANA IS A BIG PLACE.
HOW WILL WE EVER FIND LUFFY!?
DON'T WORRY, VIVI.
JUST LOOK FOR THE NOISIEST PLACE IN TOWN.
HE'S BOUND TO BE THERE.
HA HA HA. YOU GOT THAT RIGHT!
NOD NOD NOD
LET'S HOPE NOT!
LUFFY NEEDS TO REMEMBER HE'S GOT A PRICE ON HIS HEAD.
THERE COULD BE BOUNTY HUNTERS AROUND!!
DON'T WORRY ABOUT LUFFY.
LET'S EAT. WE CAN MAKE PLANS AFTER THAT.

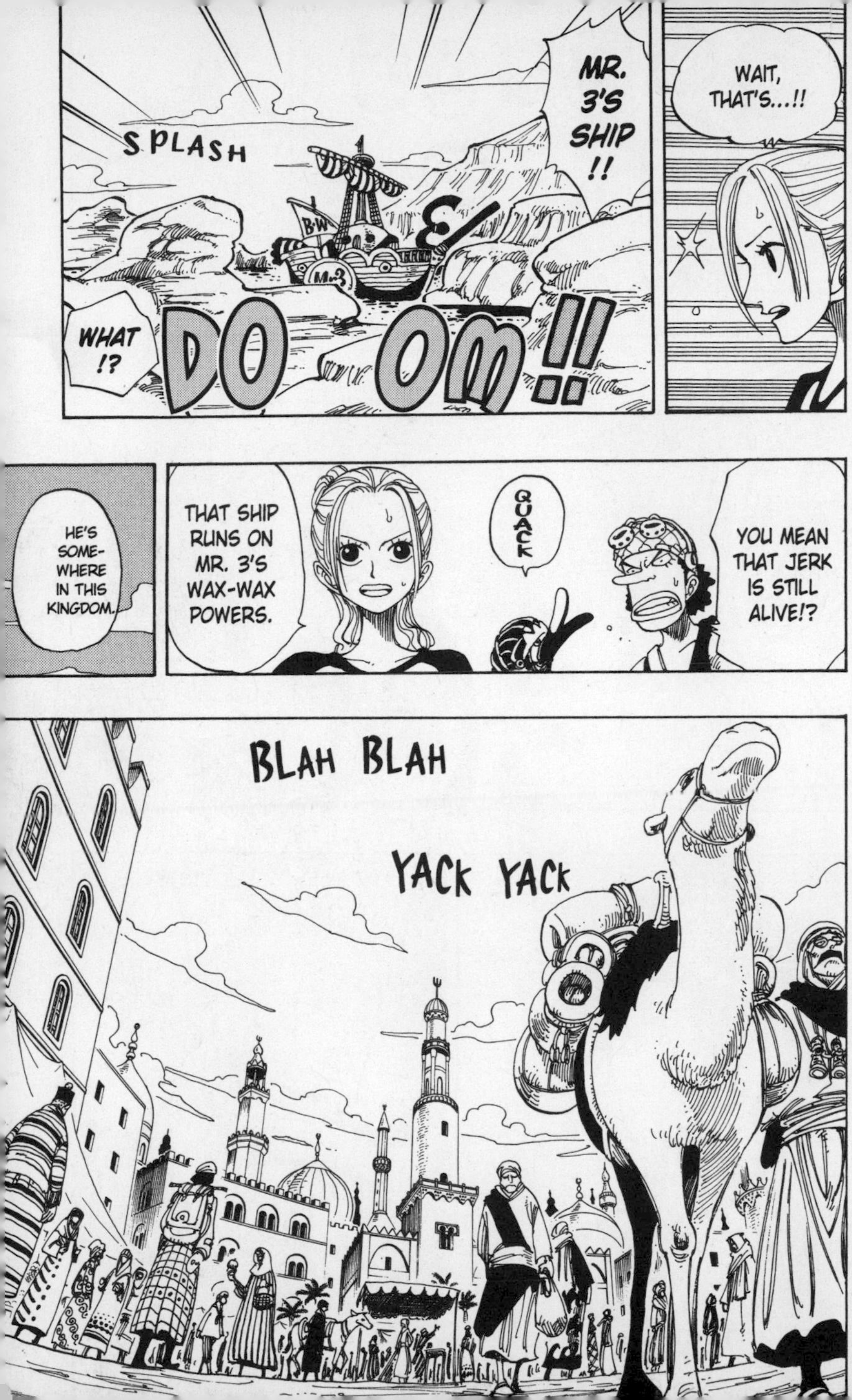
WAIT, THAT'S...!!
MR. 3'S SHIP !!
SPLASH
WHAT !?
DOOM!!
YOU MEAN THAT JERK IS STILL ALIVE!?
QUACK
THAT SHIP RUNS ON MR. 3'S WAX-WAX POWERS.
HE'S SOME-WHERE IN THIS KINGDOM.
BLAH BLAH
YACK YACK

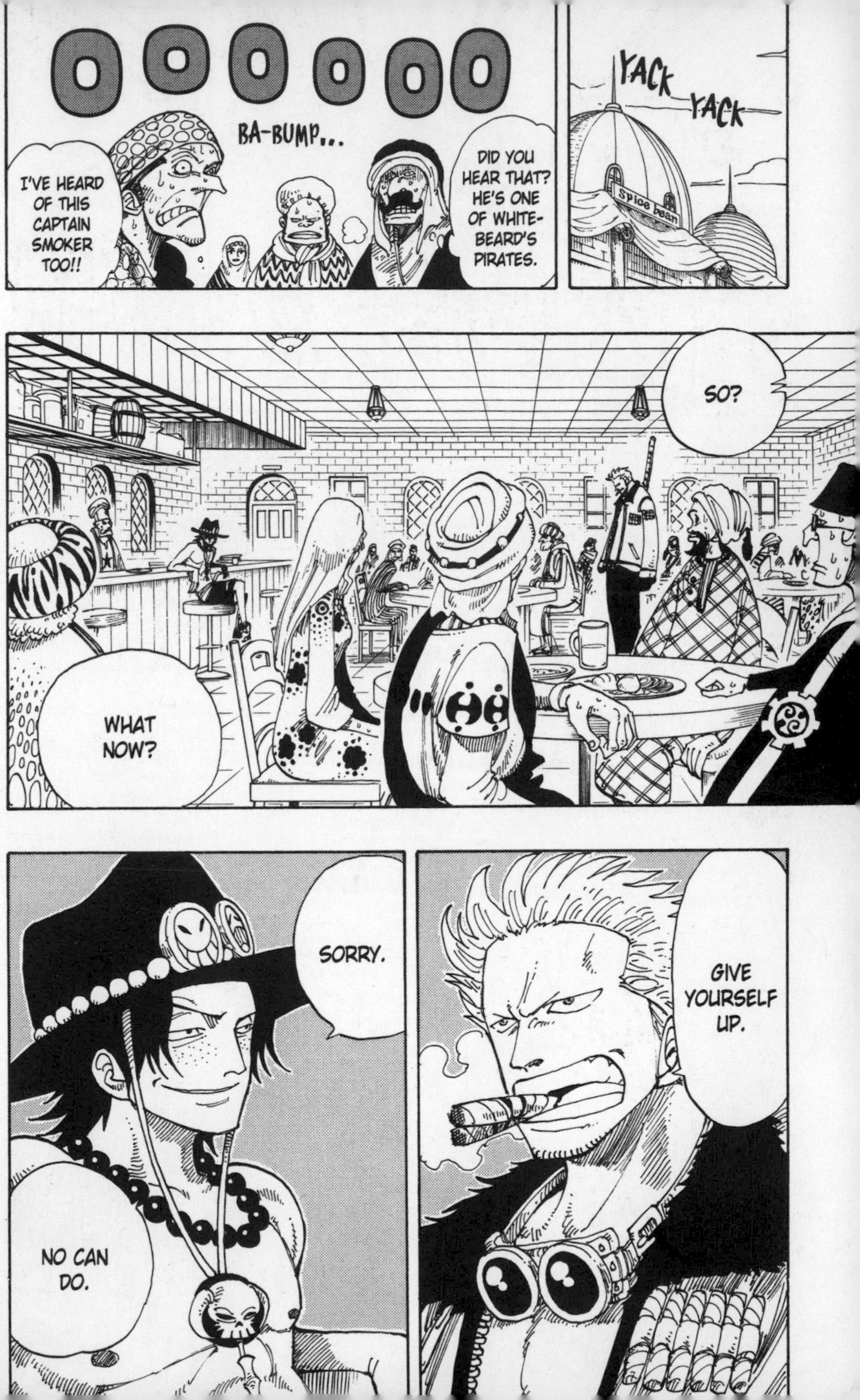
YACK
YACK
Spice bean
OOOOOO
DID YOU HEAR THAT? HE'S ONE OF WHITE-BEARD'S PIRATES.
BA-BUMP...
I'VE HEARD OF THIS CAPTAIN SMOKER TOO!!
SO?
WHAT NOW?
GIVE YOURSELF UP.
SORRY.
NO CAN DO.

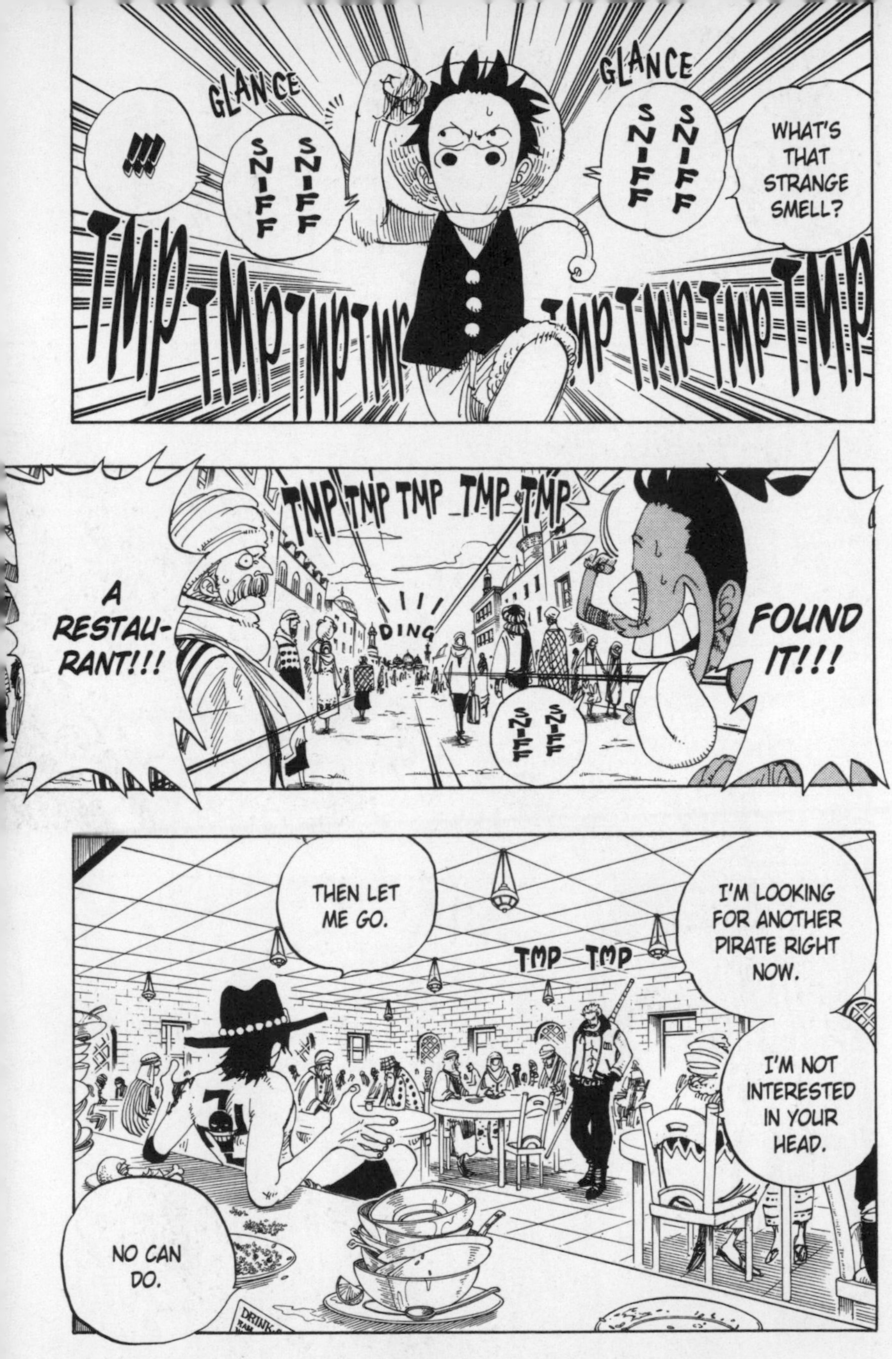
WHAT'S THAT STRANGE SMELL?
SNIFF SNIFF
GLANCE
SNIFF SNIFF
GLANCE
!!!
TMP TMP TMP TMP
TMP TMP TMP TMP
FOUND IT!!!
SNIFF SNIFF
TMP TMP TMP TMP TMP
DING
A RESTAU-RANT!!!
I'M LOOKING FOR ANOTHER PIRATE RIGHT NOW.
I'M NOT INTERESTED IN YOUR HEAD.
TMP TMP
THEN LET ME GO.
NO CAN DO.
DRINK

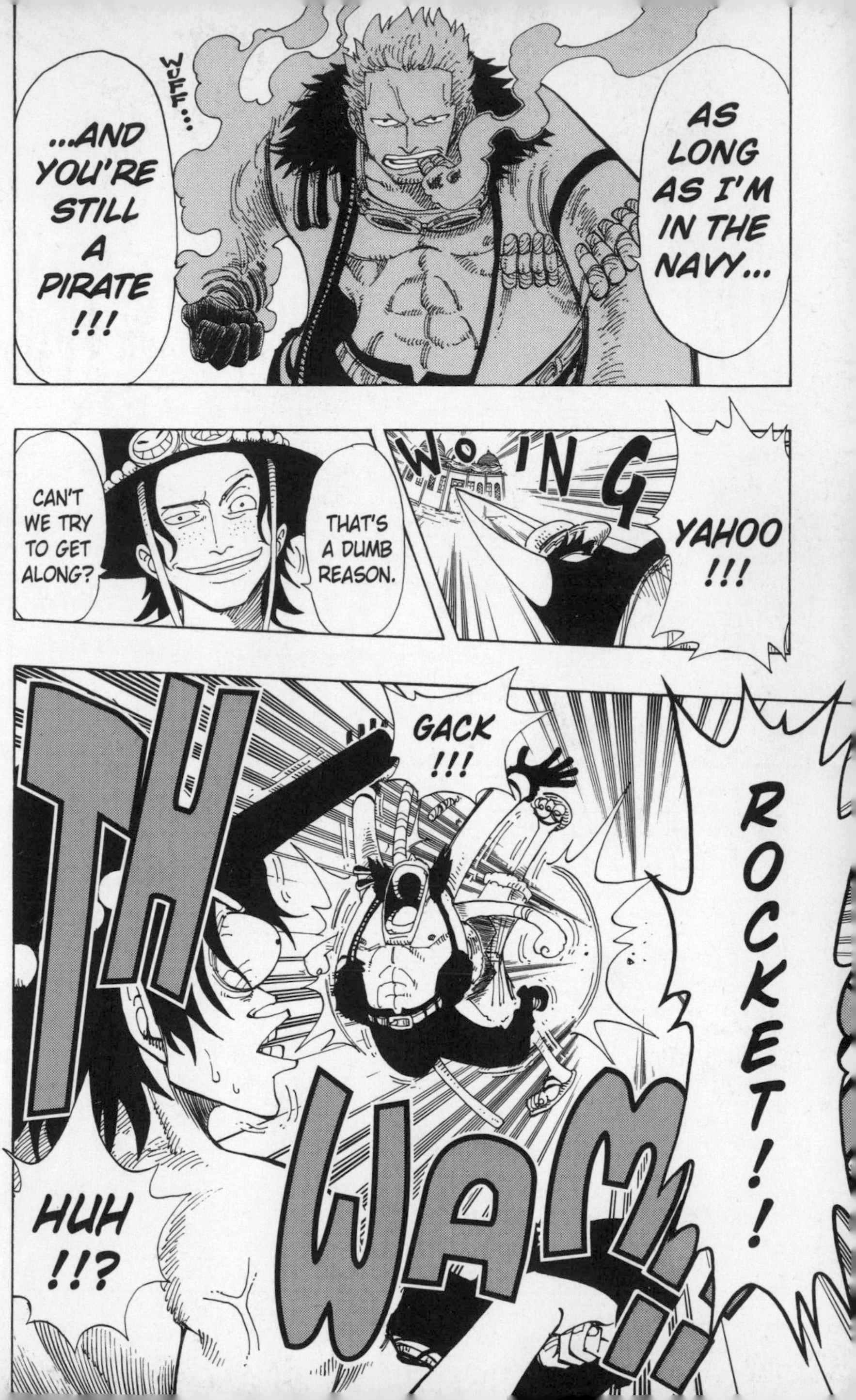
AS LONG AS I'M IN THE NAVY...
WUFF...
...AND YOU'RE STILL A PIRATE!!!
WOING
YAHOO!!!
THAT'S A DUMB REASON.
CAN'T WE TRY TO GET ALONG?
ROCKET!!
GACK!!!
THWAM!!
HUH!!?

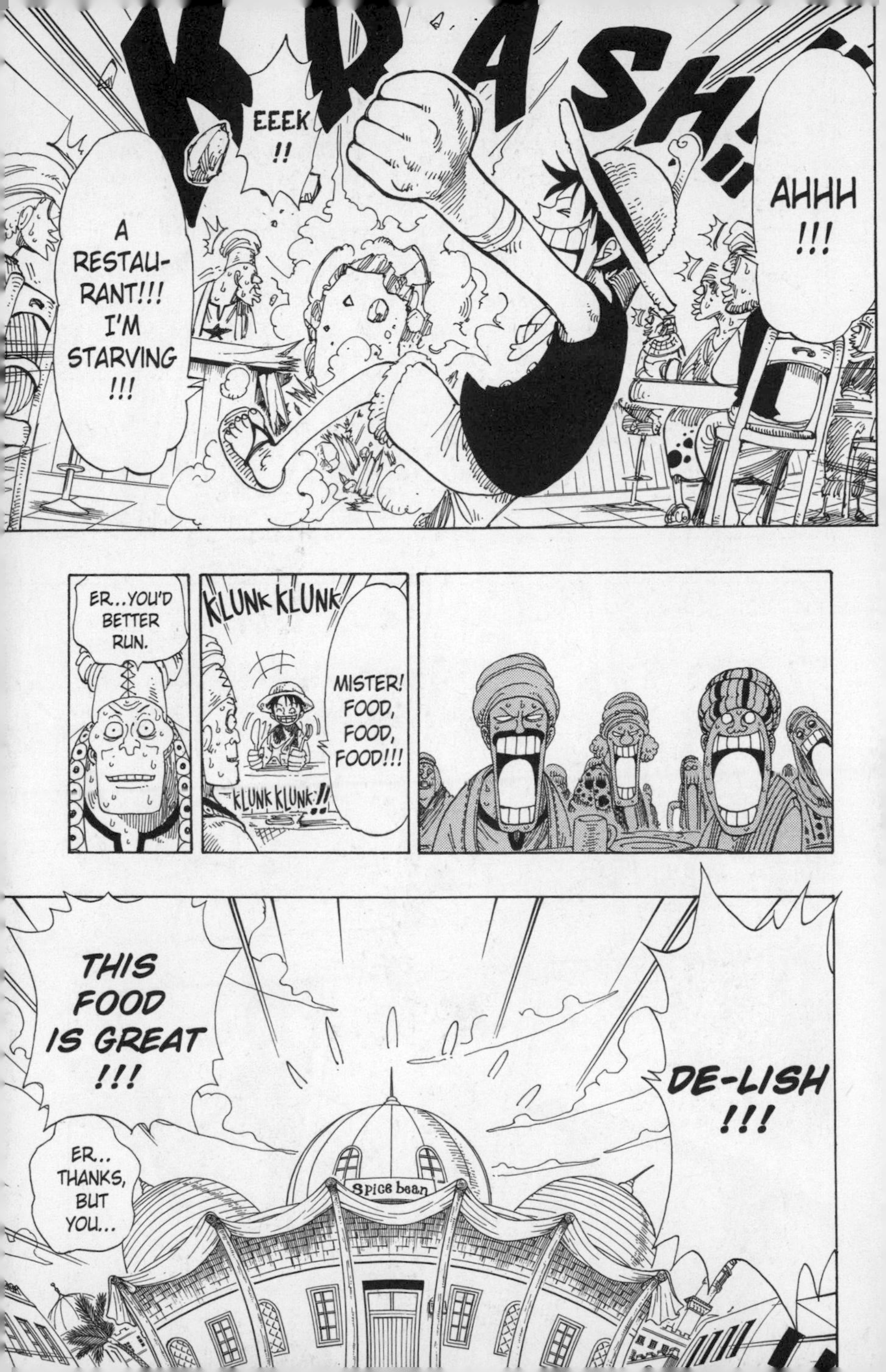
KRASH!!
AHHH!!!
EEEK!!
A RESTAU-RANT!!! I'M STARVING!!!
KLUNK KLUNK
MISTER! FOOD, FOOD, FOOD!!!
KLUNK KLUNK!!
ER...YOU'D BETTER RUN.
DE-LISH!!!
THIS FOOD IS GREAT!!!
Spice bean
ER... THANKS, BUT YOU...

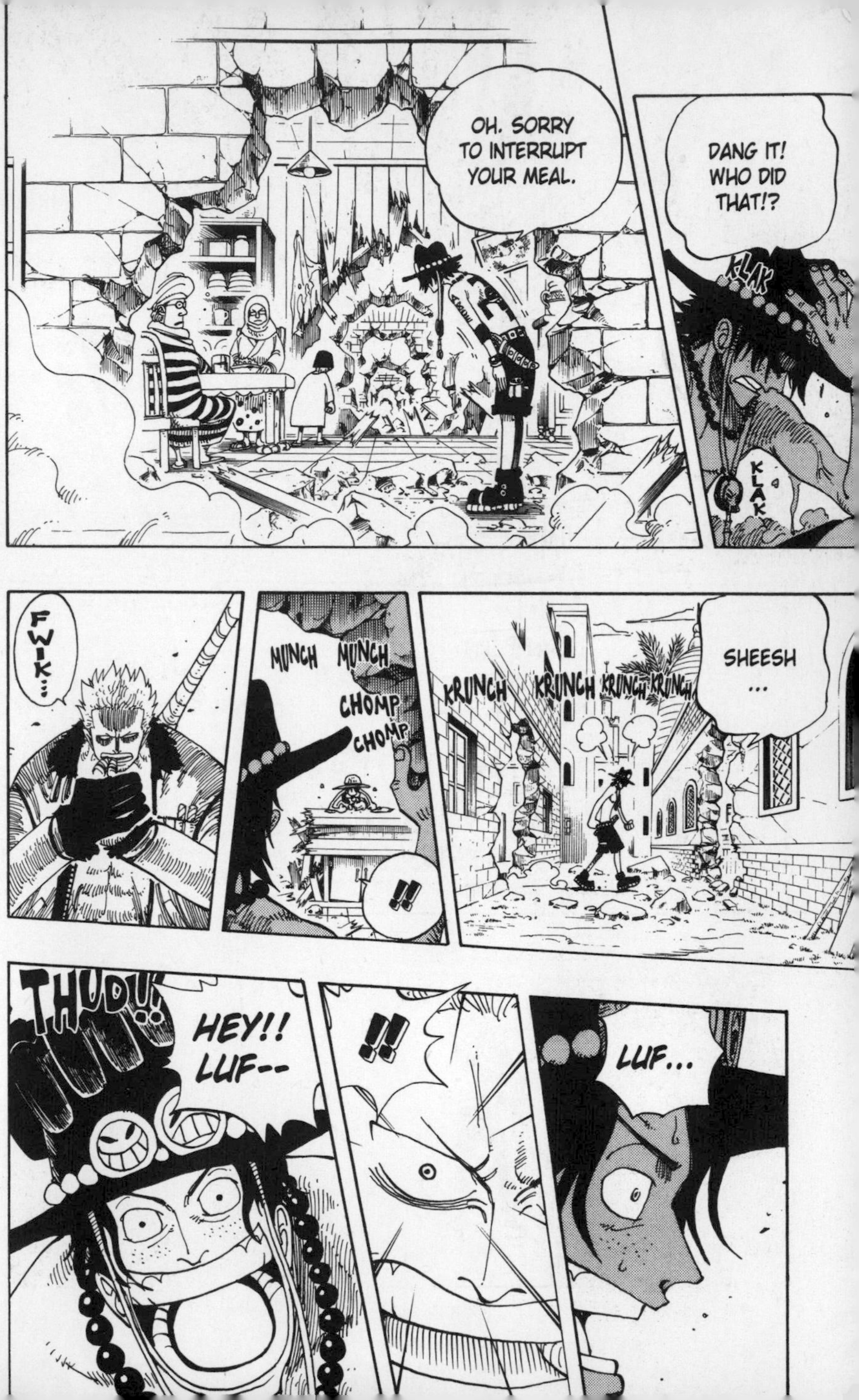
DANG IT! WHO DID THAT!?
KLAK
KLAK
OH. SORRY TO INTERRUPT YOUR MEAL.
SHEESH ...
KRUNCH
KRUNCH
KRUNCH
KRUNCH
MUNCH MUNCH
CHOMP CHOMP
!!
FWIK...
LUF...
!!
HEY!! LUF--
THUD!!

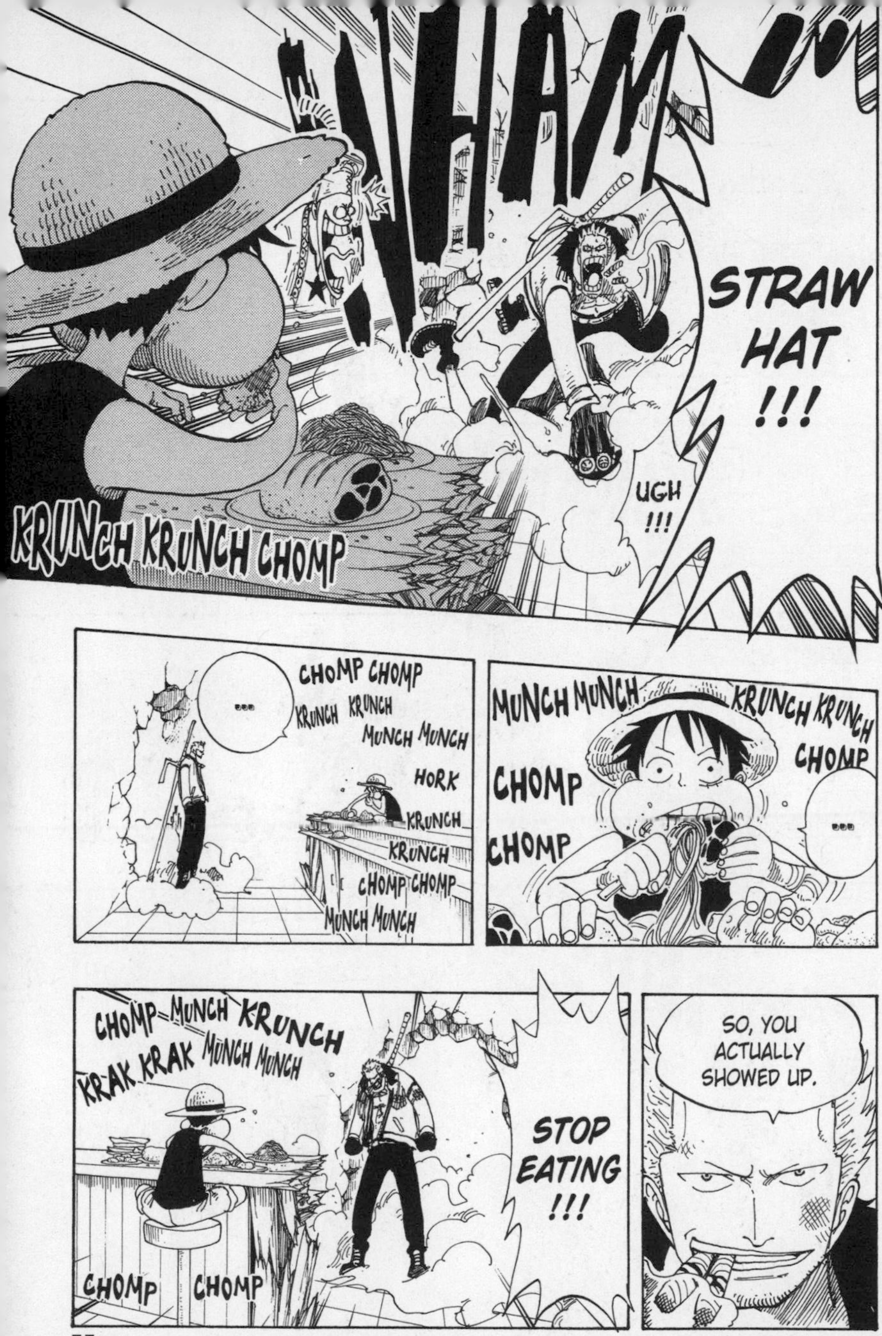
WHAM
STRAW HAT!!!
UGH!!!
KRUNCH KRUNCH CHOMP
KRUNCH KRUNCH CHOMP
MUNCH MUNCH
...
CHOMP
CHOMP
...
CHOMP CHOMP
KRUNCH KRUNCH
MUNCH MUNCH
HORK
KRUNCH
KRUNCH
CHOMP CHOMP
MUNCH MUNCH
SO, YOU ACTUALLY SHOWED UP.
STOP EATING!!!
CHOMP MUNCH KRUNCH
KRAK KRAK MUNCH MUNCH
CHOMP CHOMP

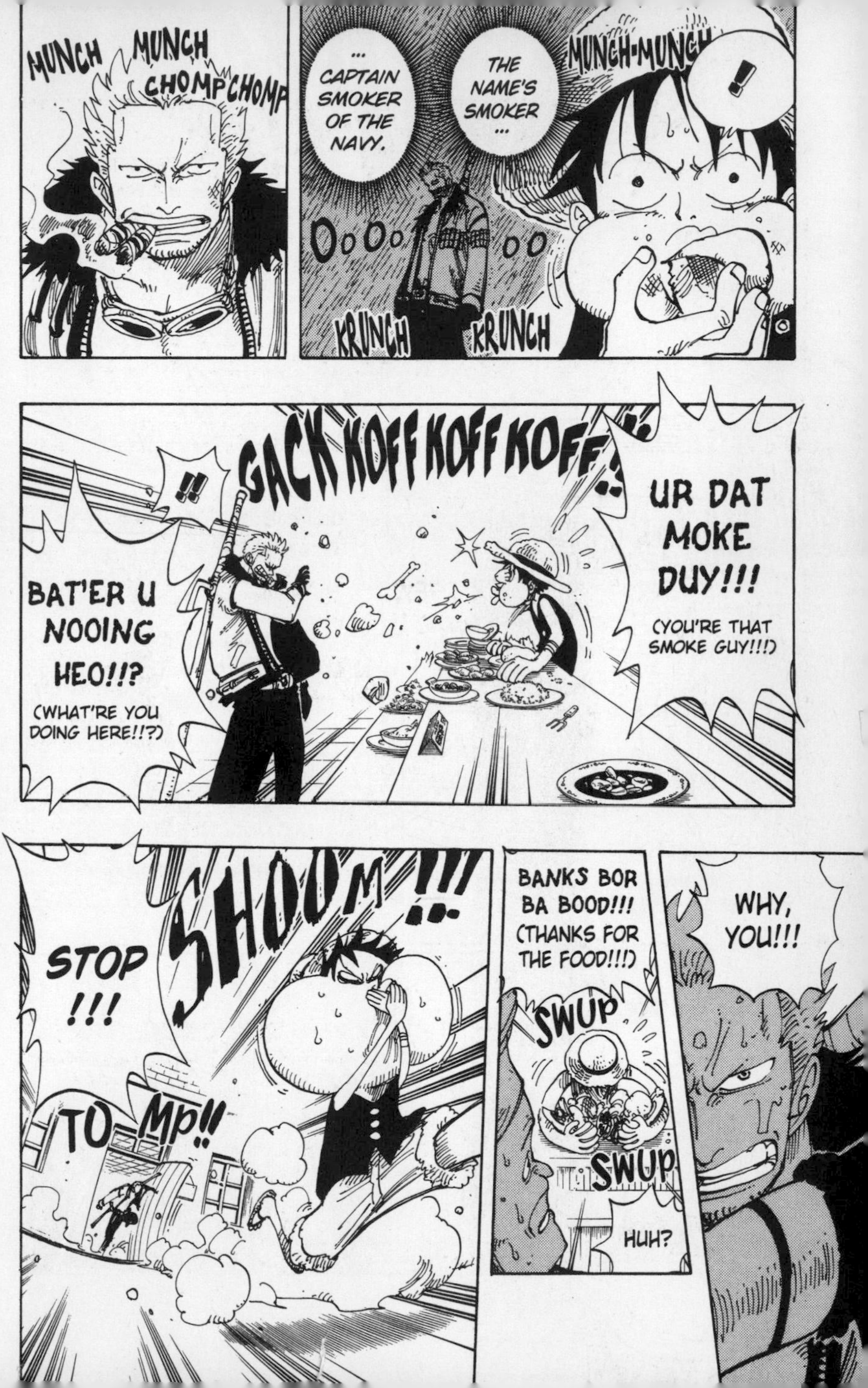
MUNCH-MUNCH
!
THE NAME'S SMOKER ...
... CAPTAIN SMOKER OF THE NAVY.
OoOo
OO
KRUNCH
KRUNCH
MUNCH MUNCH
CHOMP CHOMP
GACK KOFF KOFF KOFF
UR DAT MOKE DUY!!!
(YOU'RE THAT SMOKE GUY!!!)
!!
BAT'ER U NOOING HEO!!?
(WHAT'RE YOU DOING HERE!!?)
WHY, YOU!!!
BANKS BOR BA BOOD!!! (THANKS FOR THE FOOD!!!)
SWUP
SWUP
HUH?
SHOOM!!!
STOP !!!
TO-Mp!!

READ THIS WAY

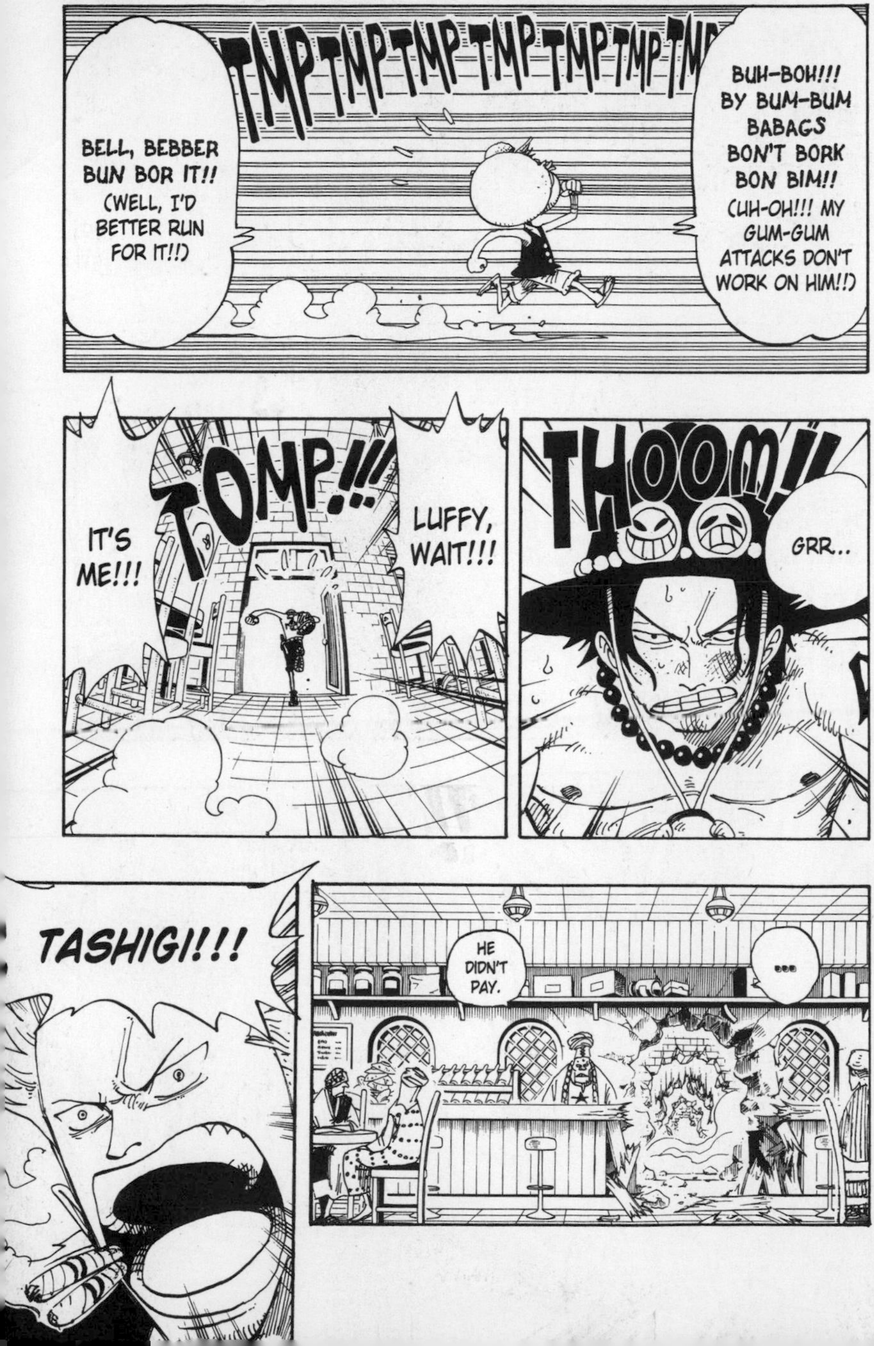
BUH-BOH!!! BY BUM-BUM BABAGS BON'T BORK BON BIM!! (UH-OH!!! MY GUM-GUM ATTACKS DON'T WORK ON HIM!!)
TMP TMP TMP TMP TMP TMP TMP
BELL, BEBBER BUN BOR IT!! (WELL, I'D BETTER RUN FOR IT!!)
THOOM!!
GRR...
LUFFY, WAIT!!!
TOMP!!!
IT'S ME!!!
...
HE DIDN'T PAY.
TASHIGI!!!

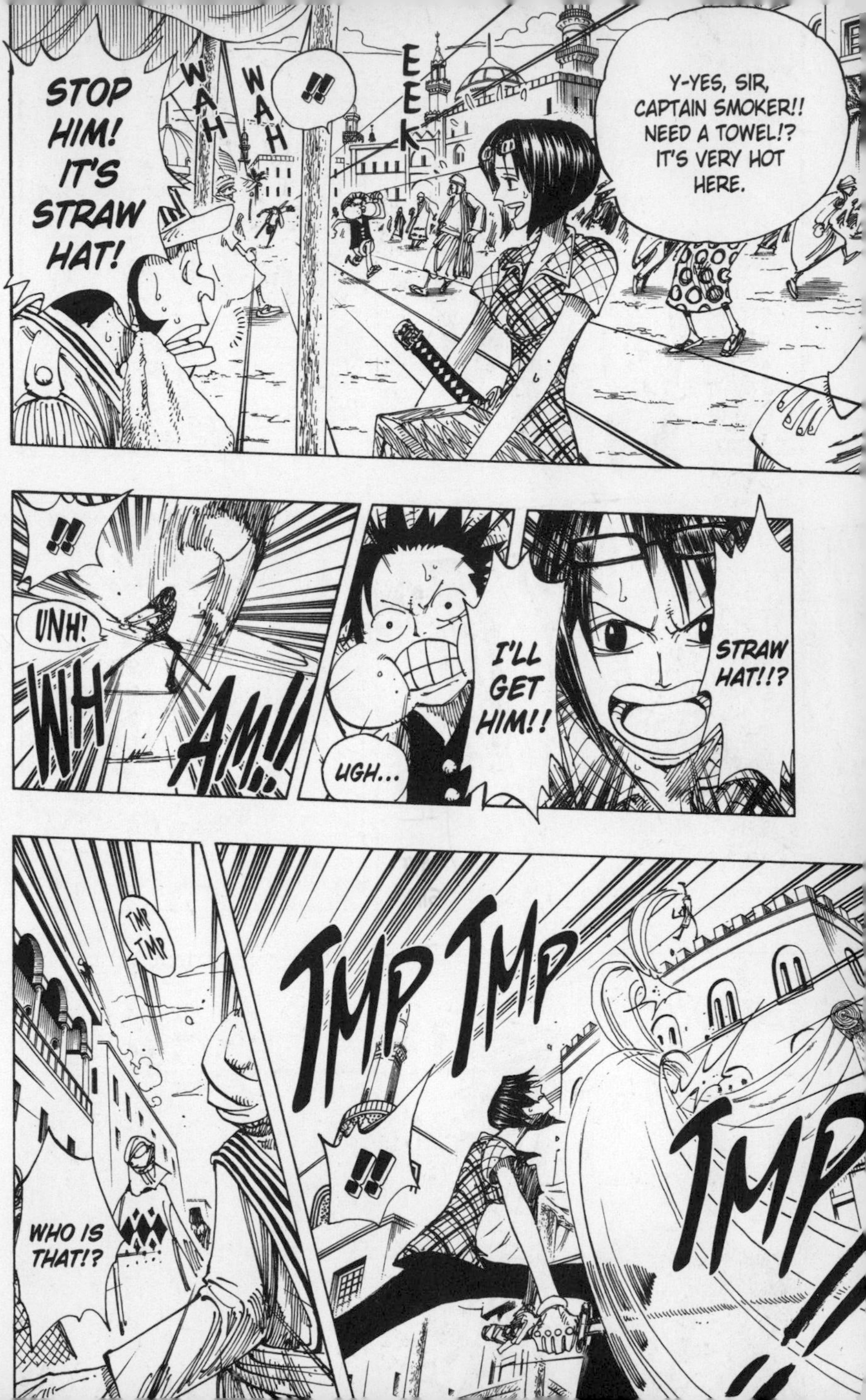
Y-YES, SIR, CAPTAIN SMOKER!! NEED A TOWEL!? IT'S VERY HOT HERE.
EEK
!!
WAH
WAH
STOP HIM! IT'S STRAW HAT!
STRAW HAT!!?
I'LL GET HIM!!
UGH...
!!
UNH!
WHAM!!
TMP
TMP TMP
!!
TMP TMP
WHO IS THAT!?

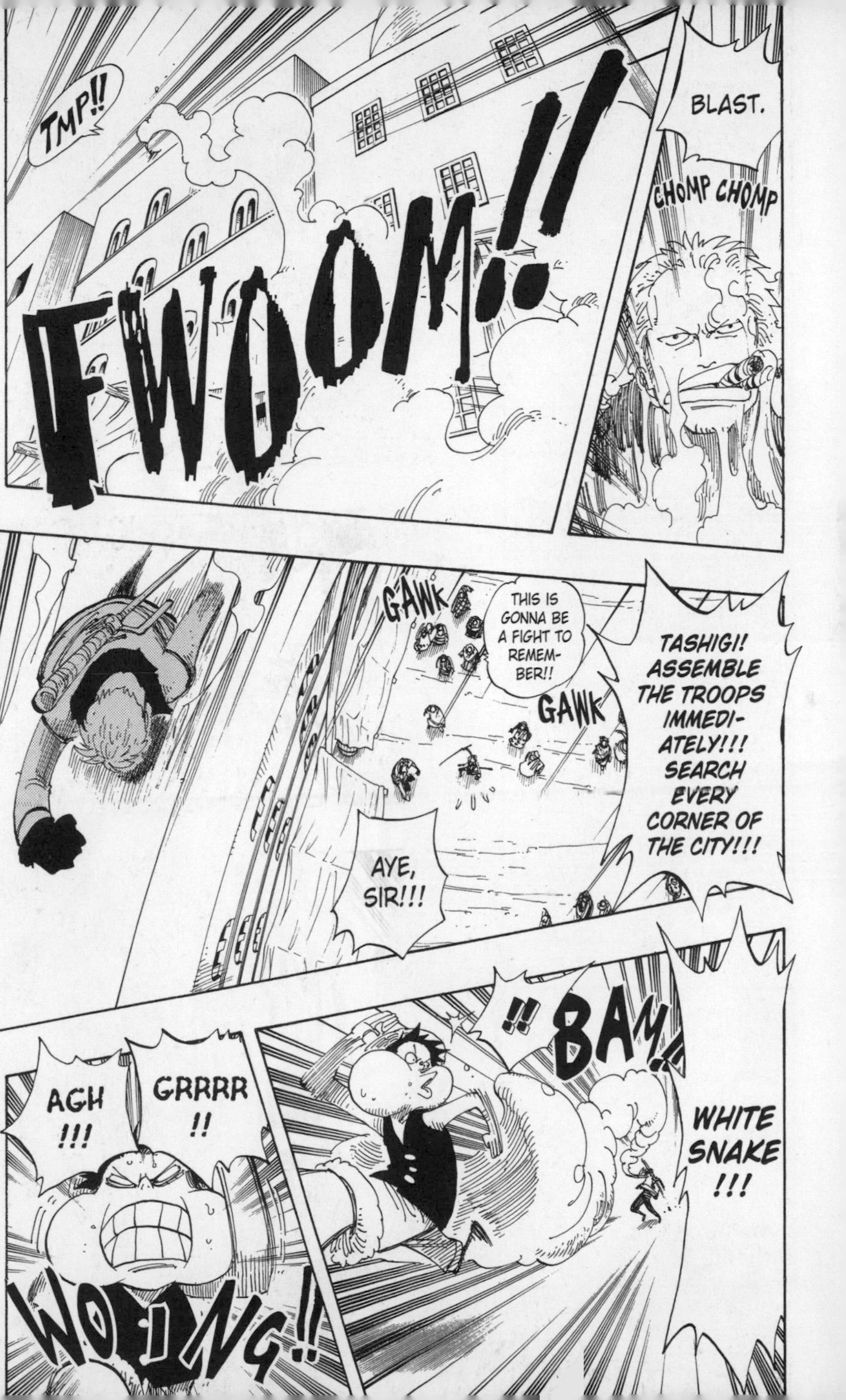
BLAST.
CHOMP CHOMP
TMP!!
FWOOM!!
TASHIGI! ASSEMBLE THE TROOPS IMMEDI-ATELY!!! SEARCH EVERY CORNER OF THE CITY!!!
AYE, SIR!!!
GAWK
THIS IS GONNA BE A FIGHT TO REMEM-BER!!
GAWK
WHITE SNAKE !!!
BAM!!
!!
GRRRR !!
AGH !!!
WOING!!

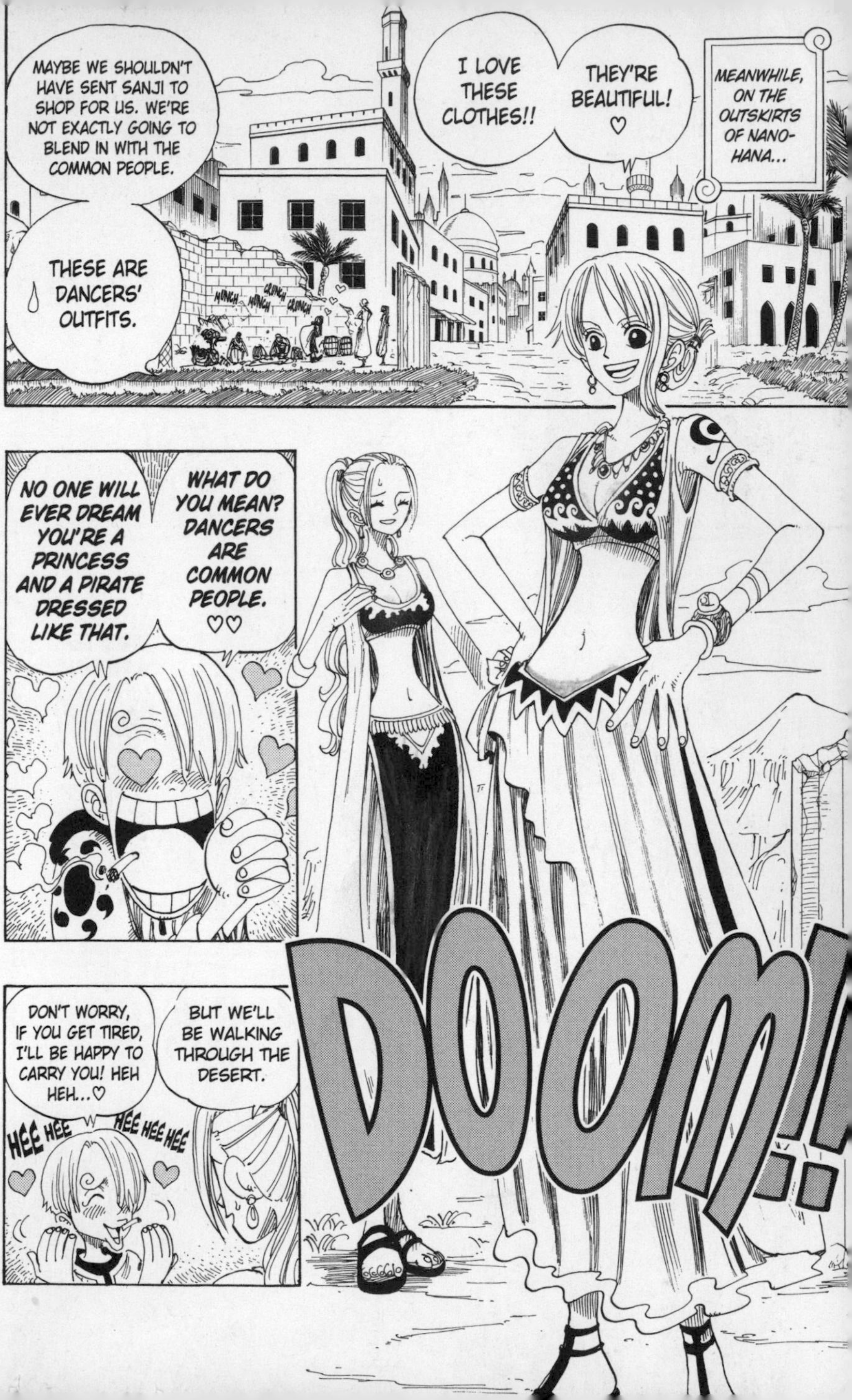
MEANWHILE, ON THE OUTSKIRTS OF NANO-HANA...
THEY'RE BEAUTIFUL! ♡
I LOVE THESE CLOTHES!!
MAYBE WE SHOULDN'T HAVE SENT SANJI TO SHOP FOR US. WE'RE NOT EXACTLY GOING TO BLEND IN WITH THE COMMON PEOPLE.
THESE ARE DANCERS' OUTFITS.
CRUNCH CRUNCH
MUNCH MUNCH
DOOM!!
WHAT DO YOU MEAN? DANCERS ARE COMMON PEOPLE. ♡♡
NO ONE WILL EVER DREAM YOU'RE A PRINCESS AND A PIRATE DRESSED LIKE THAT.
BUT WE'LL BE WALKING THROUGH THE DESERT.
DON'T WORRY, IF YOU GET TIRED, I'LL BE HAPPY TO CARRY YOU! HEH HEH...♡
HEE HEE HEE
HEE HEE

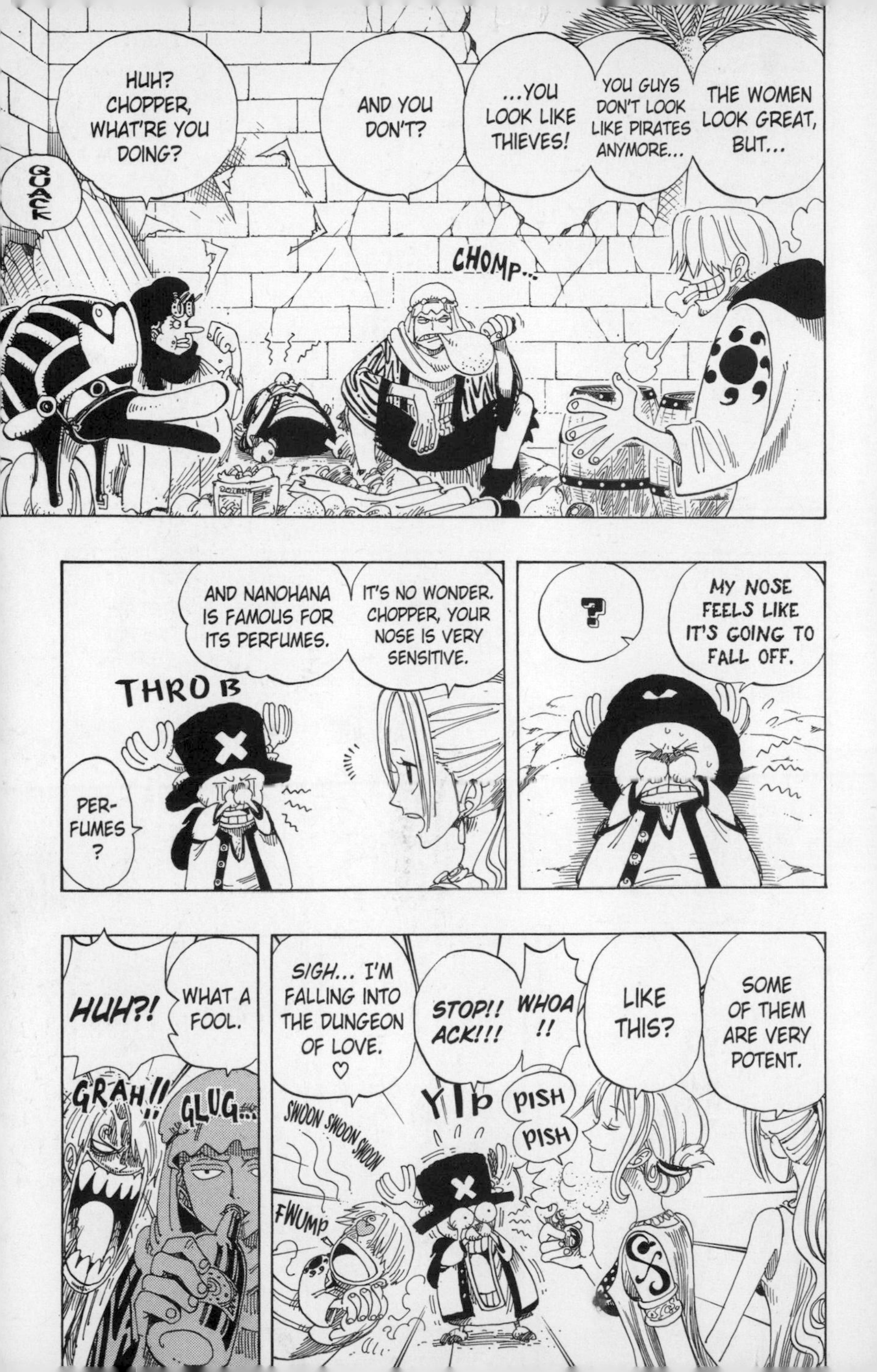
THE WOMEN LOOK GREAT, BUT...
YOU GUYS DON'T LOOK LIKE PIRATES ANYMORE...
...YOU LOOK LIKE THIEVES!
AND YOU DON'T?
HUH? CHOPPER, WHAT'RE YOU DOING?
QUACK
CHOMP...
MY NOSE FEELS LIKE IT'S GOING TO FALL OFF.
?
IT'S NO WONDER. CHOPPER, YOUR NOSE IS VERY SENSITIVE.
AND NANOHANA IS FAMOUS FOR ITS PERFUMES.
THROB
PER-FUMES?
SOME OF THEM ARE VERY POTENT.
LIKE THIS?
WHOA!!
STOP!! ACK!!!
YIP
PISH
PISH
SIGH... I'M FALLING INTO THE DUNGEON OF LOVE. ♡
SWOON SWOON SWOON
FWUMP
WHAT A FOOL.
HUH?!
GRAH!!
GLUG...

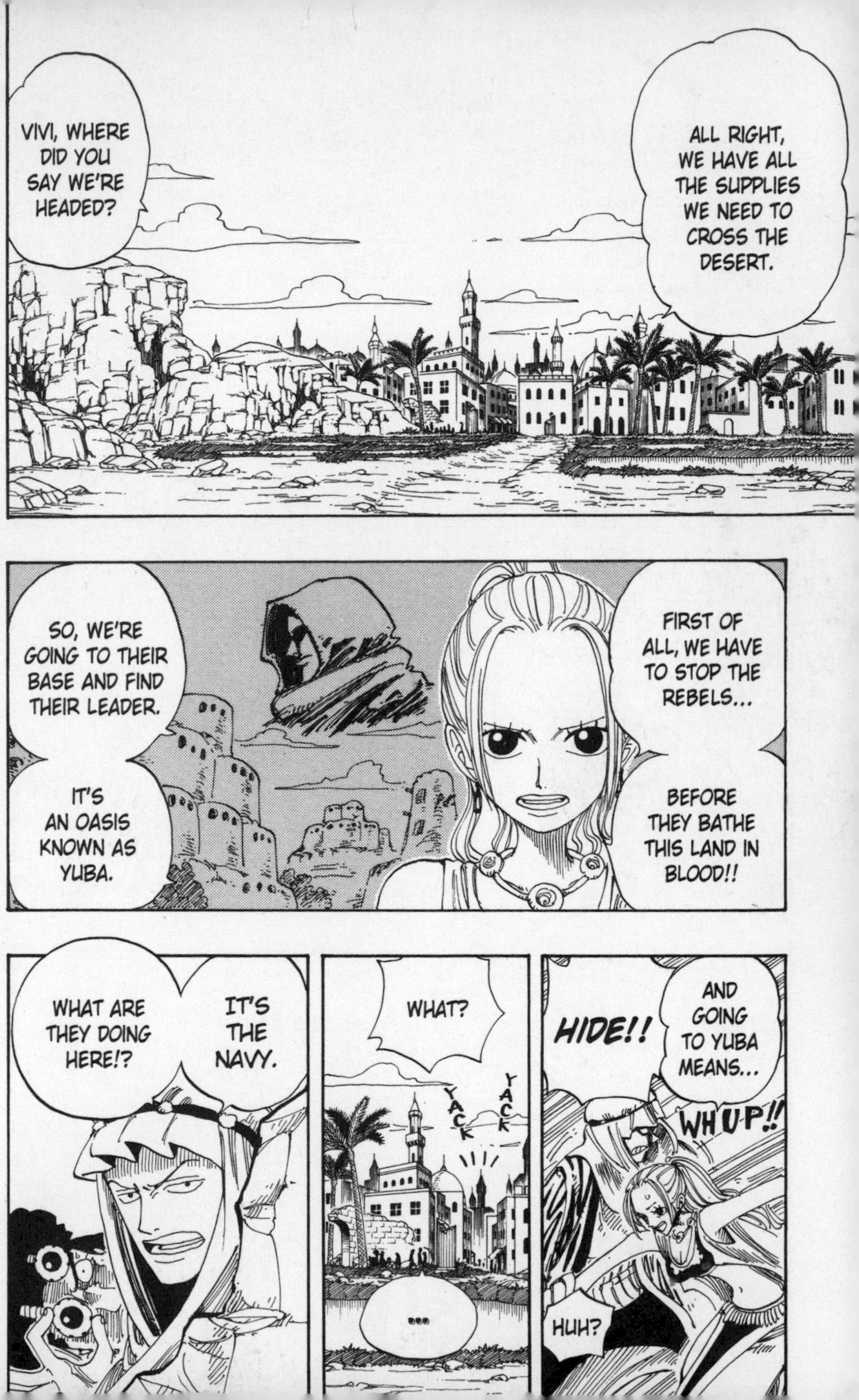
ALL RIGHT, WE HAVE ALL THE SUPPLIES WE NEED TO CROSS THE DESERT.
VIVI, WHERE DID YOU SAY WE'RE HEADED?
FIRST OF ALL, WE HAVE TO STOP THE REBELS...
BEFORE THEY BATHE THIS LAND IN BLOOD!!
SO, WE'RE GOING TO THEIR BASE AND FIND THEIR LEADER.
IT'S AN OASIS KNOWN AS YUBA.
AND GOING TO YUBA MEANS...
HIDE!!
WHUP!!
HUH?
WHAT?
YACK
YACK
...
IT'S THE NAVY.
WHAT ARE THEY DOING HERE!?

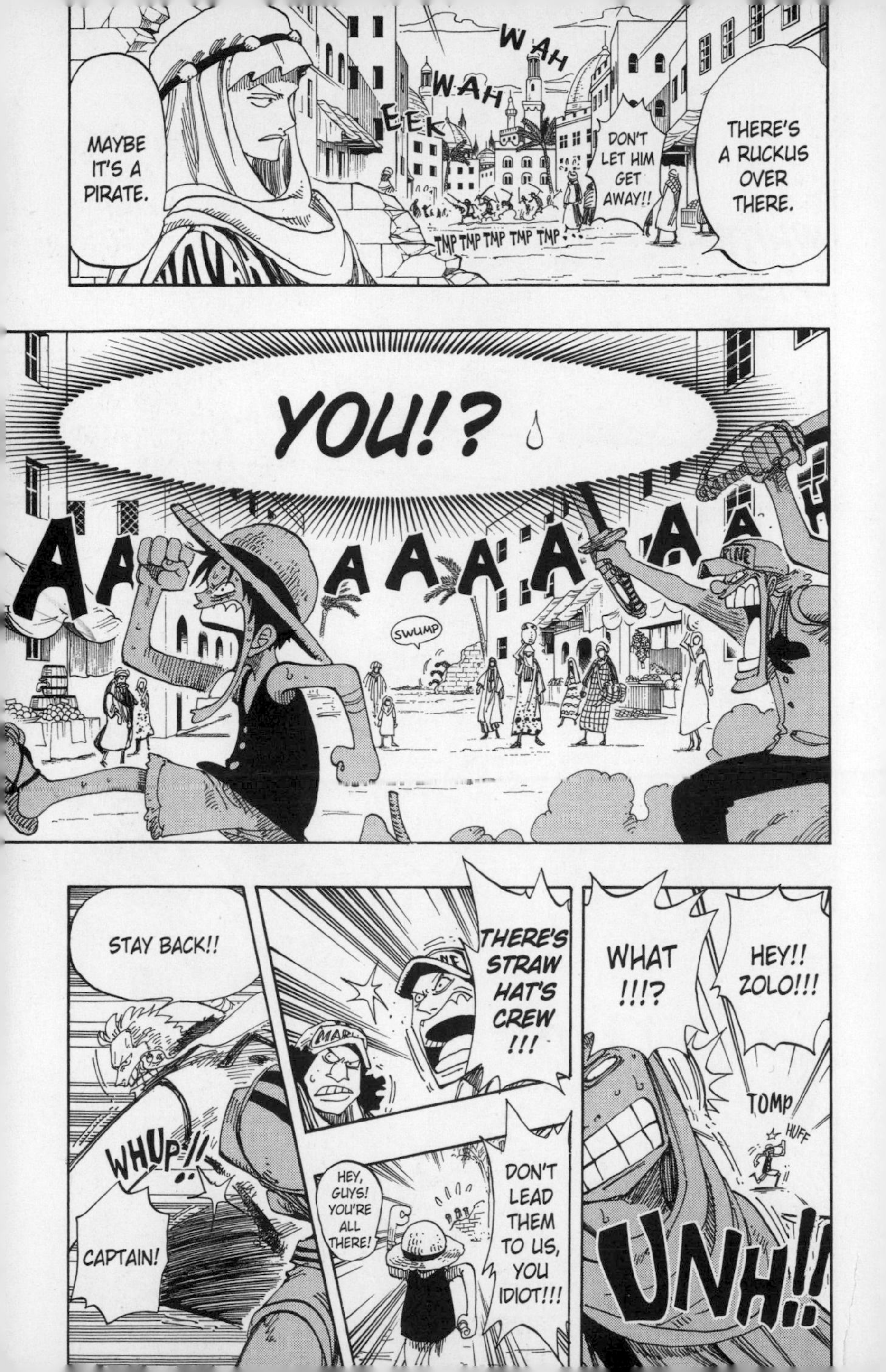
THERE'S A RUCKUS OVER THERE.
DON'T LET HIM GET AWAY!!
WAH
WAH
EEK
TMP TMP TMP TMP TMP
MAYBE IT'S A PIRATE.
YOU!?
AAAAAAAA
SWUMP
HEY!! ZOLO!!!
WHAT!!!?
TOMP
HUFF
UNH!!
THERE'S STRAW HAT'S CREW!!!
DON'T LEAD THEM TO US, YOU IDIOT!!!
HEY, GUYS! YOU'RE ALL THERE!
STAY BACK!!
WHUP!!
CAPTAIN!

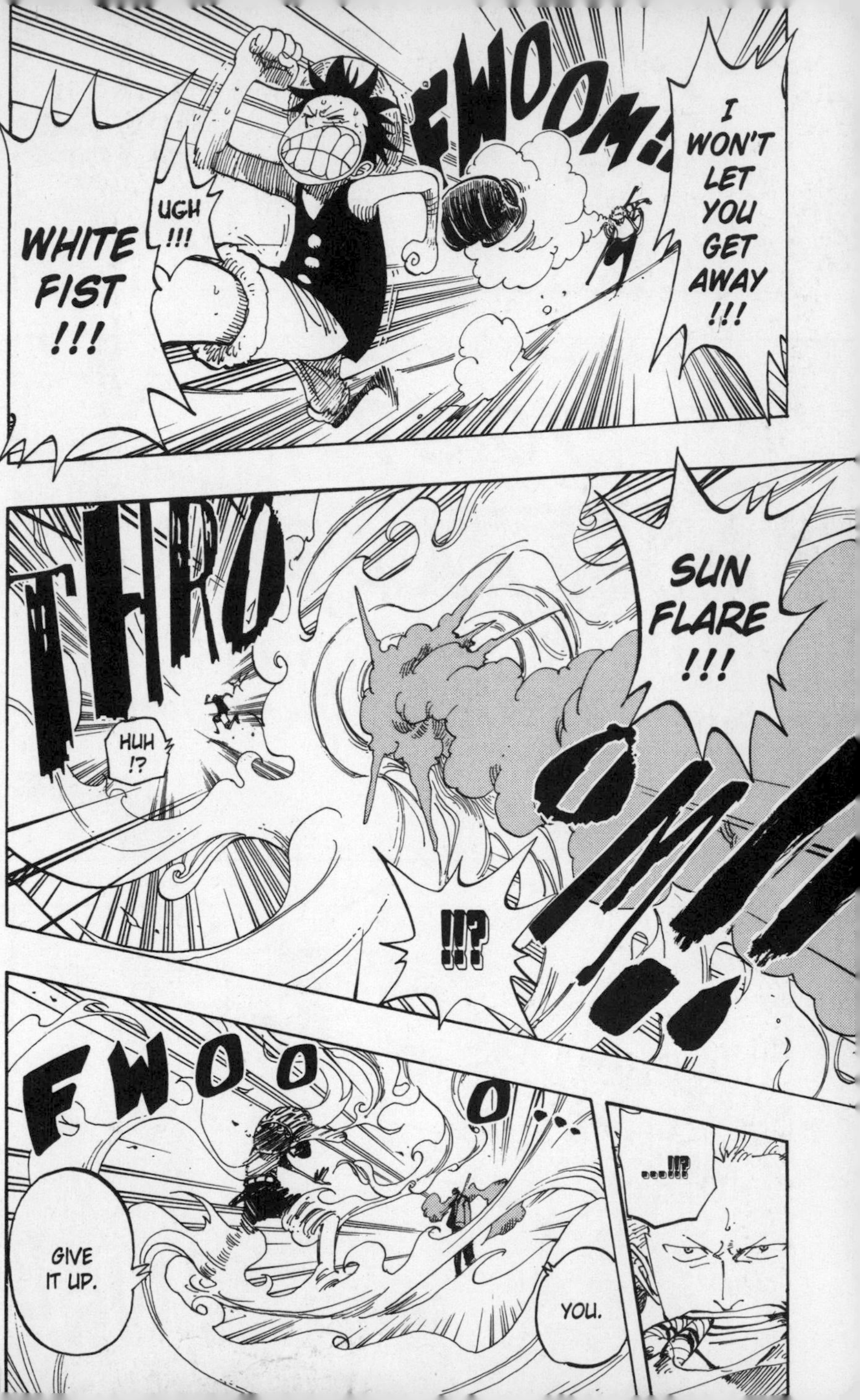
I WON'T LET YOU GET AWAY!!!
FWOOM!!
UGH!!!
WHITE FIST!!!
SUN FLARE!!!
OM!!
!!?
THRO
HUH!?
...!!?
FWOOO...
YOU.
GIVE IT UP.

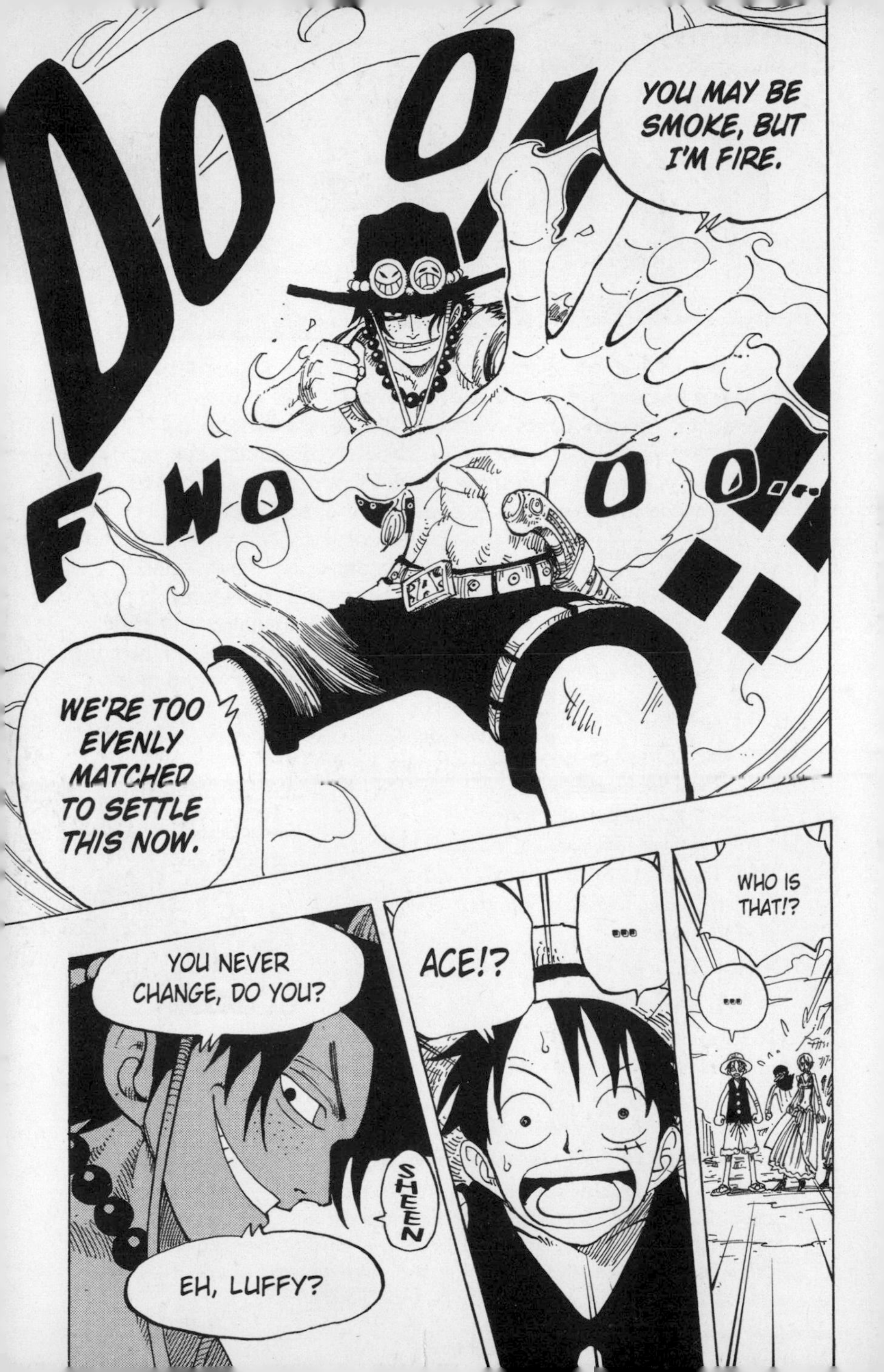
YOU MAY BE SMOKE, BUT I'M FIRE.
DOO...
FWOOO...!!
WE'RE TOO EVENLY MATCHED TO SETTLE THIS NOW.
WHO IS THAT!?
...
...
ACE!?
YOU NEVER CHANGE, DO YOU?
SHEEN
EH, LUFFY?

Question Corner

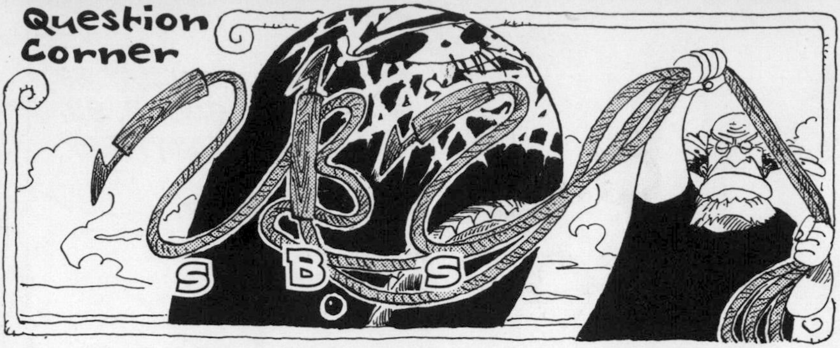

S B S

Oda: Yes, um, I'd like to...clarify something for a few of our readers about the last issue, volume 17. There was a character named "Chessmarimo." He was a fusion of "Chess" and "Kuromarimo," so when he spoke, you could hear both of their voices at the same time. In order to illustrate that, I made their dialogue overlap. And, boy, did I get it.

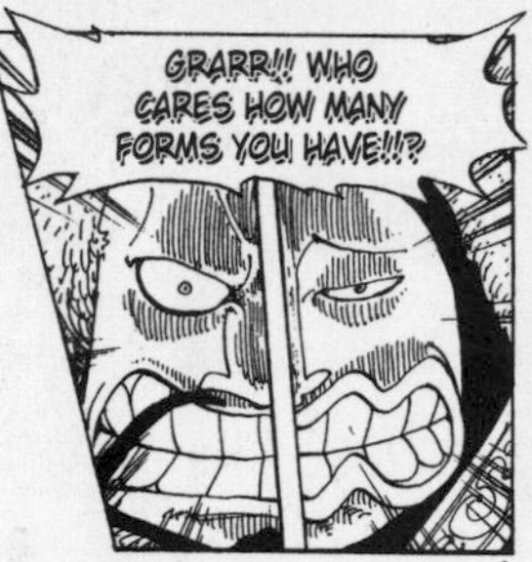

GRARR!! WHO CARES HOW MANY FORMS YOU HAVE!!?

Tons of complaints from parents of little kids screaming, "Your quality control is terrible!!" They even complained to the publisher of this comic. I'm very sorry, Mothers, but I did it on purpose!! Please, read the comic. It's "Chessmarimo." Isn't that hilarious!? (not much repentance here)

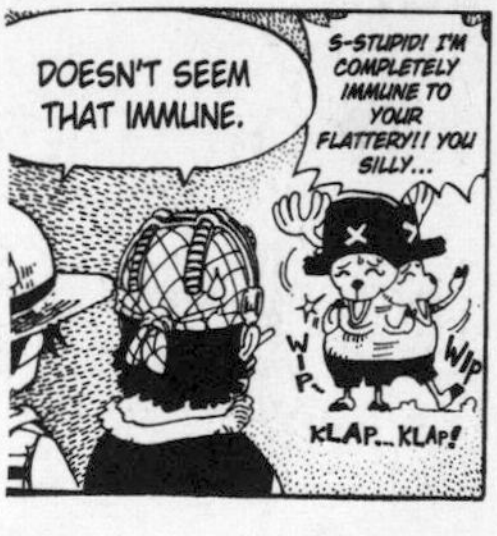

S-STUPID! I'M COMPLETELY IMMUNE TO YOUR FLATTERY!! YOU SILLY...
DOESN'T SEEM THAT IMMUNE.
WIP
WIP
KLAP...KLAP!

Q: Oda Honey, I have a question…
In vol. 17, page 176, panel 6, what is Chopper doing? It looks to me like he's doing that "dirty old man" dance that Ken Shimura* does!! Am I right? Please tell me!!

A: Oh, you figured it out.

Q: Hi, Oda Sensei. → I think *One Piece* is just too much fun!!
During class → I drew → Buggy! In my notebook!!
I have Buggy-itis →!
Oh yes, yes… Young Shanks and Buggy once argued about whether the South Pole or the North Pole was colder. Which is it? → Well, *sayonara.*

A: Oh, that was Buggy's flashback in Volume 3. The answer is the South Pole. The North Pole isn't a continent, it's an ice formation. Between land and ocean, land is colder, so the South Pole wins. Shanks was right. By the way, did you know that the coldest place in the world is not the South Pole?

* Famous Japanese Comedian - Ed.

Chapter 159:
COME ON

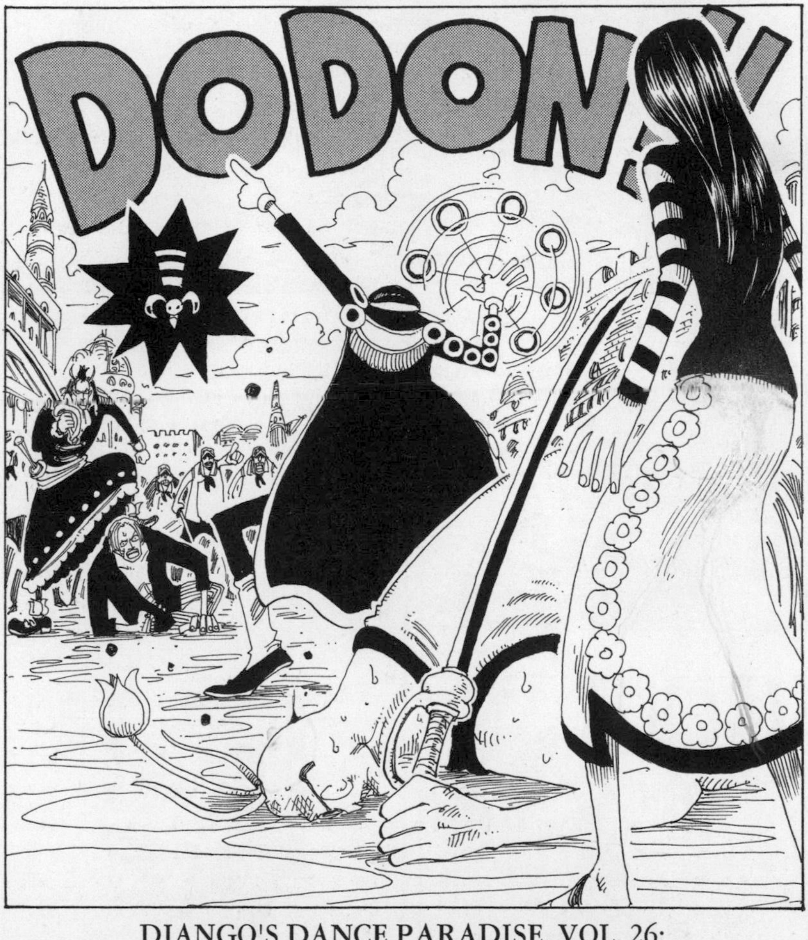
DODON

DJANGO'S DANCE PARADISE, VOL. 26:
"THE MAN WHO ENDED UP COMING BACK"

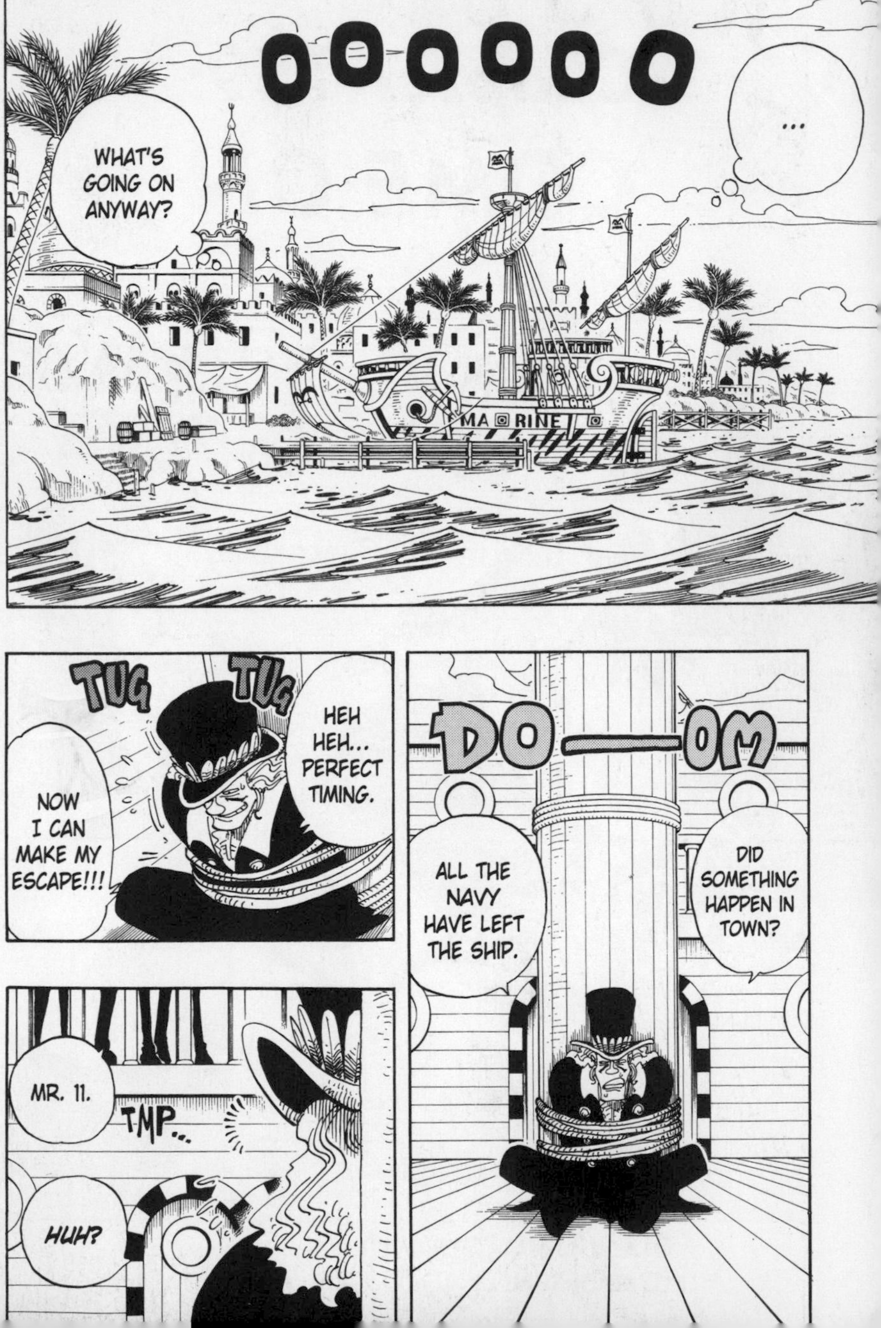
OOOOOO
...
WHAT'S GOING ON ANYWAY?
DO—OM
DID SOMETHING HAPPEN IN TOWN?
ALL THE NAVY HAVE LEFT THE SHIP.
TUG TUG
HEH HEH... PERFECT TIMING.
NOW I CAN MAKE MY ESCAPE!!!
MR. 11.
TMP...
HUH?

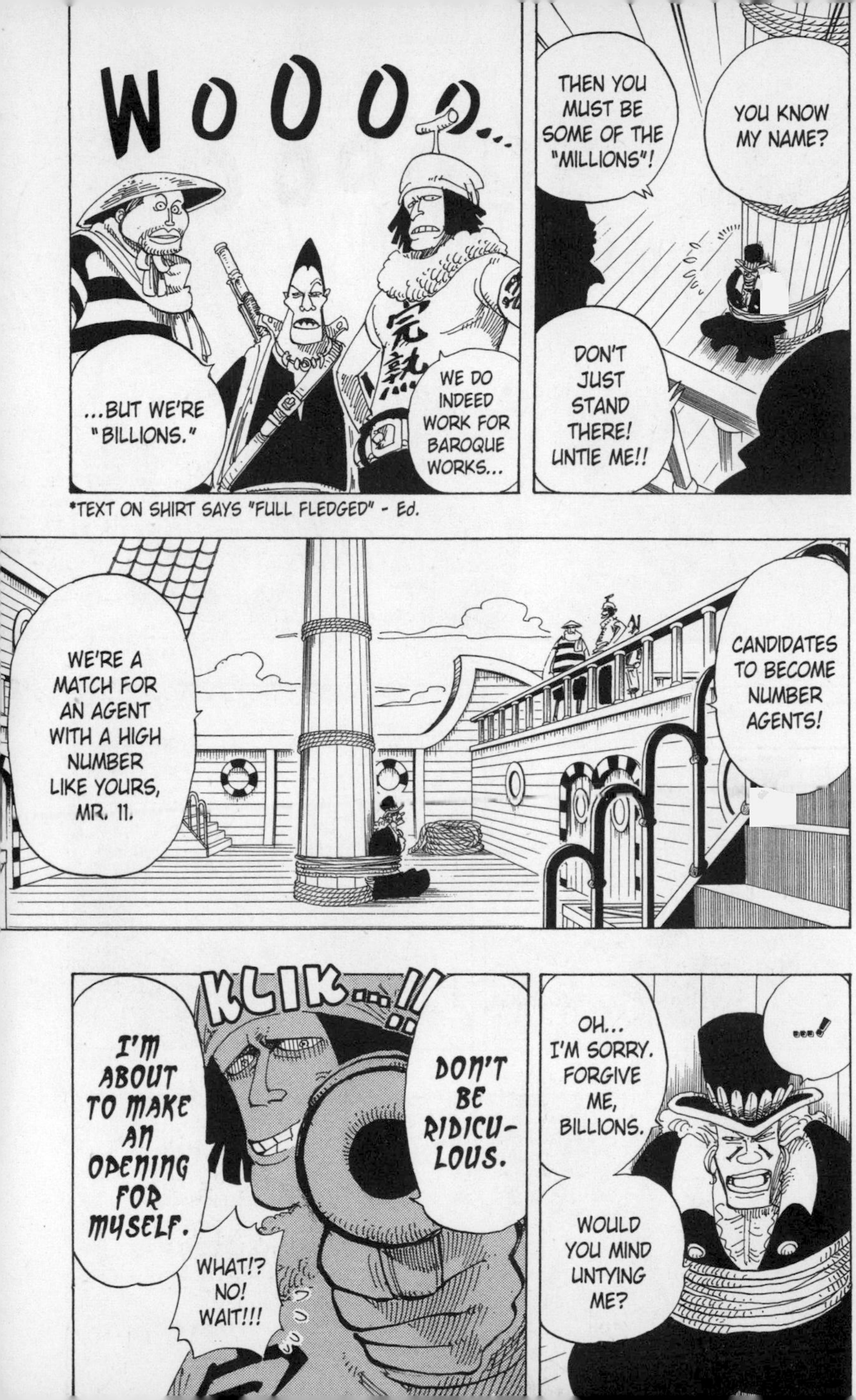
YOU KNOW MY NAME?
THEN YOU MUST BE SOME OF THE "MILLIONS"!
DON'T JUST STAND THERE! UNTIE ME!!
WOOOO...
完熟
WE DO INDEED WORK FOR BAROQUE WORKS...
...BUT WE'RE "BILLIONS."
*TEXT ON SHIRT SAYS "FULL FLEDGED" - Ed.
CANDIDATES TO BECOME NUMBER AGENTS!
WE'RE A MATCH FOR AN AGENT WITH A HIGH NUMBER LIKE YOURS, MR. 11.
...!
OH... I'M SORRY. FORGIVE ME, BILLIONS.
WOULD YOU MIND UNTYING ME?
KLIK...!!
DON'T BE RIDICULOUS.
I'M ABOUT TO MAKE AN OPENING FOR MYSELF.
WHAT!? NO! WAIT!!!

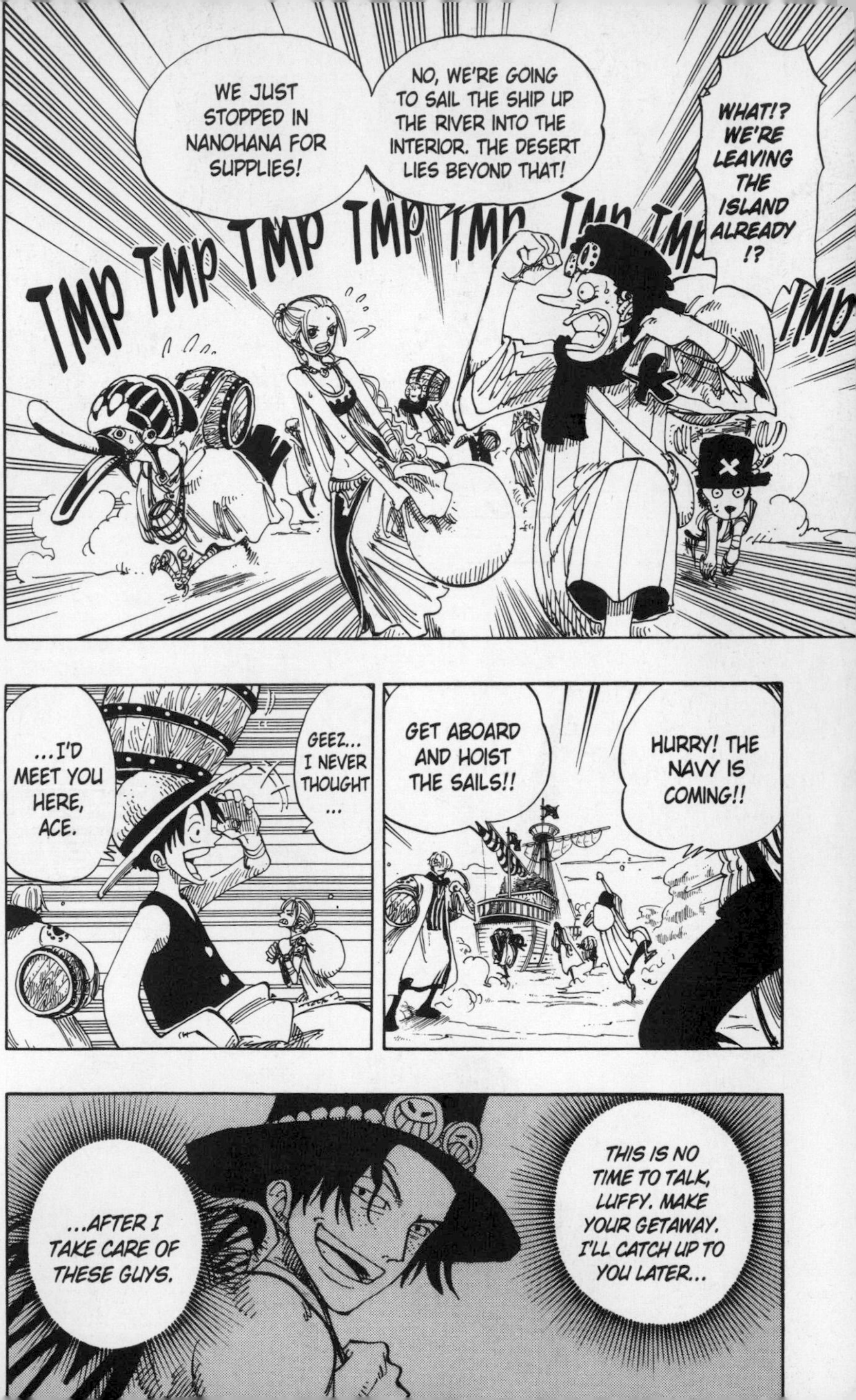
WHAT!? WE'RE LEAVING THE ISLAND ALREADY !?
NO, WE'RE GOING TO SAIL THE SHIP UP THE RIVER INTO THE INTERIOR. THE DESERT LIES BEYOND THAT!
WE JUST STOPPED IN NANOHANA FOR SUPPLIES!
TMP TMP TMP TMP TMP TMP TMP TMP TMP
HURRY! THE NAVY IS COMING!!
GET ABOARD AND HOIST THE SAILS!!
GEEZ... I NEVER THOUGHT ...
...I'D MEET YOU HERE, ACE.
THIS IS NO TIME TO TALK, LUFFY. MAKE YOUR GETAWAY. I'LL CATCH UP TO YOU LATER...
...AFTER I TAKE CARE OF THESE GUYS.

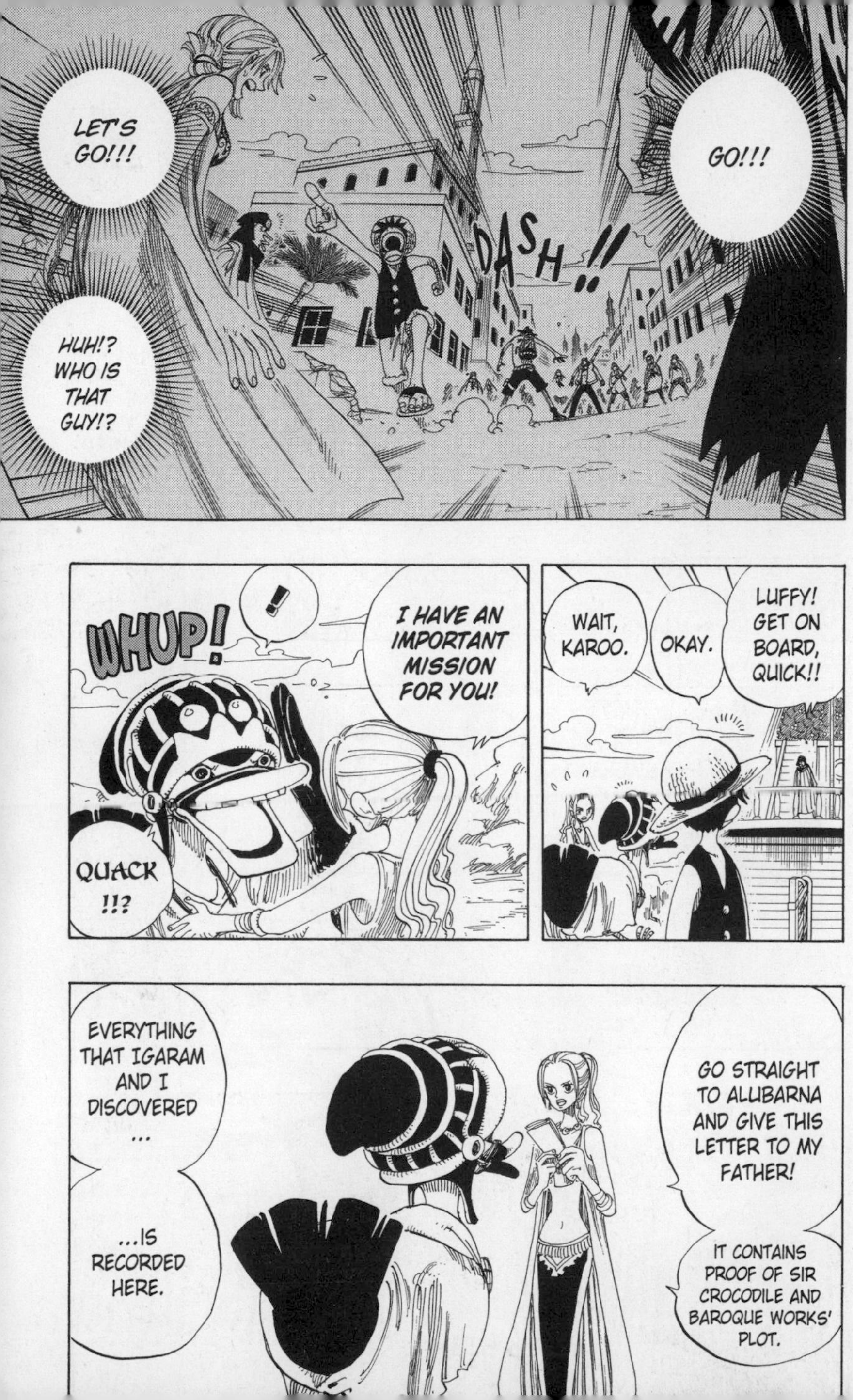
GO!!!
LET'S GO!!!
DASH!!
HUH!? WHO IS THAT GUY!?
LUFFY! GET ON BOARD, QUICK!!
OKAY.
WAIT, KAROO.
I HAVE AN IMPORTANT MISSION FOR YOU!
!
WHUP!
QUACK!!?
GO STRAIGHT TO ALUBARNA AND GIVE THIS LETTER TO MY FATHER!
IT CONTAINS PROOF OF SIR CROCODILE AND BAROQUE WORKS' PLOT.
EVERYTHING THAT IGARAM AND I DISCOVERED ...
...IS RECORDED HERE.

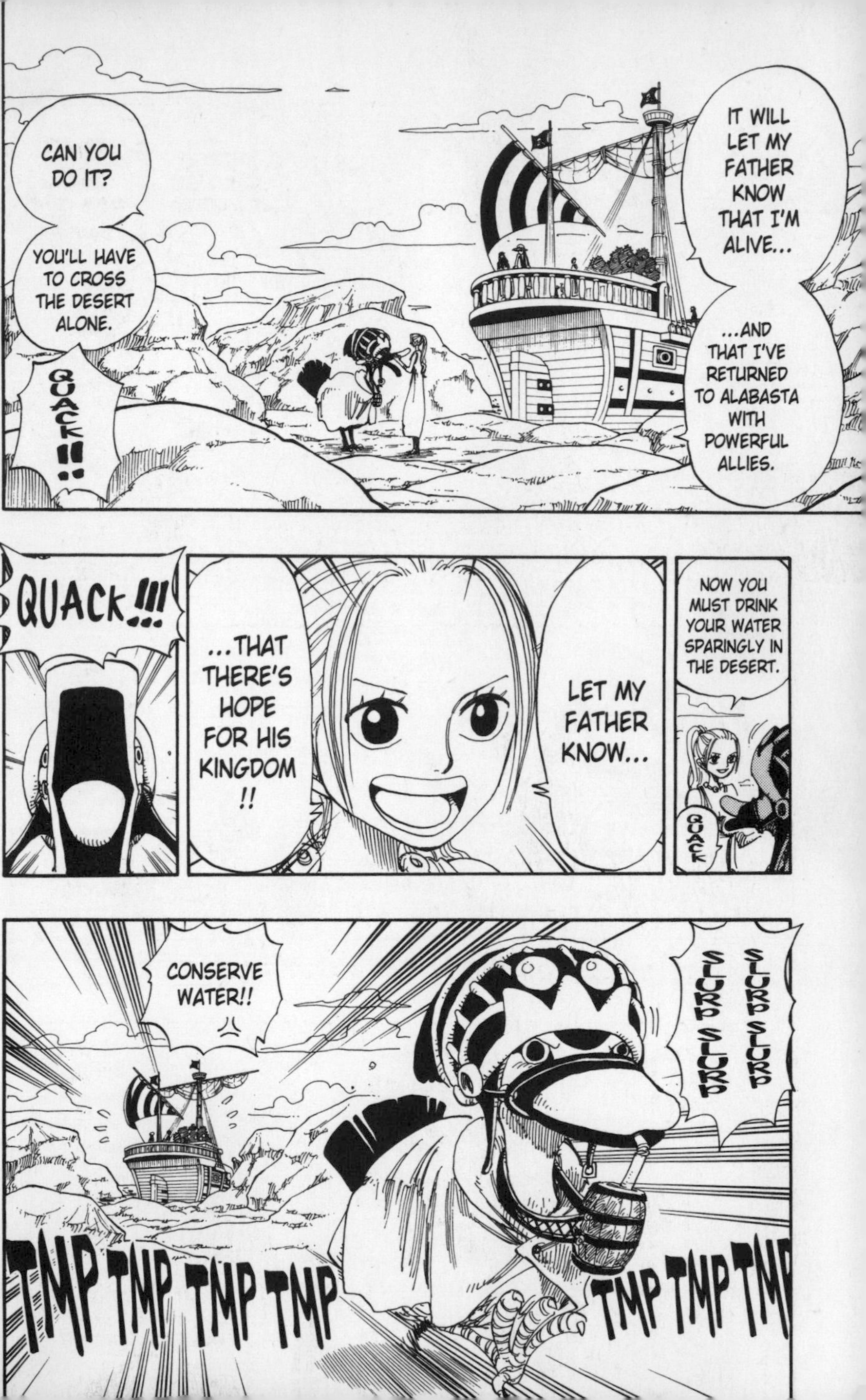
IT WILL LET MY FATHER KNOW THAT I'M ALIVE...
...AND THAT I'VE RETURNED TO ALABASTA WITH POWERFUL ALLIES.
CAN YOU DO IT?
YOU'LL HAVE TO CROSS THE DESERT ALONE.
QUACK!!
NOW YOU MUST DRINK YOUR WATER SPARINGLY IN THE DESERT.
QUACK
LET MY FATHER KNOW...
...THAT THERE'S HOPE FOR HIS KINGDOM!!
QUACK!!!
SLURP SLURP
SLURP SLURP
CONSERVE WATER!!
TMP TMP TMP
TMP TMP TMP TMP

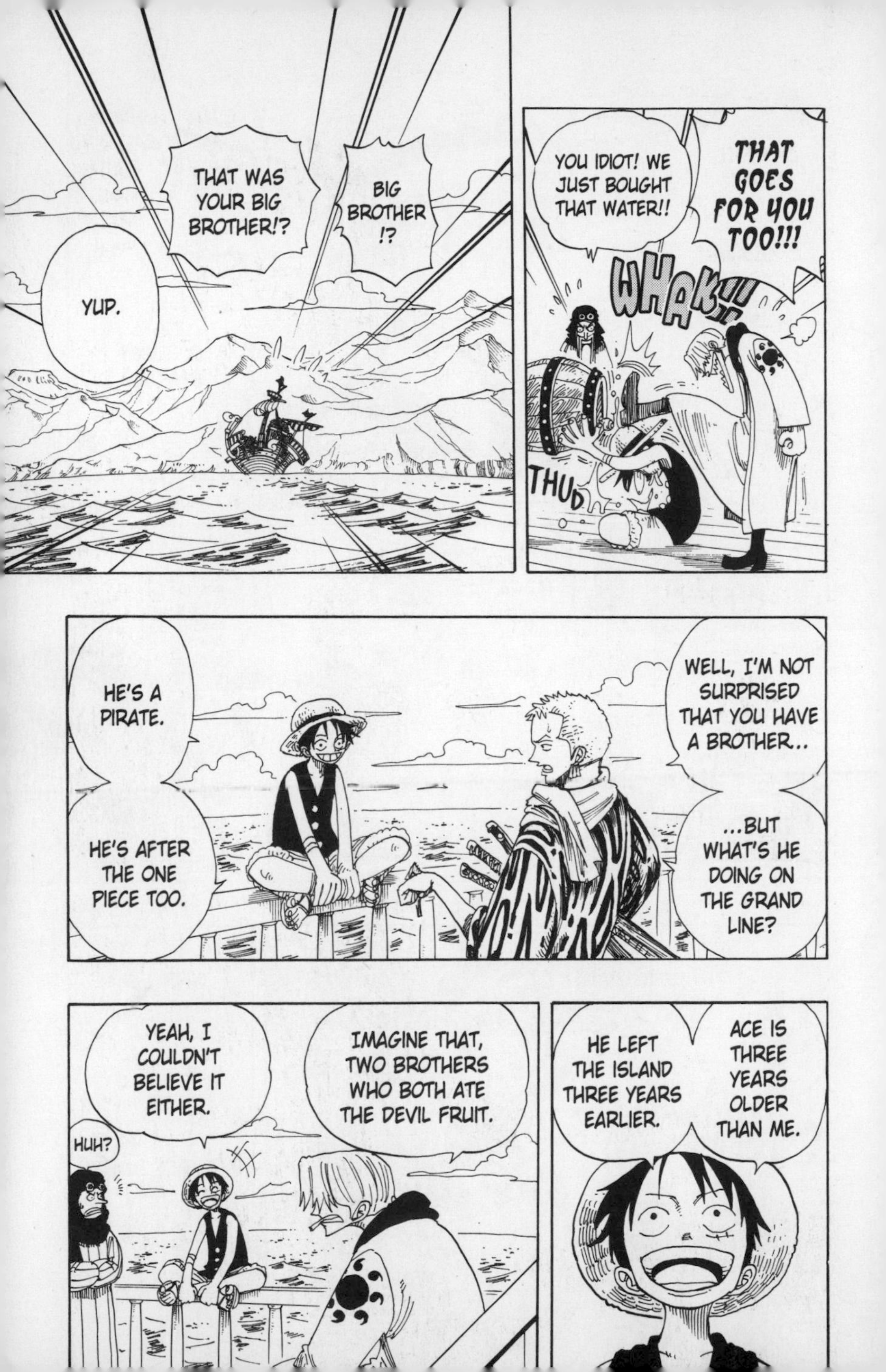
YOU IDIOT! WE JUST BOUGHT THAT WATER!!
THAT GOES FOR YOU TOO!!!
WHAK!!
THUD
BIG BROTHER !?
THAT WAS YOUR BIG BROTHER!?
YUP.
WELL, I'M NOT SURPRISED THAT YOU HAVE A BROTHER...
...BUT WHAT'S HE DOING ON THE GRAND LINE?
HE'S A PIRATE.
HE'S AFTER THE ONE PIECE TOO.
ACE IS THREE YEARS OLDER THAN ME.
HE LEFT THE ISLAND THREE YEARS EARLIER.
IMAGINE THAT, TWO BROTHERS WHO BOTH ATE THE DEVIL FRUIT.
YEAH, I COULDN'T BELIEVE IT EITHER.
HUH?

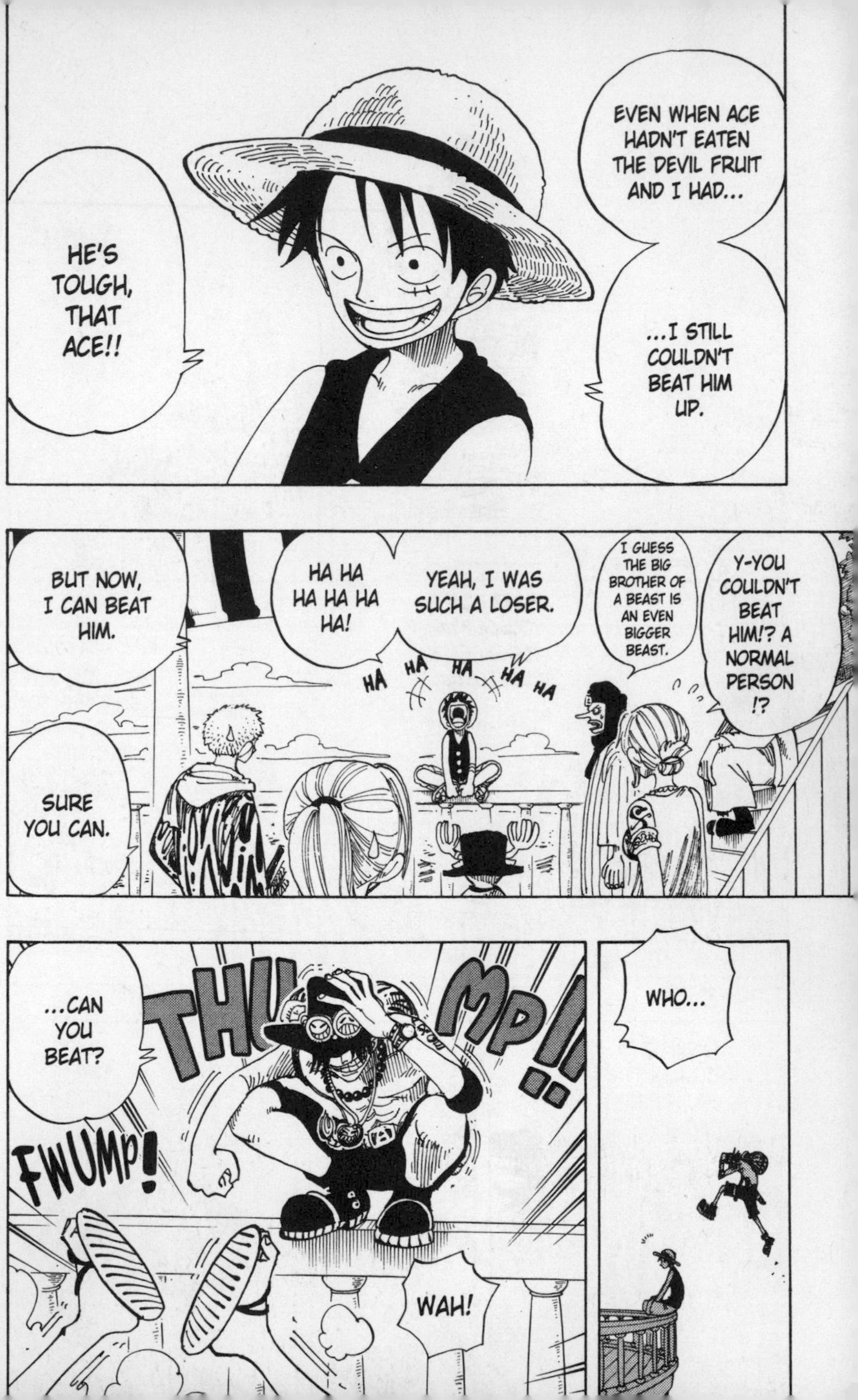
EVEN WHEN ACE HADN'T EATEN THE DEVIL FRUIT AND I HAD...
...I STILL COULDN'T BEAT HIM UP.
HE'S TOUGH, THAT ACE!!
Y-YOU COULDN'T BEAT HIM!? A NORMAL PERSON!?
I GUESS THE BIG BROTHER OF A BEAST IS AN EVEN BIGGER BEAST.
YEAH, I WAS SUCH A LOSER.
HA HA HA HA HA HA!
BUT NOW, I CAN BEAT HIM.
HA HA HA HA HA
SURE YOU CAN.
WHO...
...CAN YOU BEAT?
THUMP!!
FWUMP!
WAH!

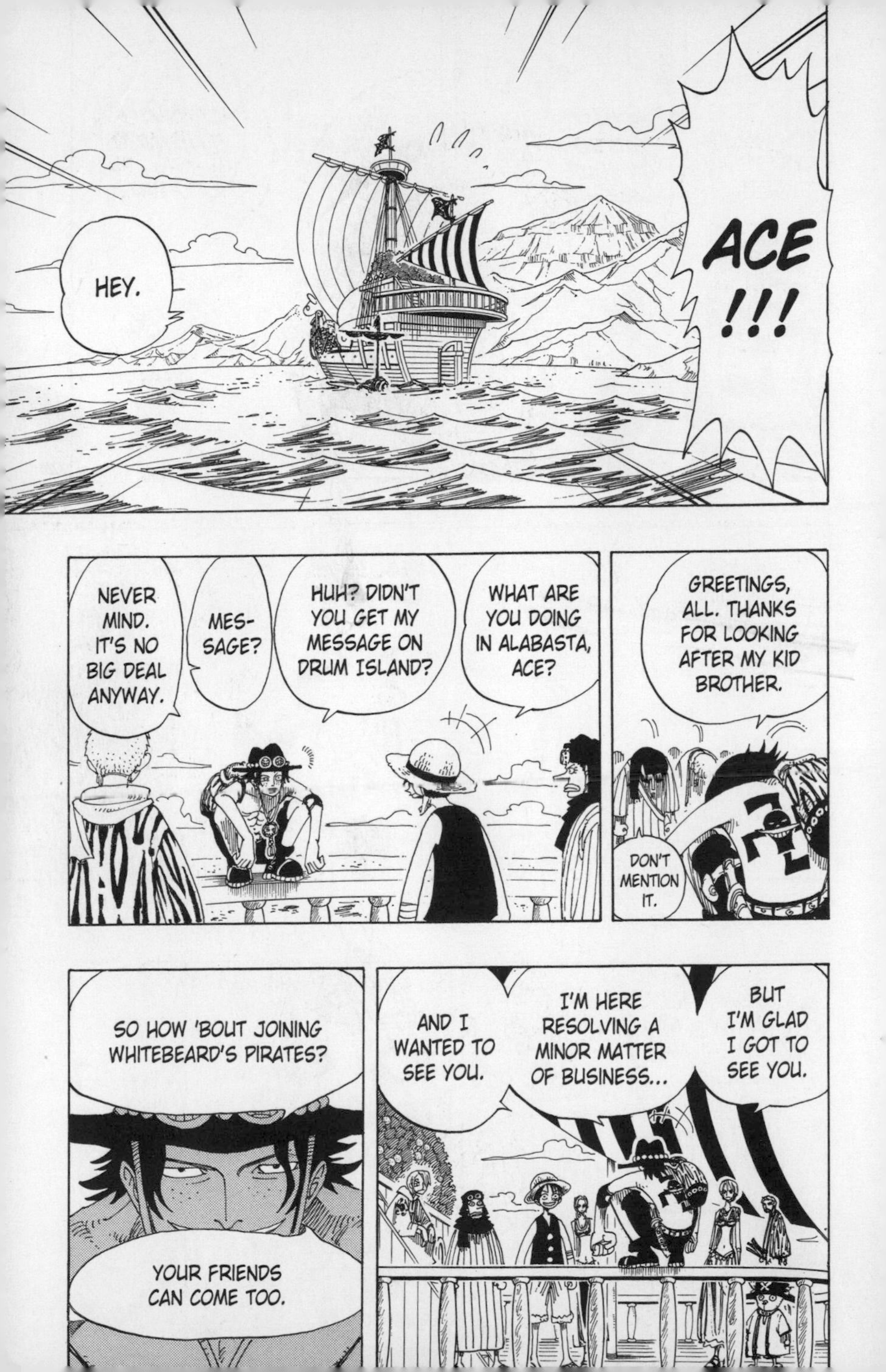
ACE !!!
HEY.
GREETINGS, ALL. THANKS FOR LOOKING AFTER MY KID BROTHER.
DON'T MENTION IT.
WHAT ARE YOU DOING IN ALABASTA, ACE?
HUH? DIDN'T YOU GET MY MESSAGE ON DRUM ISLAND?
MES-SAGE?
NEVER MIND. IT'S NO BIG DEAL ANYWAY.
BUT I'M GLAD I GOT TO SEE YOU.
I'M HERE RESOLVING A MINOR MATTER OF BUSINESS...
AND I WANTED TO SEE YOU.
SO HOW 'BOUT JOINING WHITEBEARD'S PIRATES?
YOUR FRIENDS CAN COME TOO.

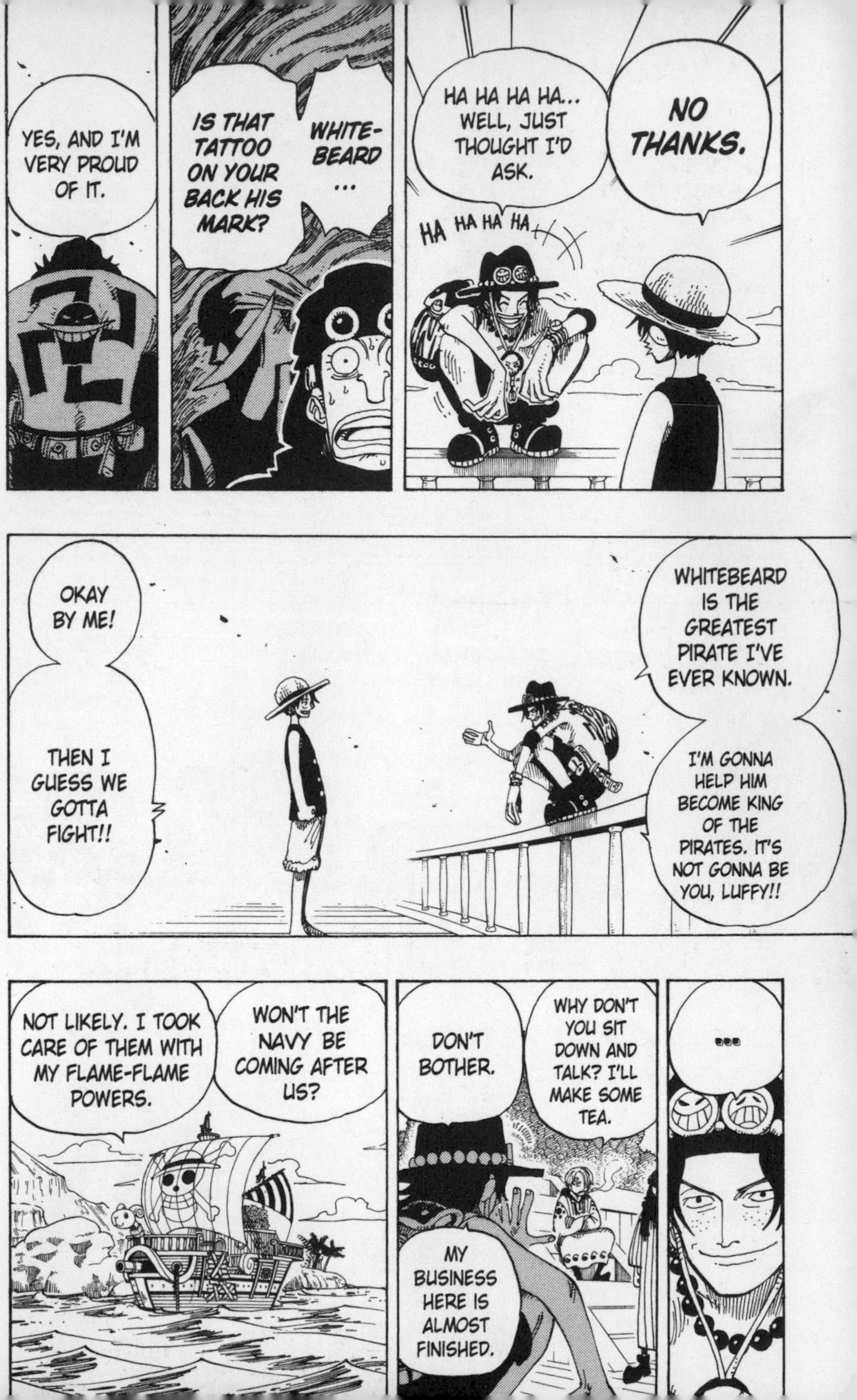
NO THANKS.
HA HA HA HA... WELL, JUST THOUGHT I'D ASK.
HA HA HA HA
WHITE-BEARD ...
IS THAT TATTOO ON YOUR BACK HIS MARK?
YES, AND I'M VERY PROUD OF IT.
WHITEBEARD IS THE GREATEST PIRATE I'VE EVER KNOWN.
I'M GONNA HELP HIM BECOME KING OF THE PIRATES. IT'S NOT GONNA BE YOU, LUFFY!!
OKAY BY ME!
THEN I GUESS WE GOTTA FIGHT!!
...
WHY DON'T YOU SIT DOWN AND TALK? I'LL MAKE SOME TEA.
DON'T BOTHER.
MY BUSINESS HERE IS ALMOST FINISHED.
WON'T THE NAVY BE COMING AFTER US?
NOT LIKELY. I TOOK CARE OF THEM WITH MY FLAME-FLAME POWERS.

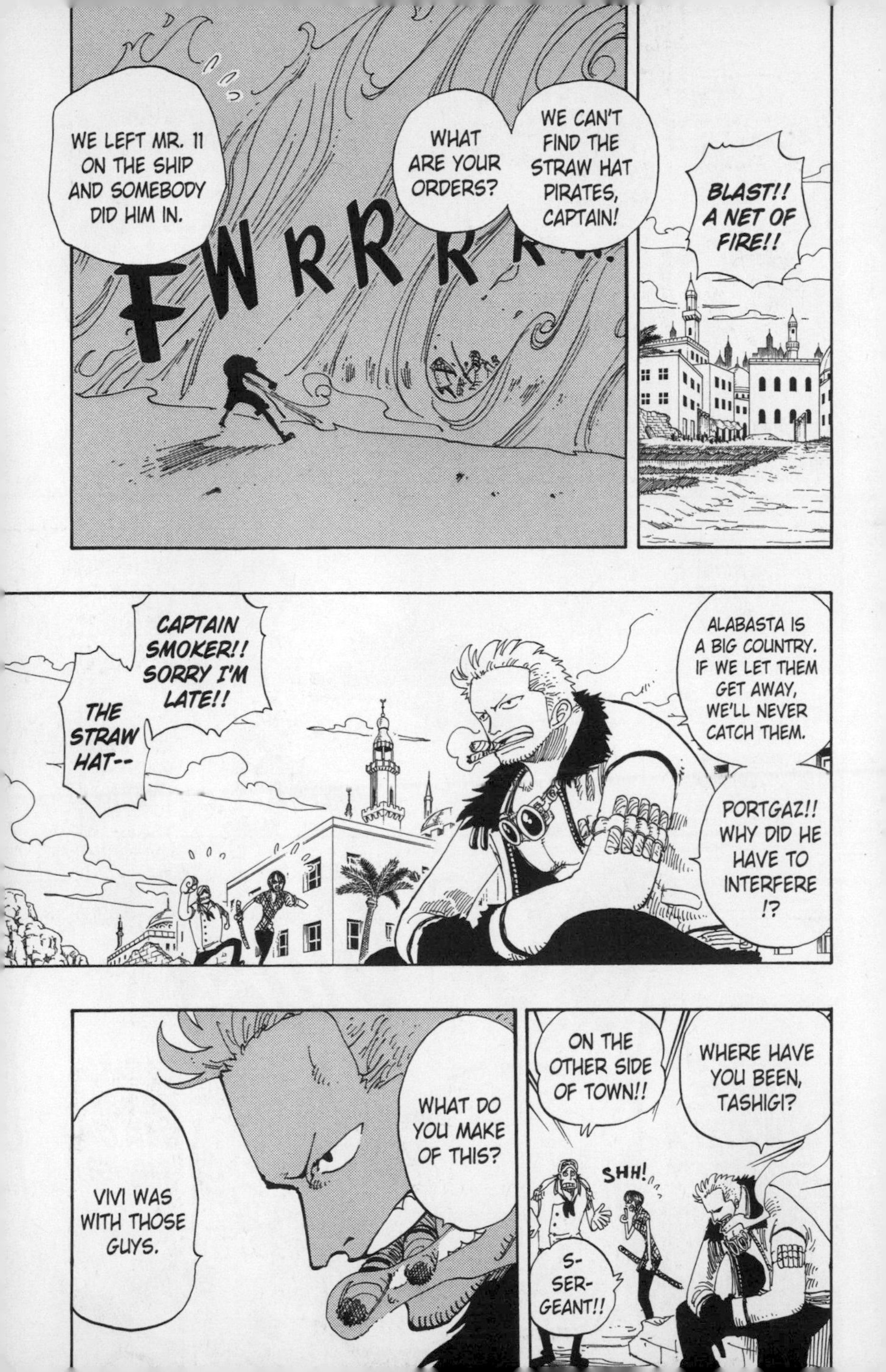
BLAST!! A NET OF FIRE!!
WE CAN'T FIND THE STRAW HAT PIRATES, CAPTAIN!
WHAT ARE YOUR ORDERS?
WE LEFT MR. 11 ON THE SHIP AND SOMEBODY DID HIM IN.
FWRRRR...
ALABASTA IS A BIG COUNTRY. IF WE LET THEM GET AWAY, WE'LL NEVER CATCH THEM.
PORTGAZ!! WHY DID HE HAVE TO INTERFERE!?
CAPTAIN SMOKER!! SORRY I'M LATE!!
THE STRAW HAT--
WHERE HAVE YOU BEEN, TASHIGI?
ON THE OTHER SIDE OF TOWN!!
SHH!
S-SER-GEANT!!
WHAT DO YOU MAKE OF THIS?
VIVI WAS WITH THOSE GUYS.

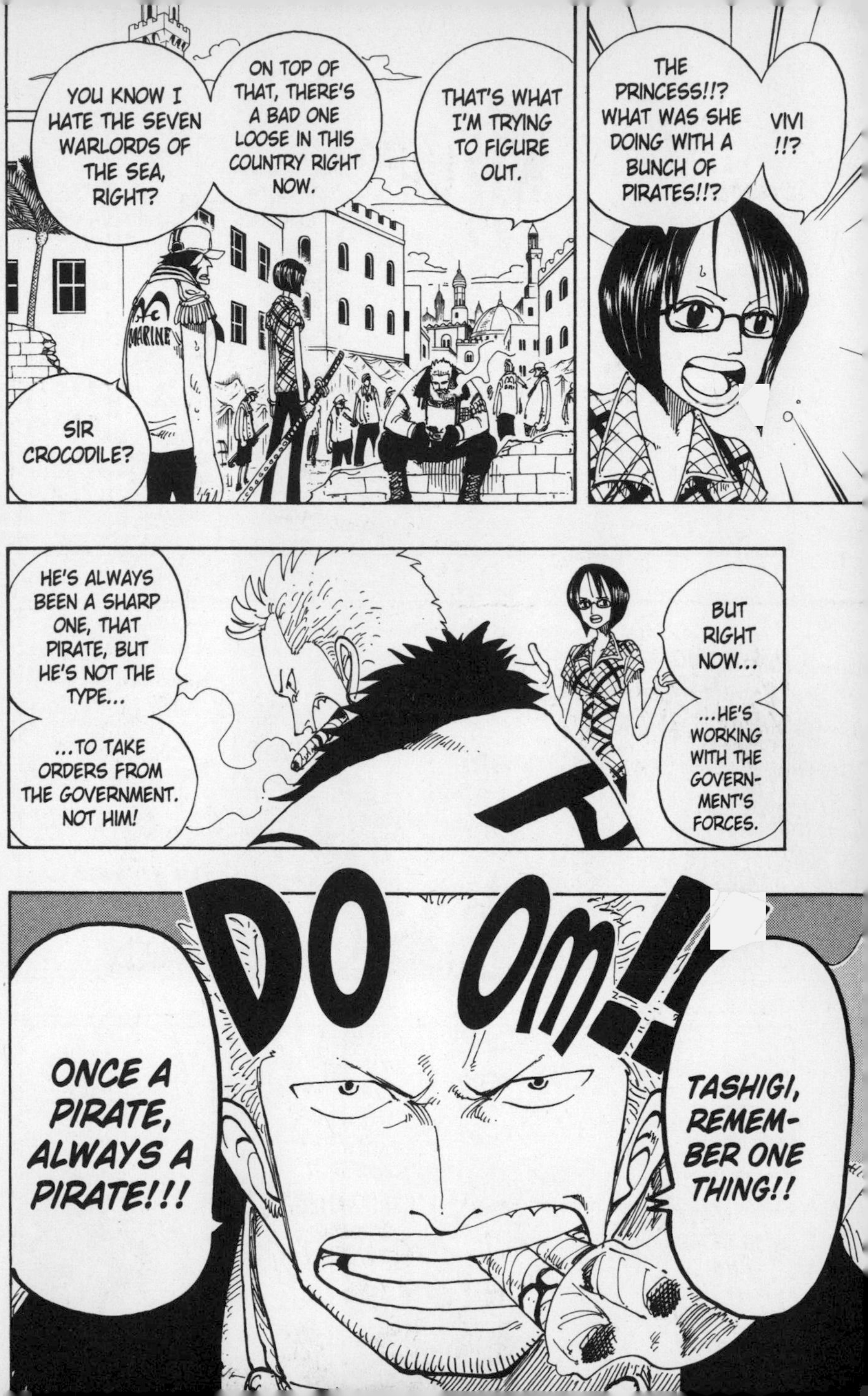
VIVI !!?
THE PRINCESS!!? WHAT WAS SHE DOING WITH A BUNCH OF PIRATES!!?
THAT'S WHAT I'M TRYING TO FIGURE OUT.
ON TOP OF THAT, THERE'S A BAD ONE LOOSE IN THIS COUNTRY RIGHT NOW.
YOU KNOW I HATE THE SEVEN WARLORDS OF THE SEA, RIGHT?
SIR CROCODILE?
BUT RIGHT NOW...
...HE'S WORKING WITH THE GOVERN-MENT'S FORCES.
HE'S ALWAYS BEEN A SHARP ONE, THAT PIRATE, BUT HE'S NOT THE TYPE...
...TO TAKE ORDERS FROM THE GOVERNMENT. NOT HIM!
DOOM!!
TASHIGI, REMEM-BER ONE THING!!
ONCE A PIRATE, ALWAYS A PIRATE!!!

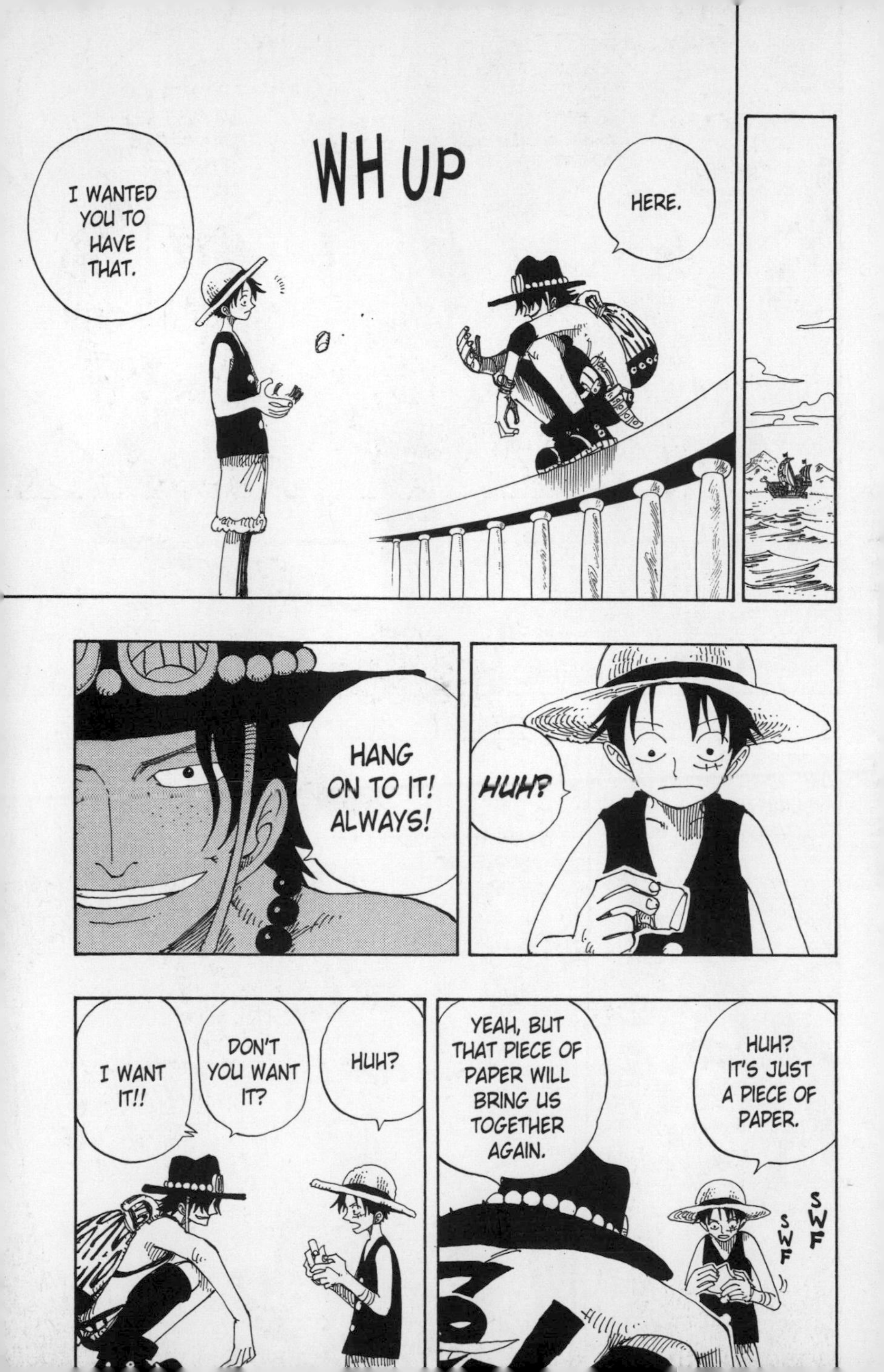
HERE.
WH UP
I WANTED YOU TO HAVE THAT.
HUH?
HANG ON TO IT! ALWAYS!
HUH? IT'S JUST A PIECE OF PAPER.
SWF
SWF
YEAH, BUT THAT PIECE OF PAPER WILL BRING US TOGETHER AGAIN.
HUH?
DON'T YOU WANT IT?
I WANT IT!!

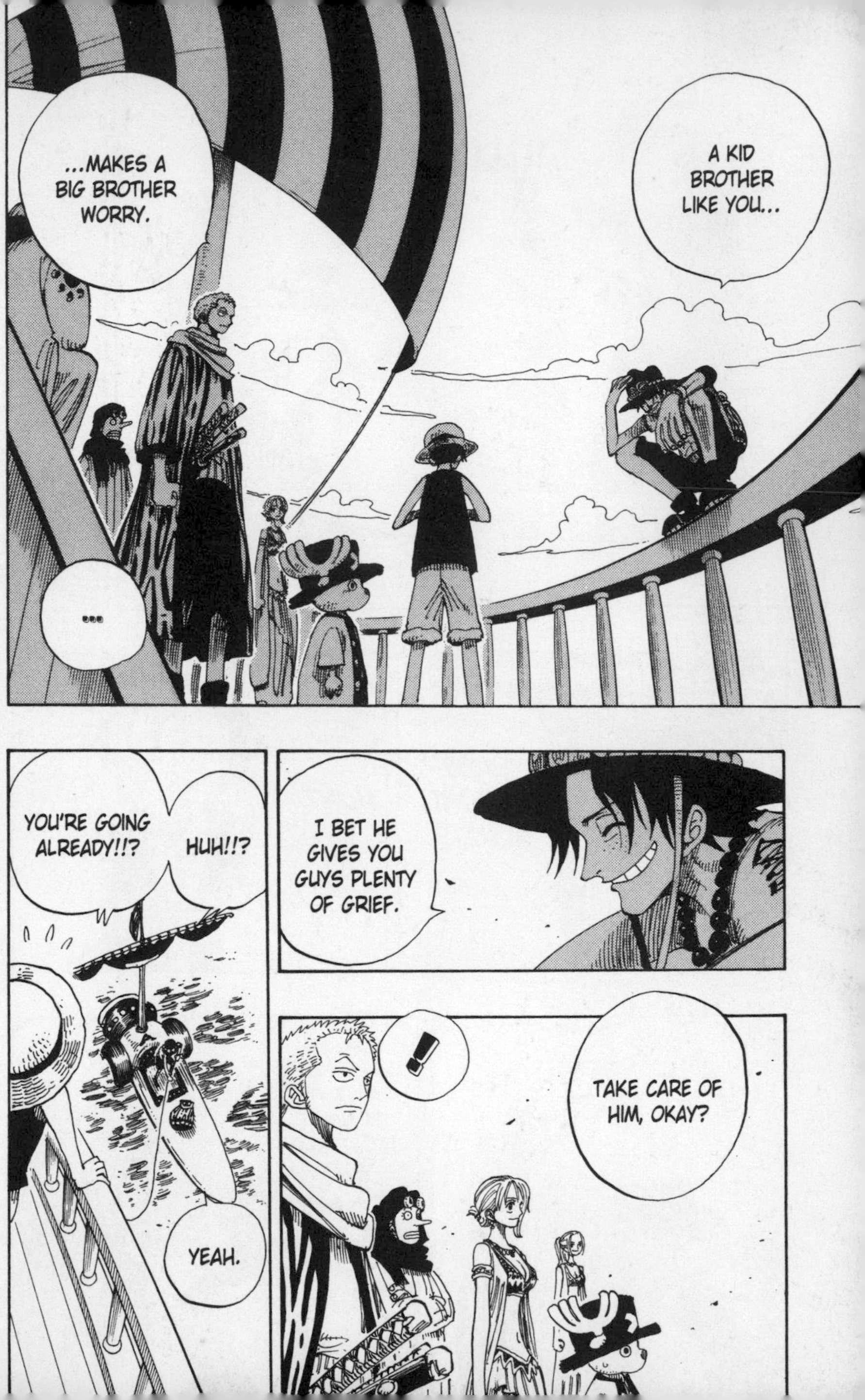
A KID BROTHER LIKE YOU...
...MAKES A BIG BROTHER WORRY.
...
I BET HE GIVES YOU GUYS PLENTY OF GRIEF.
TAKE CARE OF HIM, OKAY?
!
HUH!!?
YOU'RE GOING ALREADY!!?
YEAH.

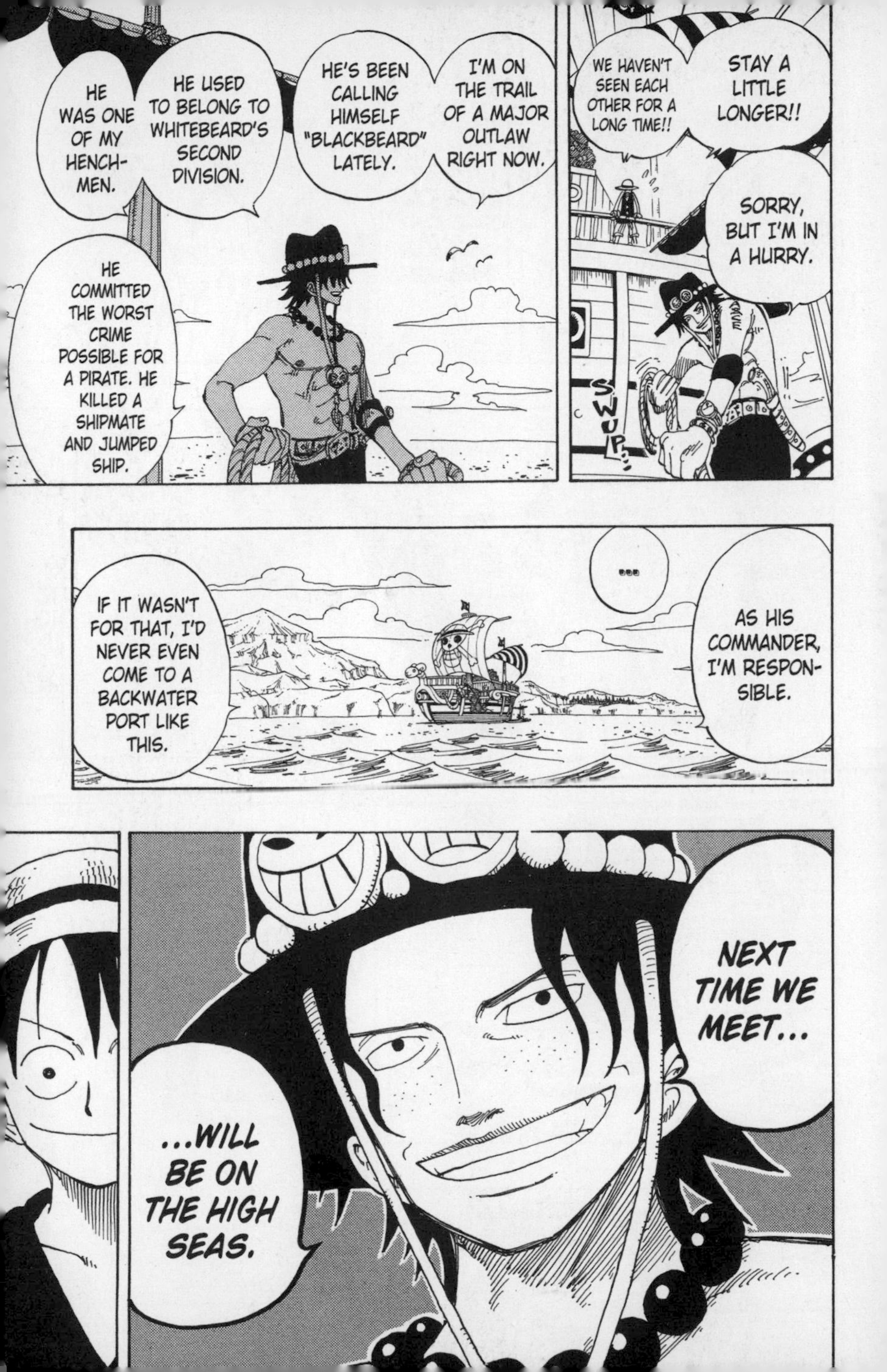
STAY A LITTLE LONGER!!
WE HAVEN'T SEEN EACH OTHER FOR A LONG TIME!!
SORRY, BUT I'M IN A HURRY.
SWUP...
I'M ON THE TRAIL OF A MAJOR OUTLAW RIGHT NOW.
HE'S BEEN CALLING HIMSELF "BLACKBEARD" LATELY.
HE USED TO BELONG TO WHITEBEARD'S SECOND DIVISION.
HE WAS ONE OF MY HENCH-MEN.
HE COMMITTED THE WORST CRIME POSSIBLE FOR A PIRATE. HE KILLED A SHIPMATE AND JUMPED SHIP.
AS HIS COMMANDER, I'M RESPON-SIBLE.
...
IF IT WASN'T FOR THAT, I'D NEVER EVEN COME TO A BACKWATER PORT LIKE THIS.
NEXT TIME WE MEET...
...WILL BE ON THE HIGH SEAS.

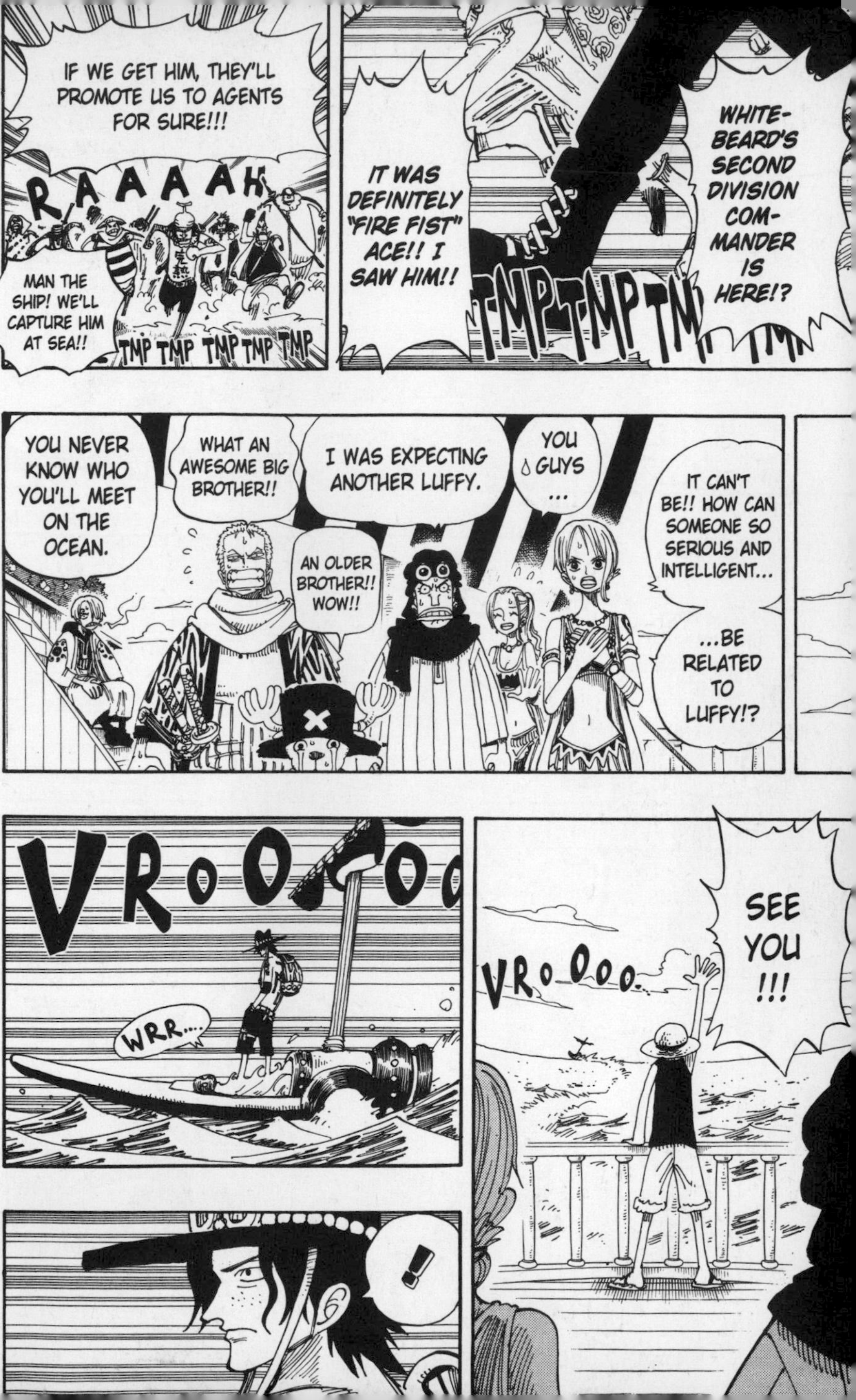
WHITE-BEARD'S SECOND DIVISION COM-MANDER IS HERE!?
IT WAS DEFINITELY "FIRE FIST" ACE!! I SAW HIM!!
TMP TMP TM
TM
IF WE GET HIM, THEY'LL PROMOTE US TO AGENTS FOR SURE!!!
RAAAAH
MAN THE SHIP! WE'LL CAPTURE HIM AT SEA!!
TMP TMP TMP TMP TMP
IT CAN'T BE!! HOW CAN SOMEONE SO SERIOUS AND INTELLIGENT...
...BE RELATED TO LUFFY!?
YOU GUYS ...
I WAS EXPECTING ANOTHER LUFFY.
AN OLDER BROTHER!! WOW!!
WHAT AN AWESOME BIG BROTHER!!
YOU NEVER KNOW WHO YOU'LL MEET ON THE OCEAN.
SEE YOU !!!
VROOOO...
VROOOO
WRR....
!

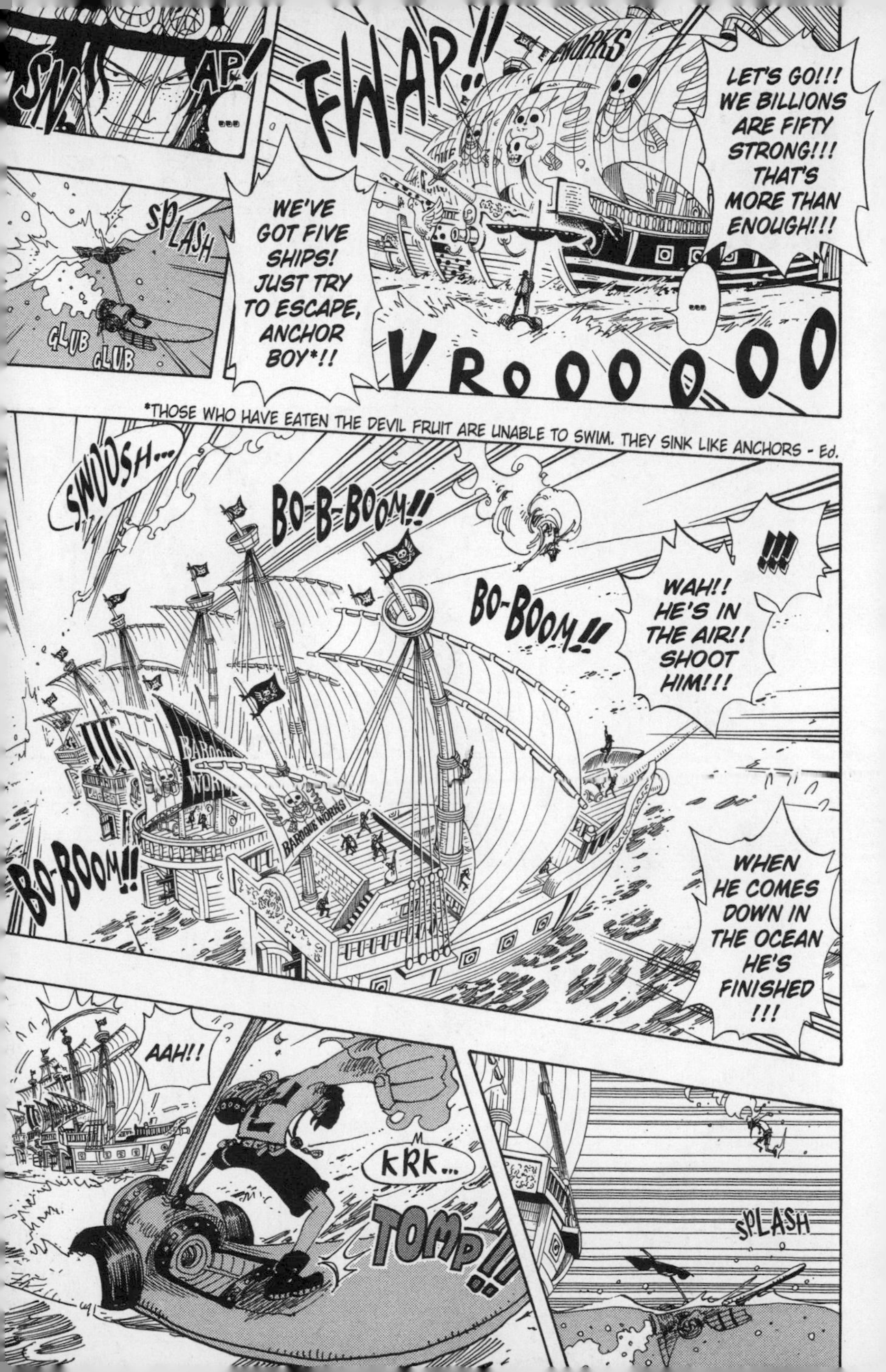

LET'S GO!!! WE BILLIONS ARE FIFTY STRONG!!! THAT'S MORE THAN ENOUGH!!!
...
VROOOOOO
FWAP!!
WE'VE GOT FIVE SHIPS! JUST TRY TO ESCAPE, ANCHOR BOY*!!
SNAP!
...
SPLASH
GLUB
GLUB
*THOSE WHO HAVE EATEN THE DEVIL FRUIT ARE UNABLE TO SWIM. THEY SINK LIKE ANCHORS - Ed.
!!!
WAH!! HE'S IN THE AIR!! SHOOT HIM!!!
BO-BOOM!!
BO-B-BOOM!!
SWOOSH...
WHEN HE COMES DOWN IN THE OCEAN HE'S FINISHED!!!
BO-BOOM!!
SPLASH
AAH!!
KRK...
TOMP!!!

KRAK KRAK KRAK!!

FIRE FIST!!!!

FWOOO...

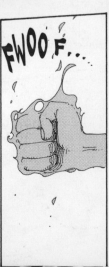

FWOOF...

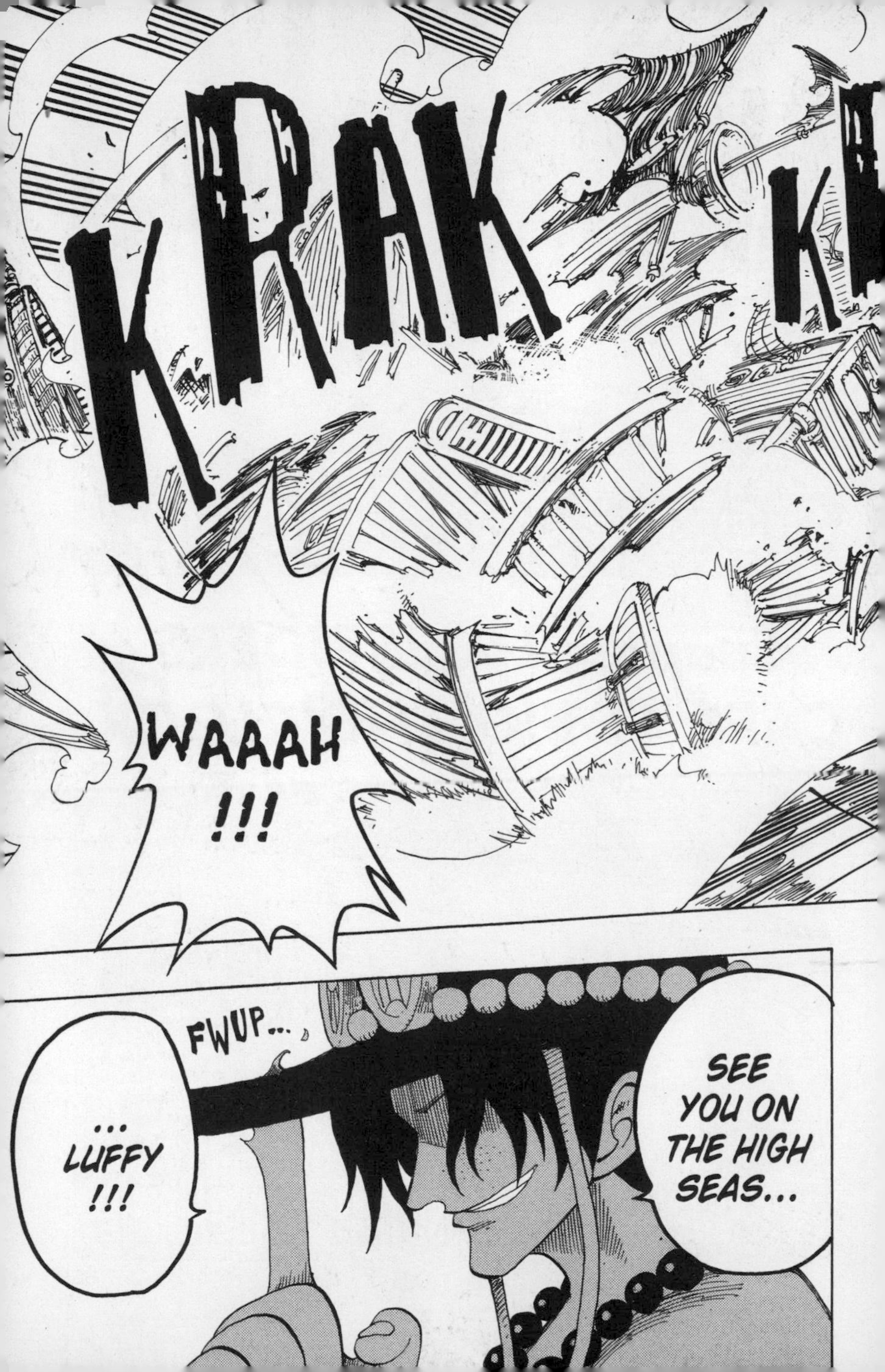
KRAK
WAAAH !!!
SEE YOU ON THE HIGH SEAS...
FWUP...
... LUFFY !!!

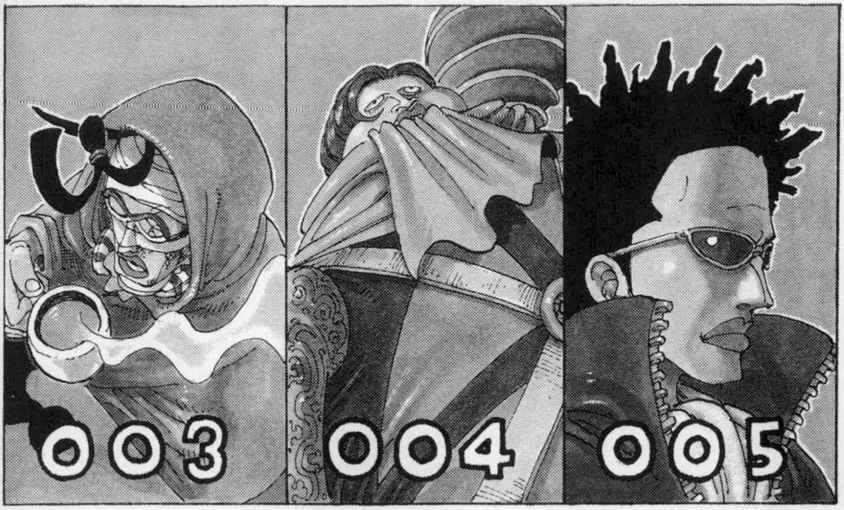
005
004
003

Chapter 160: SPIDERS CAFÉ AT EIGHT O'CLOCK

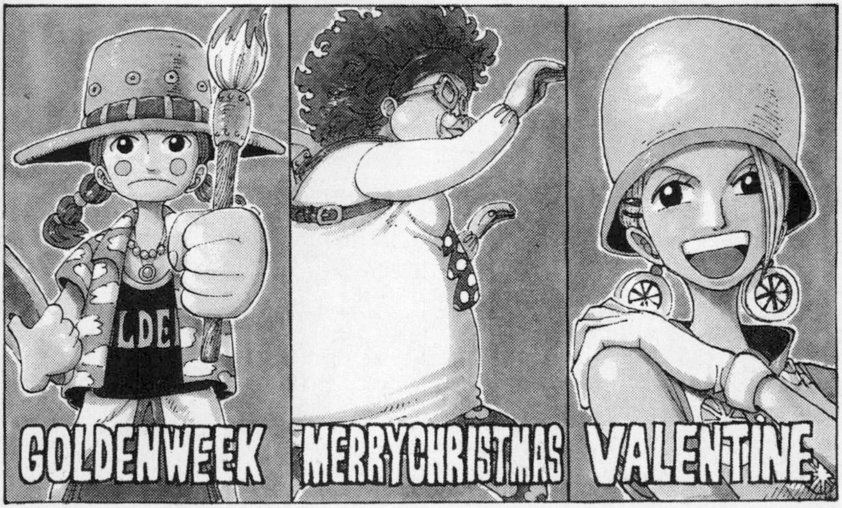
VALENTINE
MERRYCHRISTMAS
GOLDENWEEK

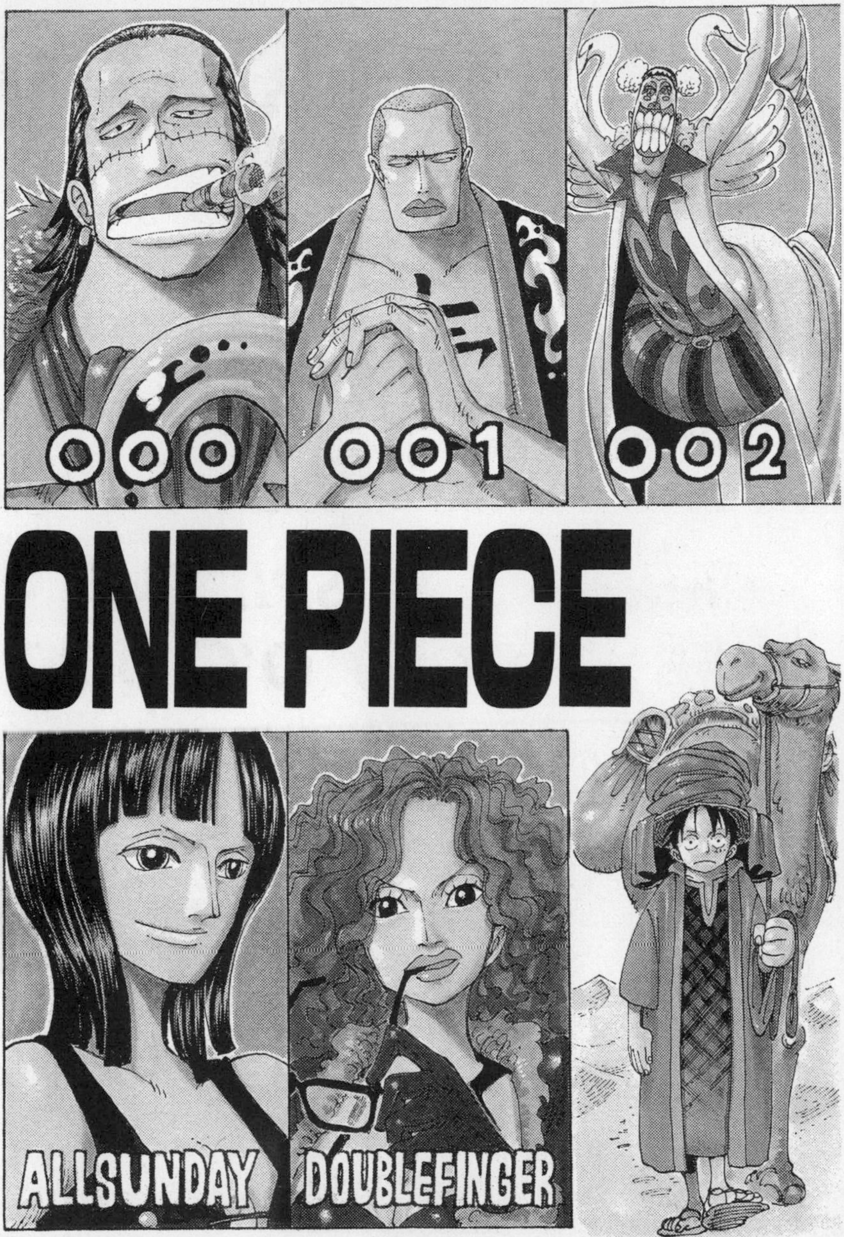

002
001
000
ONE PIECE
DOUBLEFINGER
ALLSUNDAY

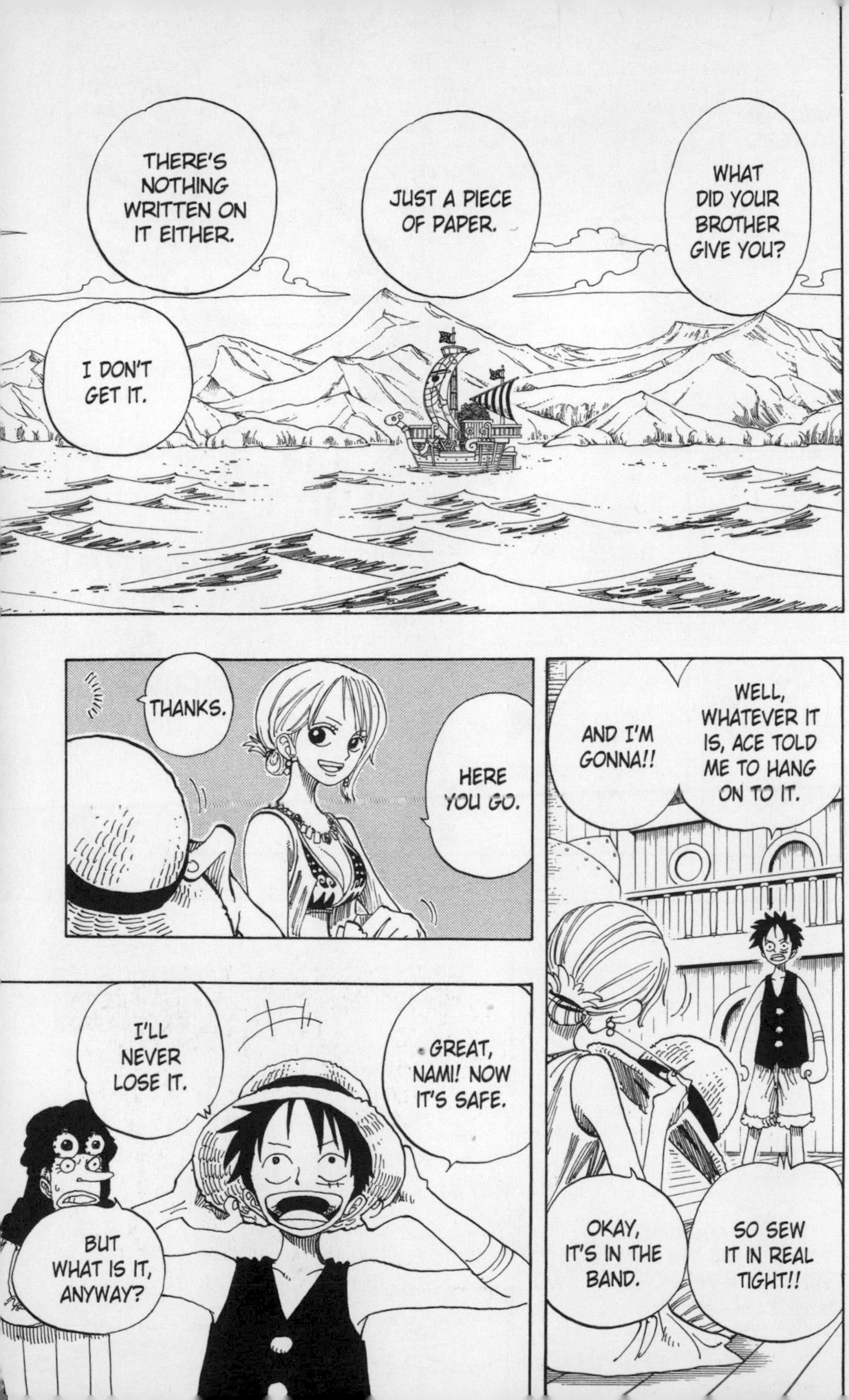
WHAT DID YOUR BROTHER GIVE YOU?
JUST A PIECE OF PAPER.
THERE'S NOTHING WRITTEN ON IT EITHER.
I DON'T GET IT.
WELL, WHATEVER IT IS, ACE TOLD ME TO HANG ON TO IT.
AND I'M GONNA!!
SO SEW IT IN REAL TIGHT!!
OKAY, IT'S IN THE BAND.
HERE YOU GO.
THANKS.
GREAT, NAMI! NOW IT'S SAFE.
I'LL NEVER LOSE IT.
BUT WHAT IS IT, ANYWAY?

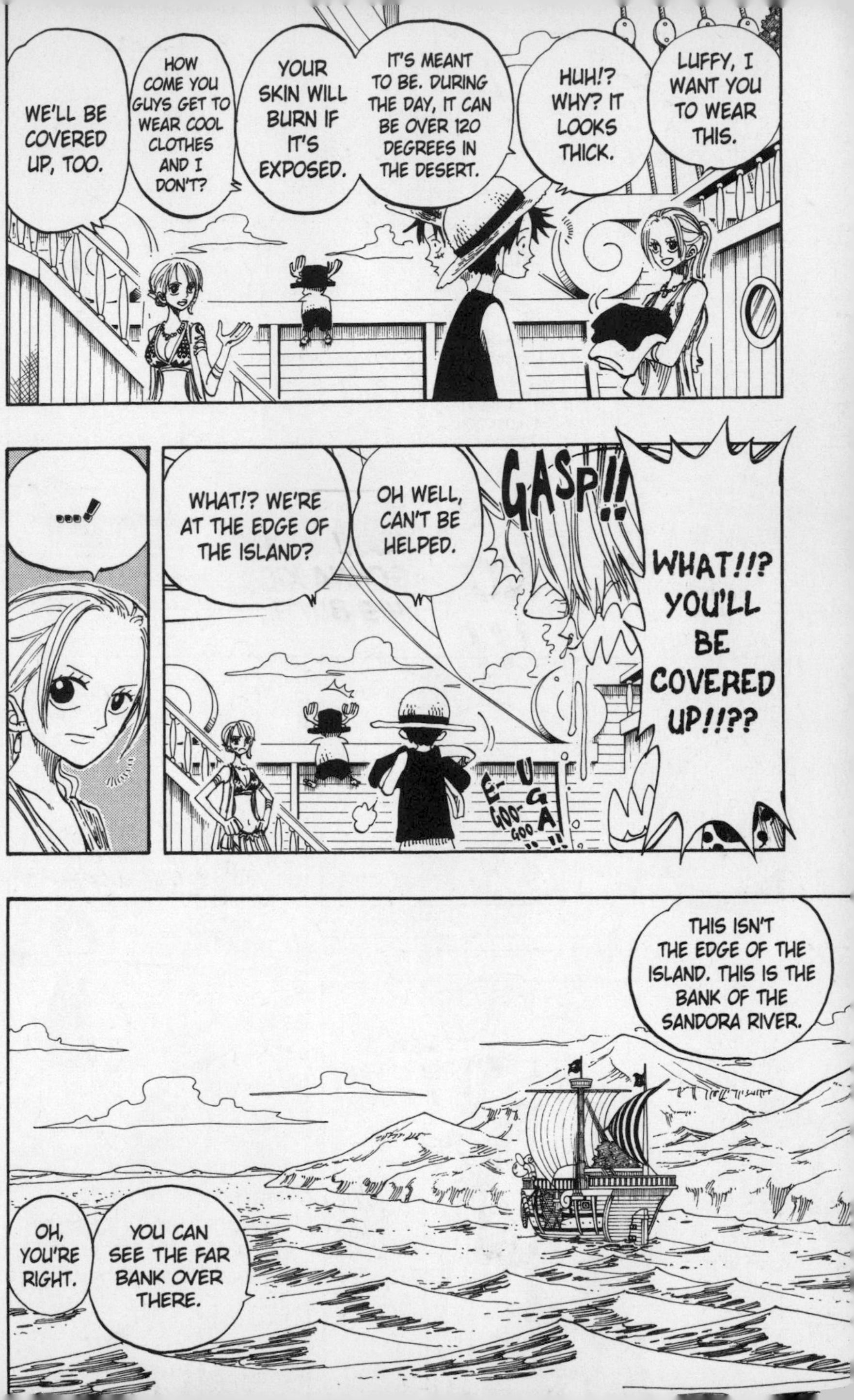
LUFFY, I WANT YOU TO WEAR THIS.
HUH!? WHY? IT LOOKS THICK.
IT'S MEANT TO BE. DURING THE DAY, IT CAN BE OVER 120 DEGREES IN THE DESERT.
YOUR SKIN WILL BURN IF IT'S EXPOSED.
HOW COME YOU GUYS GET TO WEAR COOL CLOTHES AND I DON'T?
WE'LL BE COVERED UP, TOO.
GASP!!
WHAT!!? YOU'LL BE COVERED UP!!??
OH WELL, CAN'T BE HELPED.
WHAT!? WE'RE AT THE EDGE OF THE ISLAND?
UGA!!
E-GOO GOO!!
...!
THIS ISN'T THE EDGE OF THE ISLAND. THIS IS THE BANK OF THE SANDORA RIVER.
YOU CAN SEE THE FAR BANK OVER THERE.
OH, YOU'RE RIGHT.

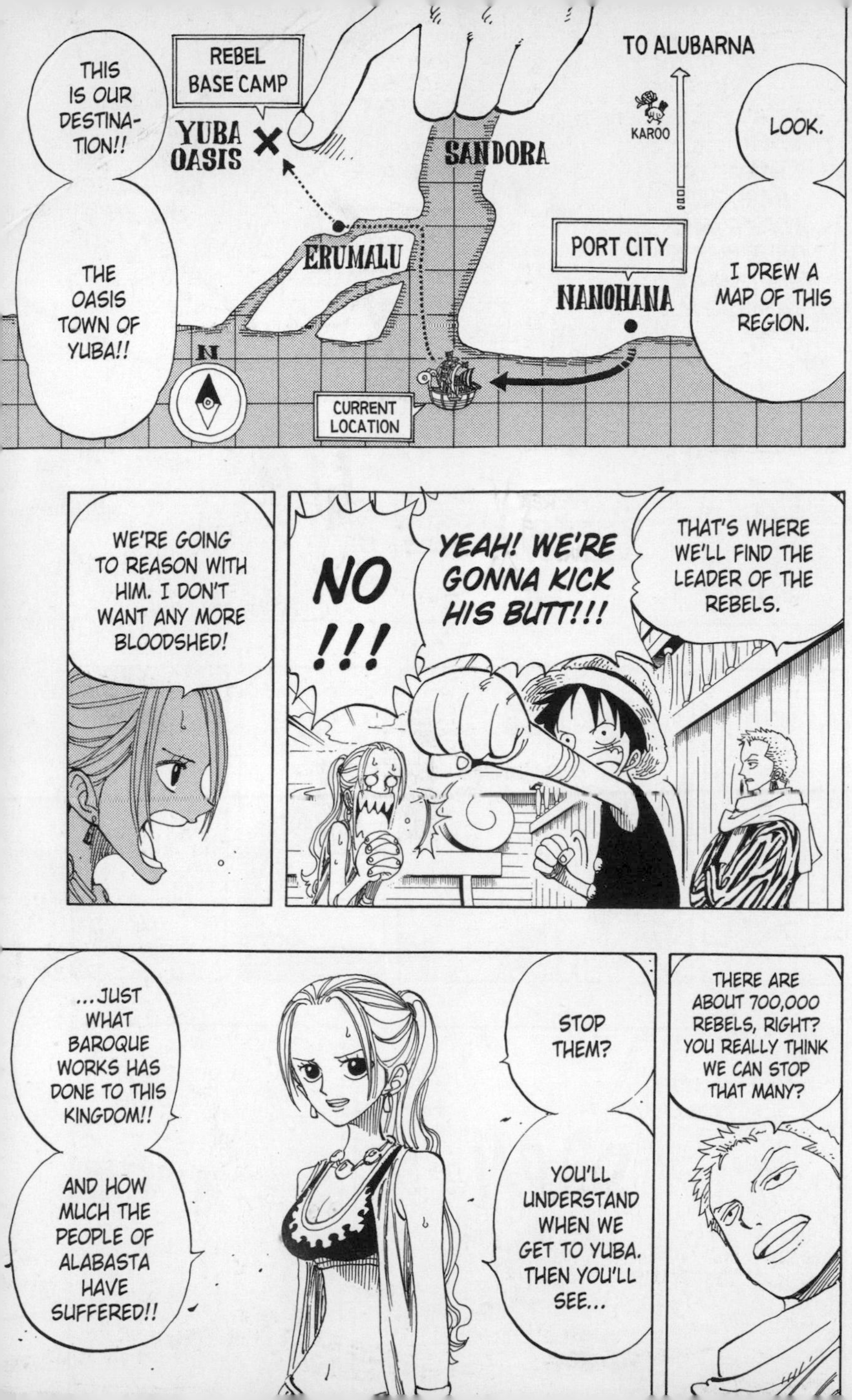
LOOK.
I DREW A MAP OF THIS REGION.
TO ALUBARNA
KAROO
PORT CITY
NANOHANA
SANDORA
REBEL BASE CAMP
YUBA OASIS
ERUMALU
N
CURRENT LOCATION
THIS IS OUR DESTINATION!!
THE OASIS TOWN OF YUBA!!
THAT'S WHERE WE'LL FIND THE LEADER OF THE REBELS.
YEAH! WE'RE GONNA KICK HIS BUTT!!!
NO !!!
WE'RE GOING TO REASON WITH HIM. I DON'T WANT ANY MORE BLOODSHED!
THERE ARE ABOUT 700,000 REBELS, RIGHT? YOU REALLY THINK WE CAN STOP THAT MANY?
STOP THEM?
YOU'LL UNDERSTAND WHEN WE GET TO YUBA. THEN YOU'LL SEE...
...JUST WHAT BAROQUE WORKS HAS DONE TO THIS KINGDOM!!
AND HOW MUCH THE PEOPLE OF ALABASTA HAVE SUFFERED!!

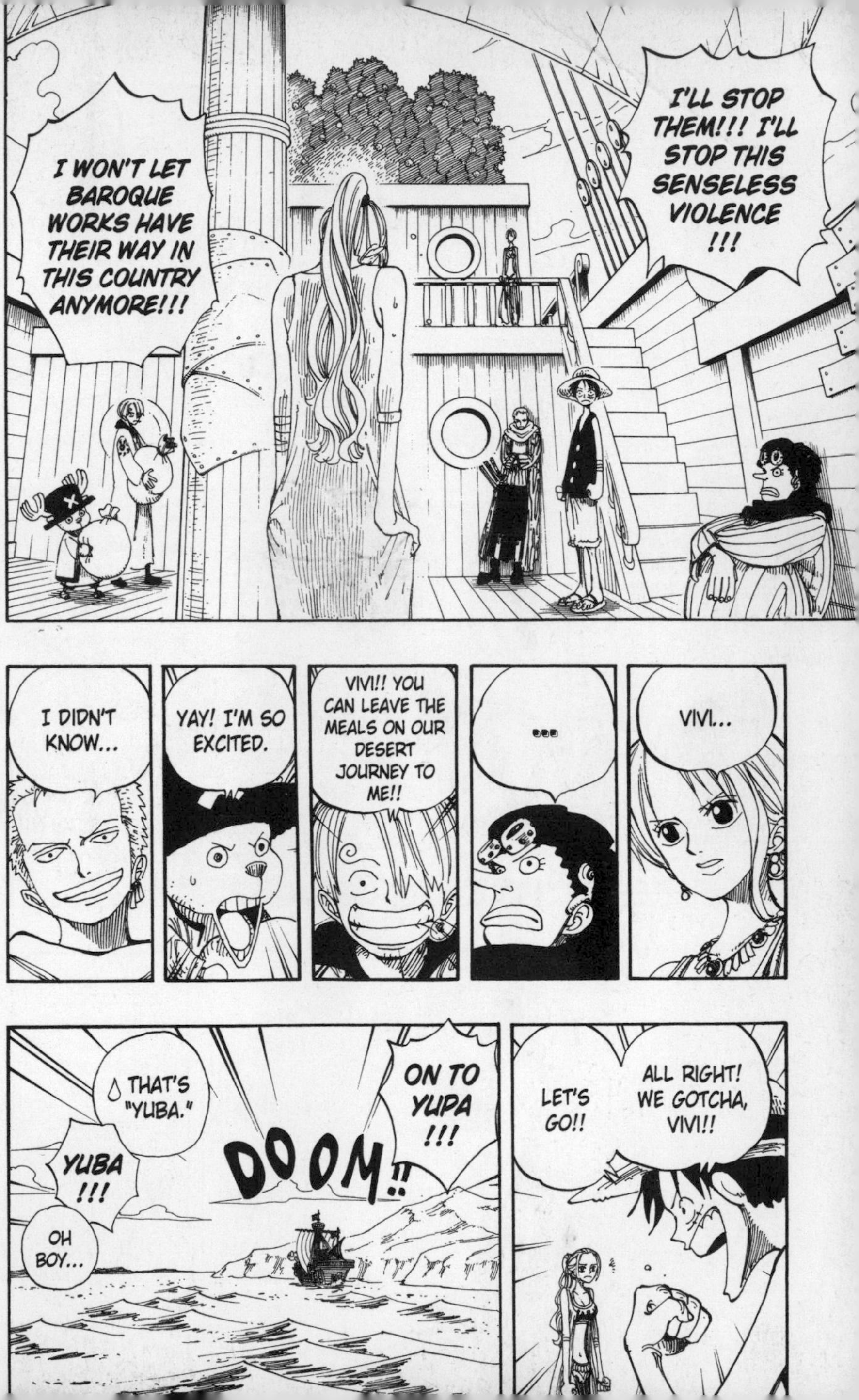
I'LL STOP THEM!!! I'LL STOP THIS SENSELESS VIOLENCE !!!
I WON'T LET BAROQUE WORKS HAVE THEIR WAY IN THIS COUNTRY ANYMORE!!!
VIVI...
...
VIVI!! YOU CAN LEAVE THE MEALS ON OUR DESERT JOURNEY TO ME!!
YAY! I'M SO EXCITED.
I DIDN'T KNOW...
ALL RIGHT! WE GOTCHA, VIVI!!
LET'S GO!!
ON TO YUPA !!!
DOOM!!
THAT'S "YUBA."
YUBA !!!
OH BOY...

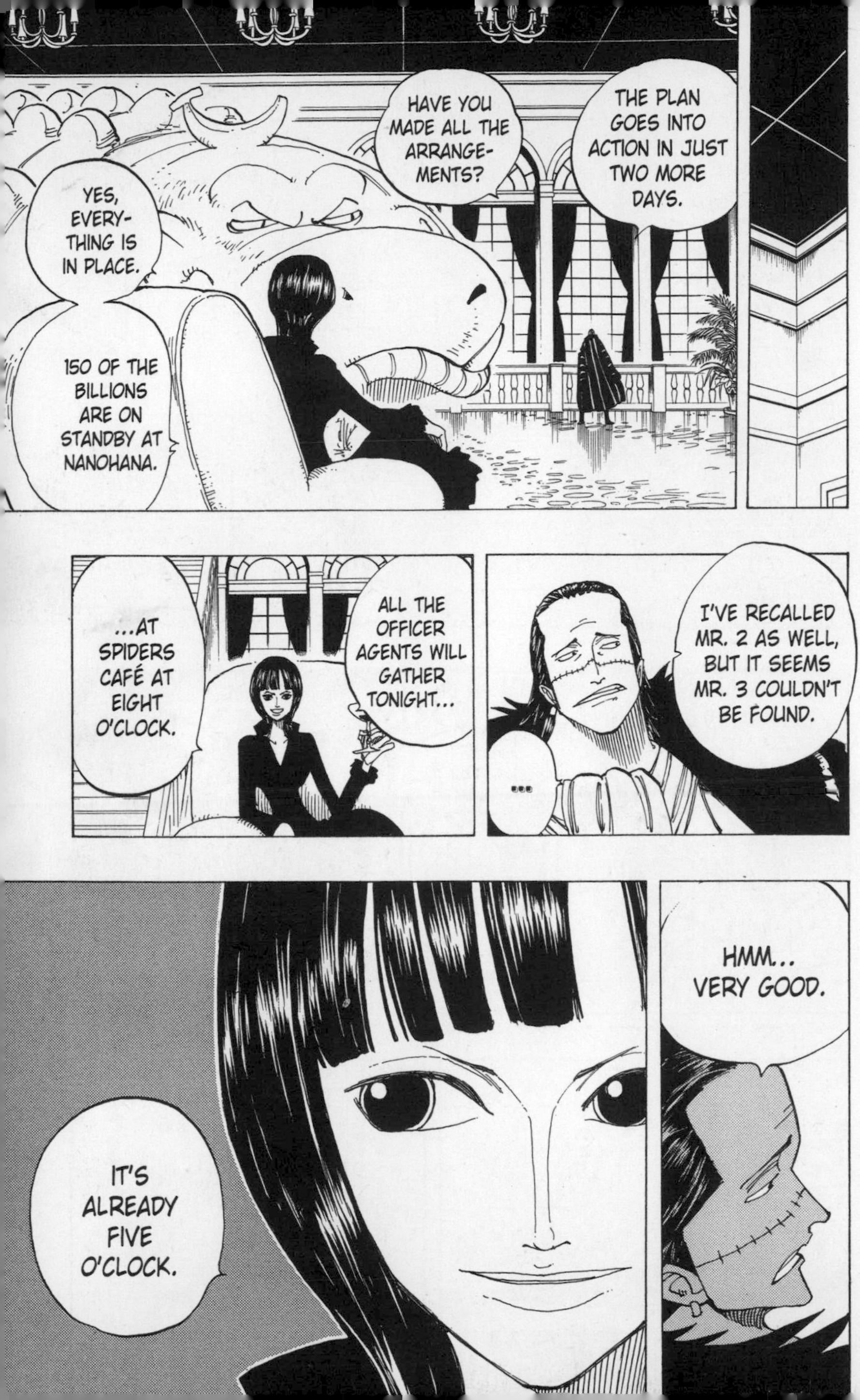
THE PLAN GOES INTO ACTION IN JUST TWO MORE DAYS.
HAVE YOU MADE ALL THE ARRANGE-MENTS?
YES, EVERY-THING IS IN PLACE.
150 OF THE BILLIONS ARE ON STANDBY AT NANOHANA.
I'VE RECALLED MR. 2 AS WELL, BUT IT SEEMS MR. 3 COULDN'T BE FOUND.
...
ALL THE OFFICER AGENTS WILL GATHER TONIGHT...
...AT SPIDERS CAFÉ AT EIGHT O'CLOCK.
HMM... VERY GOOD.
IT'S ALREADY FIVE O'CLOCK.

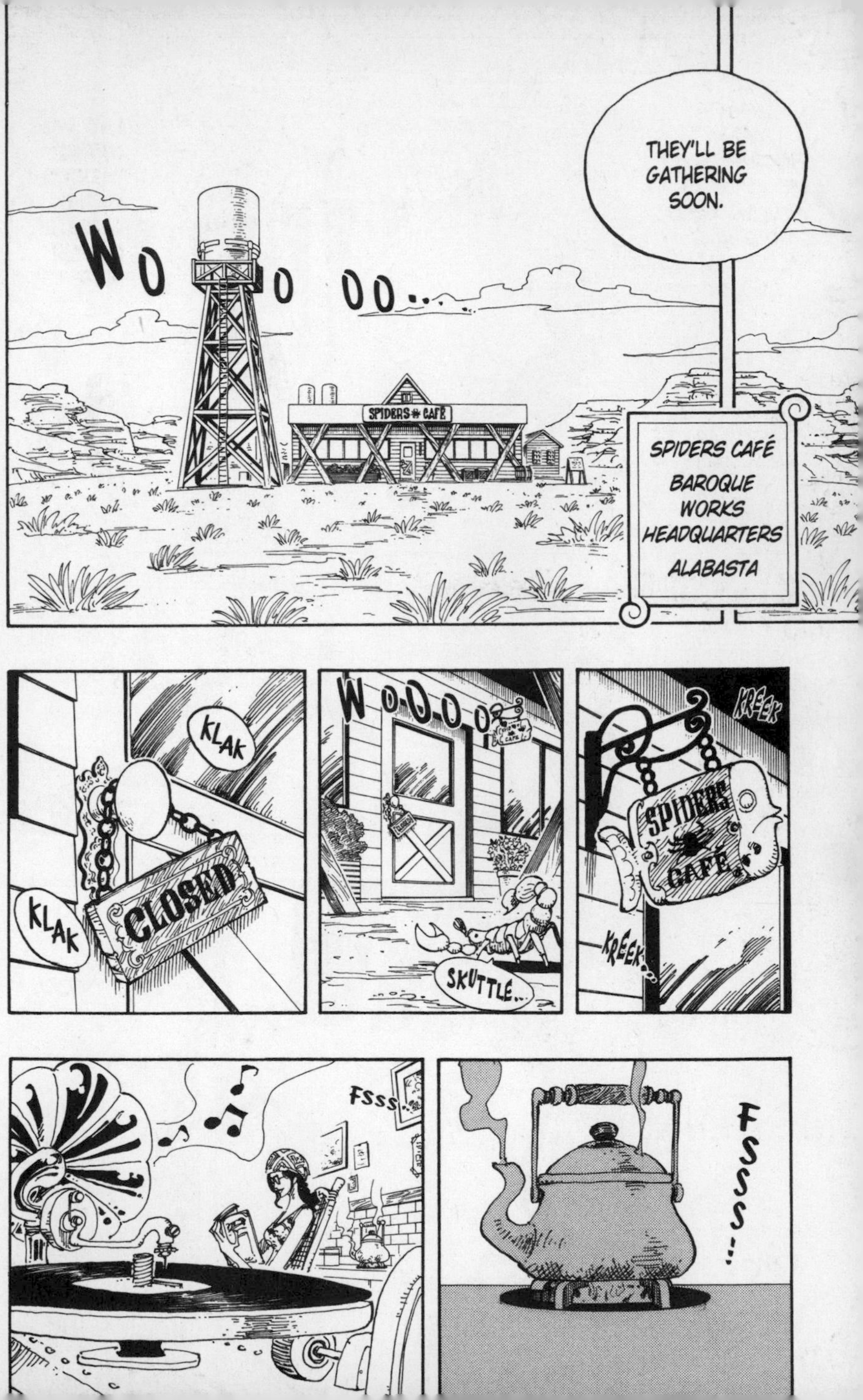
THEY'LL BE GATHERING SOON.
SPIDERS CAFÉ
BAROQUE WORKS HEADQUARTERS
ALABASTA
WO O OO...
SPIDERS CAFÉ
KREEK
SPIDERS CAFÉ
KREEK
WOOOOO
SKUTTLE...
KLAK
CLOSED
KLAK
FSSS!!
FSSS..

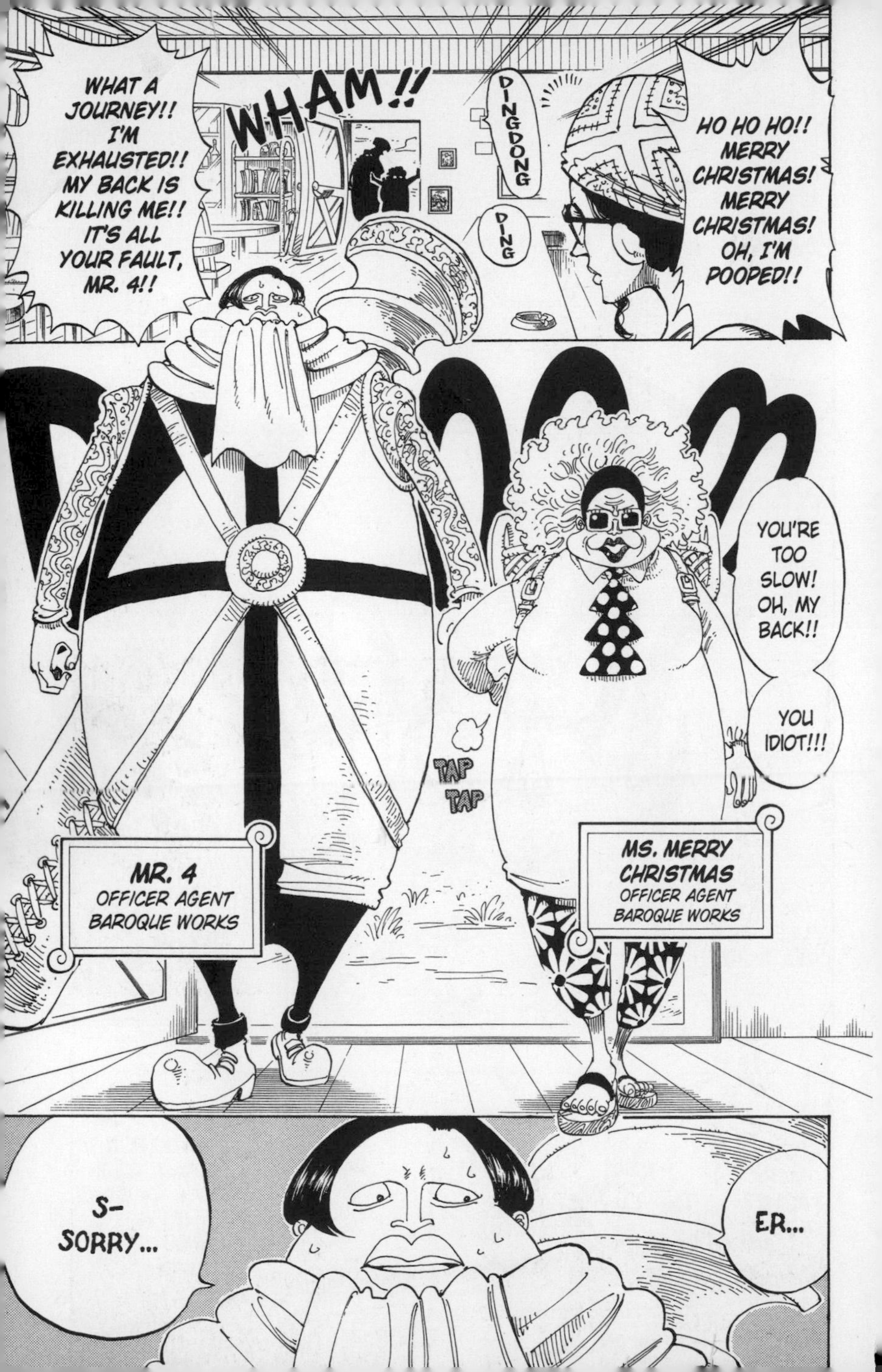
HO HO HO!! MERRY CHRISTMAS! MERRY CHRISTMAS! OH, I'M POOPED!!
DING
DINGDONG
WHAM!!
WHAT A JOURNEY!! I'M EXHAUSTED!! MY BACK IS KILLING ME!! IT'S ALL YOUR FAULT, MR. 4!!
YOU'RE TOO SLOW! OH, MY BACK!!
YOU IDIOT!!!
MS. MERRY CHRISTMAS OFFICER AGENT BAROQUE WORKS
TAP TAP
MR. 4 OFFICER AGENT BAROQUE WORKS
ER...
S- SORRY...

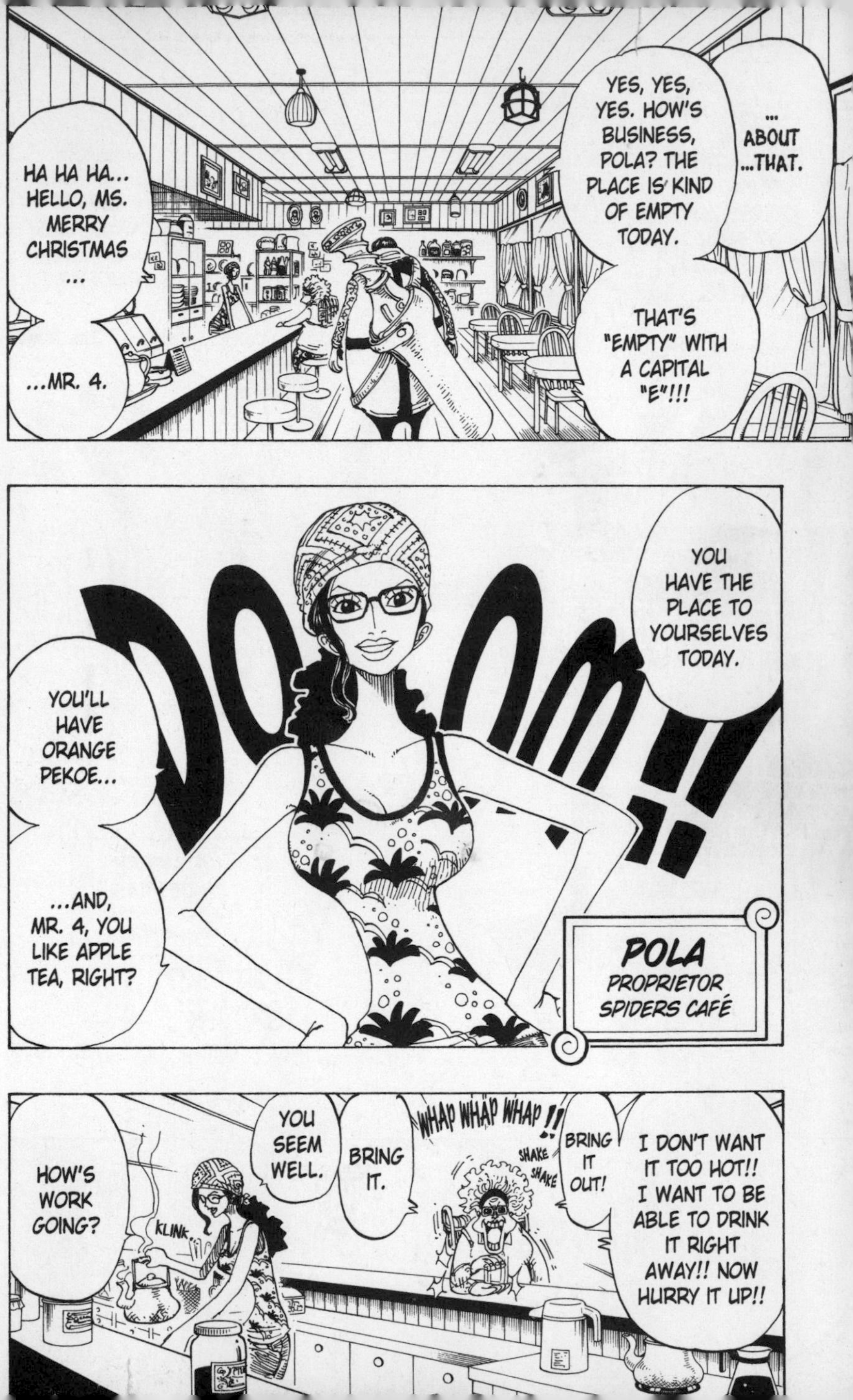

... ABOUT ...THAT.
YES, YES, YES. HOW'S BUSINESS, POLA? THE PLACE IS KIND OF EMPTY TODAY.
THAT'S "EMPTY" WITH A CAPITAL "E"!!!
HA HA HA... HELLO, MS. MERRY CHRISTMAS ...
...MR. 4.
YOU HAVE THE PLACE TO YOURSELVES TODAY.
DOOM!!
YOU'LL HAVE ORANGE PEKOE...
...AND, MR. 4, YOU LIKE APPLE TEA, RIGHT?
POLA
PROPRIETOR SPIDERS CAFÉ
I DON'T WANT IT TOO HOT!! I WANT TO BE ABLE TO DRINK IT RIGHT AWAY!! NOW HURRY IT UP!!
BRING IT OUT!
SHAKE SHAKE
WHAP WHAP WHAP!!
BRING IT.
YOU SEEM WELL.
HOW'S WORK GOING?
KLINK...

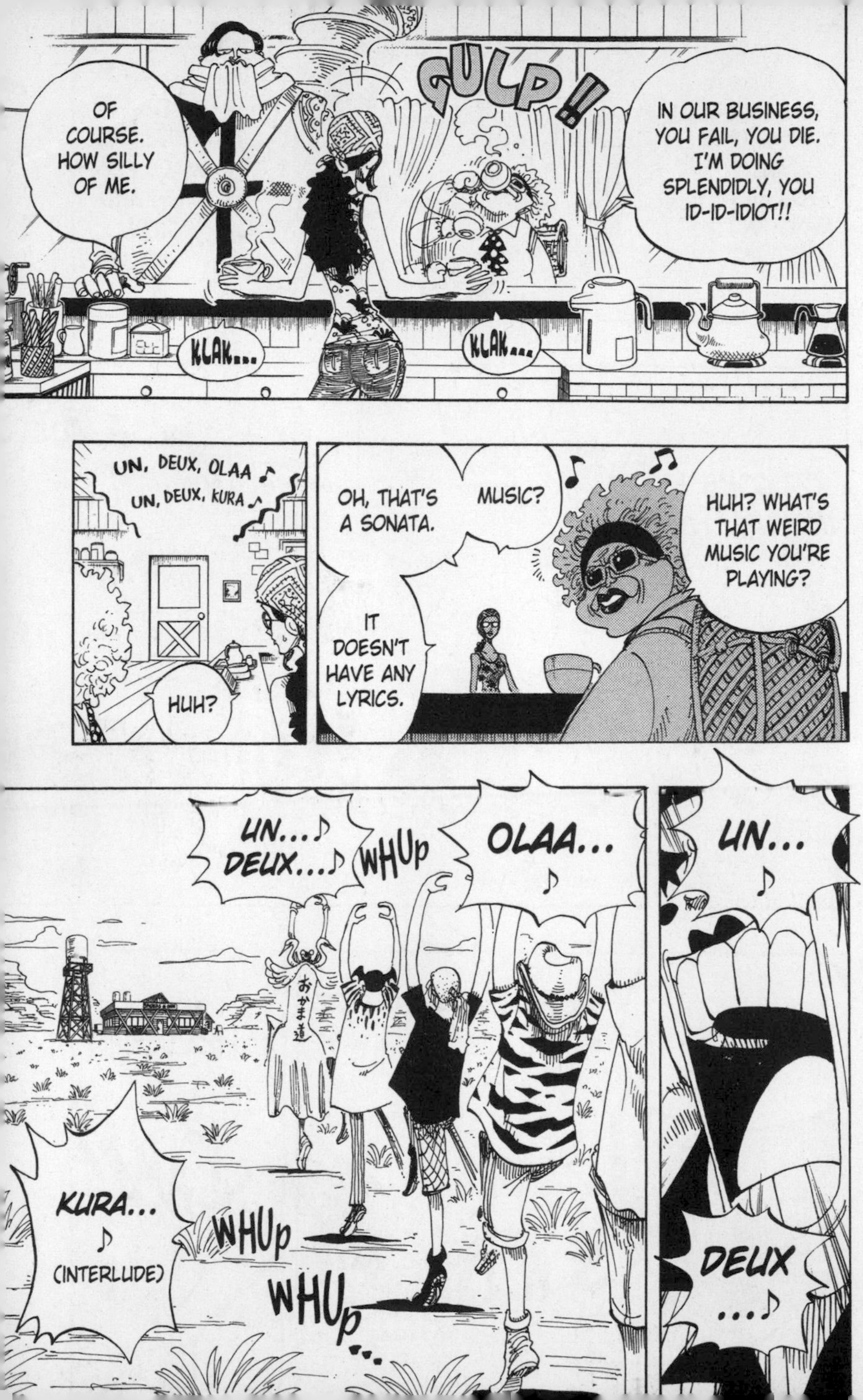
IN OUR BUSINESS, YOU FAIL, YOU DIE. I'M DOING SPLENDIDLY, YOU ID-ID-IDIOT!!
GULP!!
OF COURSE. HOW SILLY OF ME.
KLAK...
KLAK...
HUH? WHAT'S THAT WEIRD MUSIC YOU'RE PLAYING?
MUSIC?
OH, THAT'S A SONATA.
IT DOESN'T HAVE ANY LYRICS.
UN, DEUX, OLAA ♪
UN, DEUX, KURA ♪
HUH?
UN... ♪
DEUX ...♪
OLAA... ♪
UN...♪ DEUX...♪
WHUp
おかま道
KURA... ♪ (INTERLUDE)
WHUp
WHUp...

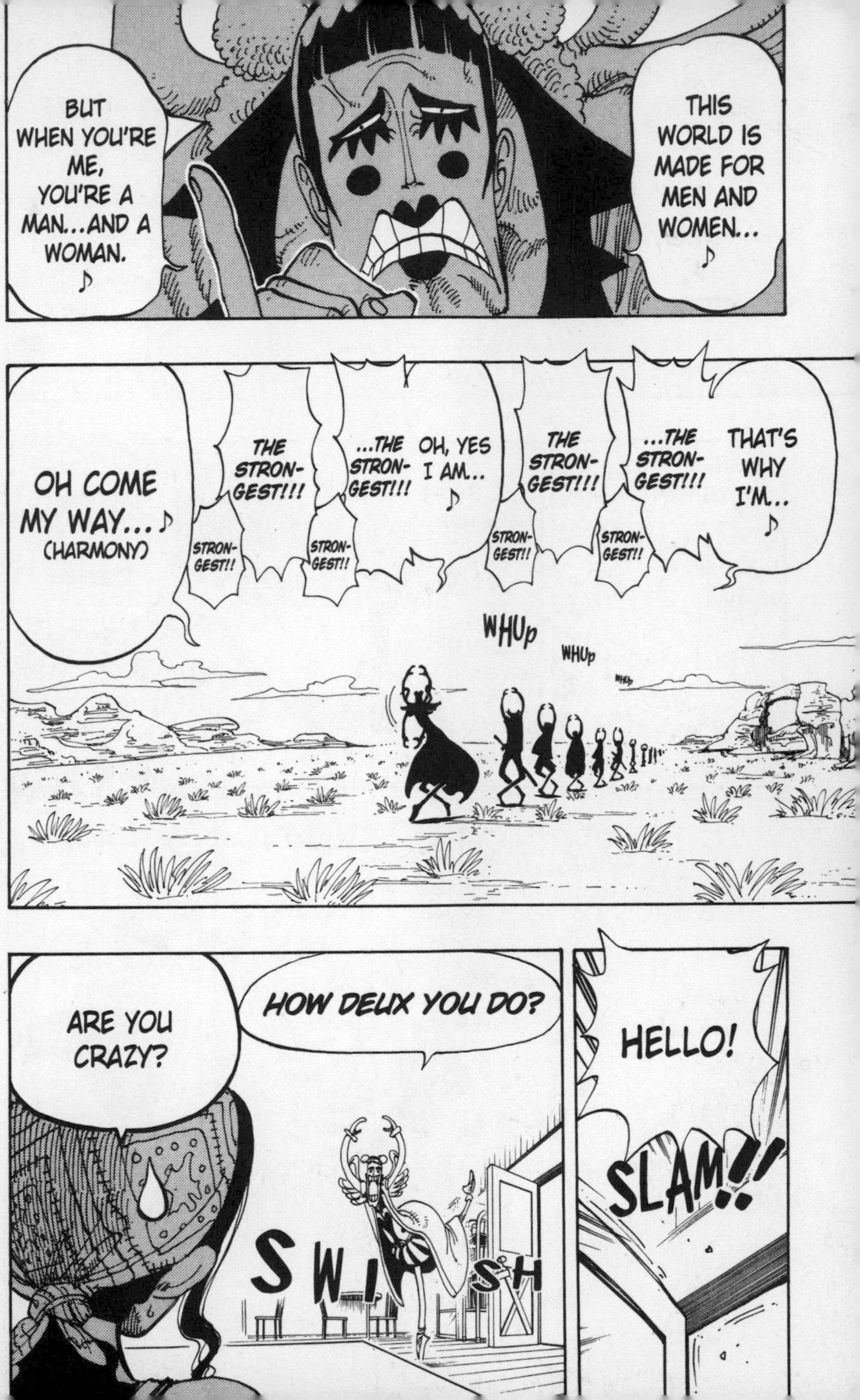
THIS WORLD IS MADE FOR MEN AND WOMEN... ♪
BUT WHEN YOU'RE ME, YOU'RE A MAN...AND A WOMAN. ♪
THAT'S WHY I'M... ♪
...THE STRON-GEST!!!
STRON-GEST!!
THE STRON-GEST!!!
STRON-GEST!!
OH, YES I AM... ♪
...THE STRON-GEST!!!
STRON-GEST!!
THE STRON-GEST!!!
STRON-GEST!!
OH COME MY WAY...♪ (HARMONY)
WHUp
WHUp
WHUp
HELLO!
SLAM!!
HOW DEUX YOU DO?
ARE YOU CRAZY?
SWISH

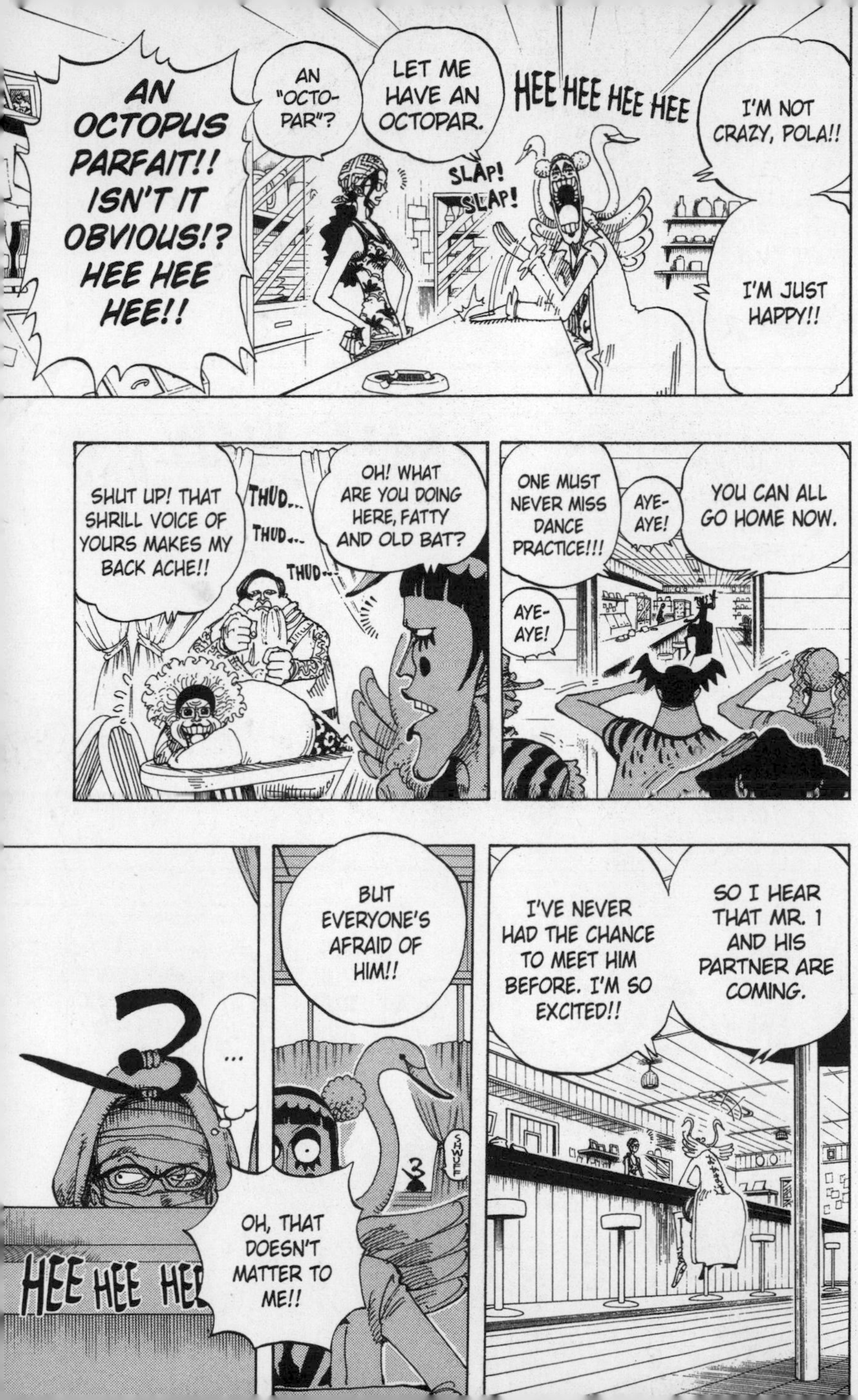
I'M NOT CRAZY, POLA!!
I'M JUST HAPPY!!
HEE HEE HEE HEE
LET ME HAVE AN OCTOPAR.
AN "OCTO-PAR"?
SLAP! SLAP!
AN OCTOPUS PARFAIT!! ISN'T IT OBVIOUS!? HEE HEE HEE!!
YOU CAN ALL GO HOME NOW.
AYE-AYE!
ONE MUST NEVER MISS DANCE PRACTICE!!!
AYE-AYE!
OH! WHAT ARE YOU DOING HERE, FATTY AND OLD BAT?
THUD... THUD... THUD...
SHUT UP! THAT SHRILL VOICE OF YOURS MAKES MY BACK ACHE!!
SO I HEAR THAT MR. 1 AND HIS PARTNER ARE COMING.
I'VE NEVER HAD THE CHANCE TO MEET HIM BEFORE. I'M SO EXCITED!!
BUT EVERYONE'S AFRAID OF HIM!!
SHWUFF
OH, THAT DOESN'T MATTER TO ME!!
HEE HEE HE
...

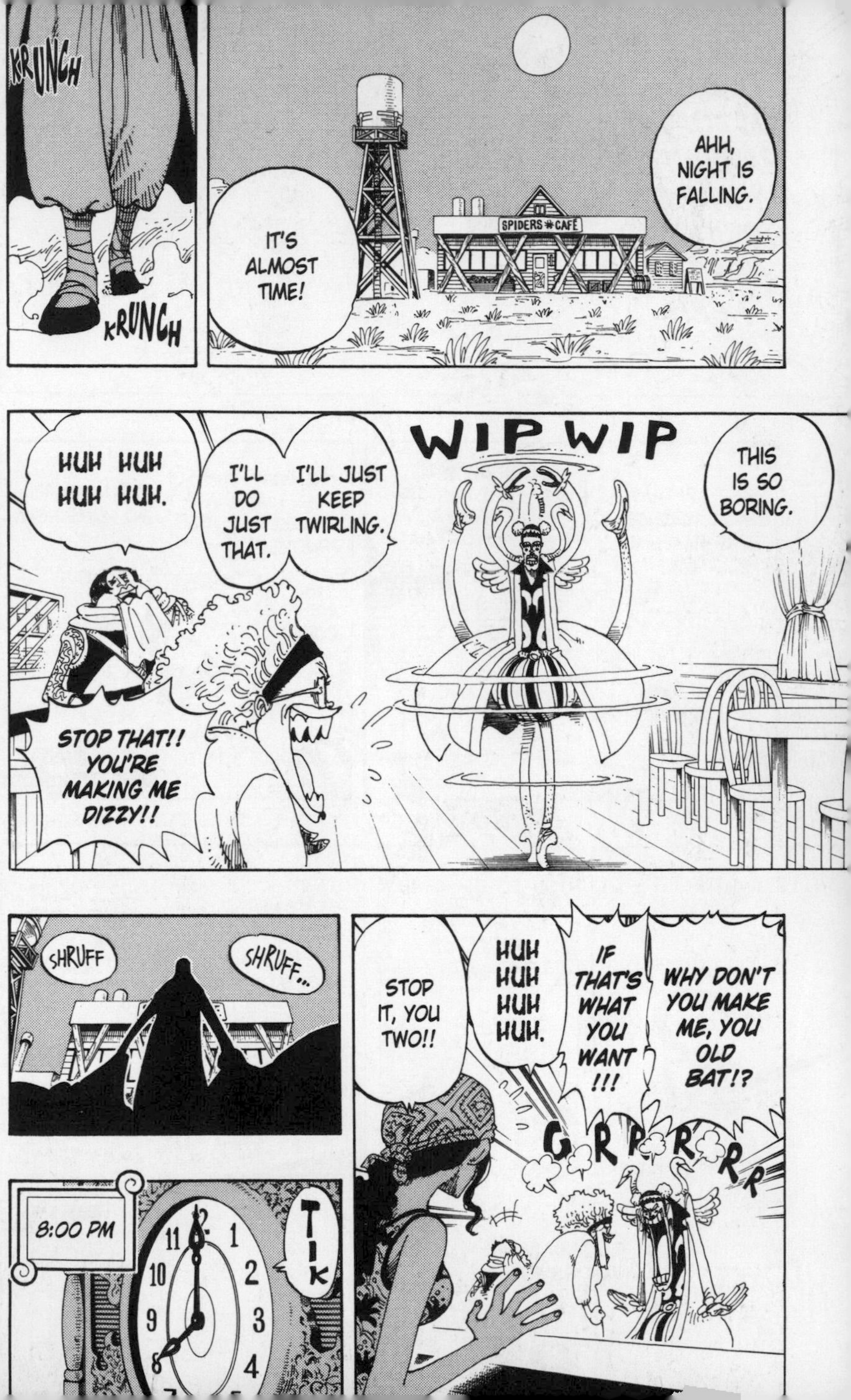

AHH, NIGHT IS FALLING.
SPIDERS CAFÉ
IT'S ALMOST TIME!
KRUNCH
KRUNCH
THIS IS SO BORING.
WIP WIP
I'LL JUST KEEP TWIRLING.
I'LL DO JUST THAT.
HUH HUH HUH HUH.
STOP THAT!! YOU'RE MAKING ME DIZZY!!
WHY DON'T YOU MAKE ME, YOU OLD BAT!?
IF THAT'S WHAT YOU WANT!!!
HUH HUH HUH HUH.
STOP IT, YOU TWO!!
GRRRRRR
SHRUFF...
SHRUFF
TIK
8:00 PM

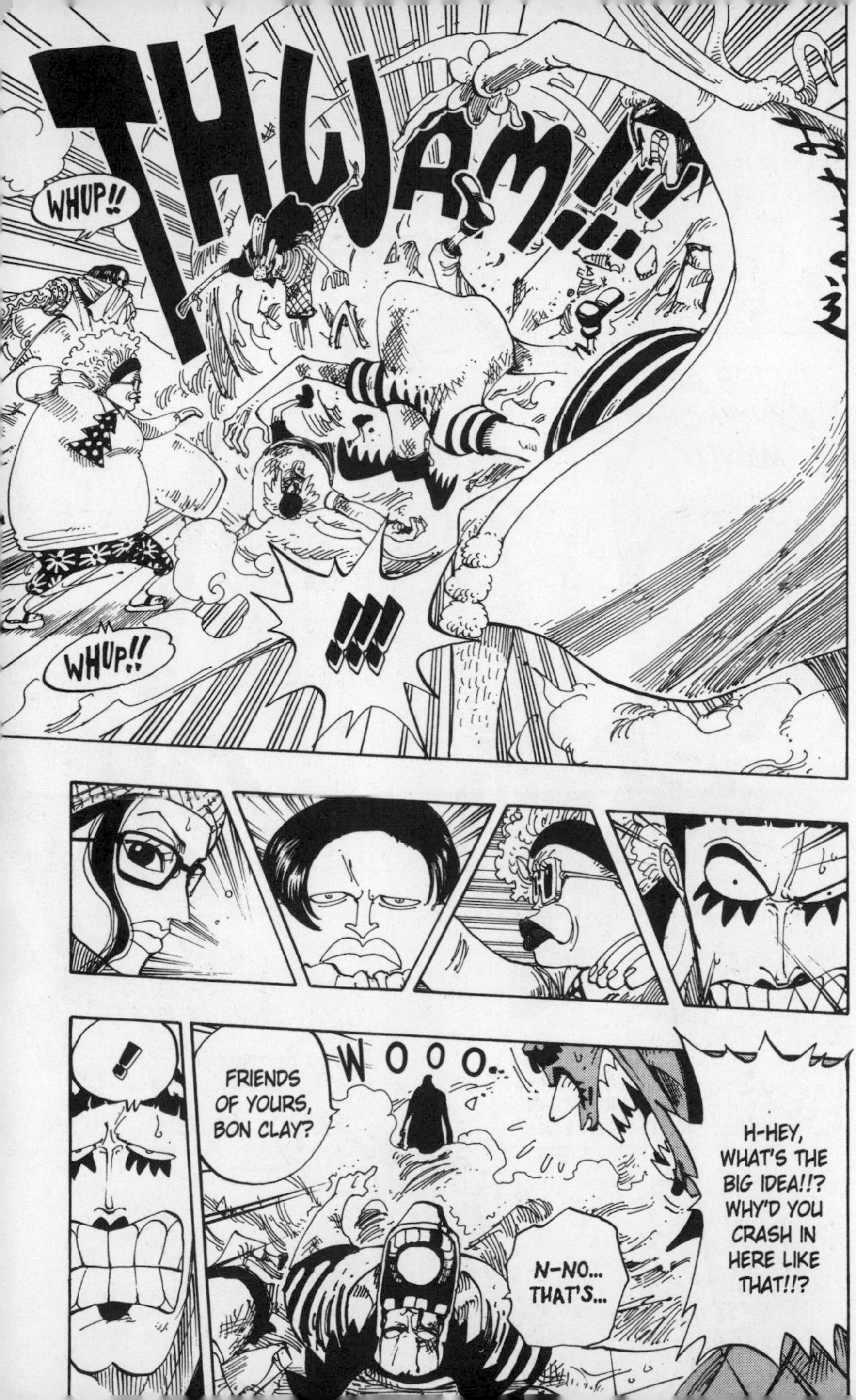
THWAM!!...
WHUP!!
WHUP!!
!!!
H-HEY, WHAT'S THE BIG IDEA!!? WHY'D YOU CRASH IN HERE LIKE THAT!!?
WOOO..
FRIENDS OF YOURS, BON CLAY?
N-NO... THAT'S...
!

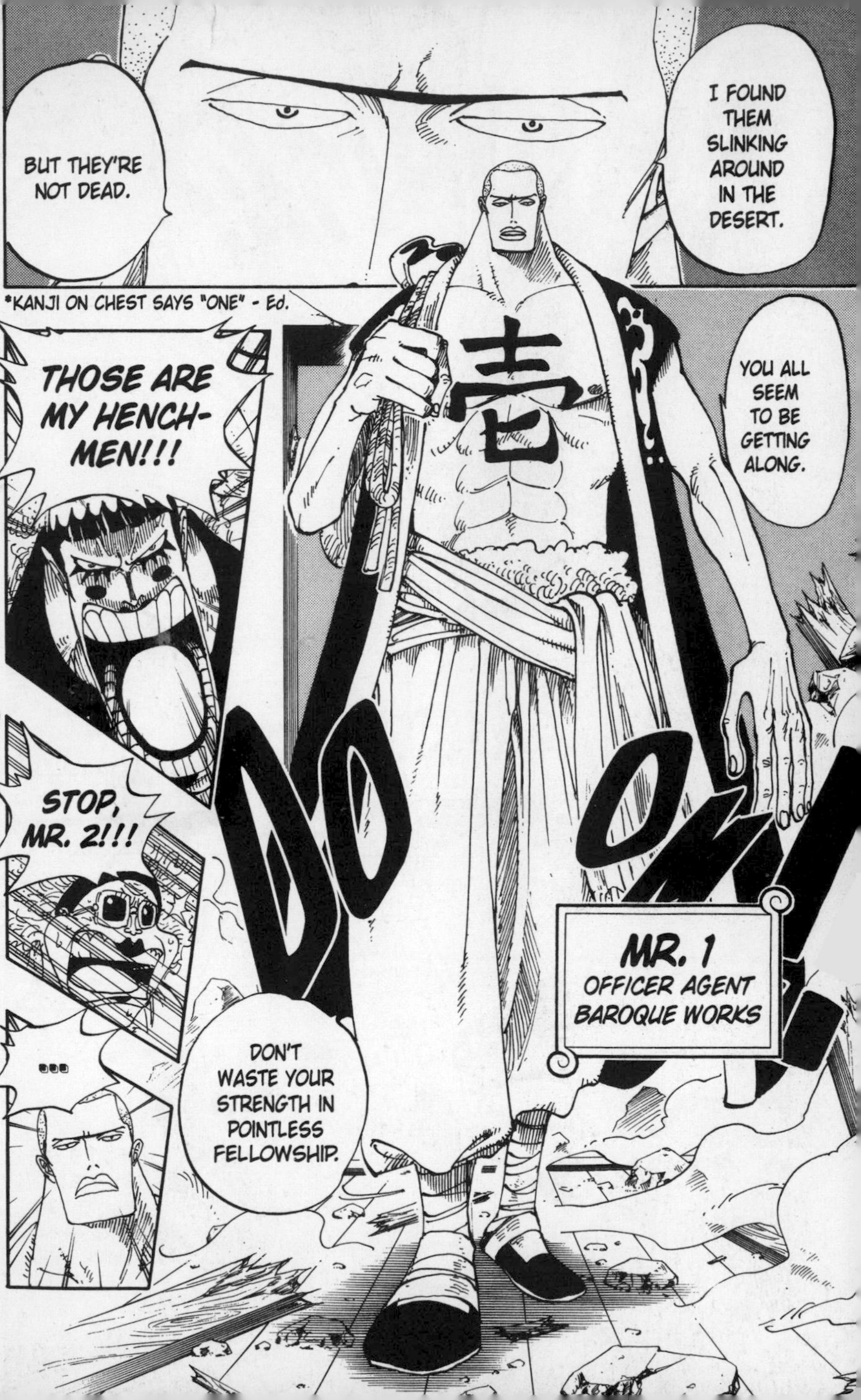
I FOUND THEM SLINKING AROUND IN THE DESERT.
BUT THEY'RE NOT DEAD.
*KANJI ON CHEST SAYS "ONE" - Ed.
YOU ALL SEEM TO BE GETTING ALONG.
壱
DOON
MR. 1
OFFICER AGENT
BAROQUE WORKS
DON'T WASTE YOUR STRENGTH IN POINTLESS FELLOWSHIP.
THOSE ARE MY HENCH-MEN!!!
STOP, MR. 2!!!
...

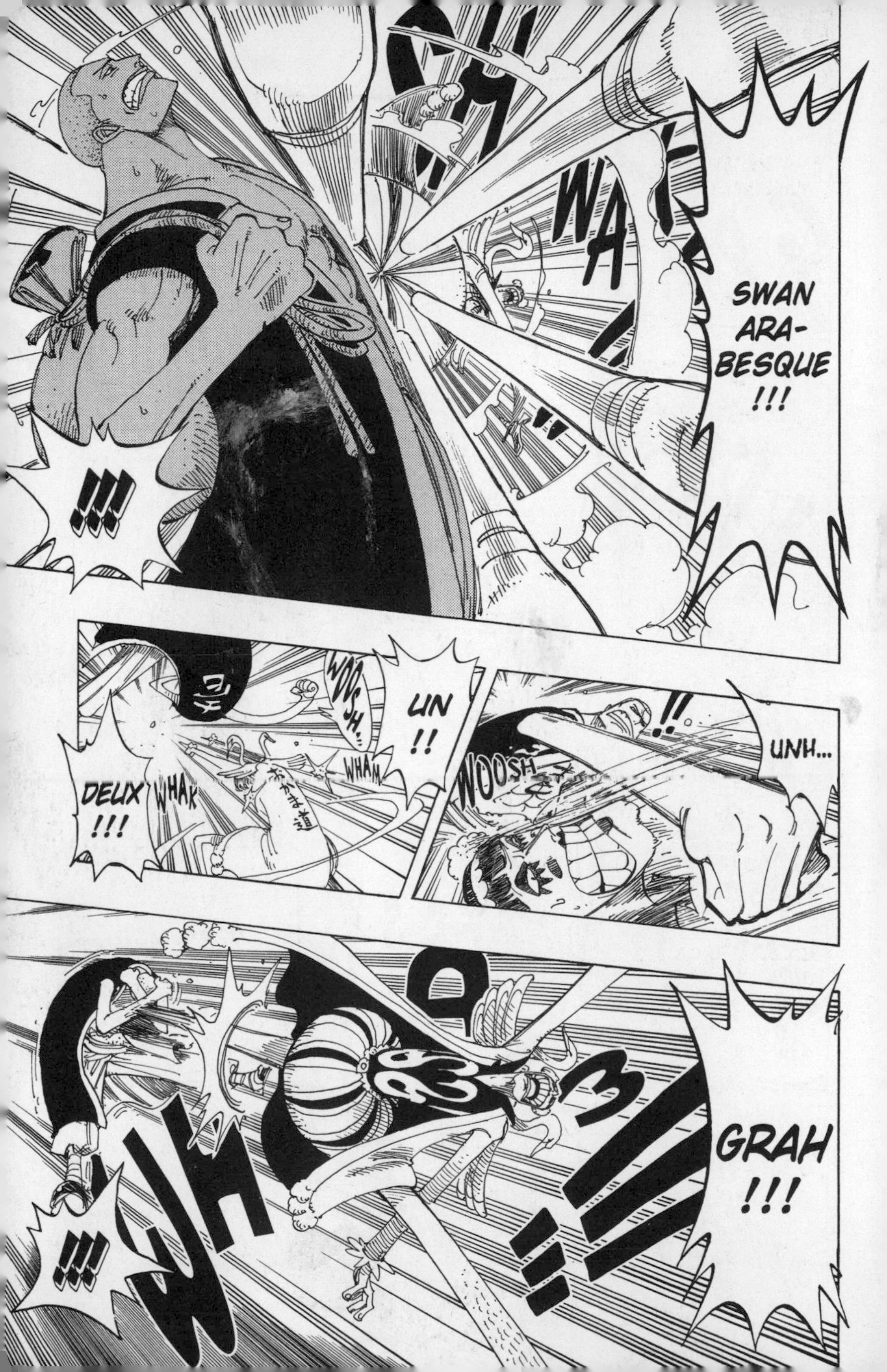
SWAN ARA-BESQUE !!!
!!!!
UNH...
!!
WOOSH
UN !!
WOOSH..
WHAM
DEUX !!!
WHAK
GRAH !!!
!!!

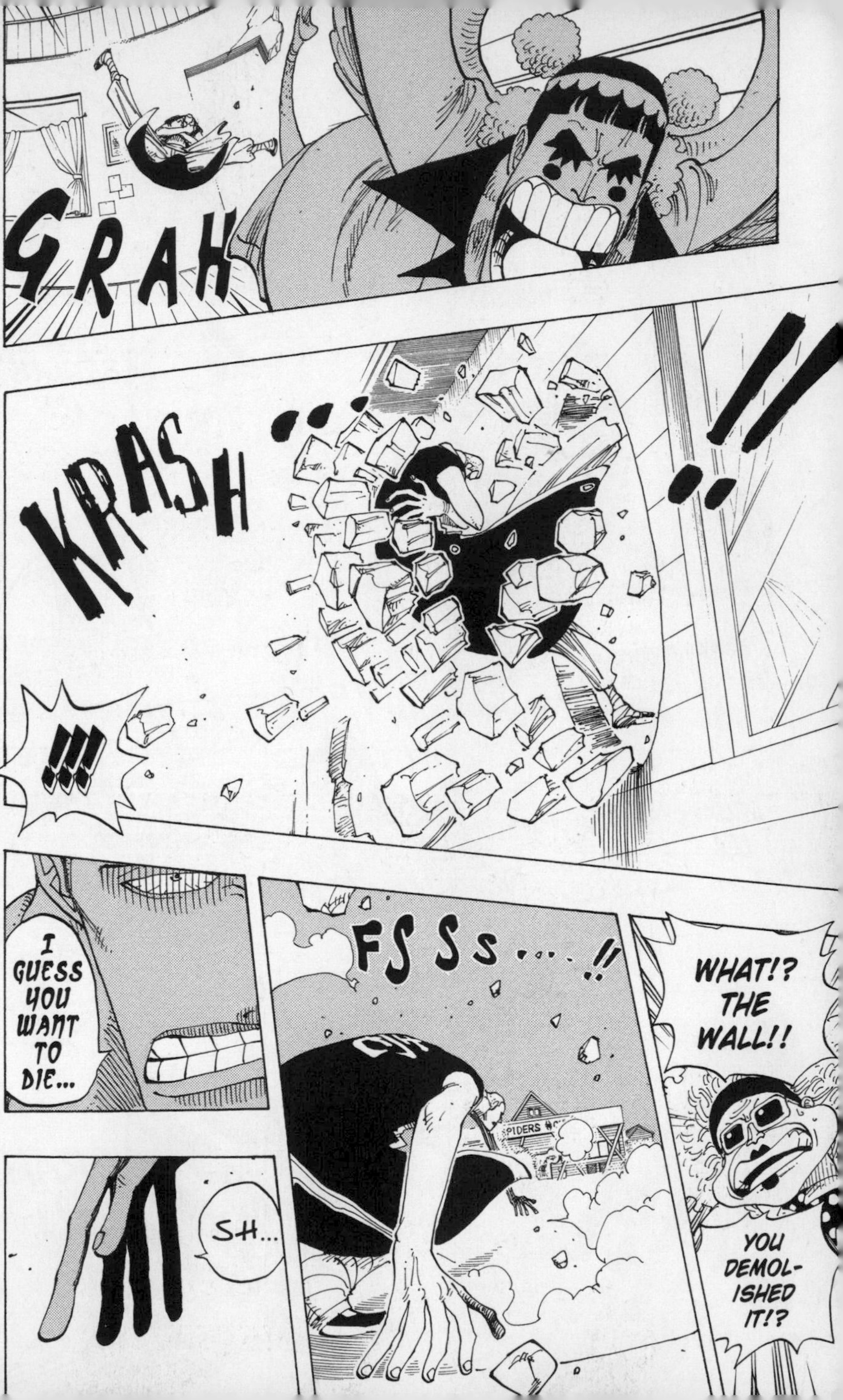
GRAH
KRASH
!!!!
WHAT!? THE WALL!!
YOU DEMOL-ISHED IT!?
FSSS...!!
I GUESS YOU WANT TO DIE...
SH...

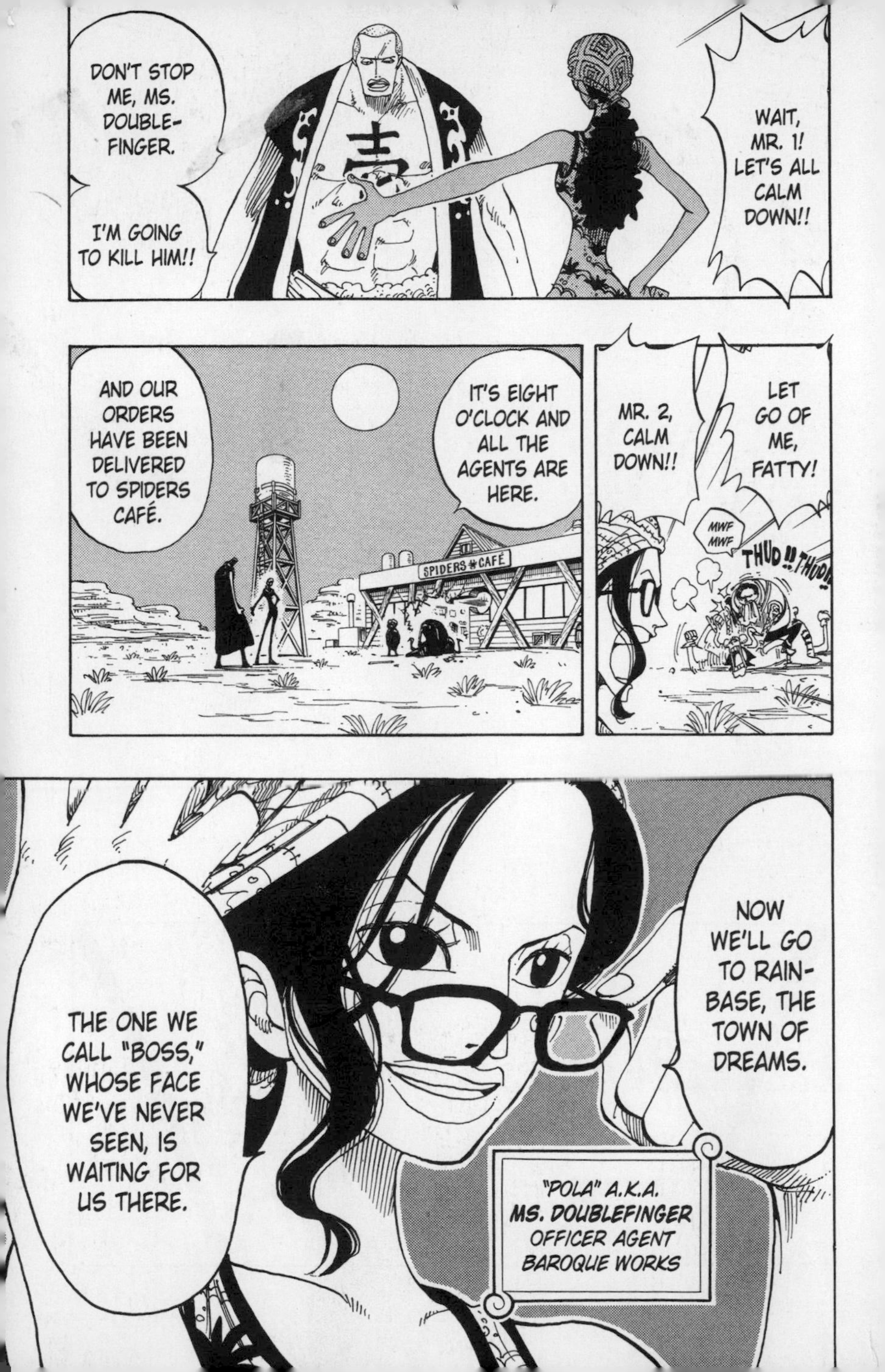

WAIT, MR. 1! LET'S ALL CALM DOWN!!
DON'T STOP ME, MS. DOUBLE-FINGER.
I'M GOING TO KILL HIM!!
LET GO OF ME, FATTY!
MR. 2, CALM DOWN!!
MWF MWF
THUD!! THUD!!
IT'S EIGHT O'CLOCK AND ALL THE AGENTS ARE HERE.
AND OUR ORDERS HAVE BEEN DELIVERED TO SPIDERS CAFÉ.
SPIDERS CAFÉ
NOW WE'LL GO TO RAIN-BASE, THE TOWN OF DREAMS.
THE ONE WE CALL "BOSS," WHOSE FACE WE'VE NEVER SEEN, IS WAITING FOR US THERE.
"POLA" A.K.A.
MS. DOUBLEFINGER
OFFICER AGENT
BAROQUE WORKS

Chapter 161:

THE GREEN CITY ERUMALU

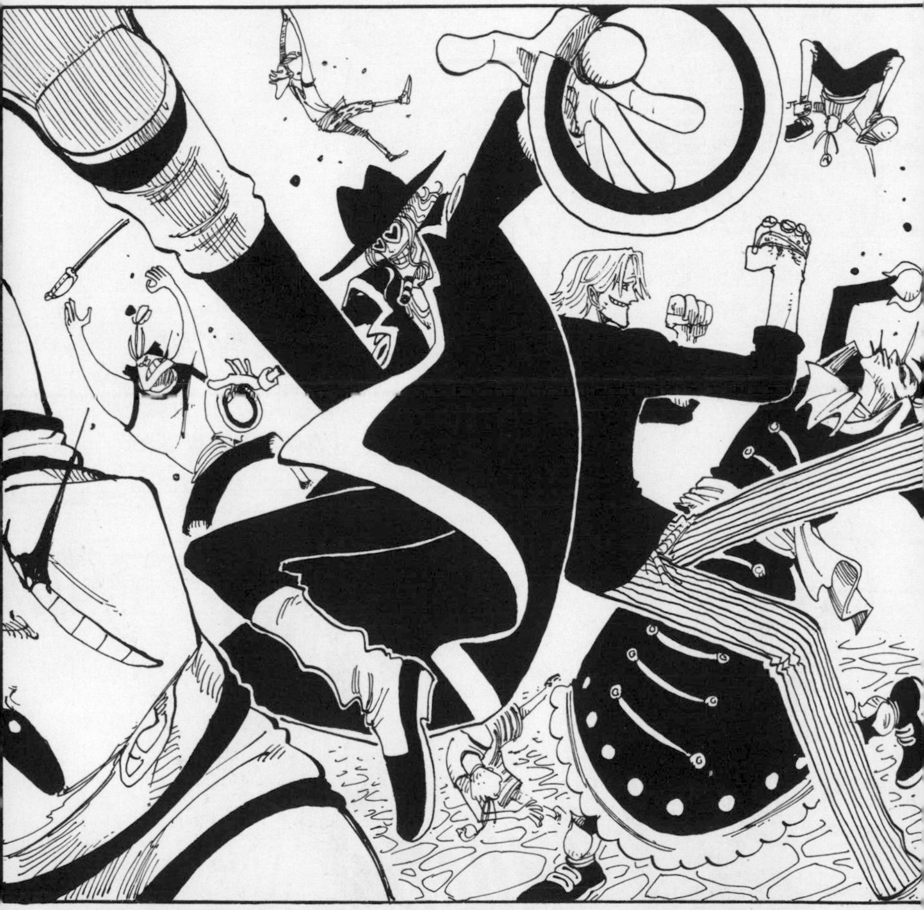

DJANGO'S DANCE PARADISE, VOL. 27: "SHALL WE DANCE?"

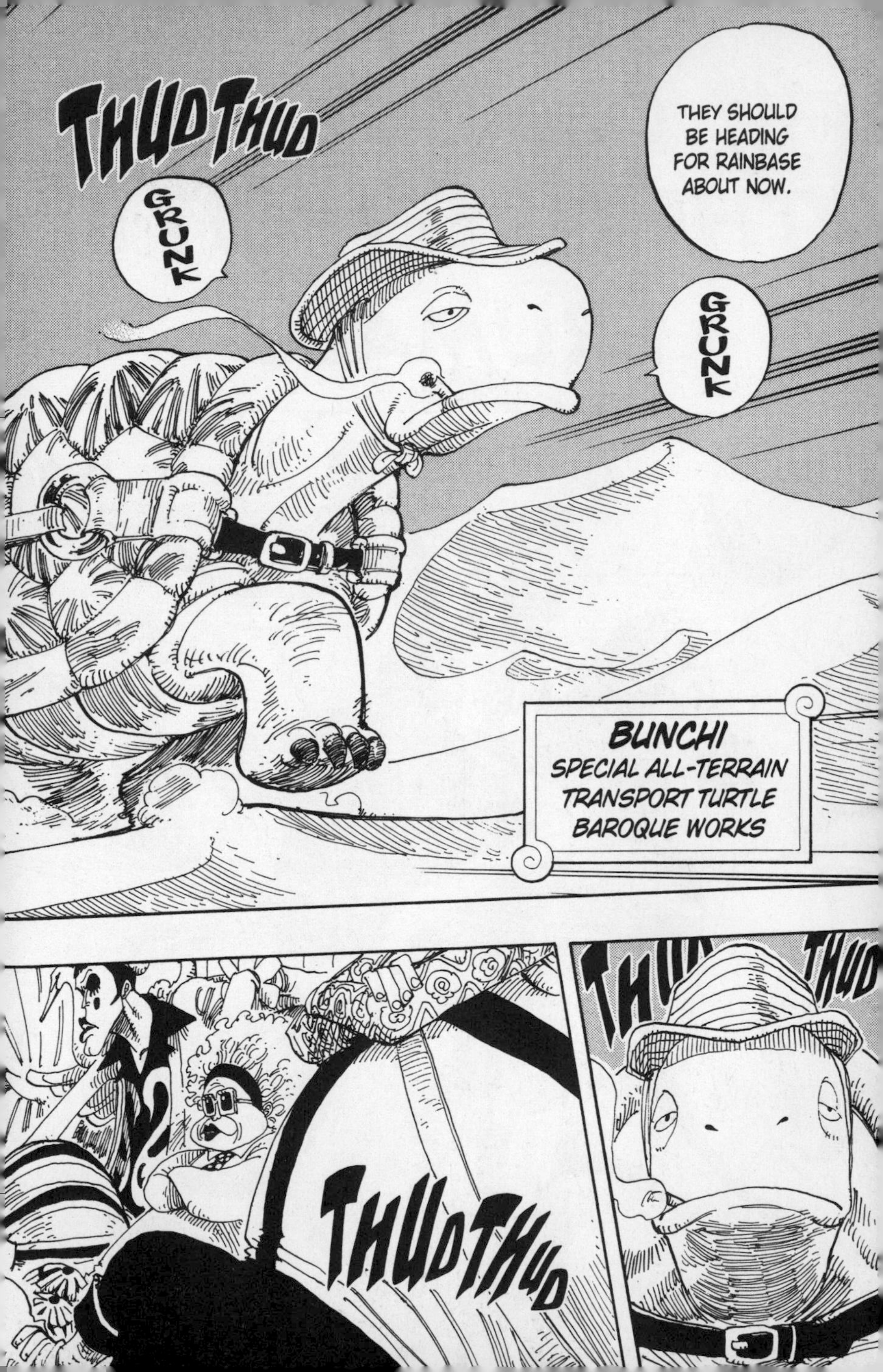
THEY SHOULD BE HEADING FOR RAINBASE ABOUT NOW.
THUD THUD
GRUNK
GRUNK
BUNCHI
SPECIAL ALL-TERRAIN TRANSPORT TURTLE
BAROQUE WORKS
THUD
THU
THUD THUD

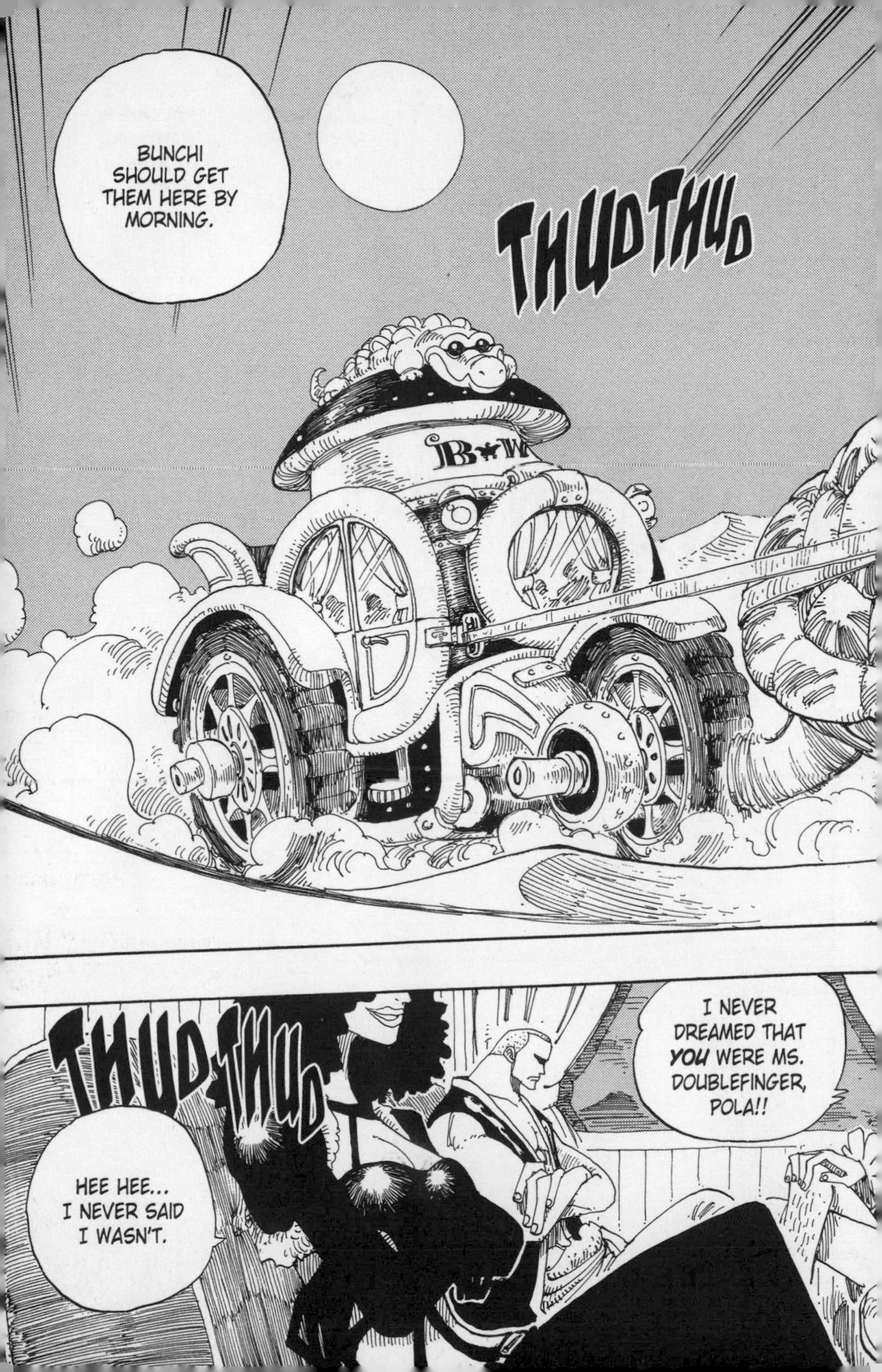
BUNCHI SHOULD GET THEM HERE BY MORNING.
THUD THUD
I NEVER DREAMED THAT ***YOU*** WERE MS. DOUBLEFINGER, POLA!!
THUD THUD
HEE HEE... I NEVER SAID I WASN'T.

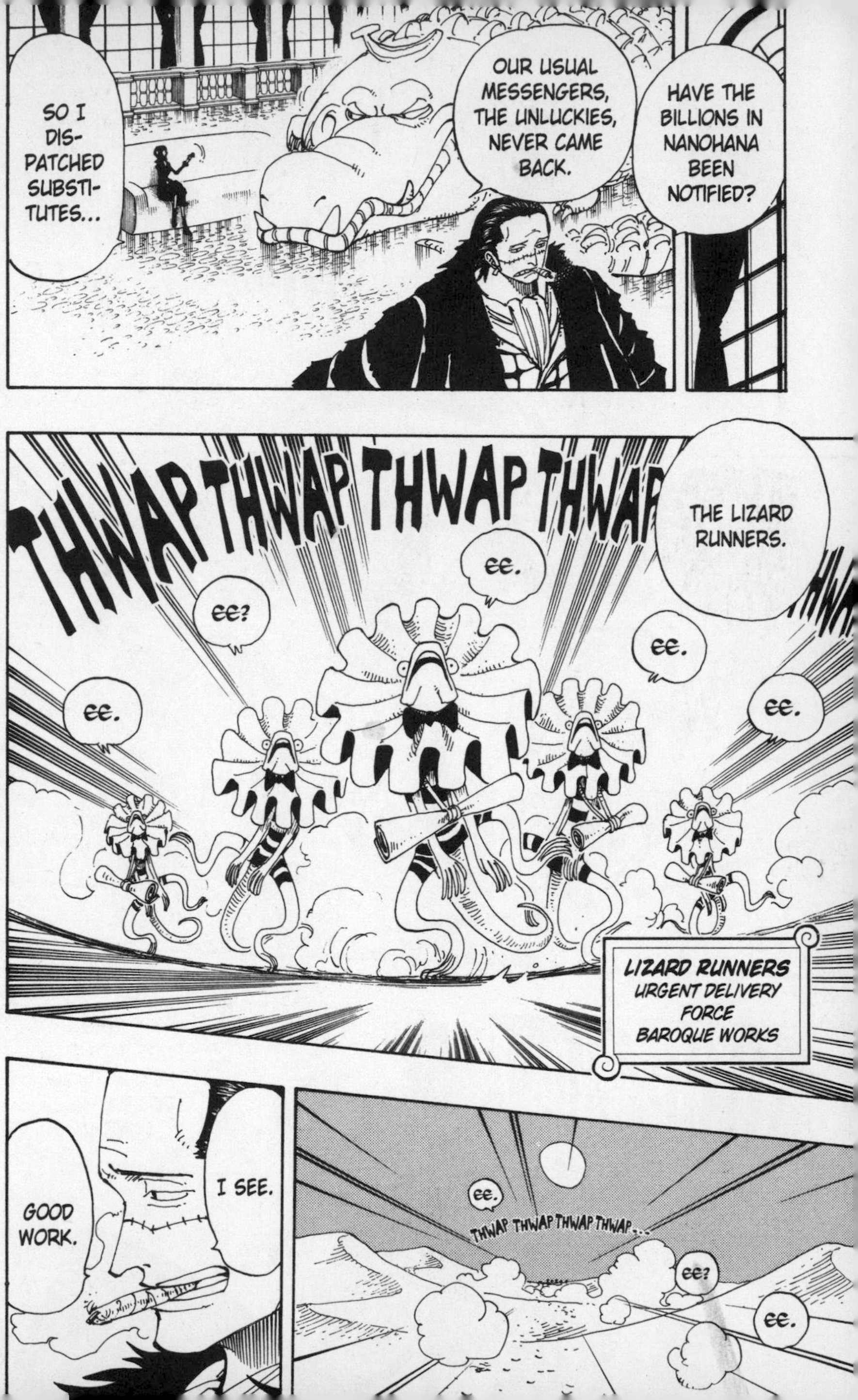
HAVE THE BILLIONS IN NANOHANA BEEN NOTIFIED?
OUR USUAL MESSENGERS, THE UNLUCKIES, NEVER CAME BACK.
SO I DISPATCHED SUBSTITUTES...
THE LIZARD RUNNERS.
THWAP THWAP THWAP THWAP
EE.
EE.
EE.
EE?
EE.
LIZARD RUNNERS
URGENT DELIVERY FORCE
BAROQUE WORKS
EE.
THWAP THWAP THWAP THWAP...
EE?
EE.
I SEE.
GOOD WORK.

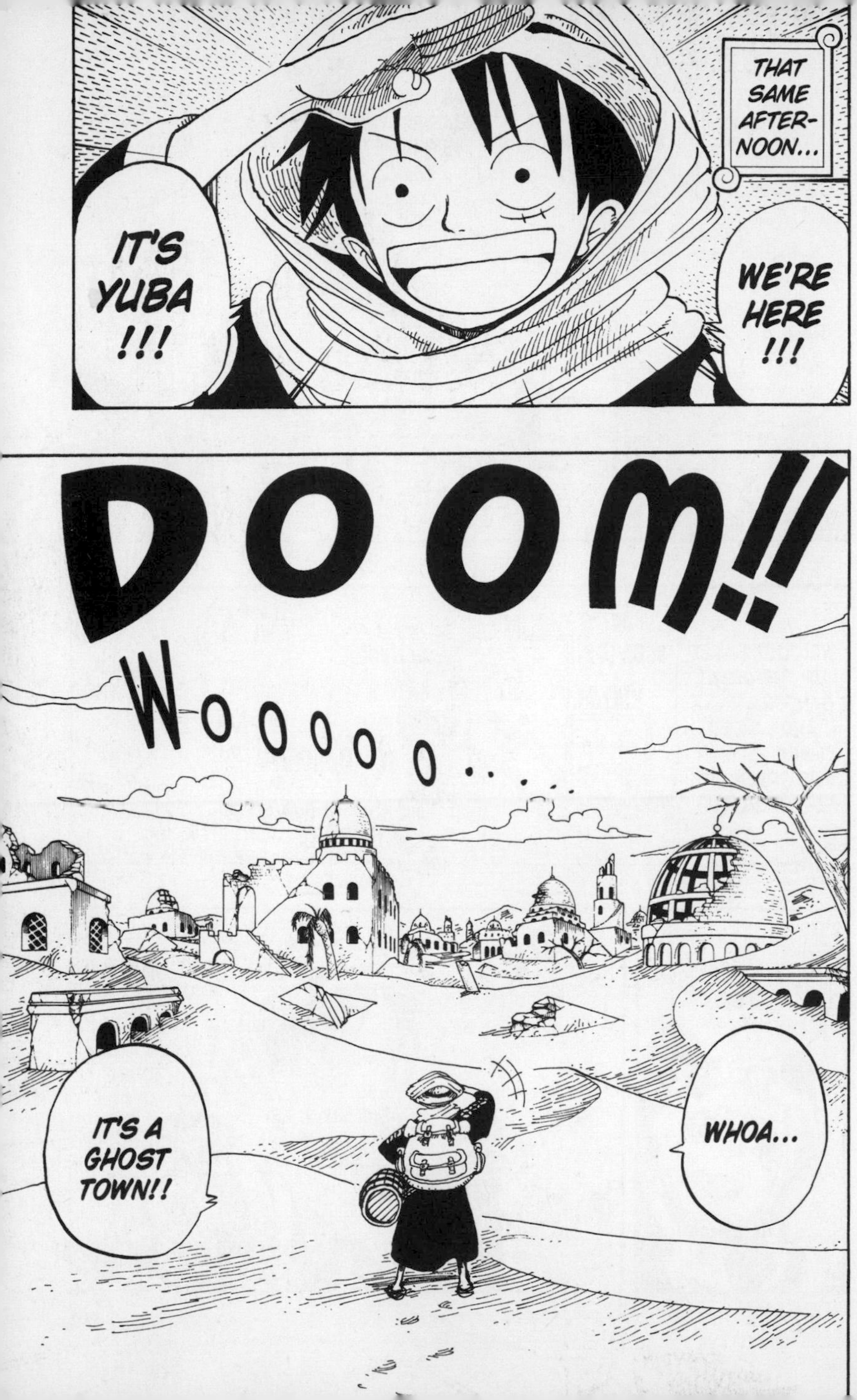
THAT SAME AFTER-NOON...
WE'RE HERE!!!
IT'S YUBA!!!
DOOM!!
WOOOOO...
WHOA...
IT'S A GHOST TOWN!!

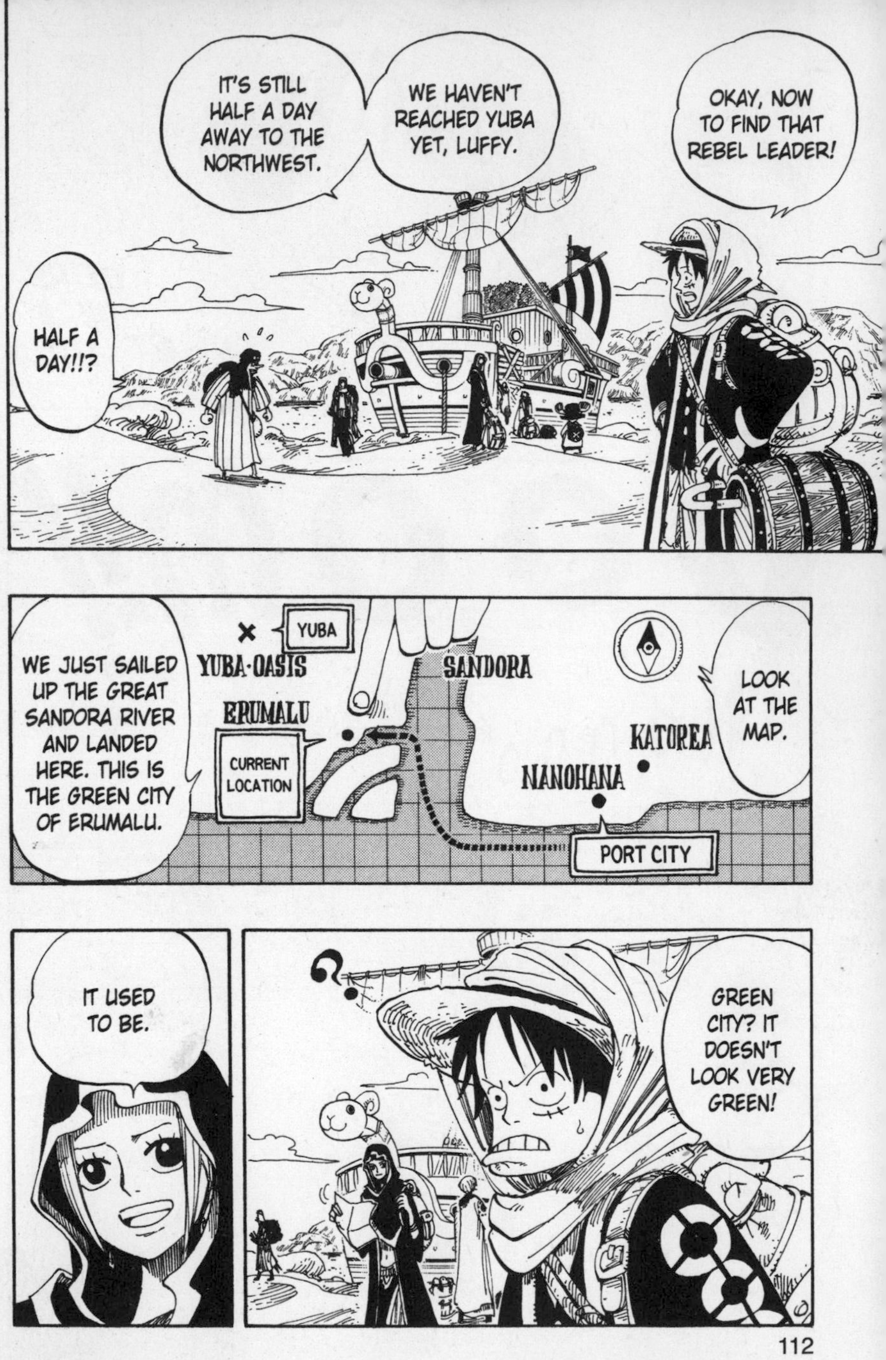
OKAY, NOW TO FIND THAT REBEL LEADER!
WE HAVEN'T REACHED YUBA YET, LUFFY.
IT'S STILL HALF A DAY AWAY TO THE NORTHWEST.
HALF A DAY!!?
LOOK AT THE MAP.
YUBA
YUBA-OASIS
SANDORA
ERUMALU
CURRENT LOCATION
KATOREA
NANOHANA
PORT CITY
WE JUST SAILED UP THE GREAT SANDORA RIVER AND LANDED HERE. THIS IS THE GREEN CITY OF ERUMALU.
GREEN CITY? IT DOESN'T LOOK VERY GREEN!
IT USED TO BE.

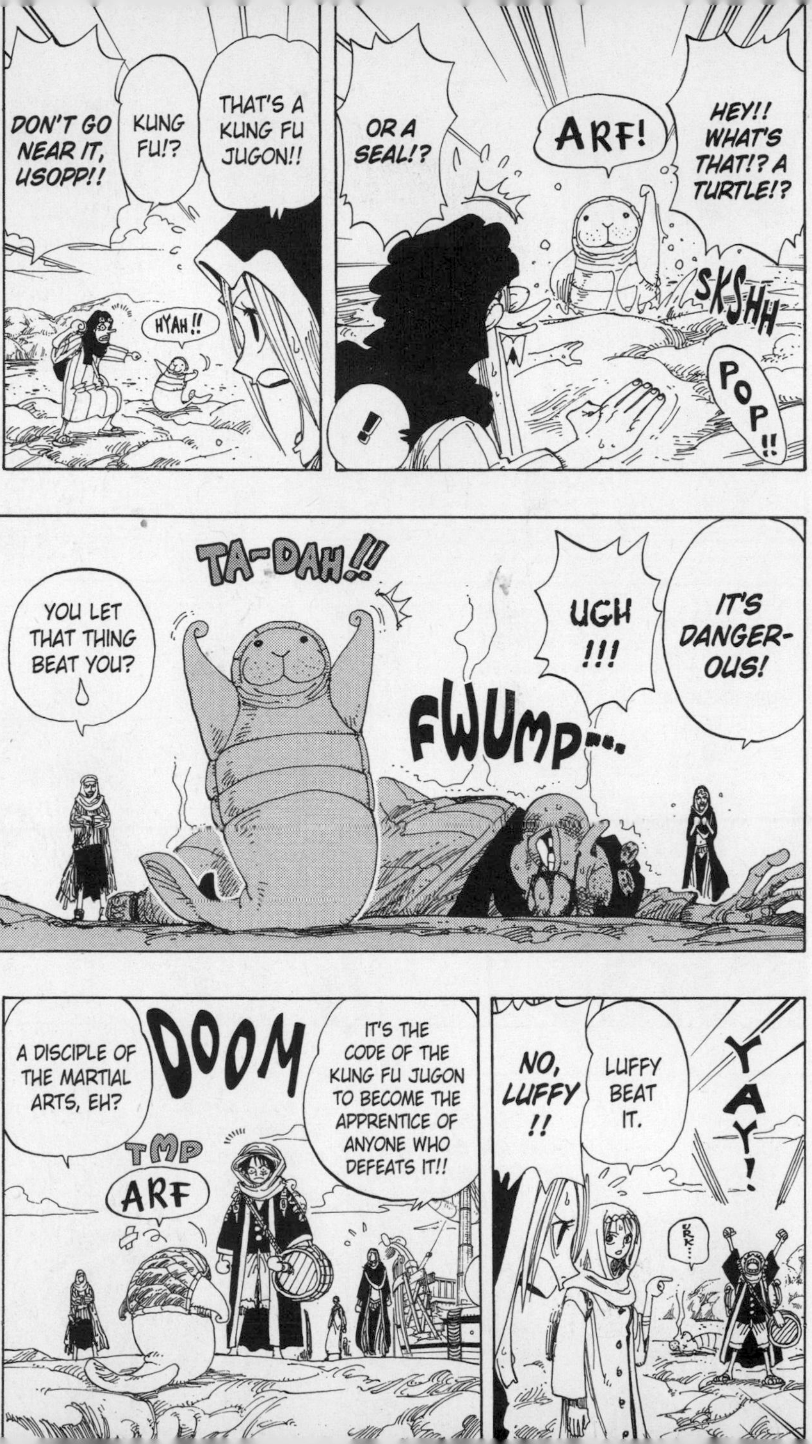
HEY!! WHAT'S THAT!? A TURTLE!?
ARF!
OR A SEAL!?
SKSHH
POP!!
!
THAT'S A KUNG FU JUGON!!
KUNG FU!?
DON'T GO NEAR IT, USOPP!!
HYAH!!
IT'S DANGER-OUS!
UGH!!!
TA-DAH!!
FWUMP...
YOU LET THAT THING BEAT YOU?
YAY!
LUFFY BEAT IT.
NO, LUFFY!!
URK...
IT'S THE CODE OF THE KUNG FU JUGON TO BECOME THE APPRENTICE OF ANYONE WHO DEFEATS IT!!
DOOM
A DISCIPLE OF THE MARTIAL ARTS, EH?
TMP
ARF

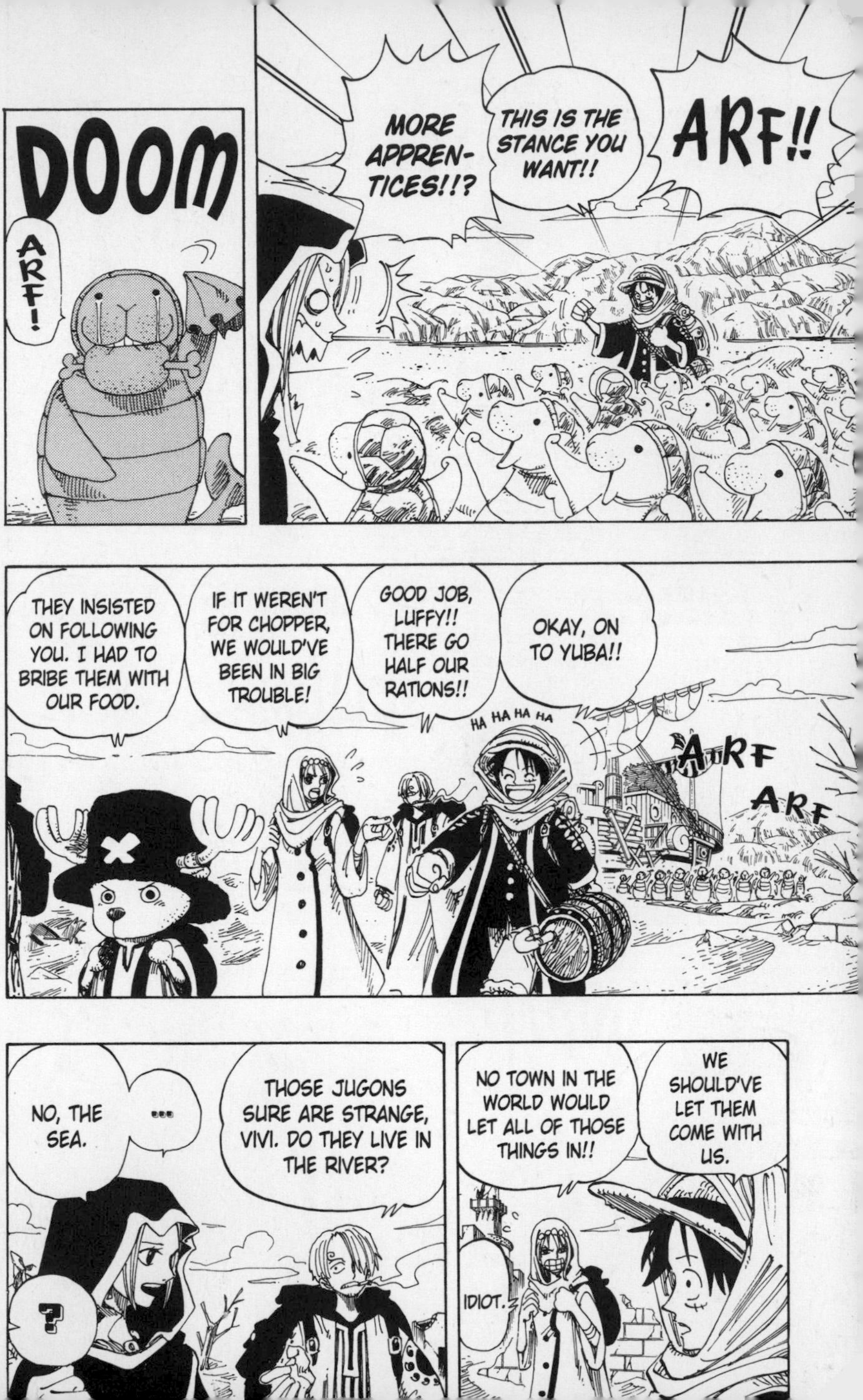
ARF!!
THIS IS THE STANCE YOU WANT!!
MORE APPRENTICES!!?
DOOM
ARF!
OKAY, ON TO YUBA!!
GOOD JOB, LUFFY!! THERE GO HALF OUR RATIONS!!
IF IT WEREN'T FOR CHOPPER, WE WOULD'VE BEEN IN BIG TROUBLE!
THEY INSISTED ON FOLLOWING YOU. I HAD TO BRIBE THEM WITH OUR FOOD.
HA HA HA HA
ARF
ARF
WE SHOULD'VE LET THEM COME WITH US.
NO TOWN IN THE WORLD WOULD LET ALL OF THOSE THINGS IN!!
IDIOT.
THOSE JUGONS SURE ARE STRANGE, VIVI. DO THEY LIVE IN THE RIVER?
...
NO, THE SEA.
?

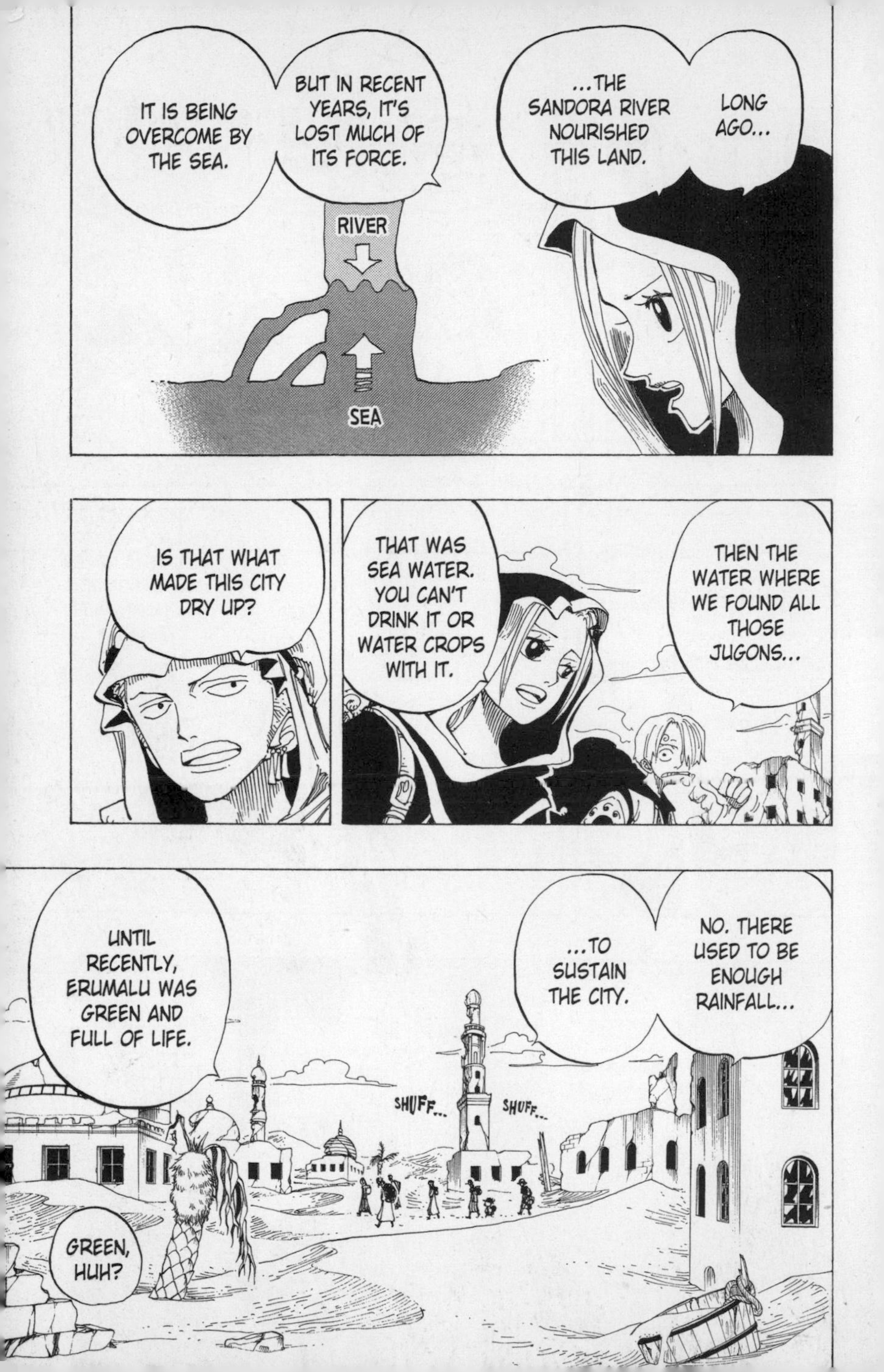
LONG AGO...
...THE SANDORA RIVER NOURISHED THIS LAND.
BUT IN RECENT YEARS, IT'S LOST MUCH OF ITS FORCE.
IT IS BEING OVERCOME BY THE SEA.
RIVER
SEA
THEN THE WATER WHERE WE FOUND ALL THOSE JUGONS...
THAT WAS SEA WATER. YOU CAN'T DRINK IT OR WATER CROPS WITH IT.
IS THAT WHAT MADE THIS CITY DRY UP?
NO. THERE USED TO BE ENOUGH RAINFALL...
...TO SUSTAIN THE CITY.
SHUFF...
SHUFF...
UNTIL RECENTLY, ERUMALU WAS GREEN AND FULL OF LIFE.
GREEN, HUH?

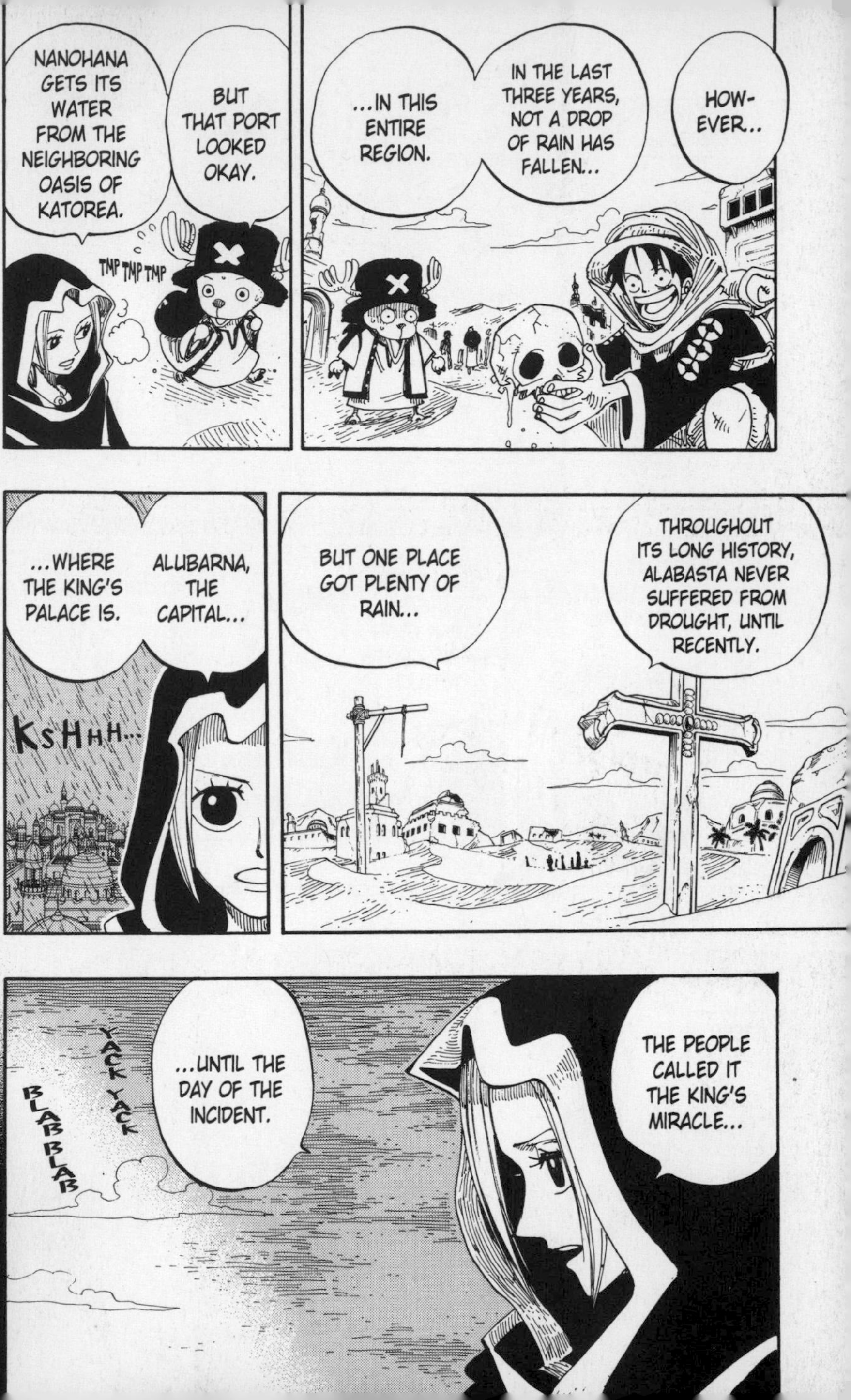
HOW-EVER...
IN THE LAST THREE YEARS, NOT A DROP OF RAIN HAS FALLEN...
...IN THIS ENTIRE REGION.
BUT THAT PORT LOOKED OKAY.
NANOHANA GETS ITS WATER FROM THE NEIGHBORING OASIS OF KATOREA.
TMP TMP TMP
THROUGHOUT ITS LONG HISTORY, ALABASTA NEVER SUFFERED FROM DROUGHT, UNTIL RECENTLY.
BUT ONE PLACE GOT PLENTY OF RAIN...
ALUBARNA, THE CAPITAL...
...WHERE THE KING'S PALACE IS.
KSHHH...
THE PEOPLE CALLED IT THE KING'S MIRACLE...
...UNTIL THE DAY OF THE INCIDENT.
YACK YACK
BLAB BLAB

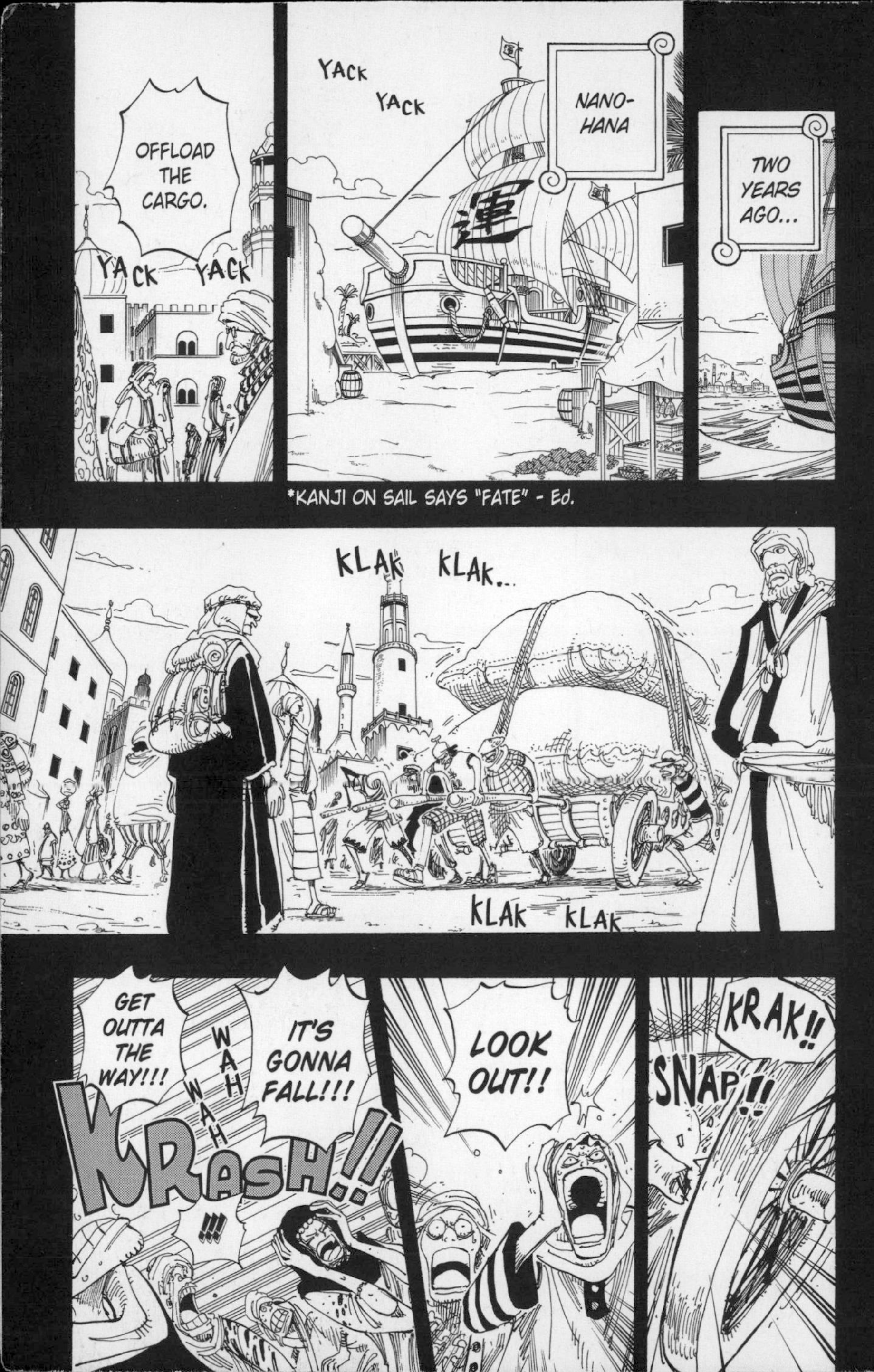
TWO YEARS AGO...
NANO-HANA
YACK YACK
OFFLOAD THE CARGO.
YACK YACK
*KANJI ON SAIL SAYS "FATE" - Ed.
KLAK KLAK...
KLAK KLAK
KRAK!!
SNAP!!
LOOK OUT!!
IT'S GONNA FALL!!!
WAH WAH
GET OUTTA THE WAY!!!
KRASH!!
!!!

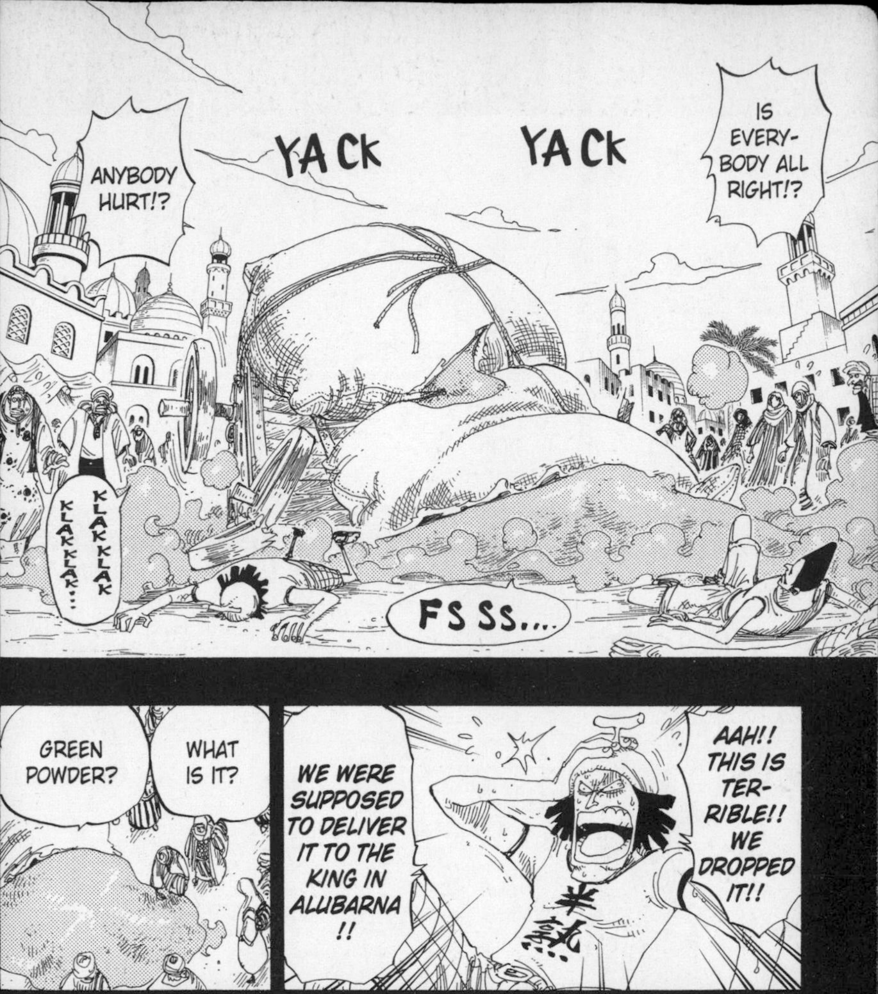
IS EVERY-BODY ALL RIGHT!?
YACK YACK
ANYBODY HURT!?
KLAK KLAK KLAK KLAK...
FS SS....
AAH!! THIS IS TER-RIBLE!! WE DROPPED IT!!
WE WERE SUPPOSED TO DELIVER IT TO THE KING IN ALUBARNA!!
WHAT IS IT?
GREEN POWDER?

*TEXT ON SHIRT SAYS "HALF-FLEDGED" - Ed.

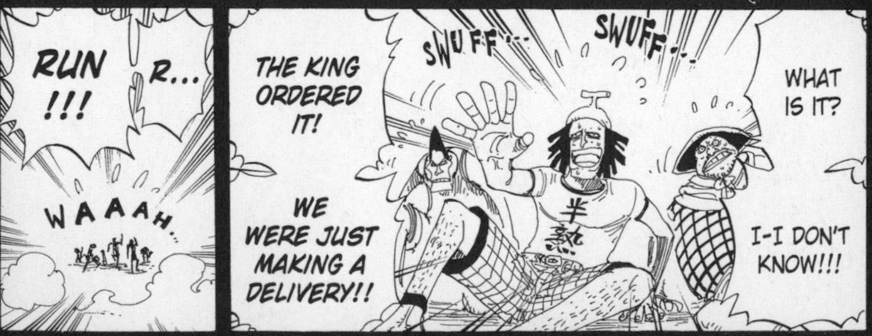
WHAT IS IT?
SWUFF...
SWUFF...
THE KING ORDERED IT!
I-I DON'T KNOW!!!
WE WERE JUST MAKING A DELIVERY!!
R...
RUN!!!
WAAAH...

READ THIS WAY

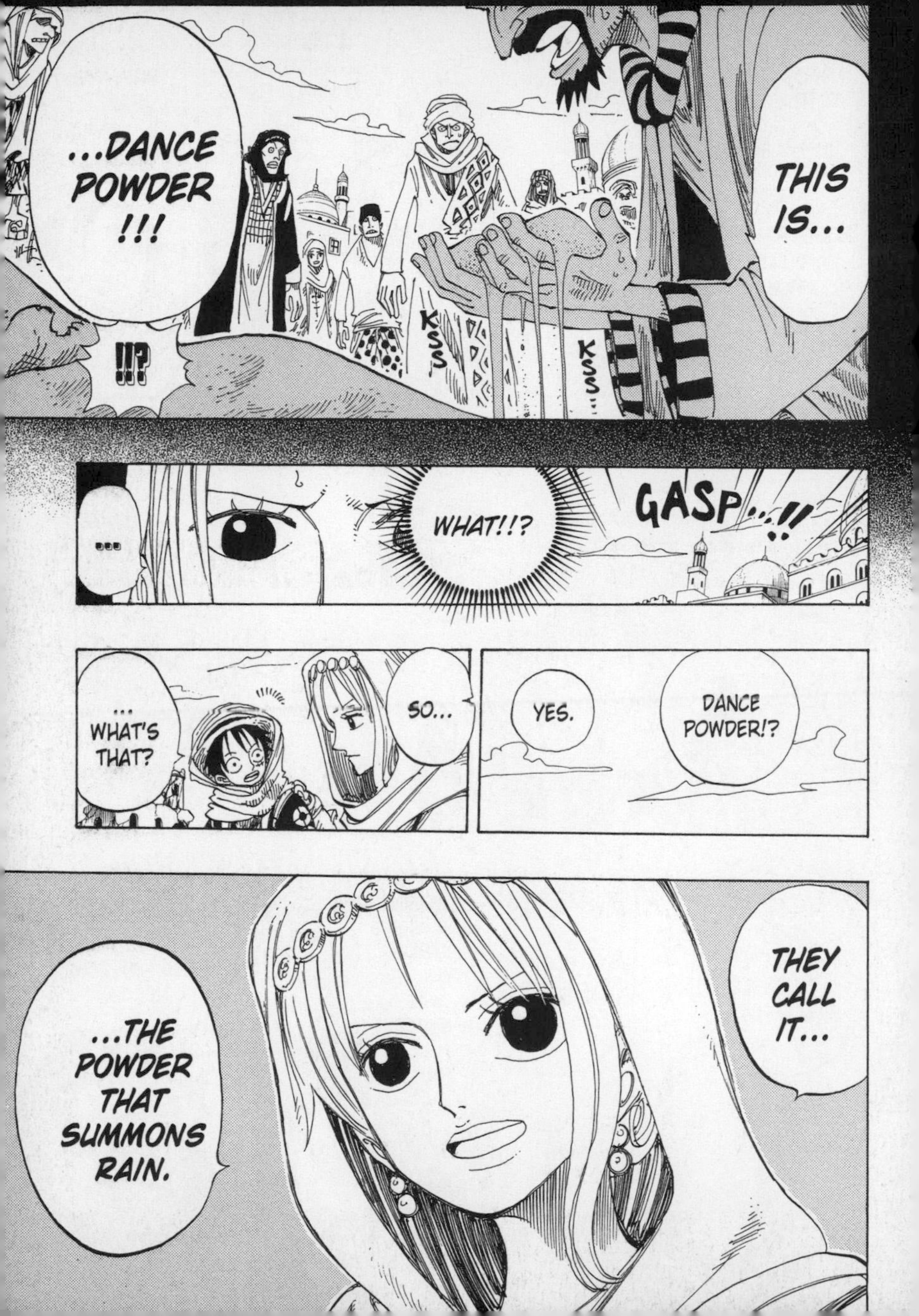

THIS IS...
...DANCE POWDER!!!
!!?
KSS
KSS...
GASP...!!
WHAT!!?
...
DANCE POWDER!?
YES.
SO...
...WHAT'S THAT?
THEY CALL IT...
...THE POWDER THAT SUMMONS RAIN.

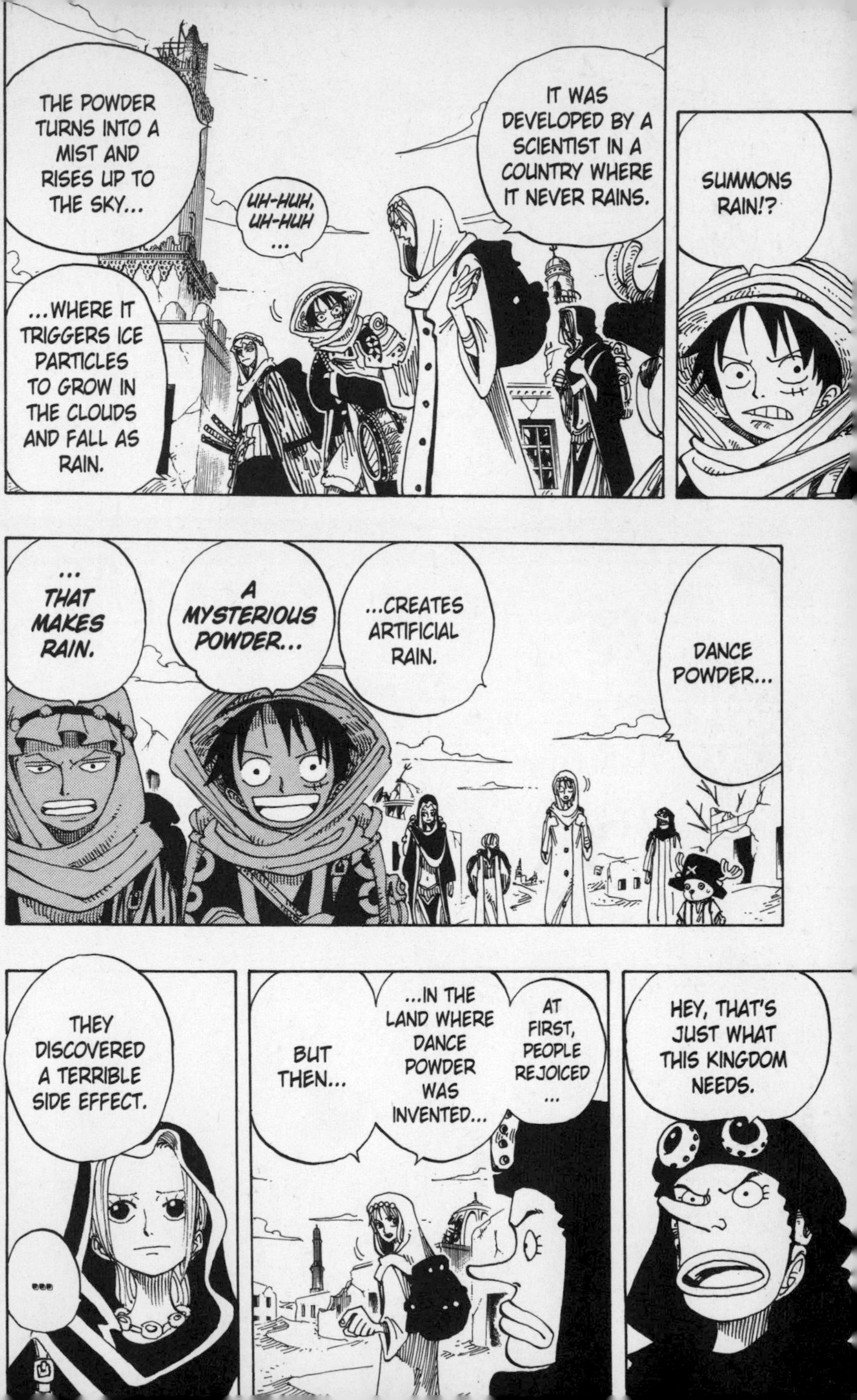
SUMMONS RAIN!?
IT WAS DEVELOPED BY A SCIENTIST IN A COUNTRY WHERE IT NEVER RAINS.
UH-HUH, UH-HUH ...
THE POWDER TURNS INTO A MIST AND RISES UP TO THE SKY...
...WHERE IT TRIGGERS ICE PARTICLES TO GROW IN THE CLOUDS AND FALL AS RAIN.
DANCE POWDER...
...CREATES ARTIFICIAL RAIN.
A MYSTERIOUS POWDER...
... *THAT MAKES RAIN.*
HEY, THAT'S JUST WHAT THIS KINGDOM NEEDS.
AT FIRST, PEOPLE REJOICED ...
...IN THE LAND WHERE DANCE POWDER WAS INVENTED...
BUT THEN...
THEY DISCOVERED A TERRIBLE SIDE EFFECT.
...

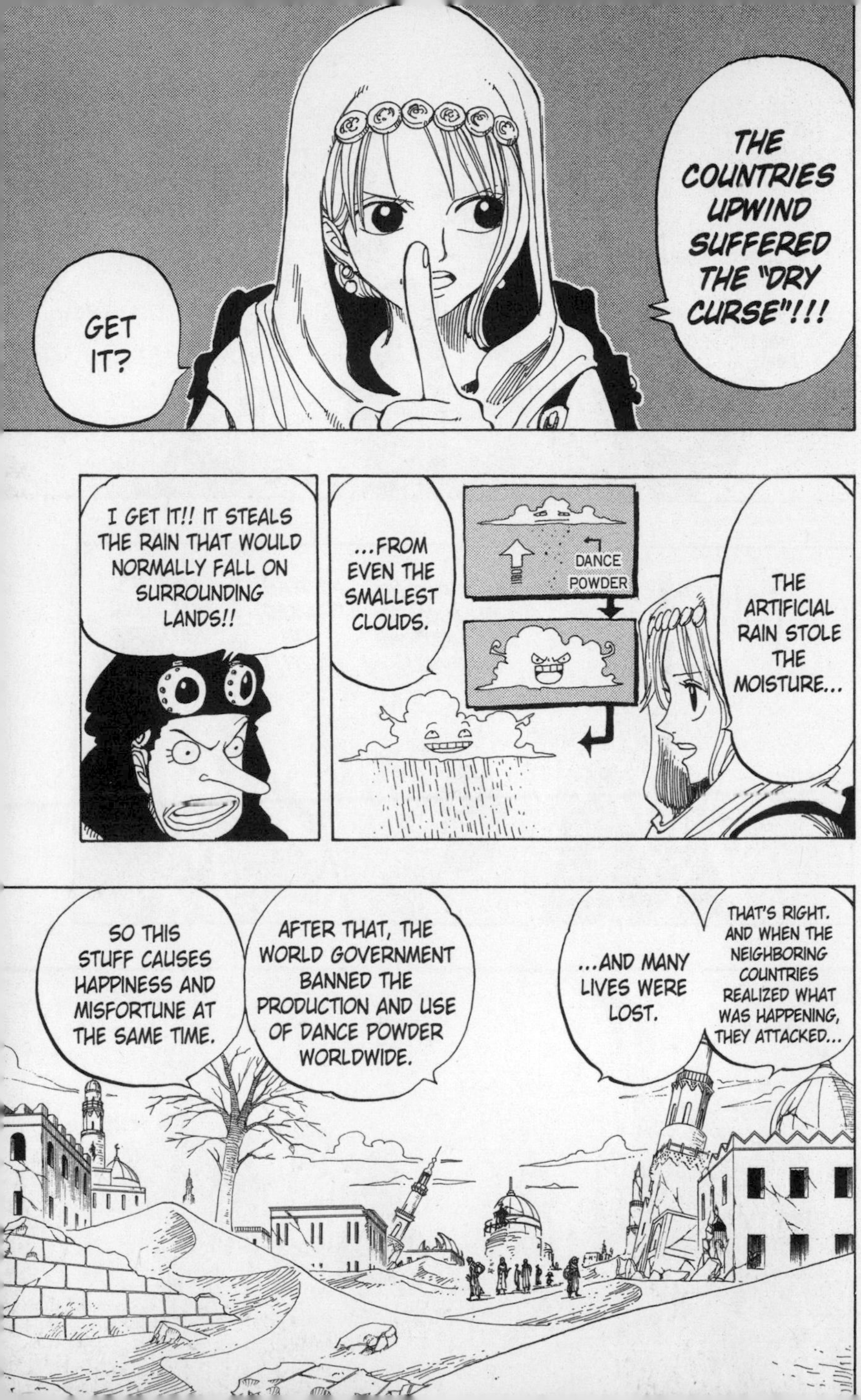
THE COUNTRIES UPWIND SUFFERED THE "DRY CURSE"!!!
GET IT?
THE ARTIFICIAL RAIN STOLE THE MOISTURE...
DANCE POWDER
...FROM EVEN THE SMALLEST CLOUDS.
I GET IT!! IT STEALS THE RAIN THAT WOULD NORMALLY FALL ON SURROUNDING LANDS!!
THAT'S RIGHT. AND WHEN THE NEIGHBORING COUNTRIES REALIZED WHAT WAS HAPPENING, THEY ATTACKED...
...AND MANY LIVES WERE LOST.
AFTER THAT, THE WORLD GOVERNMENT BANNED THE PRODUCTION AND USE OF DANCE POWDER WORLDWIDE.
SO THIS STUFF CAUSES HAPPINESS AND MISFORTUNE AT THE SAME TIME.

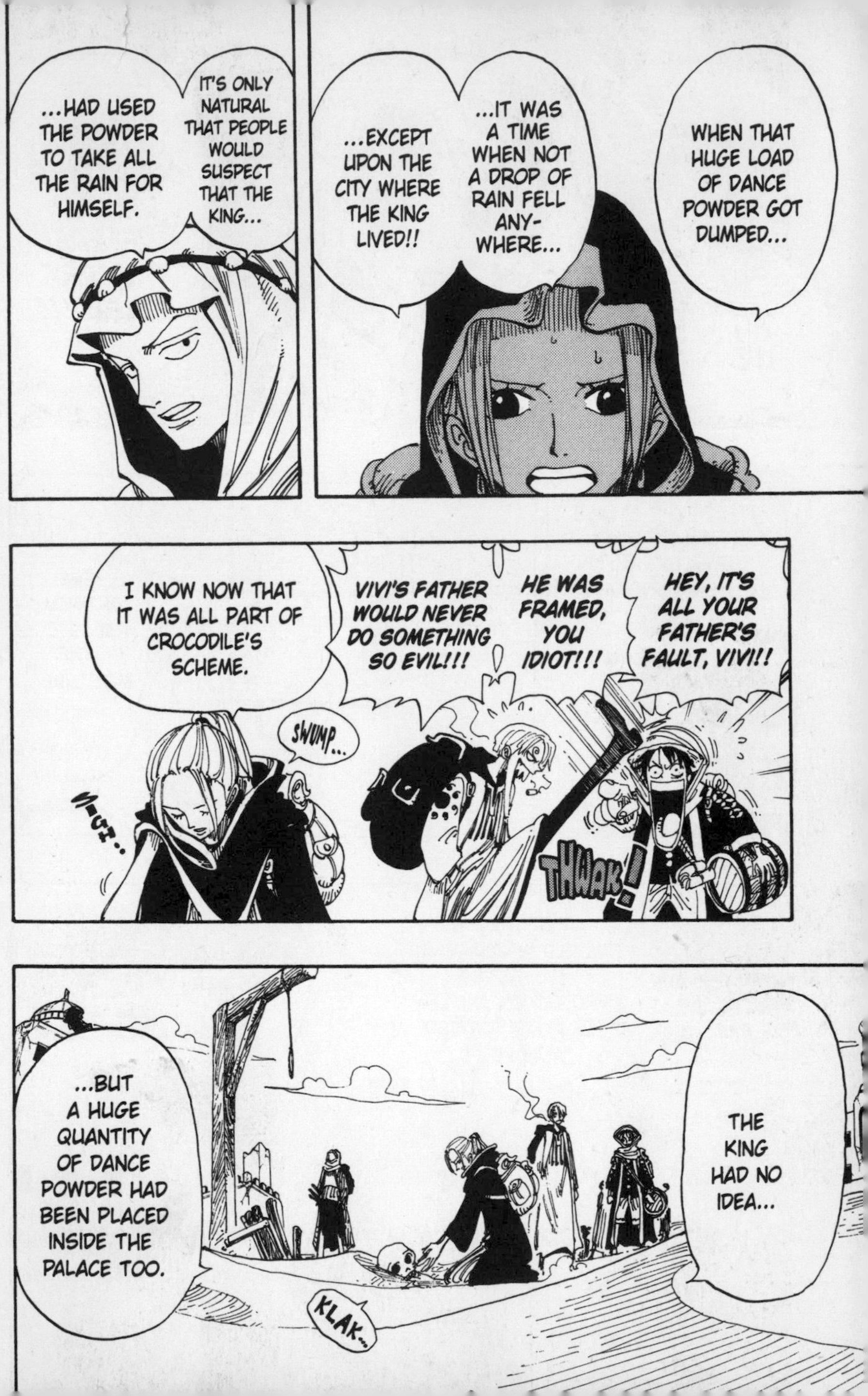
WHEN THAT HUGE LOAD OF DANCE POWDER GOT DUMPED...
...IT WAS A TIME WHEN NOT A DROP OF RAIN FELL ANY-WHERE...
...EXCEPT UPON THE CITY WHERE THE KING LIVED!!
IT'S ONLY NATURAL THAT PEOPLE WOULD SUSPECT THAT THE KING...
...HAD USED THE POWDER TO TAKE ALL THE RAIN FOR HIMSELF.
HEY, IT'S ALL YOUR FATHER'S FAULT, VIVI!!
HE WAS FRAMED, YOU IDIOT!!!
VIVI'S FATHER WOULD NEVER DO SOMETHING SO EVIL!!!
THWAK!
SWUMP...
I KNOW NOW THAT IT WAS ALL PART OF CROCODILE'S SCHEME.
SIGH...
THE KING HAD NO IDEA...
...BUT A HUGE QUANTITY OF DANCE POWDER HAD BEEN PLACED INSIDE THE PALACE TOO.
KLAK...

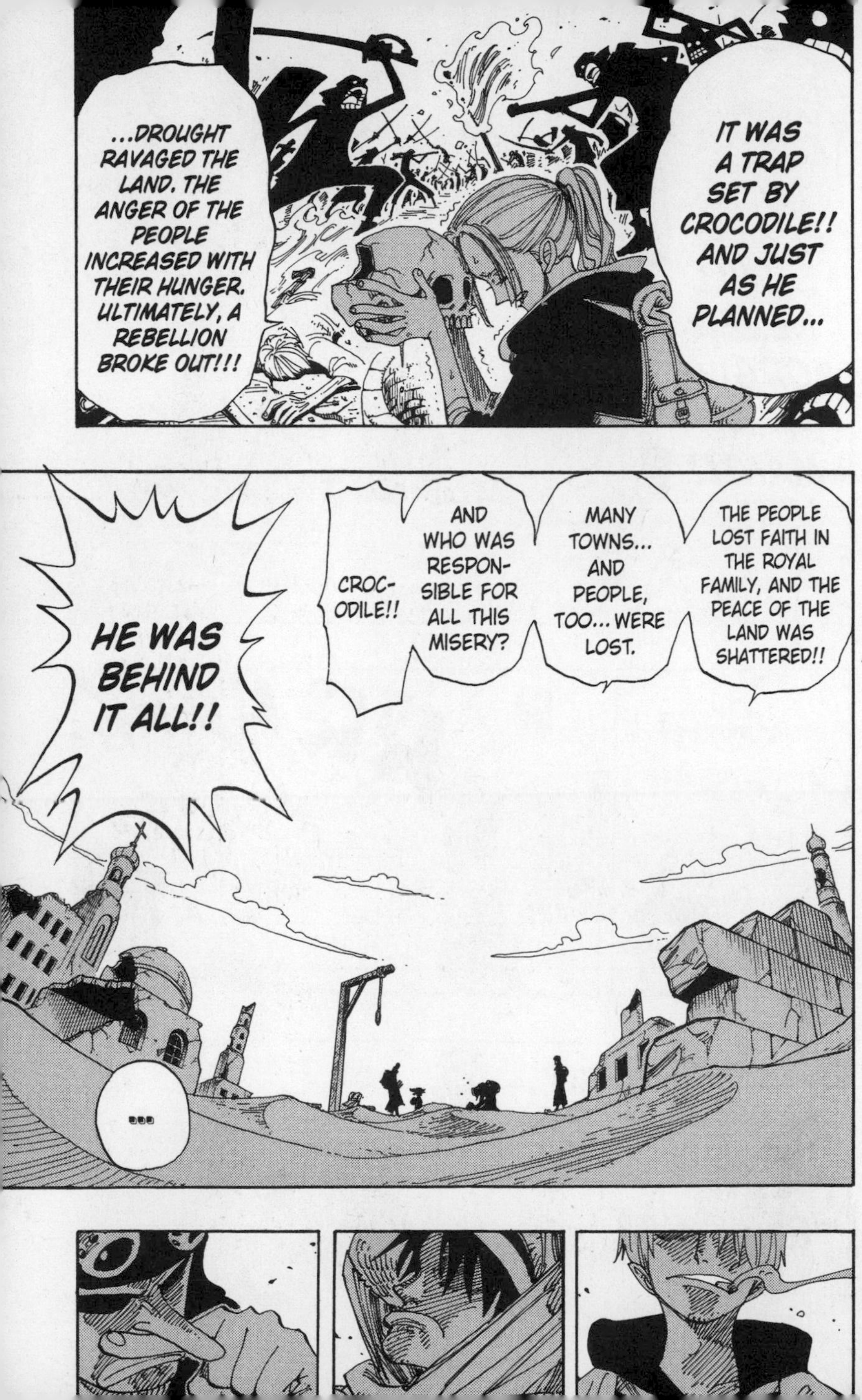
IT WAS A TRAP SET BY CROCODILE!! AND JUST AS HE PLANNED...
...DROUGHT RAVAGED THE LAND. THE ANGER OF THE PEOPLE INCREASED WITH THEIR HUNGER. ULTIMATELY, A REBELLION BROKE OUT!!!
THE PEOPLE LOST FAITH IN THE ROYAL FAMILY, AND THE PEACE OF THE LAND WAS SHATTERED!!
MANY TOWNS... AND PEOPLE, TOO... WERE LOST.
AND WHO WAS RESPONSIBLE FOR ALL THIS MISERY?
CROCODILE!!
HE WAS BEHIND IT ALL!!
...

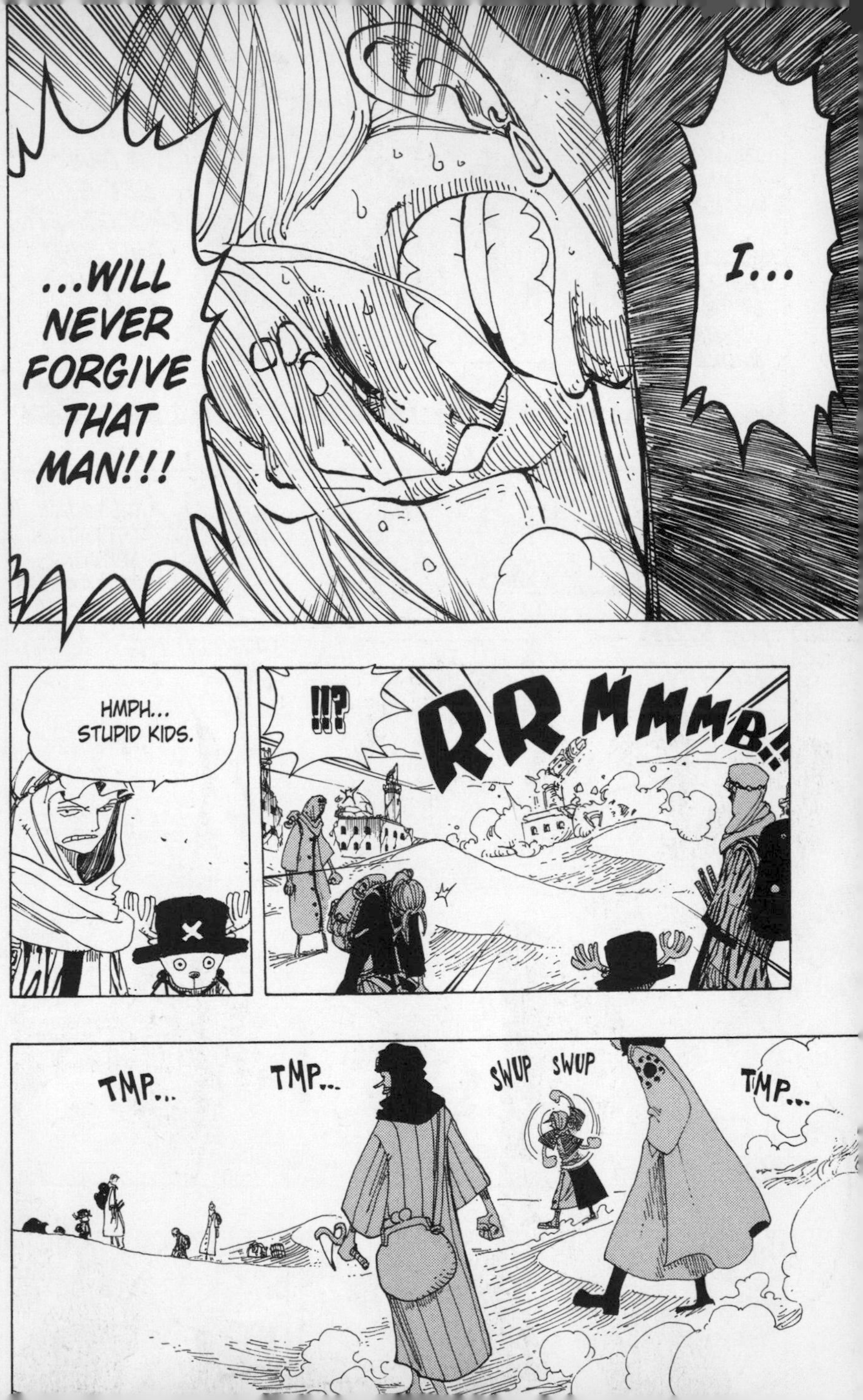
I...
...WILL NEVER FORGIVE THAT MAN!!!
!!?
RRMMMB!!
HMPH... STUPID KIDS.
TMP...
SWUP SWUP
TMP...
TMP...

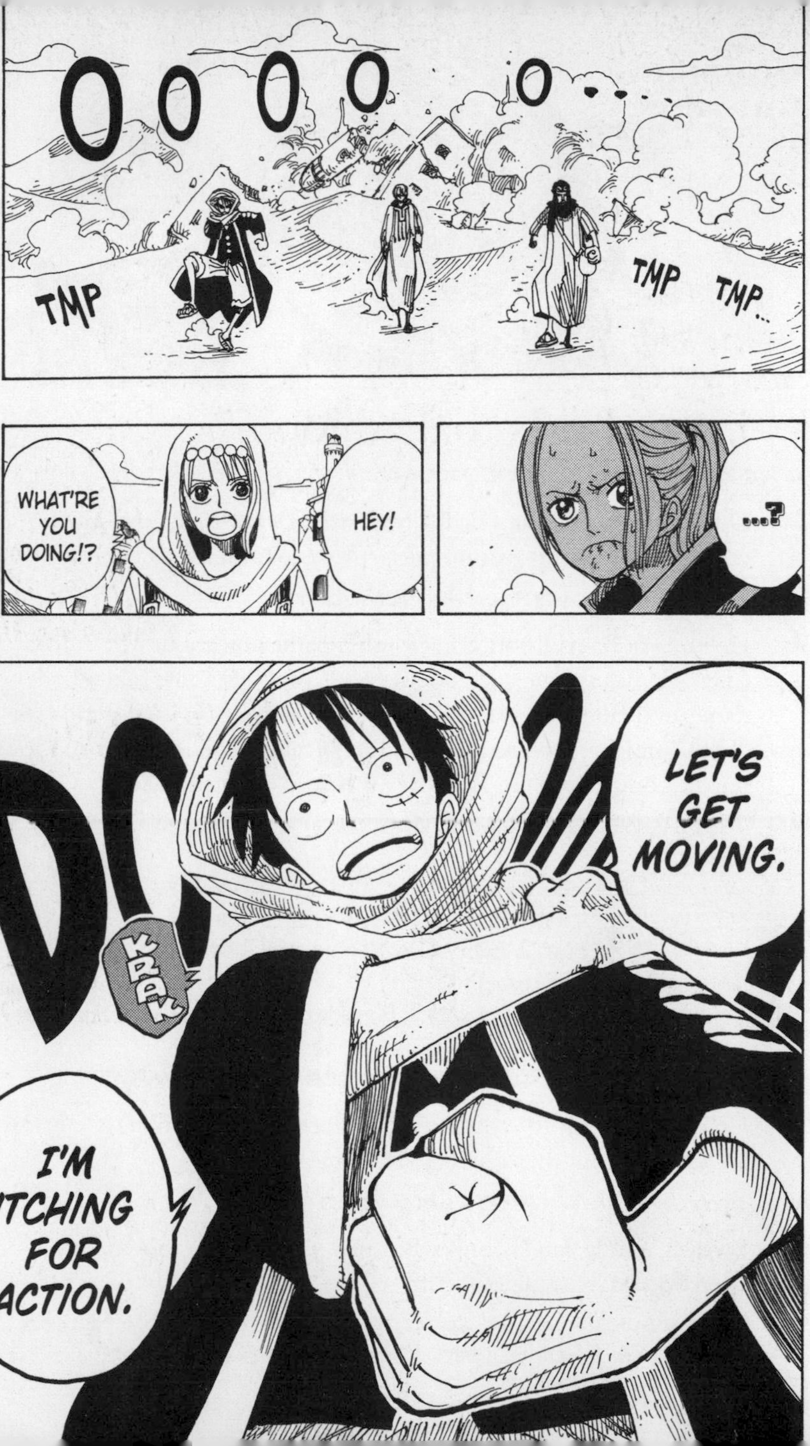
OOOOO
TMP...
TMP
TMP
...?
HEY!
WHAT'RE YOU DOING!?
LET'S GET MOVING.
KRAK
I'M ITCHING FOR ACTION.

Question Corner
S.B.S

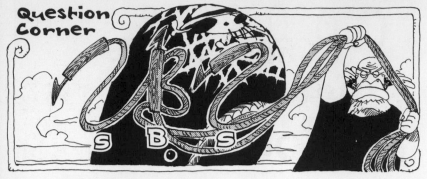

Q: Ha ha ha! Is that a hippo?

A: No. Be quiet. You're wrong.

Q: Oda Sensei, when Dr. Hiriluk was naked, how come the snow conveniently hid his private parts? Amenokawa.

A: Snow can be very useful sometimes.

Q: Hello, Oda Baby! I noticed something amazing about Mr. 2 Bon Clay!! He has an unusual code name. "Mr. 2" is a masculine code name, and Bon Clay is a feminine code name. Bon Clay stands for "bon-kure" or "Bon and year-end festivals." Holidays are used for female code names. So Bon Clay is a little of both, right?

A: That's right. The female agents are named after happy events.

0 = All Sunday (For all the Sundays)
1 = Doublefinger (New Year's Day)
2 = Mr. 2 Bon Clay (Bon and year-end festivals)
3 = Golden Week (Golden Week)
4 = Christmas (Christmas)

January 1 or 1/1
Hence two fingers
(doublefinger)

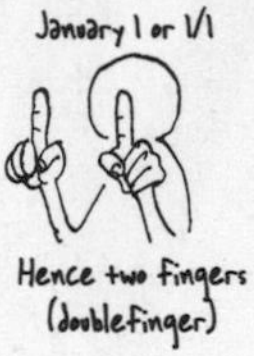

People seem confused by Doublefinger, though.

Q: Here's a question for you. Nami's older sister is Nojiko. So what's my mother's name, Mr. Manga Artist?

A: Hmm... Well...Utsubo? Utsuboko?

Q: Bwaaa!! Wrong. It's Nobuko. But that was close though. We'll do another quiz sometime.

A: Oh!! Nobuko! I get it. Just one syllable off from Nojiko. Of course, I get it... No, I don't!!!

Chapter 162:
ADVENTURE IN THE KINGDOM OF SAND

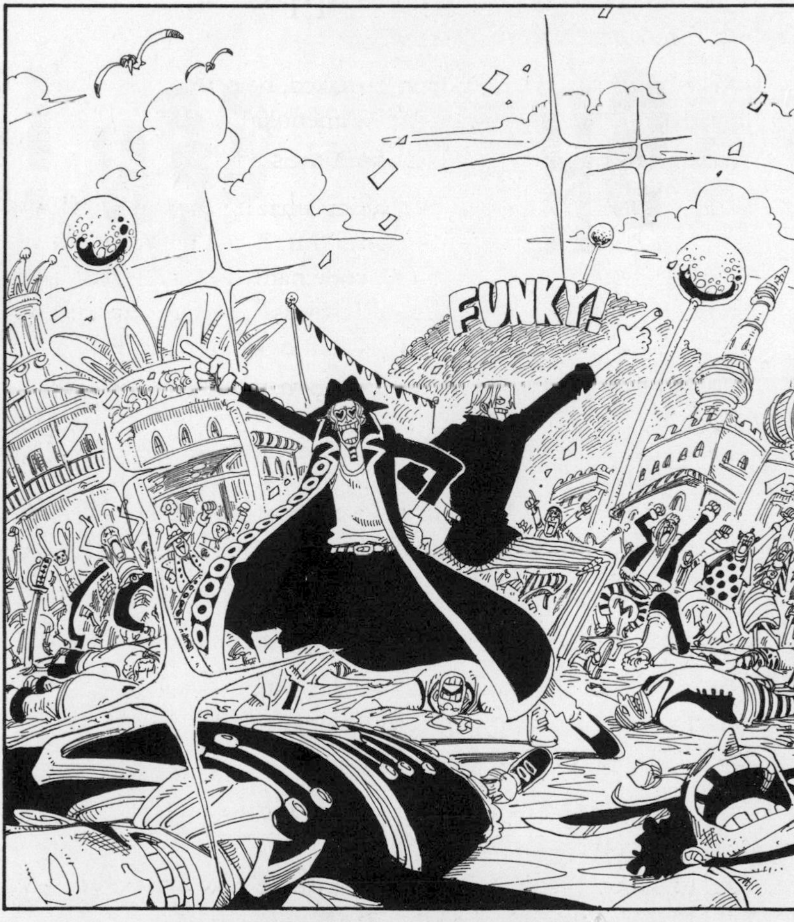
FUNKY!

DJANGO'S DANCE PARADISE, VOL. 28:
"THE TWO DANCING HEROES, BABY"

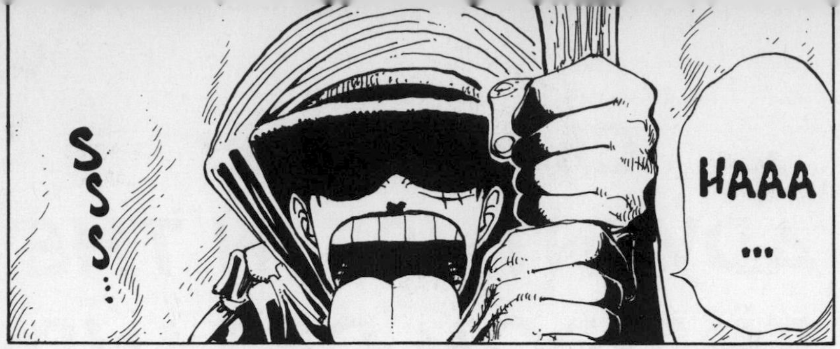
HAAA ...
SSS...

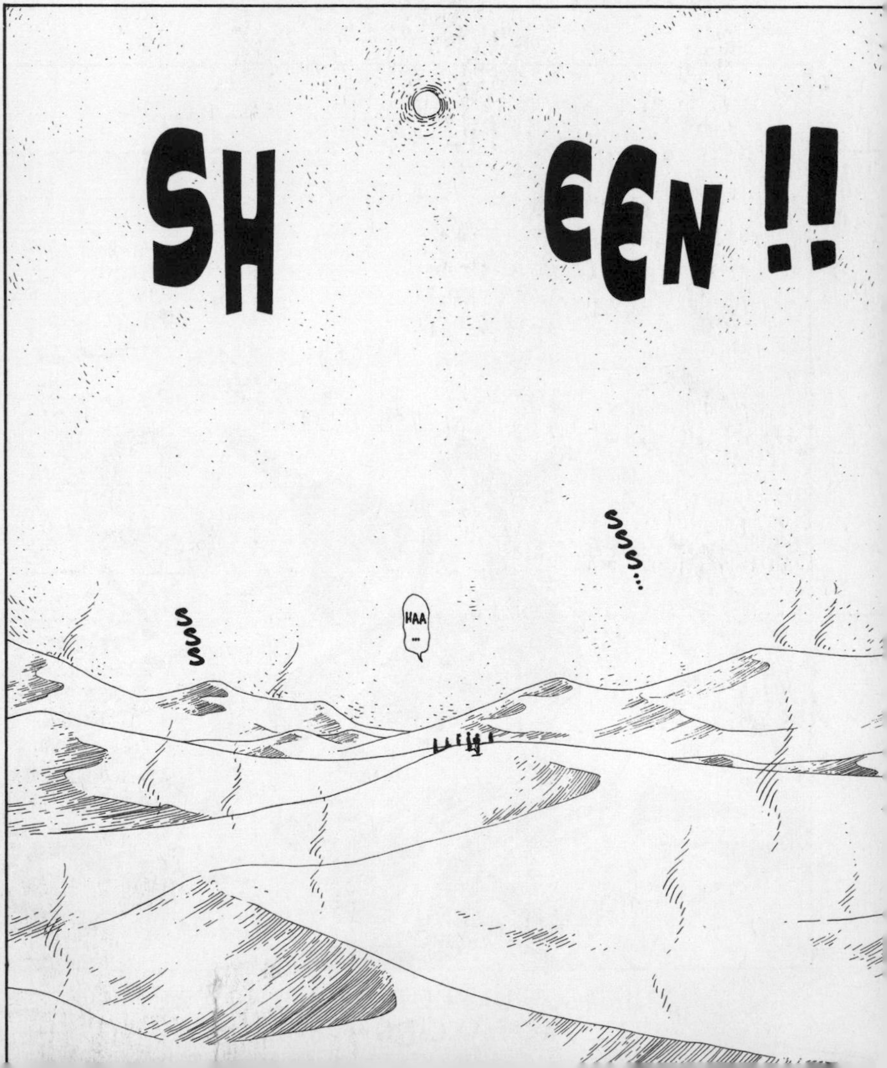
SH EEN!!
SSS...
HAA ...
SSS

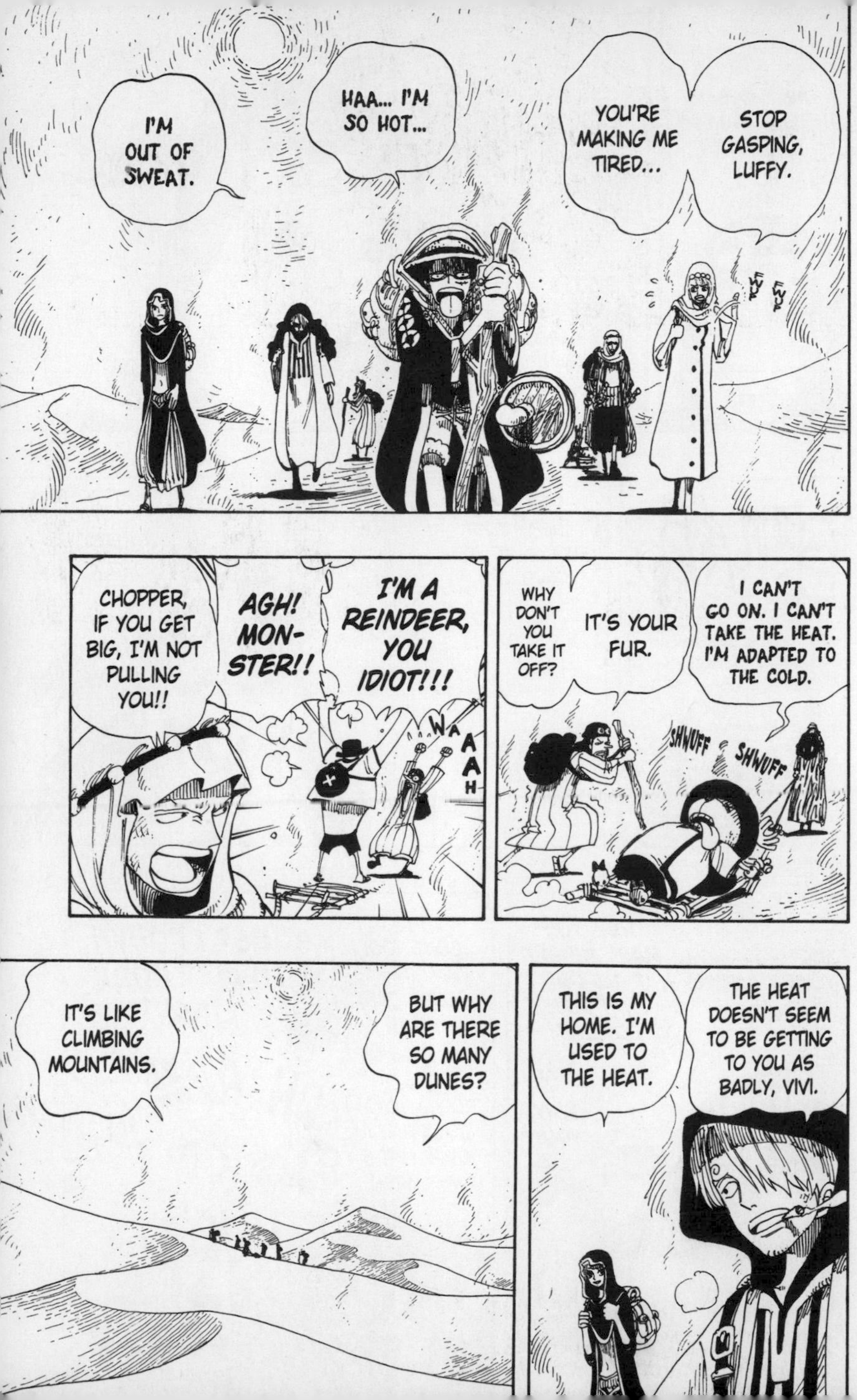
STOP GASPING, LUFFY.
YOU'RE MAKING ME TIRED...
FWUP FWUP
HAA... I'M SO HOT...
I'M OUT OF SWEAT.
I CAN'T GO ON. I CAN'T TAKE THE HEAT. I'M ADAPTED TO THE COLD.
IT'S YOUR FUR.
WHY DON'T YOU TAKE IT OFF?
SHWUFF SHWUFF
I'M A REINDEER, YOU IDIOT!!!
WAAAH
AGH! MONSTER!!
CHOPPER, IF YOU GET BIG, I'M NOT PULLING YOU!!
THE HEAT DOESN'T SEEM TO BE GETTING TO YOU AS BADLY, VIVI.
THIS IS MY HOME. I'M USED TO THE HEAT.
BUT WHY ARE THERE SO MANY DUNES?
IT'S LIKE CLIMBING MOUNTAINS.

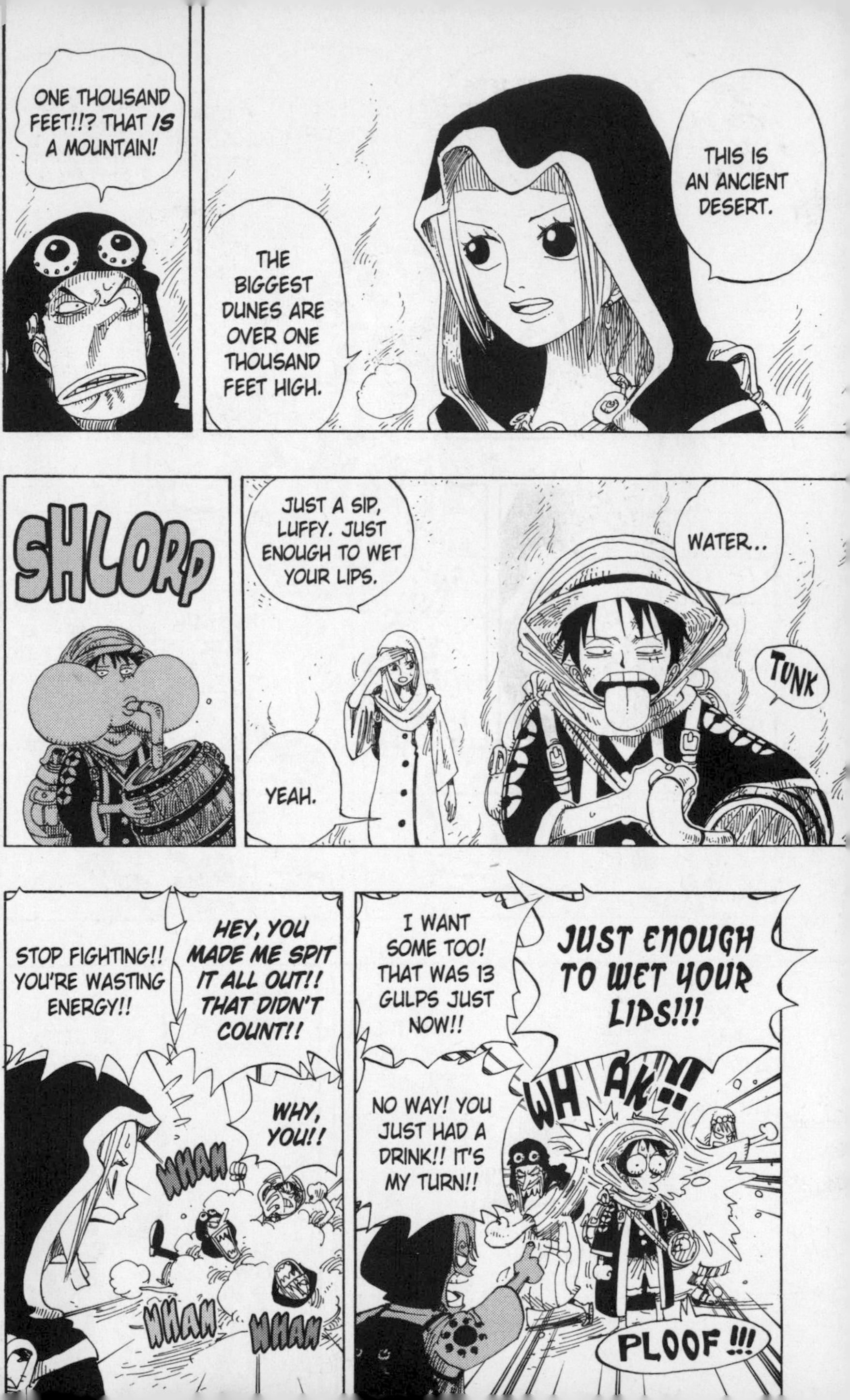
THIS IS AN ANCIENT DESERT.
THE BIGGEST DUNES ARE OVER ONE THOUSAND FEET HIGH.
ONE THOUSAND FEET!!? THAT *IS* A MOUNTAIN!
WATER...
TUNK
JUST A SIP, LUFFY. JUST ENOUGH TO WET YOUR LIPS.
YEAH.
SHLORP
JUST ENOUGH TO WET YOUR LIPS!!!
I WANT SOME TOO! THAT WAS 13 GULPS JUST NOW!!
WHAK!!
NO WAY! YOU JUST HAD A DRINK!! IT'S MY TURN!!
PLOOF!!!
HEY, YOU MADE ME SPIT IT ALL OUT!! THAT DIDN'T COUNT!!
STOP FIGHTING!! YOU'RE WASTING ENERGY!!
WHY, YOU!!
WHAM
WHAM
WHAM

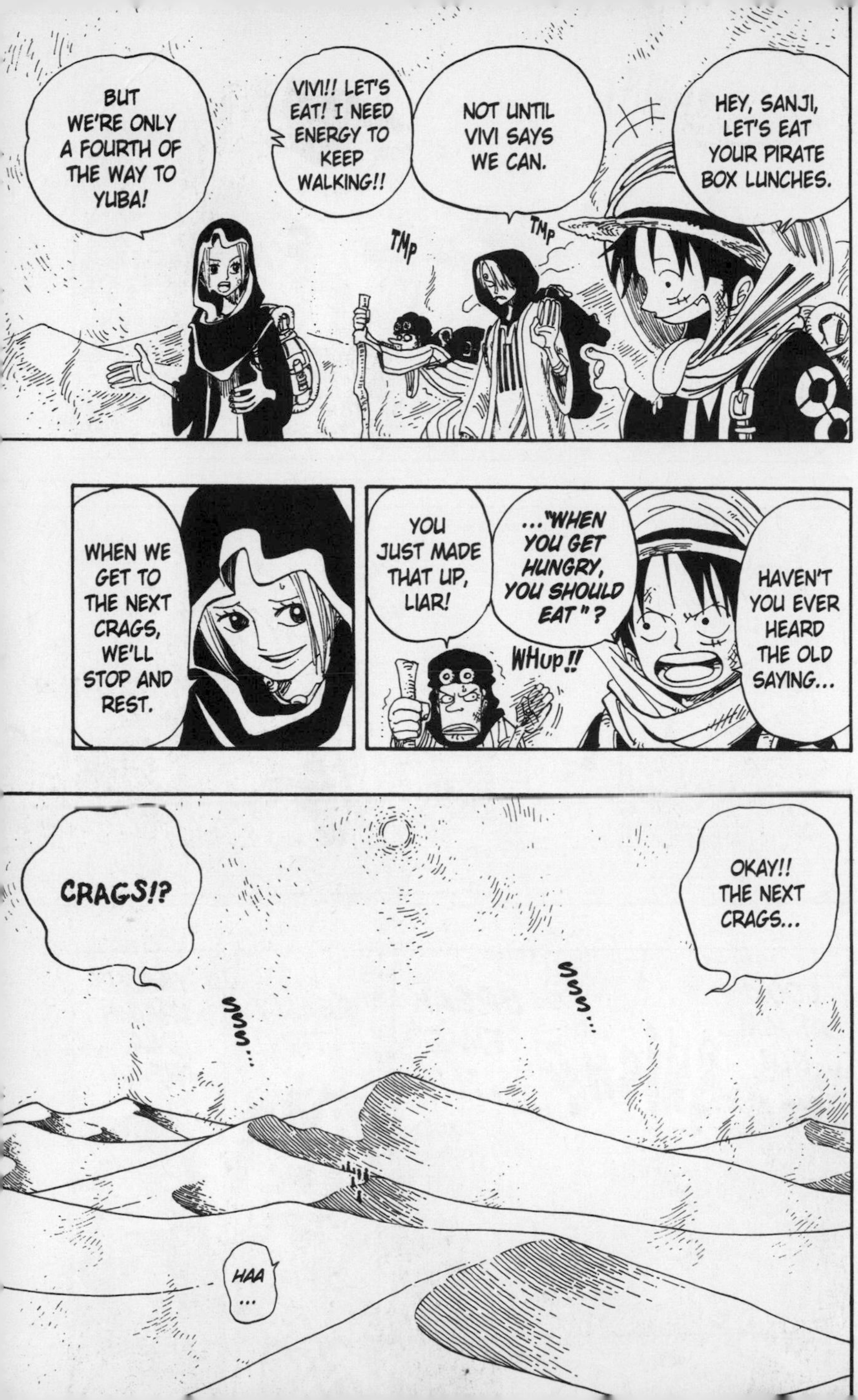
HEY, SANJI, LET'S EAT YOUR PIRATE BOX LUNCHES.
TMP
NOT UNTIL VIVI SAYS WE CAN.
TMP
VIVI!! LET'S EAT! I NEED ENERGY TO KEEP WALKING!!
BUT WE'RE ONLY A FOURTH OF THE WAY TO YUBA!
HAVEN'T YOU EVER HEARD THE OLD SAYING...
..."WHEN YOU GET HUNGRY, YOU SHOULD EAT"?
WHUP!!
YOU JUST MADE THAT UP, LIAR!
WHEN WE GET TO THE NEXT CRAGS, WE'LL STOP AND REST.
OKAY!! THE NEXT CRAGS...
CRAGS!?
SSSS...
SSSS...
HAA...

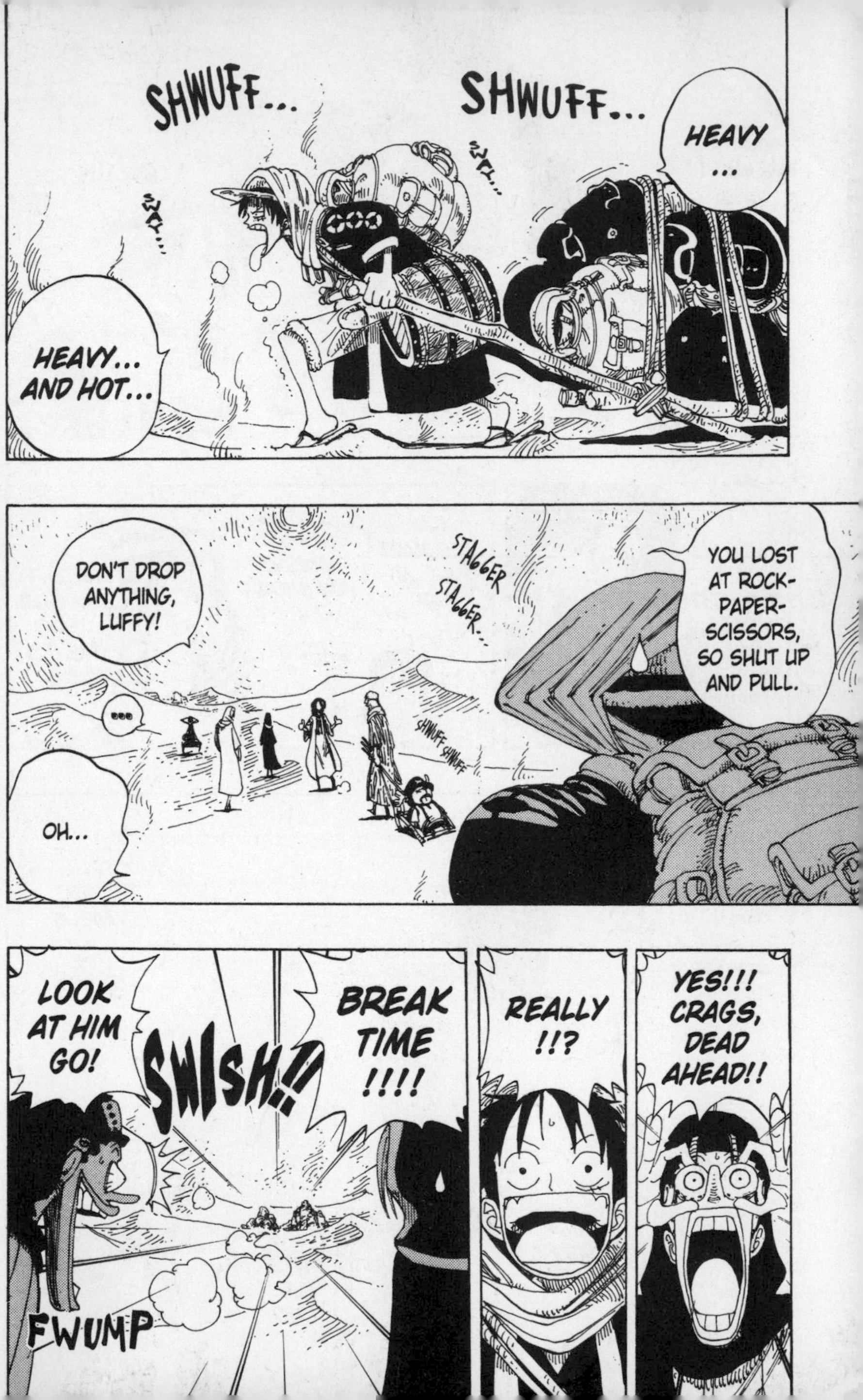
HEAVY ...
SHWUFF...
SWAY...
SHWUFF...
SWAY...
HEAVY... AND HOT...
YOU LOST AT ROCK-PAPER-SCISSORS, SO SHUT UP AND PULL.
STAGGER
STAGGER...
SHWUFF SHWUFF
DON'T DROP ANYTHING, LUFFY!
...
OH...
YES!!! CRAGS, DEAD AHEAD!!
REALLY !!?
BREAK TIME !!!!
SWISH!!
LOOK AT HIM GO!
FWUMP

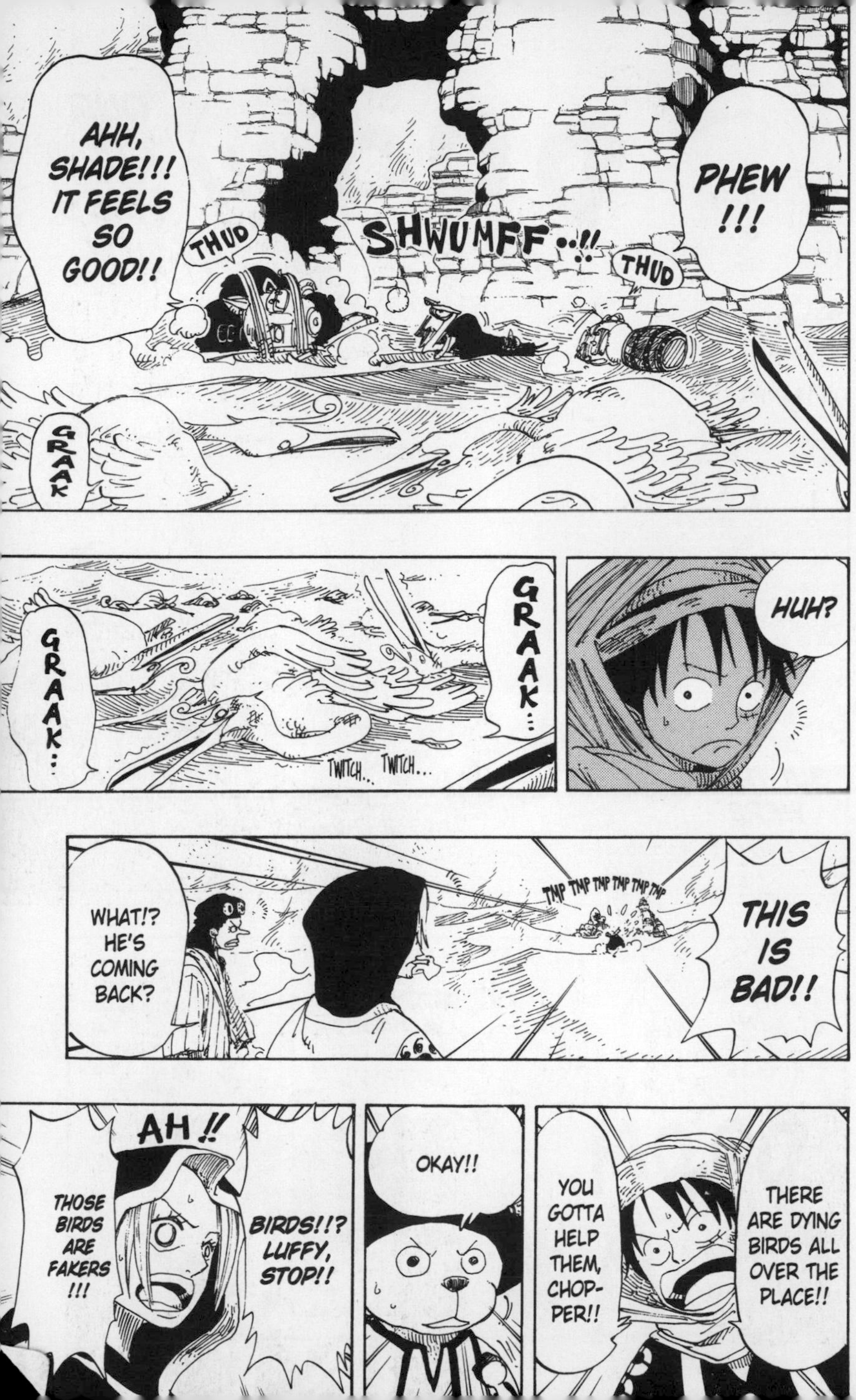
PHEW!!!
THUD
SHWUMFF..!!
THUD
AHH, SHADE!!! IT FEELS SO GOOD!!
GRAAK
HUH?
GRAAK...
GRAAK...
TWITCH... TWITCH...
THIS IS BAD!!
TMP TMP TMP TMP TMP TMP
WHAT!? HE'S COMING BACK?
THERE ARE DYING BIRDS ALL OVER THE PLACE!!
YOU GOTTA HELP THEM, CHOPPER!!
OKAY!!
AH!!
BIRDS!!? LUFFY, STOP!!
THOSE BIRDS ARE FAKERS!!!

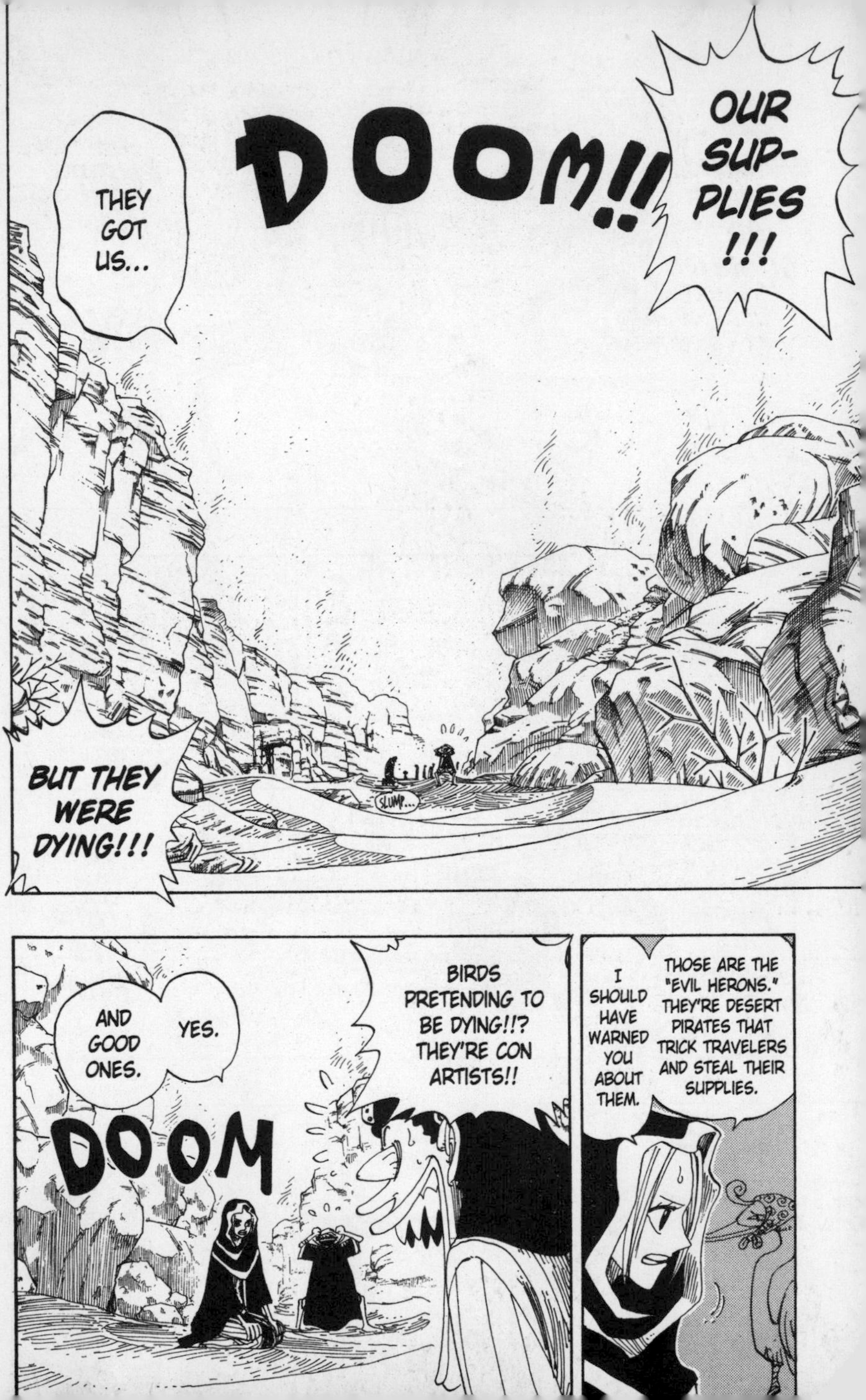
OUR SUPPLIES!!!
DOOM!!
THEY GOT US...
BUT THEY WERE DYING!!!
SLUMP...
THOSE ARE THE "EVIL HERONS." THEY'RE DESERT PIRATES THAT TRICK TRAVELERS AND STEAL THEIR SUPPLIES.
I SHOULD HAVE WARNED YOU ABOUT THEM.
BIRDS PRETENDING TO BE DYING!!? THEY'RE CON ARTISTS!!
YES.
AND GOOD ONES.
DOOM

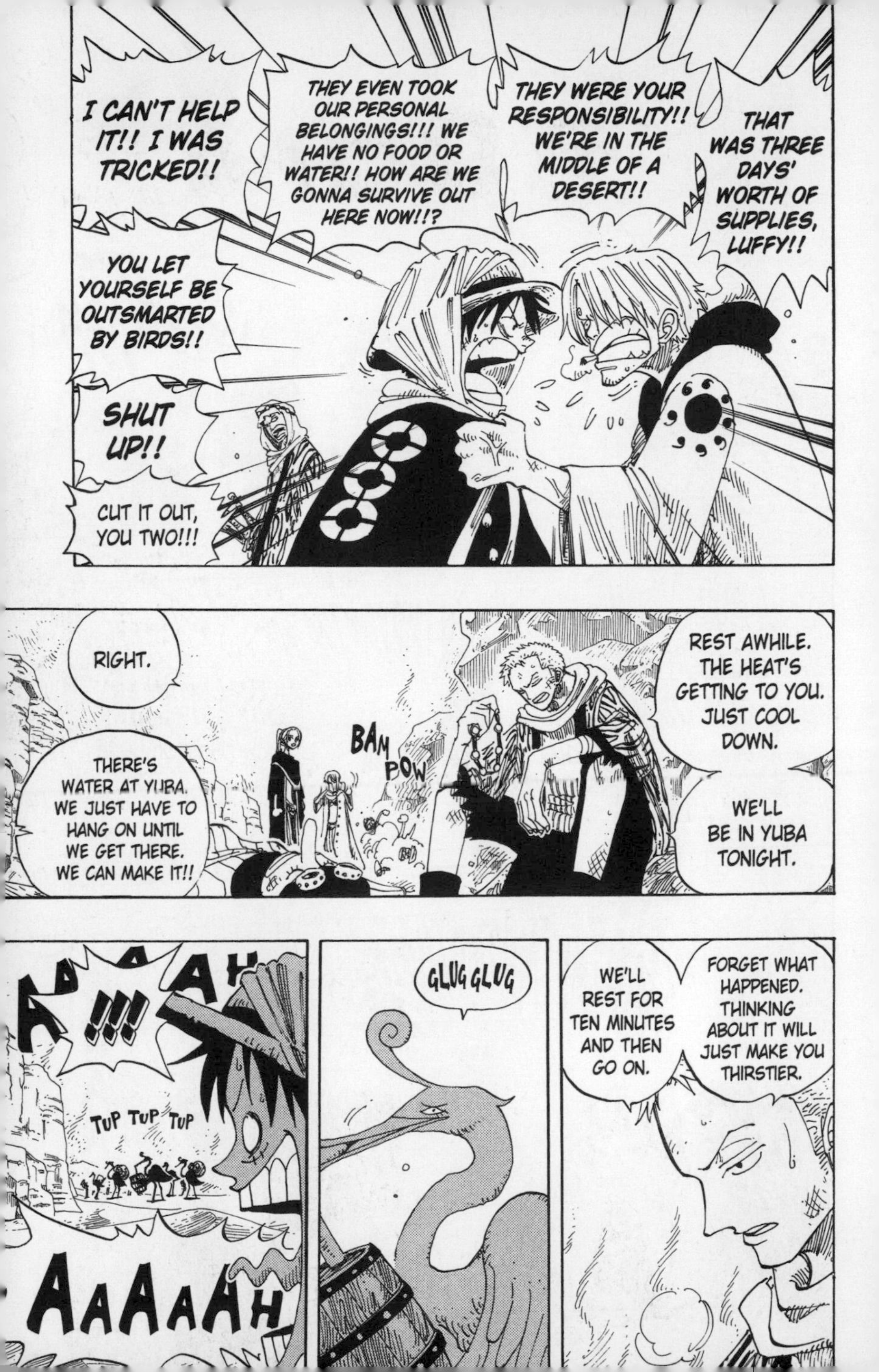
THAT WAS THREE DAYS' WORTH OF SUPPLIES, LUFFY!!
THEY WERE YOUR RESPONSIBILITY!! WE'RE IN THE MIDDLE OF A DESERT!!
THEY EVEN TOOK OUR PERSONAL BELONGINGS!!! WE HAVE NO FOOD OR WATER!! HOW ARE WE GONNA SURVIVE OUT HERE NOW!!?
I CAN'T HELP IT!! I WAS TRICKED!!
YOU LET YOURSELF BE OUTSMARTED BY BIRDS!!
SHUT UP!!
CUT IT OUT, YOU TWO!!!
REST AWHILE. THE HEAT'S GETTING TO YOU. JUST COOL DOWN.
WE'LL BE IN YUBA TONIGHT.
BAM
POW
RIGHT.
THERE'S WATER AT YUBA. WE JUST HAVE TO HANG ON UNTIL WE GET THERE. WE CAN MAKE IT!!
FORGET WHAT HAPPENED. THINKING ABOUT IT WILL JUST MAKE YOU THIRSTIER.
WE'LL REST FOR TEN MINUTES AND THEN GO ON.
GLUG GLUG
TUP TUP TUP
AAAAAH

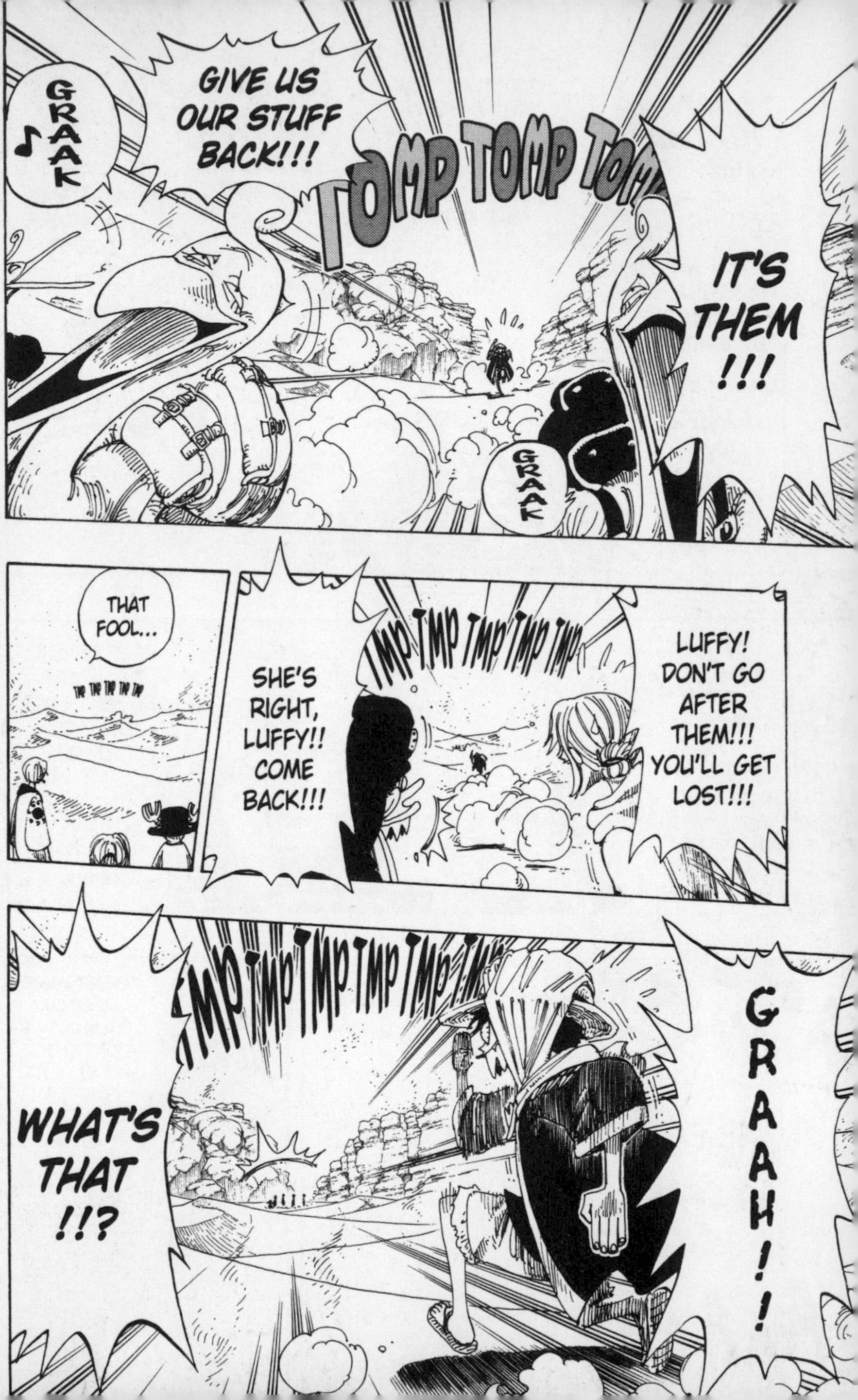

IT'S THEM!!!
GRAAK
TOMP TOMP TOM
GIVE US OUR STUFF BACK!!!
GRAAK ♪
LUFFY! DON'T GO AFTER THEM!!! YOU'LL GET LOST!!!
TMP TMP TMP TMP TMP
SHE'S RIGHT, LUFFY!! COME BACK!!!
THAT FOOL...
TMP TMP TMP TMP TMP
GRAAH!!
TMP TMP TMP TMP TMP TM
WHAT'S THAT!!?

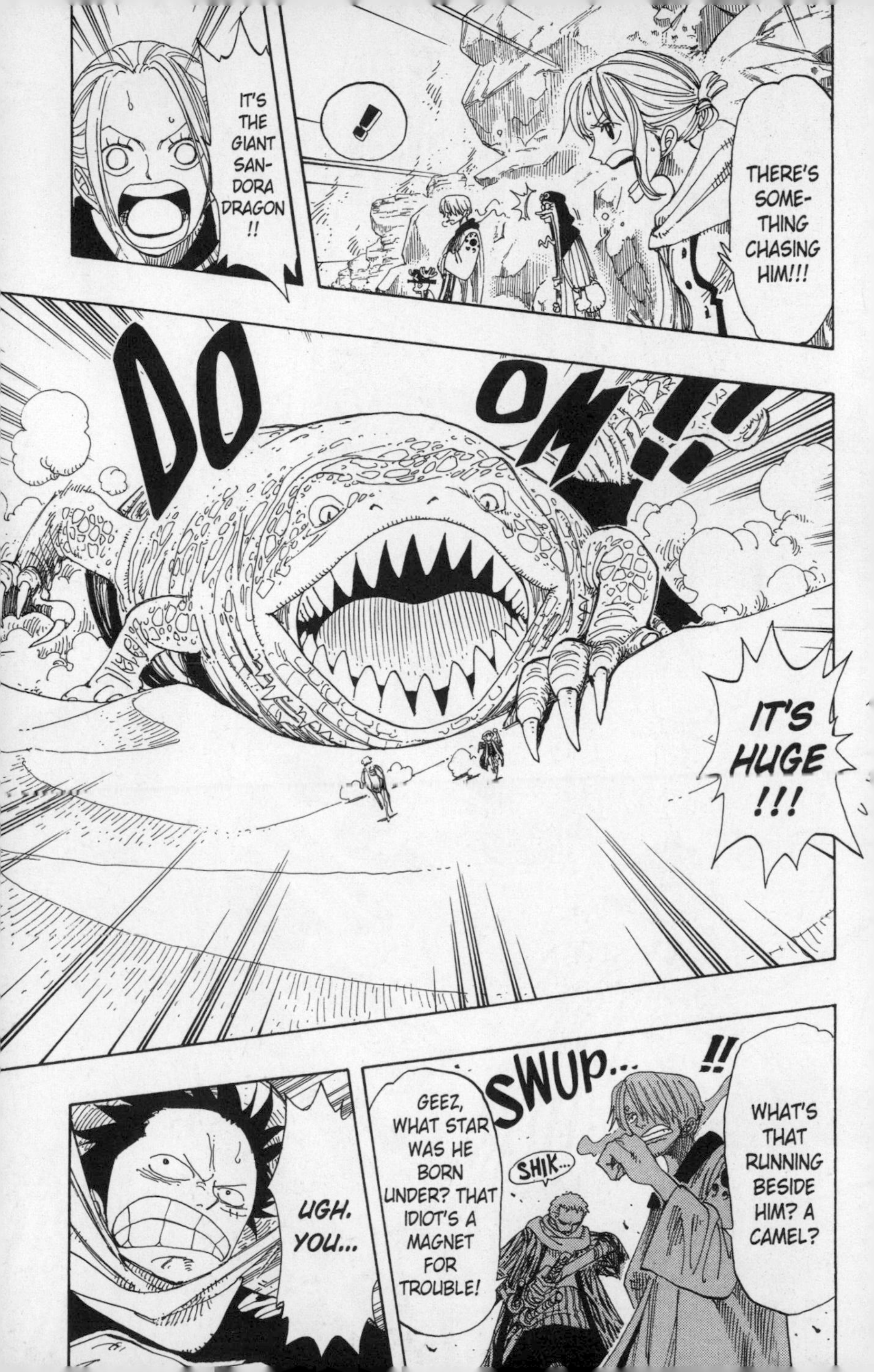

THERE'S SOME-THING CHASING HIM!!!
!
IT'S THE GIANT SAN-DORA DRAGON !!
DOOM!!
IT'S HUGE !!!
WHAT'S THAT RUNNING BESIDE HIM? A CAMEL?
!!
SWUP...
SHIK...
GEEZ, WHAT STAR WAS HE BORN UNDER? THAT IDIOT'S A MAGNET FOR TROUBLE!
UGH. YOU...

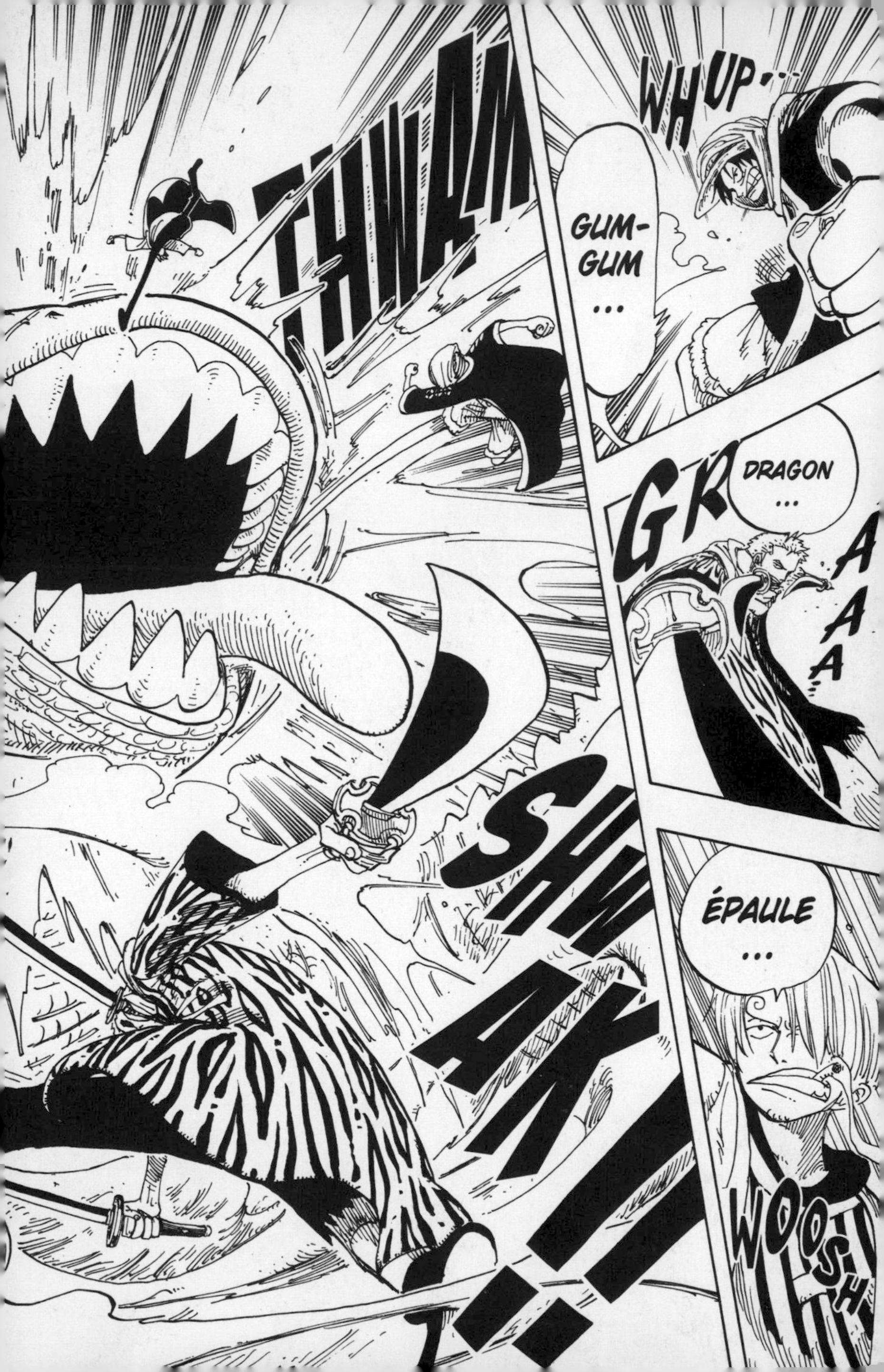
WHUP...
GUM-GUM ...
GRAAAA
DRAGON ...
ÉPAULE ...
WOOSH
THWAM
SHAK!!!

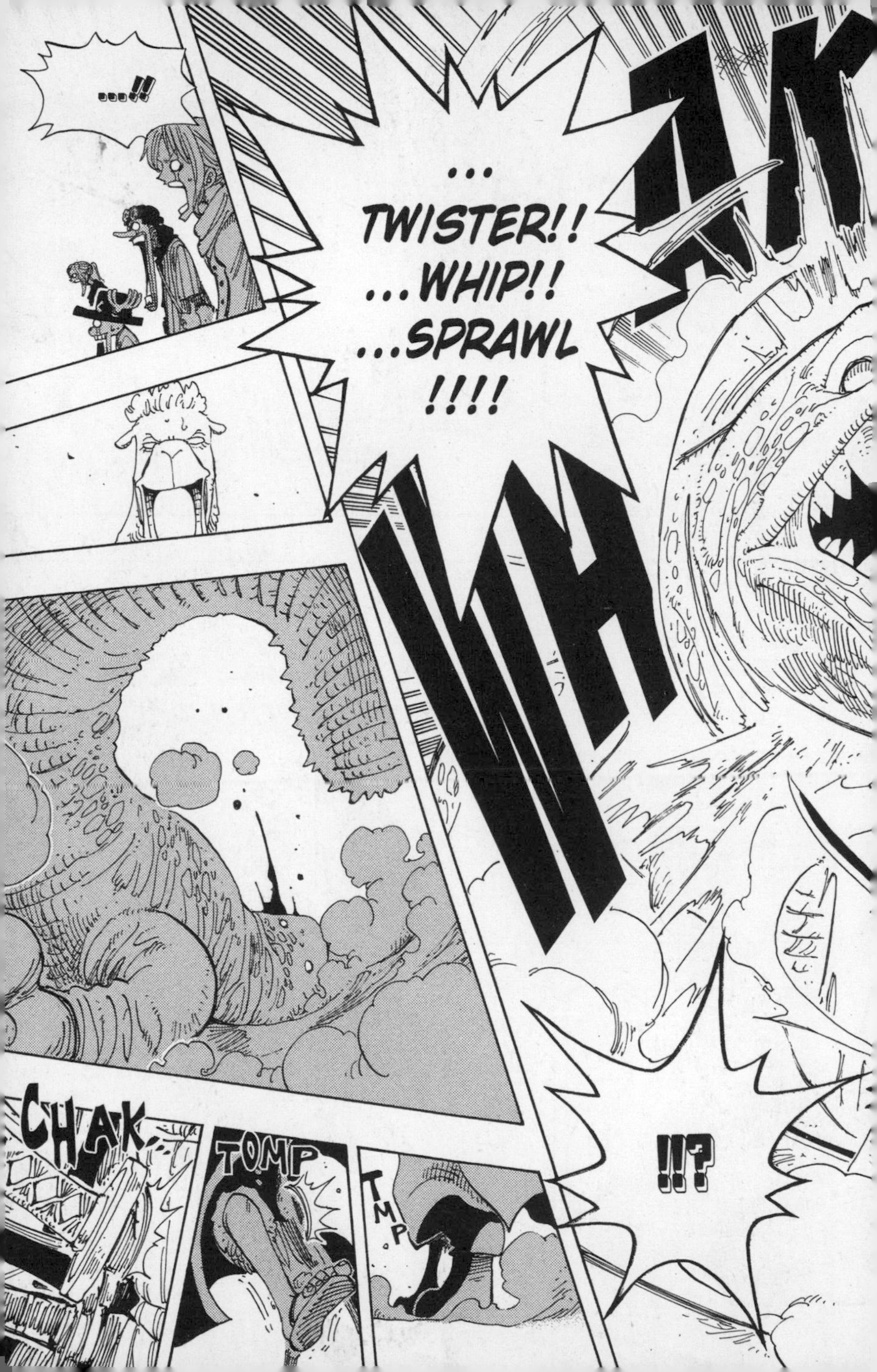

... TWISTER!! ...WHIP!! ...SPRAWL !!!!
AK
!!?
...!!
TMP
TOMP
CHAK

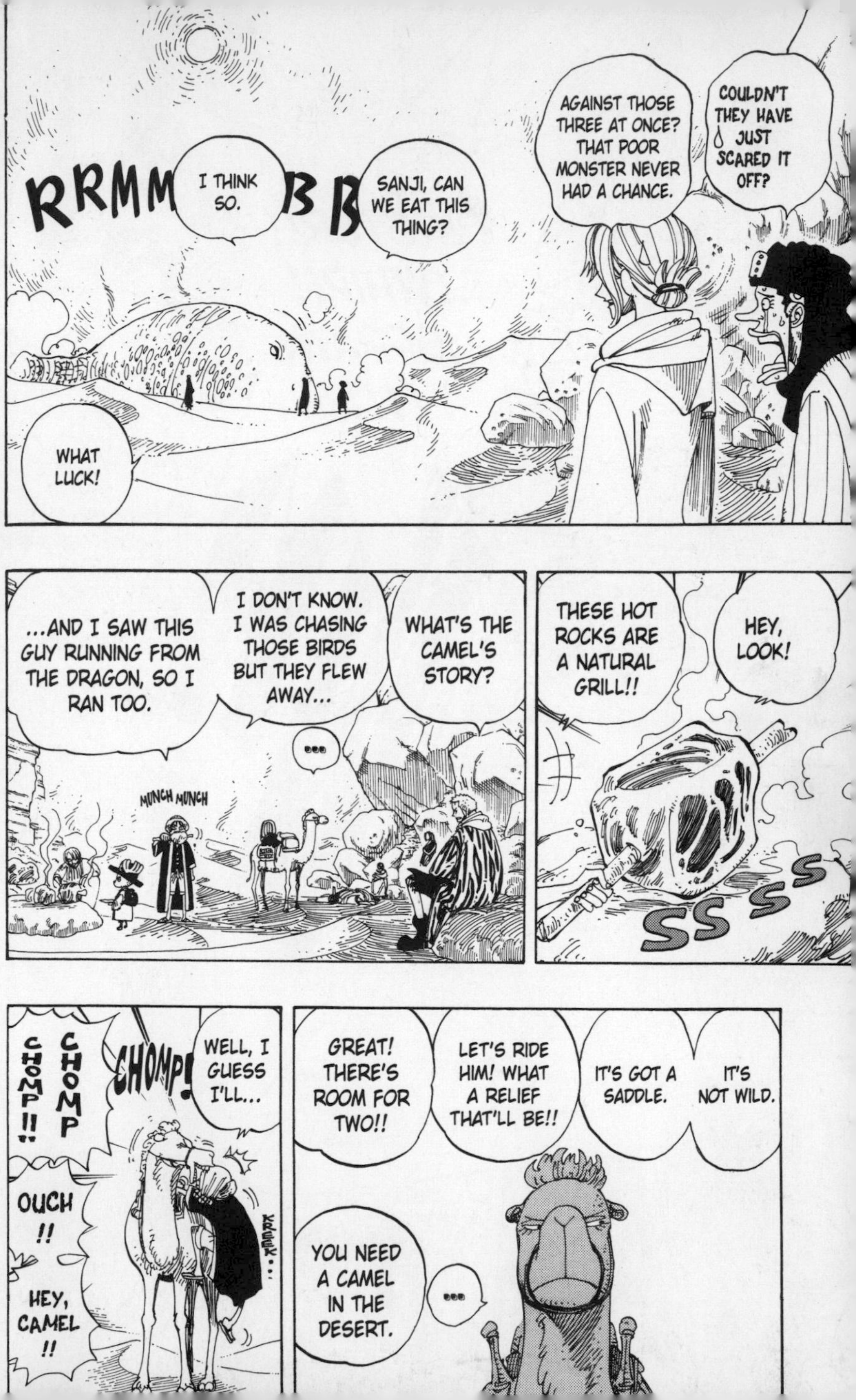
COULDN'T THEY HAVE JUST SCARED IT OFF?
AGAINST THOSE THREE AT ONCE? THAT POOR MONSTER NEVER HAD A CHANCE.
SANJI, CAN WE EAT THIS THING?
RRMMBB
I THINK SO.
WHAT LUCK!
HEY, LOOK!
THESE HOT ROCKS ARE A NATURAL GRILL!!
SSSSS
WHAT'S THE CAMEL'S STORY?
I DON'T KNOW. I WAS CHASING THOSE BIRDS BUT THEY FLEW AWAY...
...AND I SAW THIS GUY RUNNING FROM THE DRAGON, SO I RAN TOO.
...
MUNCH MUNCH
IT'S NOT WILD.
IT'S GOT A SADDLE.
LET'S RIDE HIM! WHAT A RELIEF THAT'LL BE!!
GREAT! THERE'S ROOM FOR TWO!!
YOU NEED A CAMEL IN THE DESERT.
...
WELL, I GUESS I'LL...
CHOMP!
CHOMP
CHOMP!!
KREEK...
OUCH!!
HEY, CAMEL!!

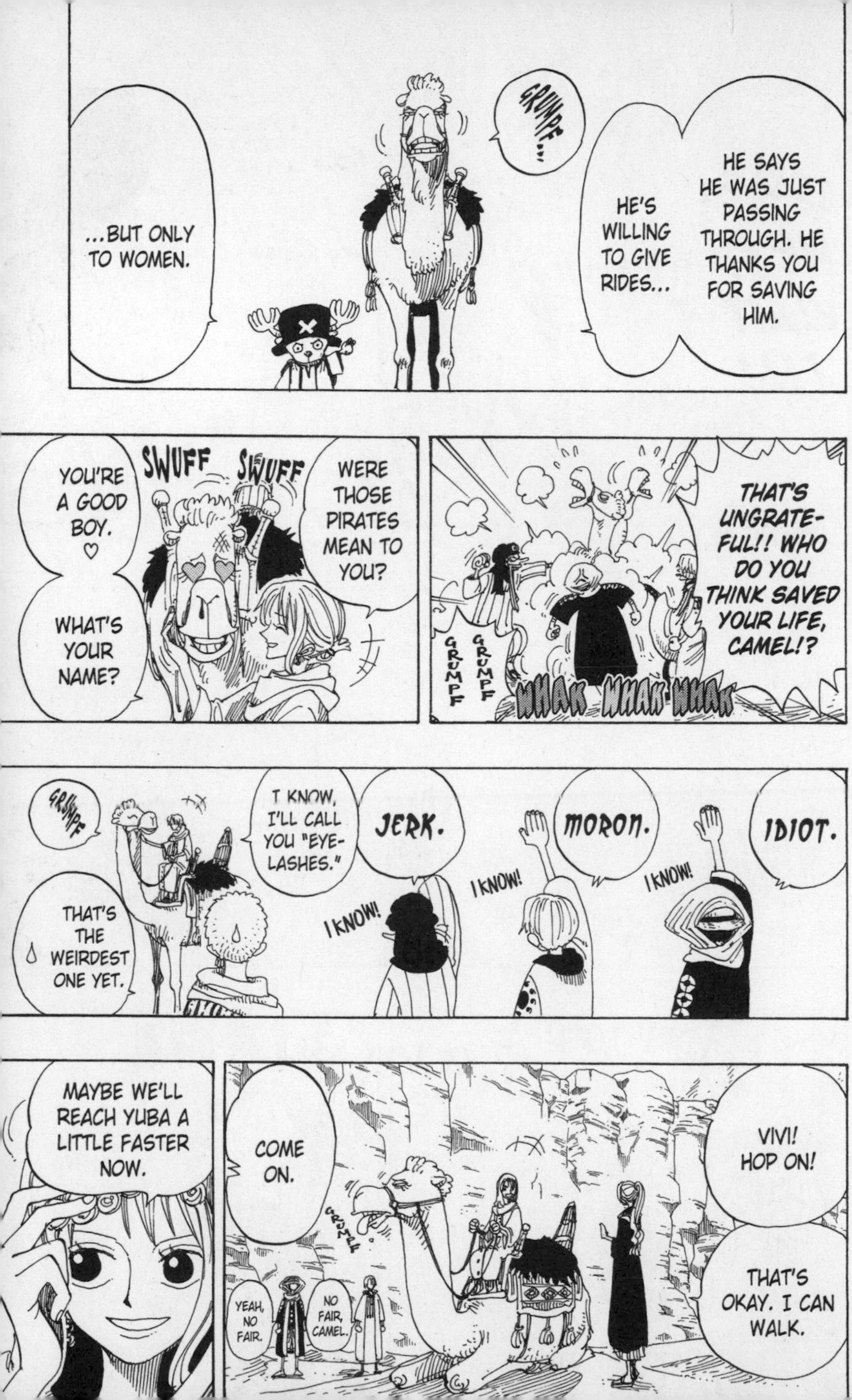
GRUMPF...
HE SAYS HE WAS JUST PASSING THROUGH. HE THANKS YOU FOR SAVING HIM.
HE'S WILLING TO GIVE RIDES...
...BUT ONLY TO WOMEN.
THAT'S UNGRATEFUL!! WHO DO YOU THINK SAVED YOUR LIFE, CAMEL!?
GRUMPF
GRUMPF
WHAK WHAK WHAK
SWUFF
SWUFF
WERE THOSE PIRATES MEAN TO YOU?
YOU'RE A GOOD BOY. ♡
WHAT'S YOUR NAME?
IDIOT.
I KNOW!
MORON.
I KNOW!
JERK.
I KNOW!
I KNOW, I'LL CALL YOU "EYE-LASHES."
GRUMPF
THAT'S THE WEIRDEST ONE YET.
VIVI! HOP ON!
THAT'S OKAY. I CAN WALK.
COME ON.
GRUMPF
NO FAIR, CAMEL.
YEAH, NO FAIR.
MAYBE WE'LL REACH YUBA A LITTLE FASTER NOW.

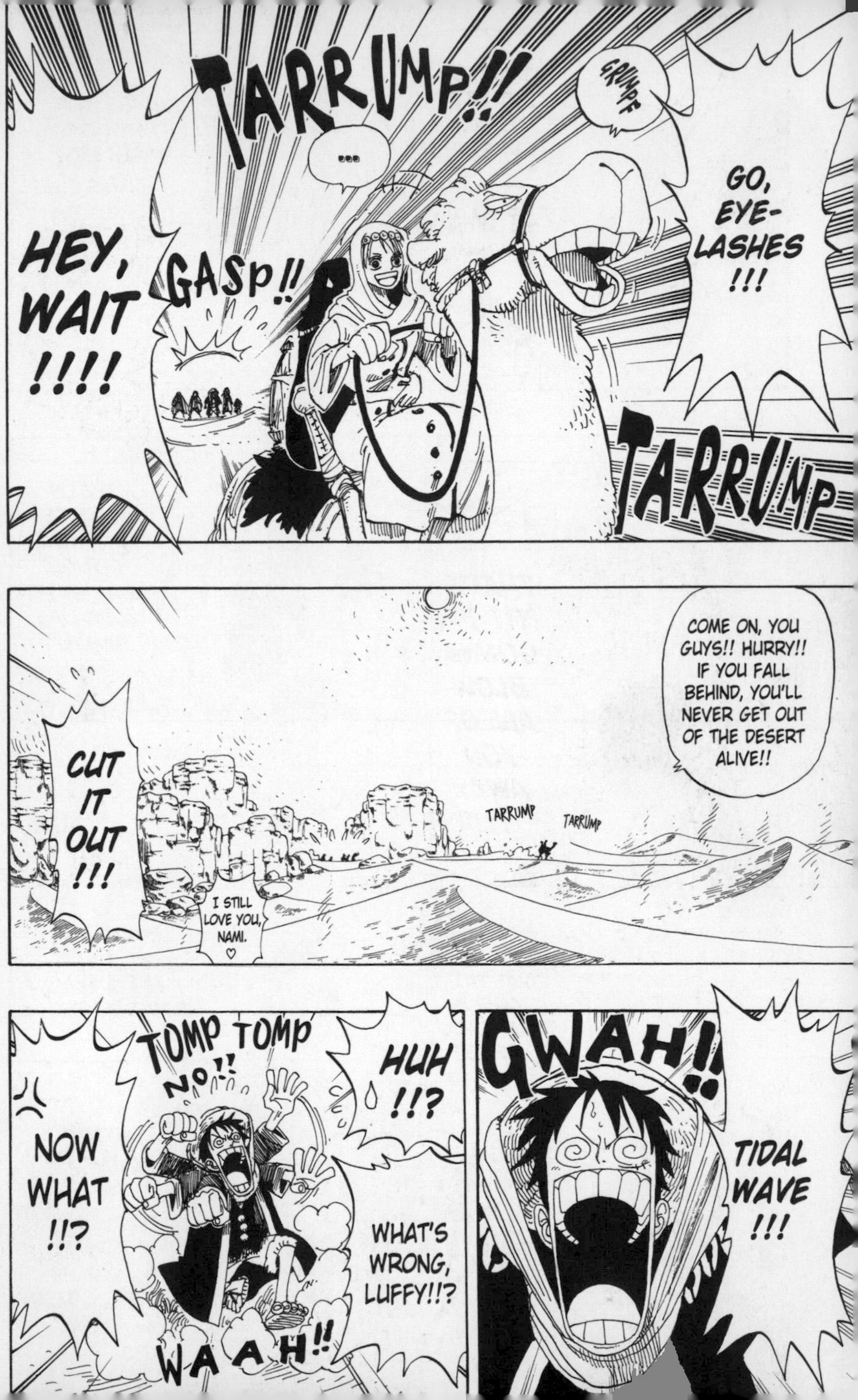
GRUMPF
GO, EYE-LASHES!!!
TARRUMP!!
...
TARRUMP
GASp!!
HEY, WAIT!!!!
COME ON, YOU GUYS!! HURRY!! IF YOU FALL BEHIND, YOU'LL NEVER GET OUT OF THE DESERT ALIVE!!
TARRUMP
TARRUMP
CUT IT OUT!!!
I STILL LOVE YOU, NAMI. ♡
GWAH!!
TIDAL WAVE!!!
HUH!!?
TOMP TOMP
NO!!
NOW WHAT!!?
WHAT'S WRONG, LUFFY!!?
WAAH!!

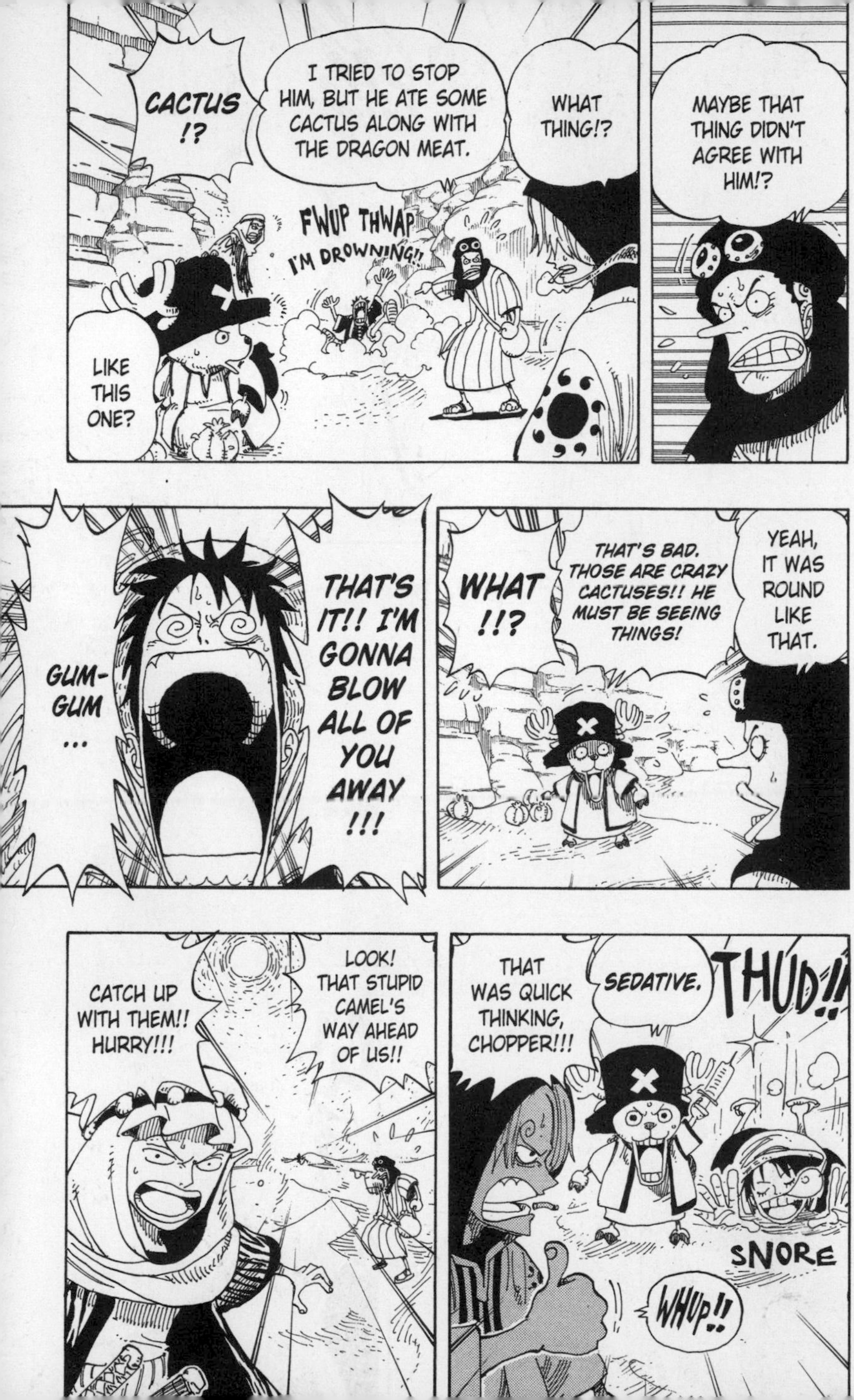
MAYBE THAT THING DIDN'T AGREE WITH HIM!?
WHAT THING!?
I TRIED TO STOP HIM, BUT HE ATE SOME CACTUS ALONG WITH THE DRAGON MEAT.
CACTUS !?
FWUP THWAP
I'M DROWNING!!
LIKE THIS ONE?
YEAH, IT WAS ROUND LIKE THAT.
THAT'S BAD. THOSE ARE CRAZY CACTUSES!! HE MUST BE SEEING THINGS!
WHAT !!?
THAT'S IT!! I'M GONNA BLOW ALL OF YOU AWAY !!!
GUM-GUM ...
THUD!!
SEDATIVE.
THAT WAS QUICK THINKING, CHOPPER!!!
SNORE
WHUP!!
LOOK! THAT STUPID CAMEL'S WAY AHEAD OF US!!
CATCH UP WITH THEM!! HURRY!!!

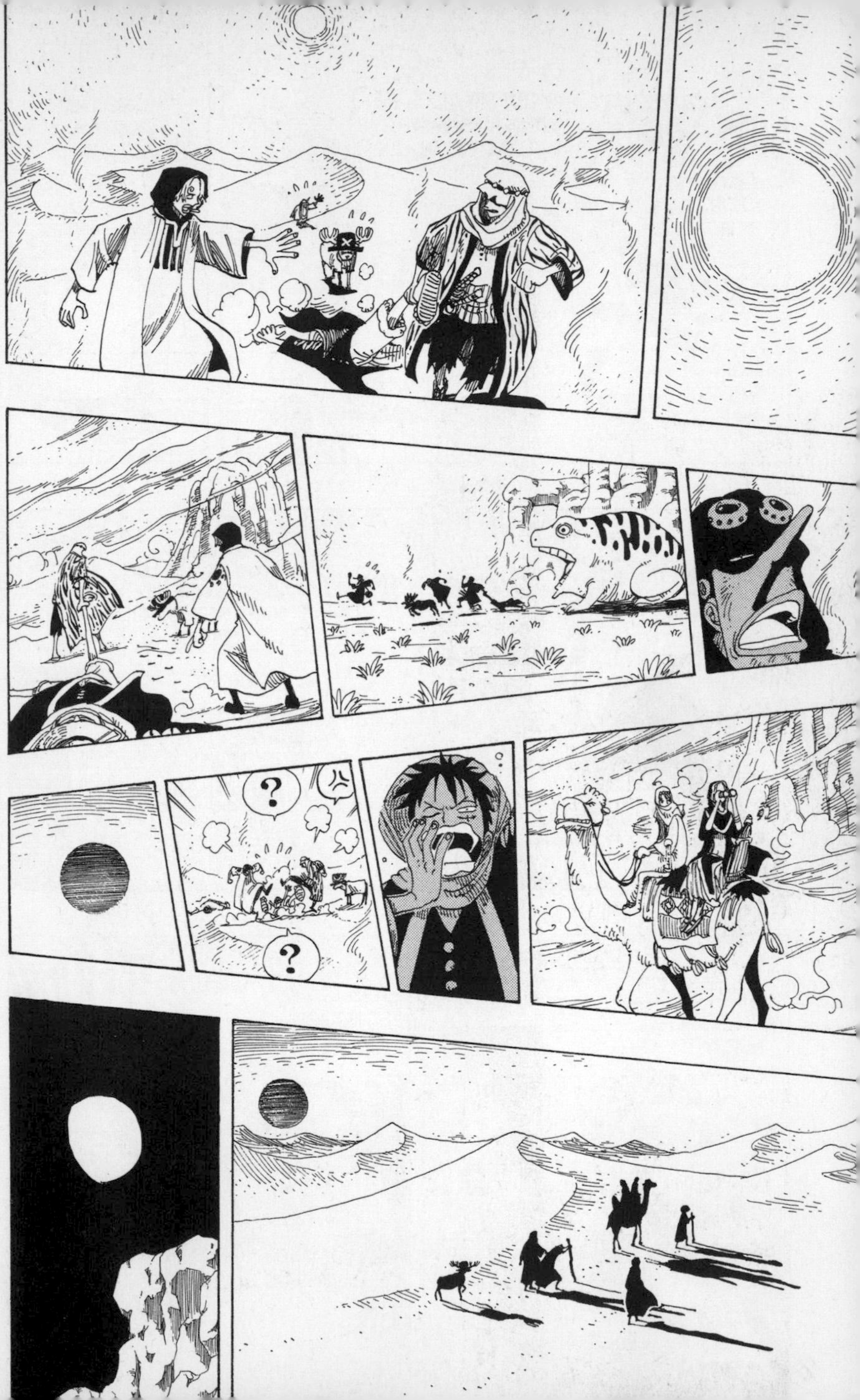
?
?

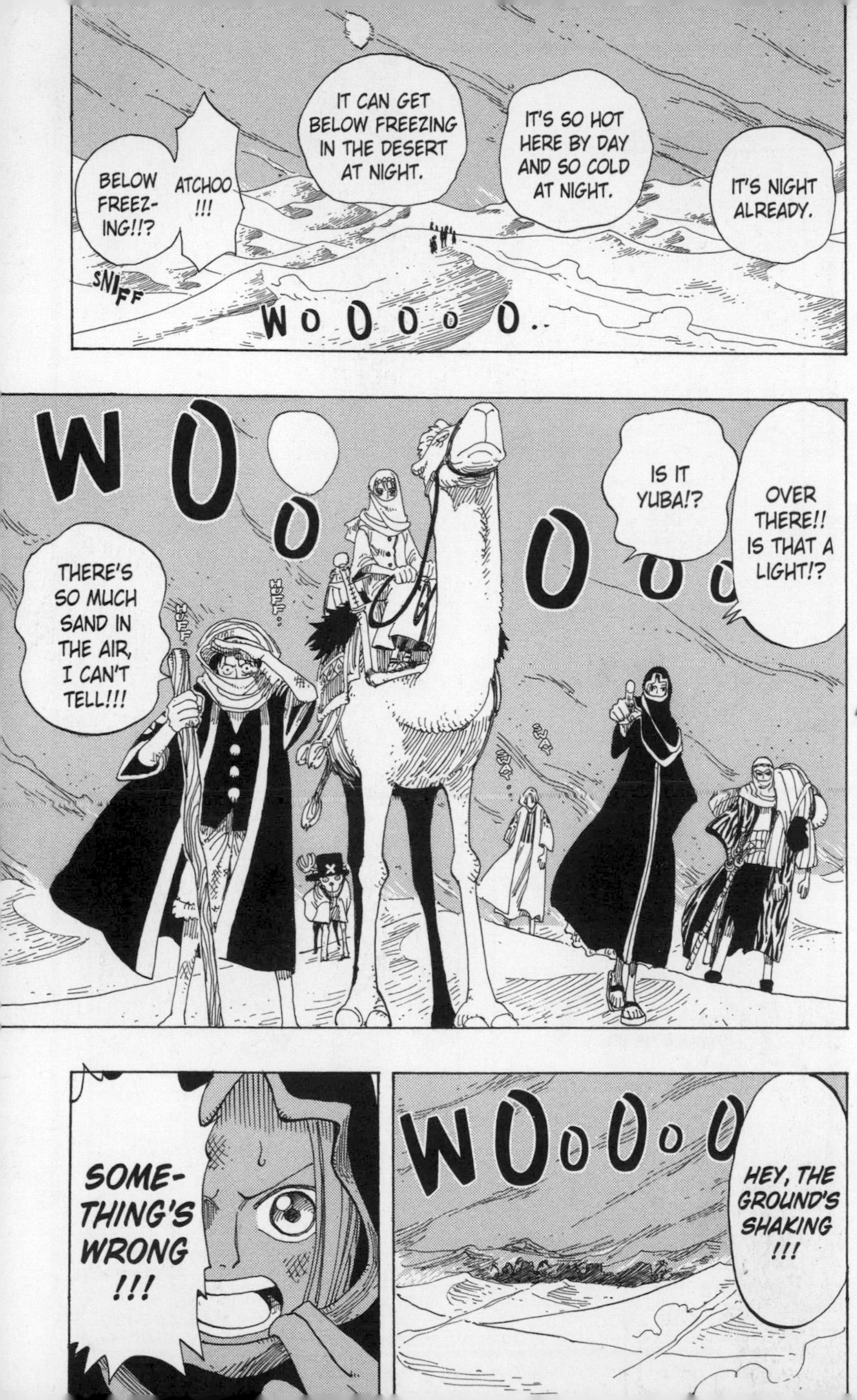
IT'S NIGHT ALREADY.
IT'S SO HOT HERE BY DAY AND SO COLD AT NIGHT.
IT CAN GET BELOW FREEZING IN THE DESERT AT NIGHT.
ATCHOO!!!
BELOW FREEZ-ING!!?
SNIFF
WOOOOO..
OVER THERE!! IS THAT A LIGHT!?
IS IT YUBA!?
WOOOOOO
HUFF..
HUFF..
THERE'S SO MUCH SAND IN THE AIR, I CAN'T TELL!!!
WOOOOOO
HEY, THE GROUND'S SHAKING!!!
SOME-THING'S WRONG!!!

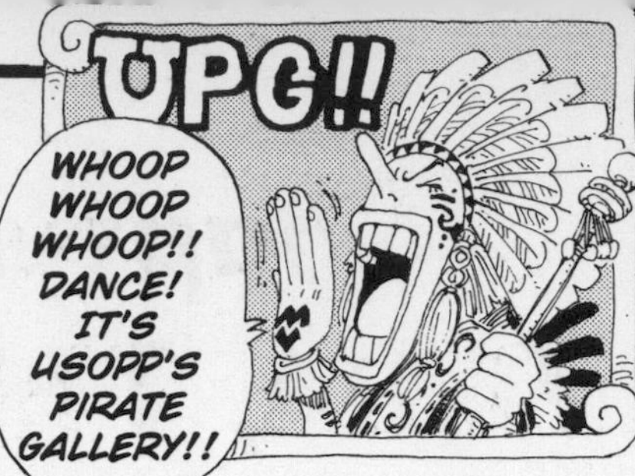
UPG!!
WHOOP WHOOP WHOOP!! DANCE! IT'S USOPP'S PIRATE GALLERY!!

OUR GUARDIAN ANGEL...

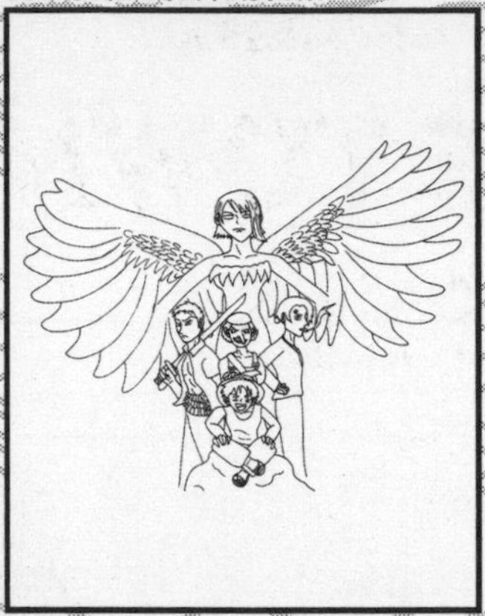

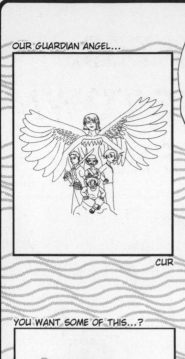

CUR

ME AND MY HERO.

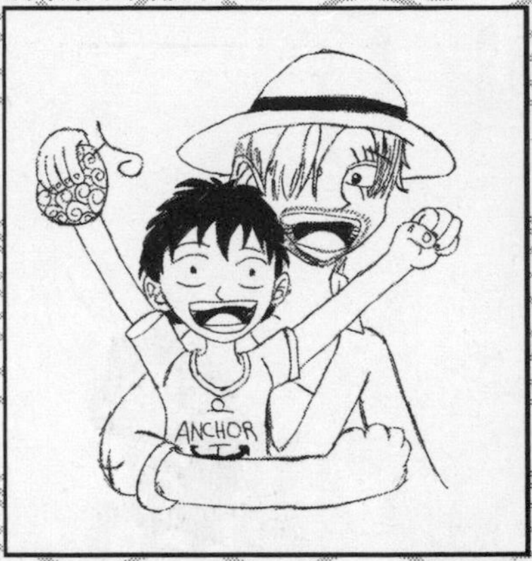
ANCHOR

AMANDA

YOU WANT SOME OF THIS...?

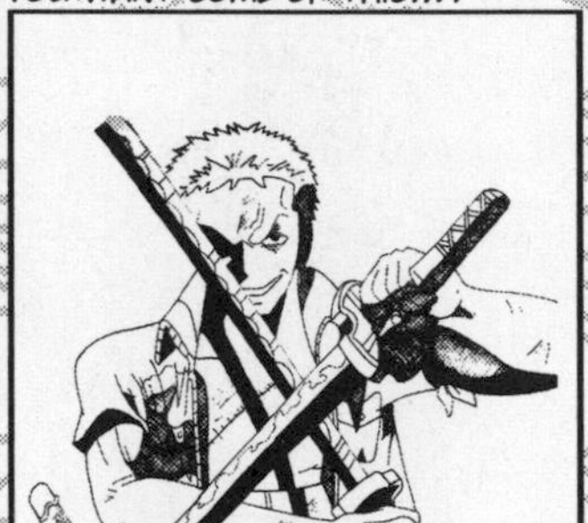

ALLAN F.

THE GREAT DEBATE.

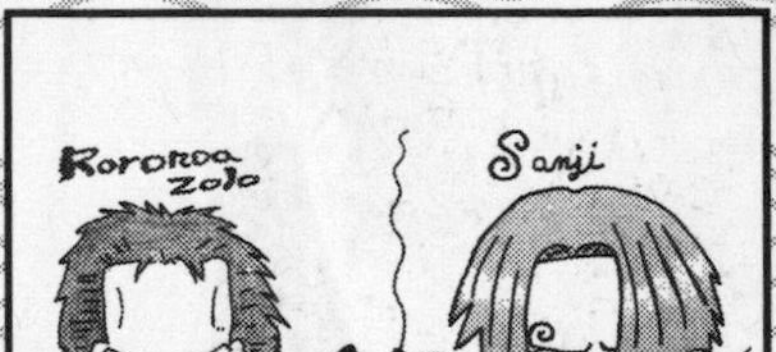
Roronoa Zolo
Sanji
V.S.
Who Will WIN?

DELANIE C., 17

SUBMIT YOUR FAN ART TO:
SHONEN JUMP C/O VIZ MEDIA, LLC P.O. BOX 77010 SAN FRANCISCO, CA 94107
*REMEMBER TO INCLUDE YOUR NAME, AGE AND PARENT RELEASE FORM!!

USOPP'S COMMENTS WERE TRANSMITTED THROUGH THE U.S. SHONEN JUMP TEAM -EDITOR

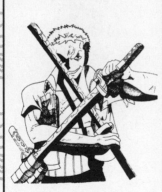

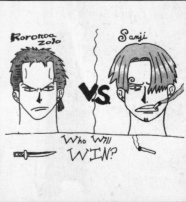

Chapter 163:
YUBA, THE TOWN OF REBELS

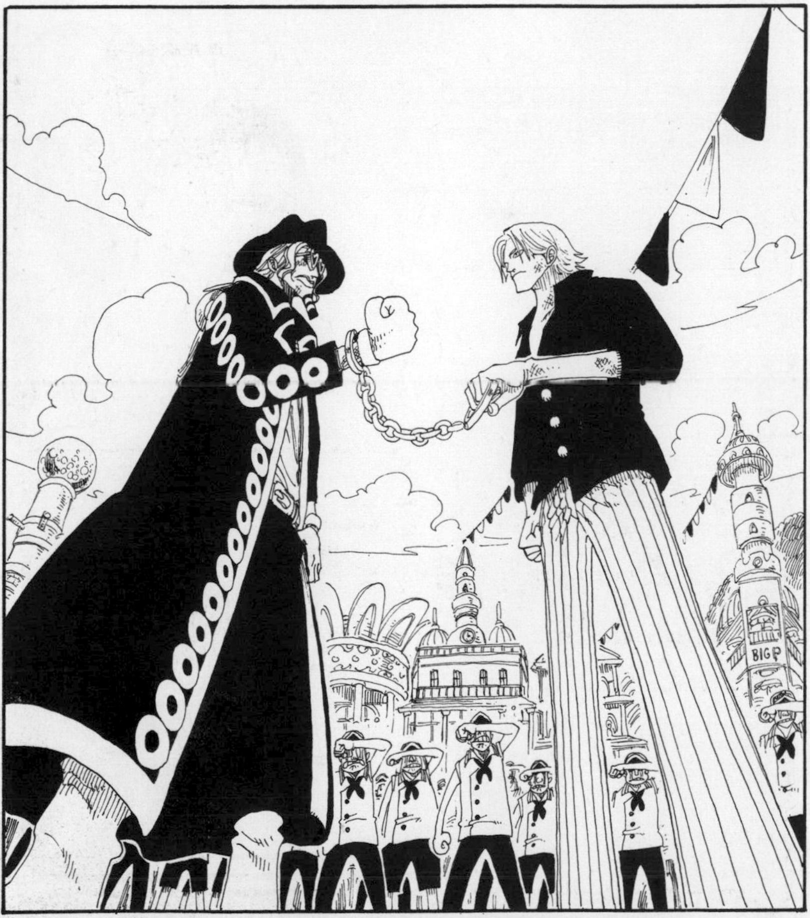

DJANGO'S DANCE PARADISE, VOL. 29:
"FRIENDSHIP, SIN AND DUTY"

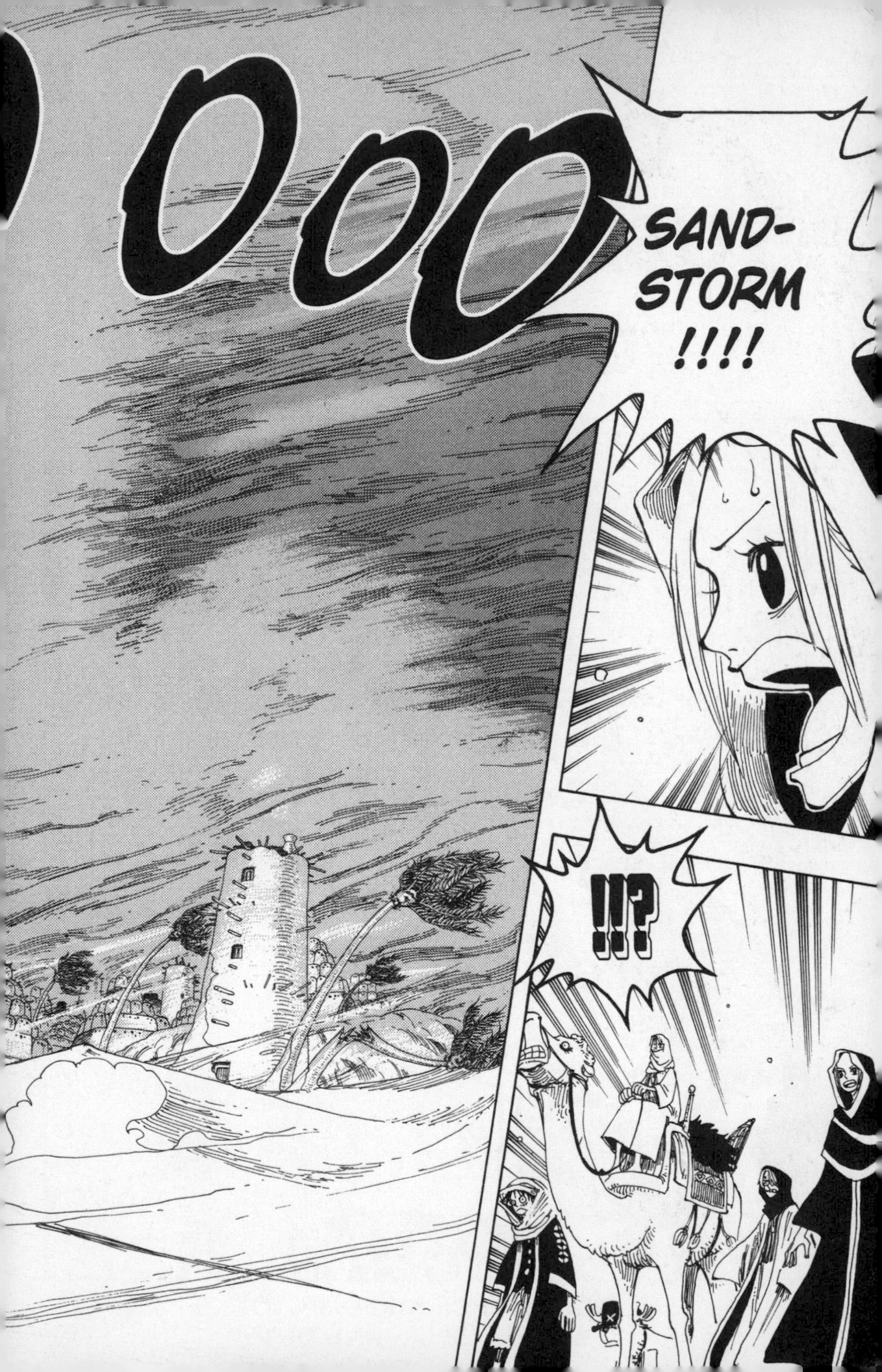
SAND-
STORM
!!!!
!!?
OOOO

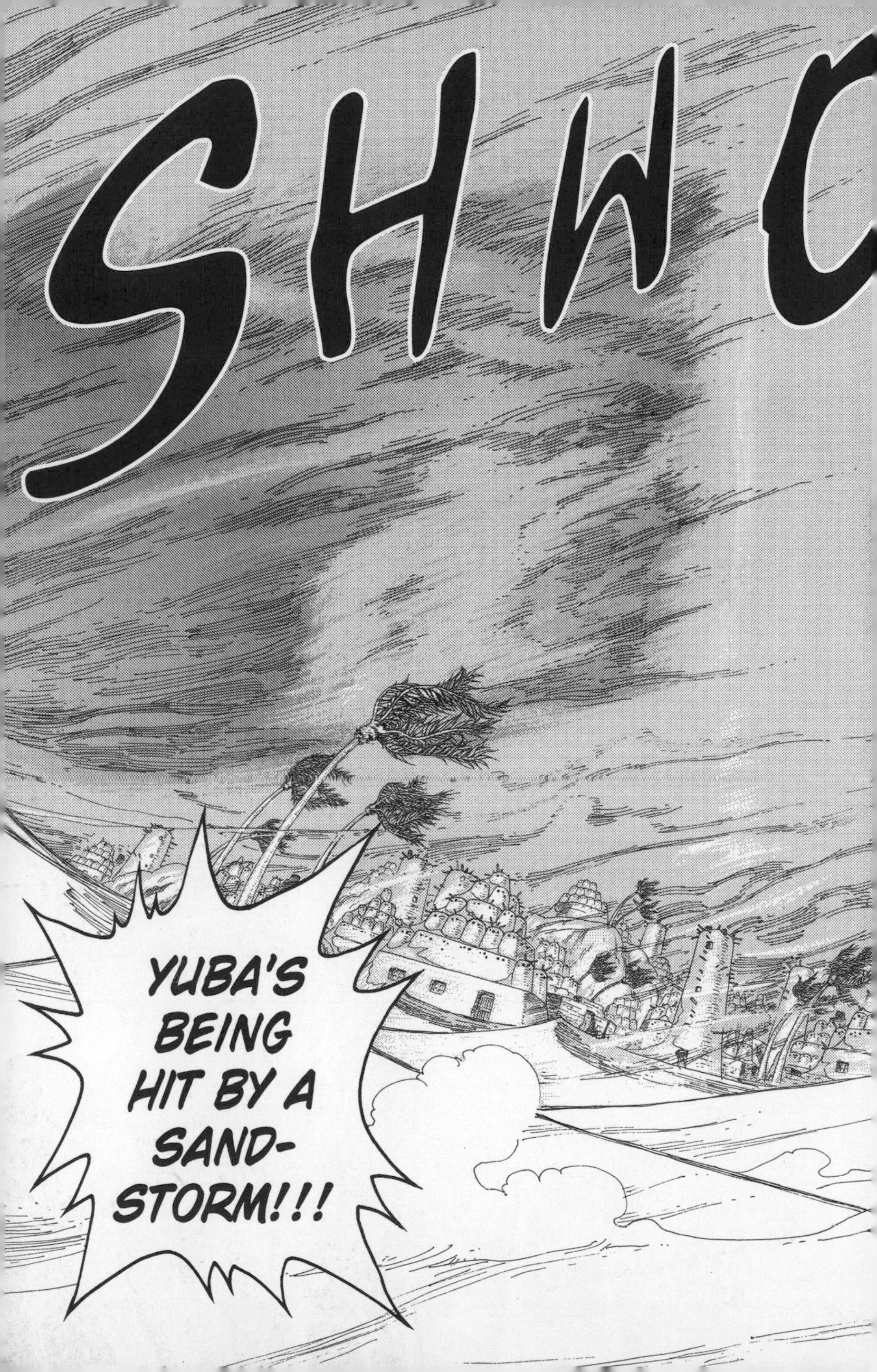
SHWO
YUBA'S BEING HIT BY A SAND-STORM!!!

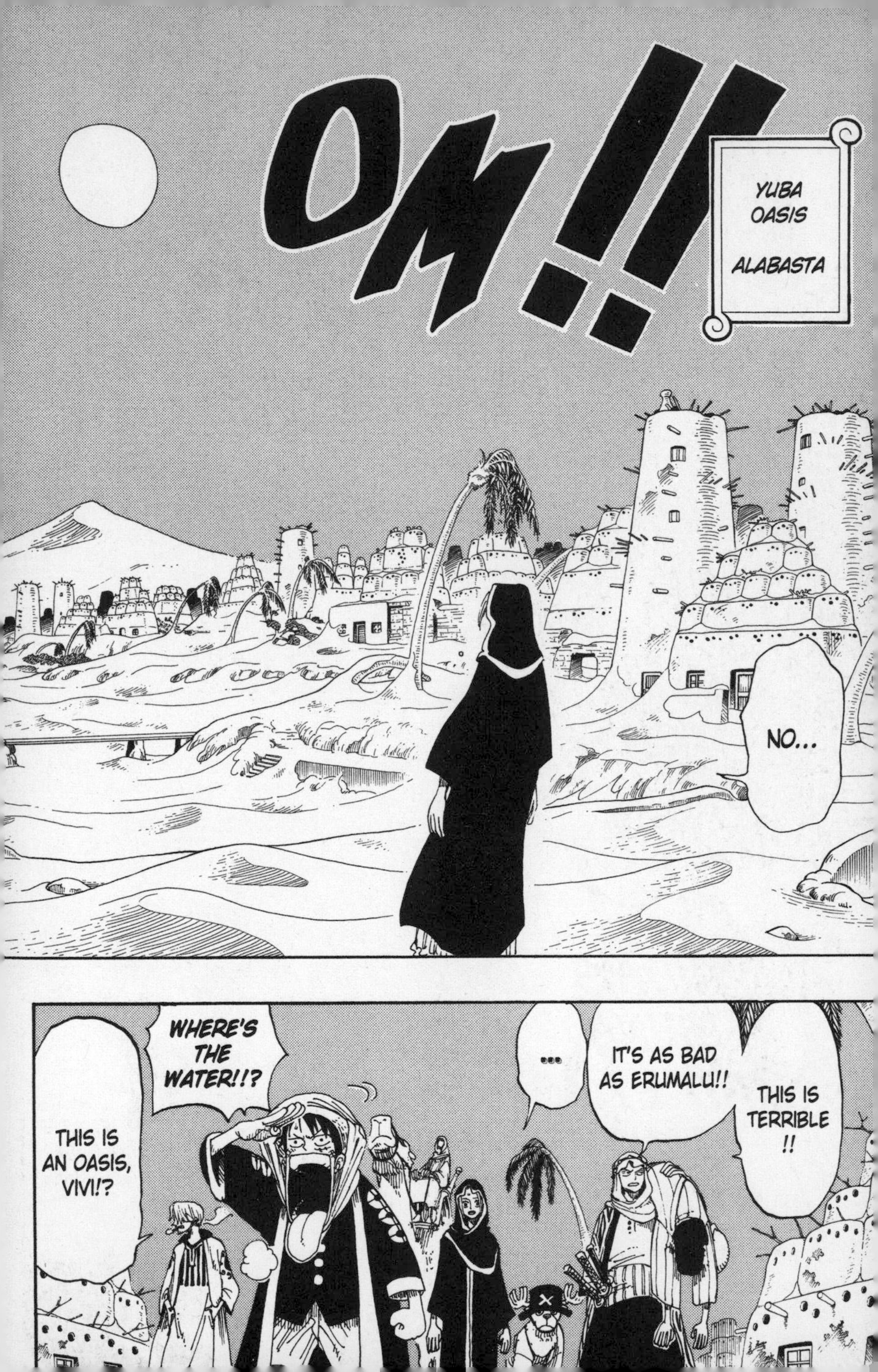
YUBA OASIS
ALABASTA
OM!!
NO...
THIS IS TERRIBLE!!
IT'S AS BAD AS ERUMALU!!
...
WHERE'S THE WATER!!?
THIS IS AN OASIS, VIVI!?

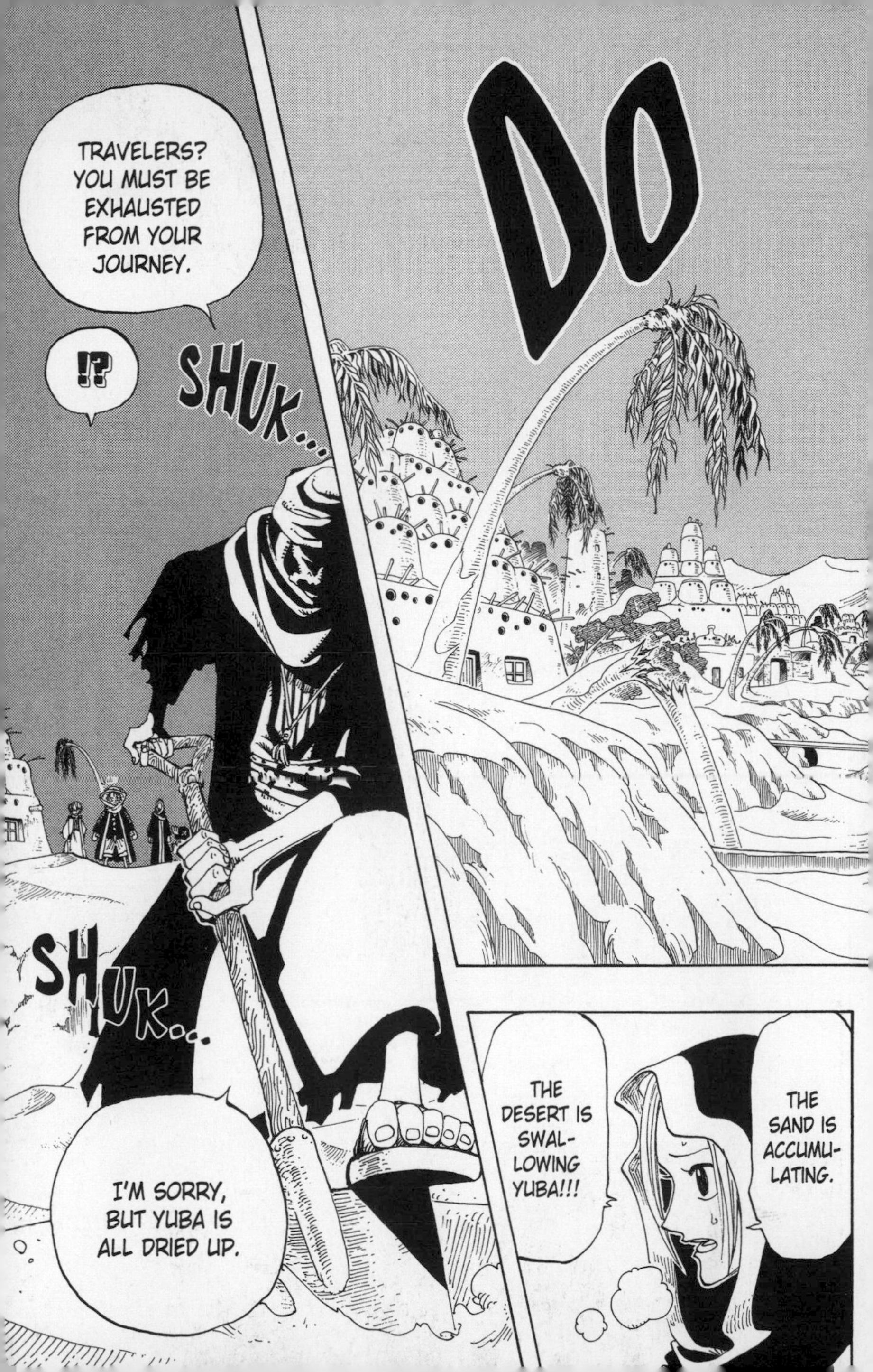
DO
THE SAND IS ACCUMULATING.
THE DESERT IS SWALLOWING YUBA!!!
SHUK...
TRAVELERS? YOU MUST BE EXHAUSTED FROM YOUR JOURNEY.
!?
SHUK...
I'M SORRY, BUT YUBA IS ALL DRIED UP.

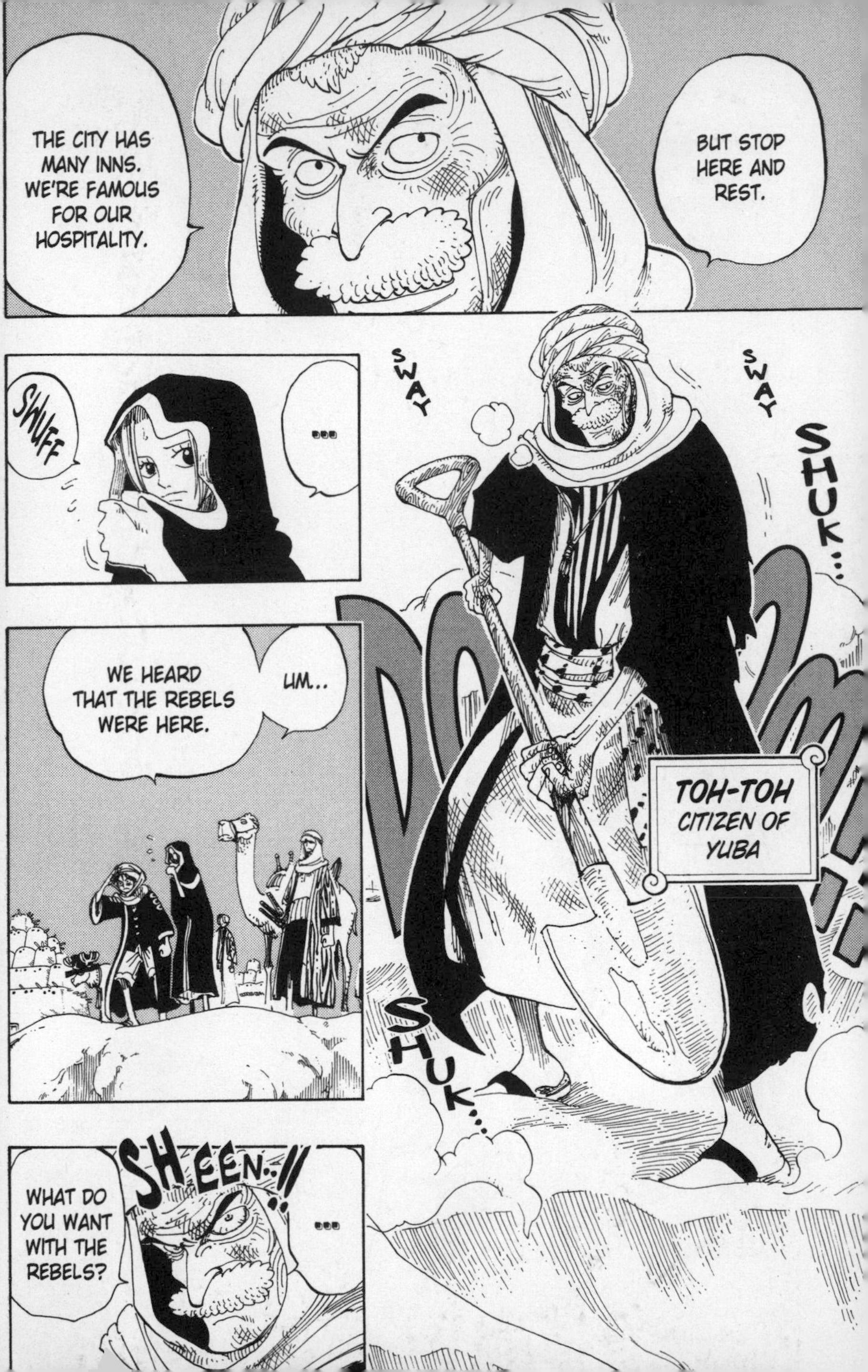
BUT STOP HERE AND REST.
THE CITY HAS MANY INNS. WE'RE FAMOUS FOR OUR HOSPITALITY.
SWAY
SWAY
SHUK...
DOOM
TOH-TOH CITIZEN OF YUBA
SHUK...
...
SNUFF
UM...
WE HEARD THAT THE REBELS WERE HERE.
...
SHEEN..!!
WHAT DO YOU WANT WITH THE REBELS?

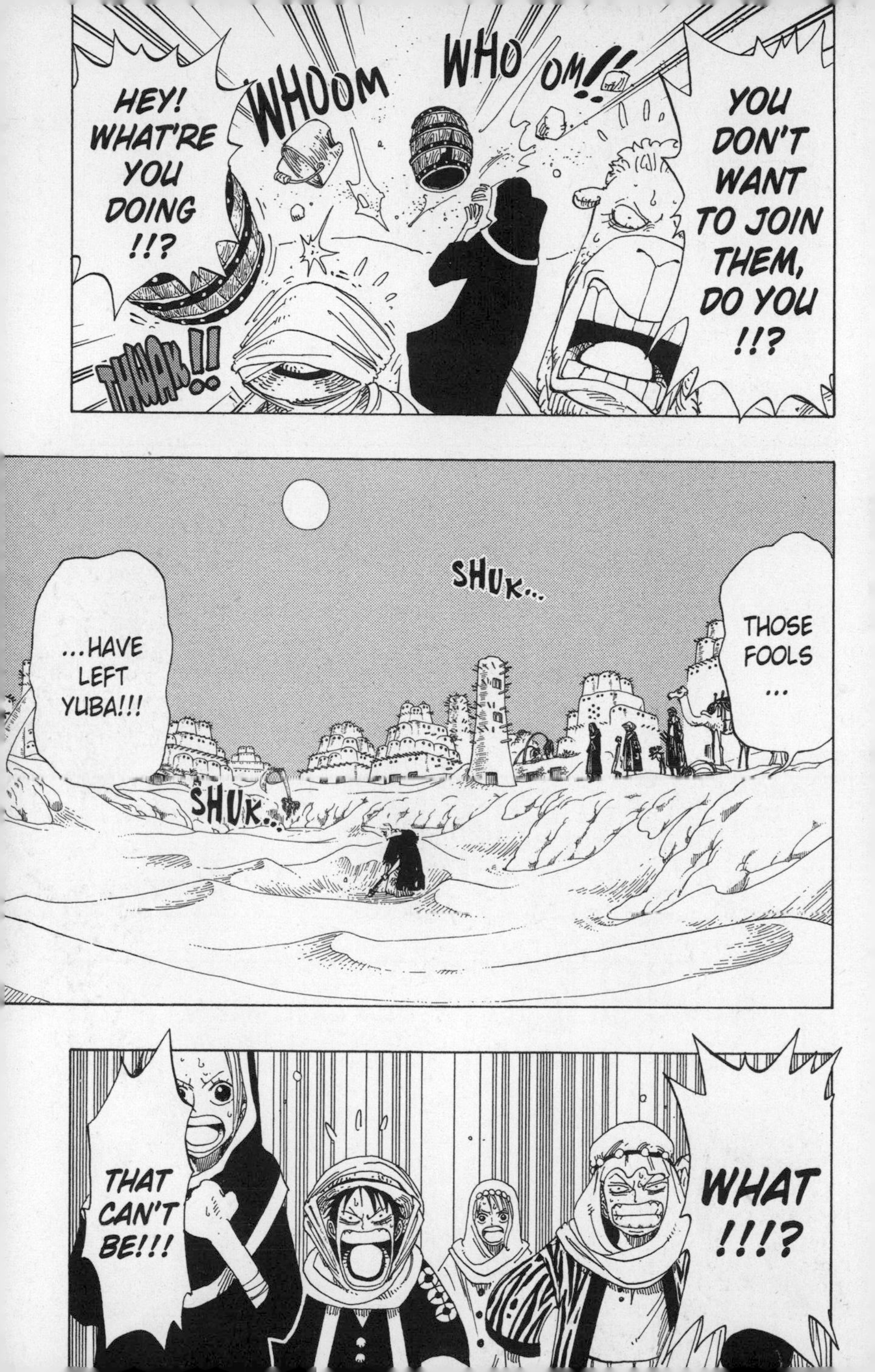
YOU DON'T WANT TO JOIN THEM, DO YOU !!?
WHO OM!!
WHOOM
HEY! WHAT'RE YOU DOING !!?
THWAK!!
THOSE FOOLS ...
SHUK...
...HAVE LEFT YUBA!!!
SHUK...
WHAT !!!?
THAT CAN'T BE!!!

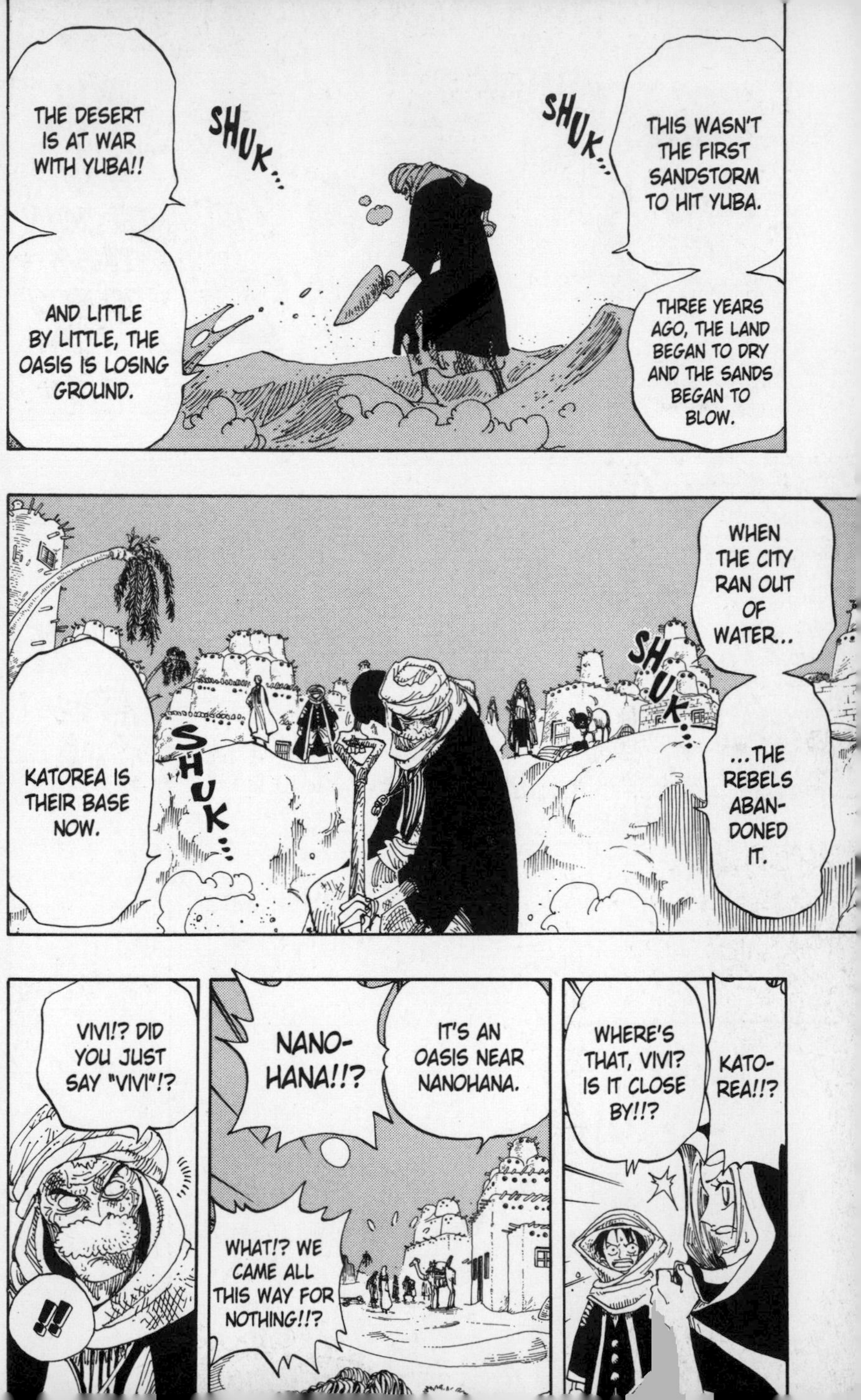
SHUK...
THIS WASN'T THE FIRST SANDSTORM TO HIT YUBA.
THREE YEARS AGO, THE LAND BEGAN TO DRY AND THE SANDS BEGAN TO BLOW.
SHUK...
THE DESERT IS AT WAR WITH YUBA!!
AND LITTLE BY LITTLE, THE OASIS IS LOSING GROUND.
WHEN THE CITY RAN OUT OF WATER...
SHUK...
...THE REBELS ABAN-DONED IT.
SHUK...
KATOREA IS THEIR BASE NOW.
KATO-REA!!?
WHERE'S THAT, VIVI? IS IT CLOSE BY!!?
IT'S AN OASIS NEAR NANOHANA.
NANO-HANA!!?
WHAT!? WE CAME ALL THIS WAY FOR NOTHING!!?
VIVI!? DID YOU JUST SAY "VIVI"!?
!!

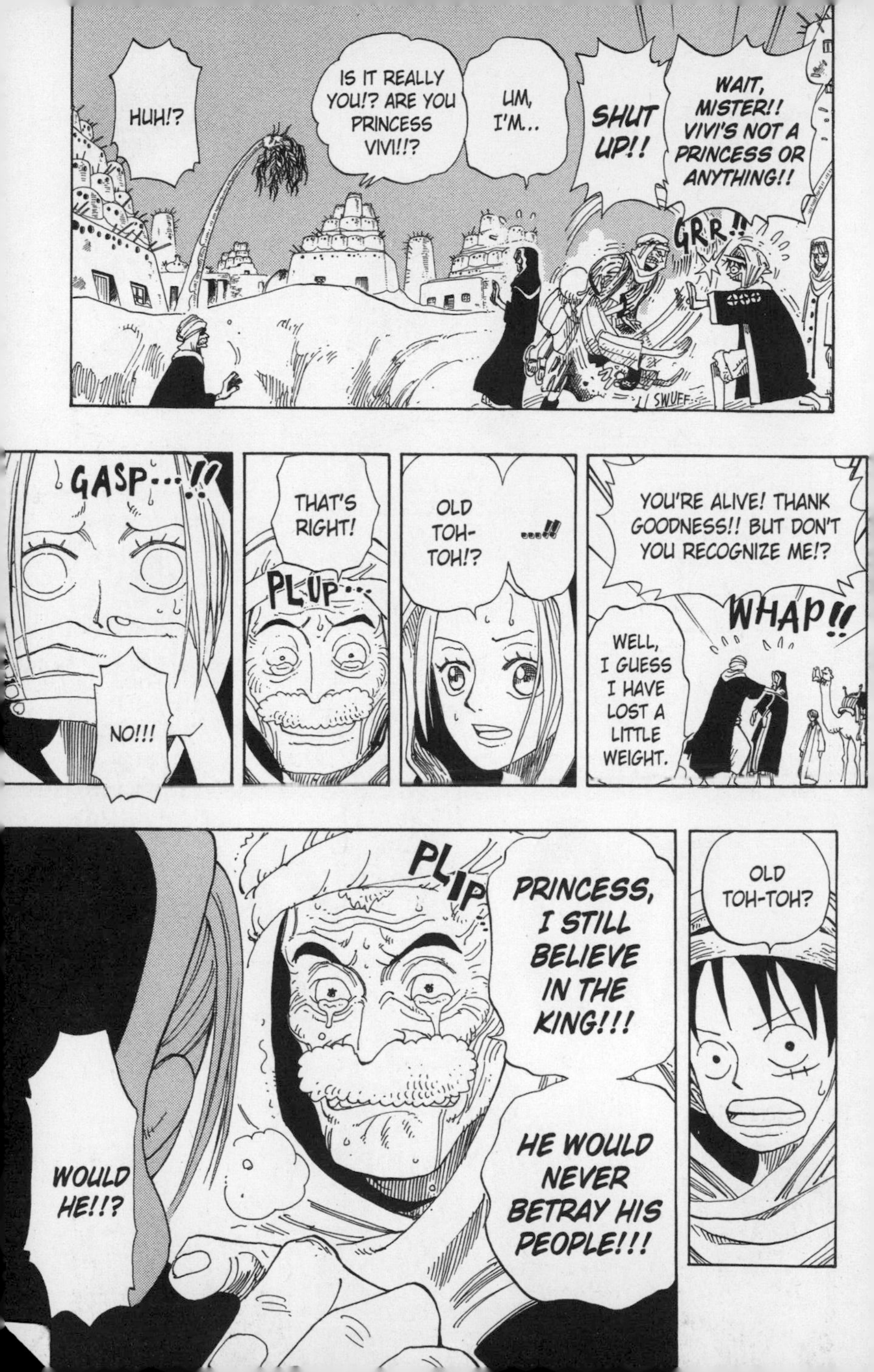
WAIT, MISTER!! VIVI'S NOT A PRINCESS OR ANYTHING!!
SHUT UP!!
UM, I'M...
IS IT REALLY YOU!? ARE YOU PRINCESS VIVI!!?
HUH!?
GRR!!
SWUFF
YOU'RE ALIVE! THANK GOODNESS!! BUT DON'T YOU RECOGNIZE ME!?
WHAP!!
WELL, I GUESS I HAVE LOST A LITTLE WEIGHT.
OLD TOH-TOH!?
...!!
THAT'S RIGHT!
PLUP...
GASP...!!
NO!!!
OLD TOH-TOH?
PLIP
PRINCESS, I STILL BELIEVE IN THE KING!!!
HE WOULD NEVER BETRAY HIS PEOPLE!!!
WOULD HE!!?

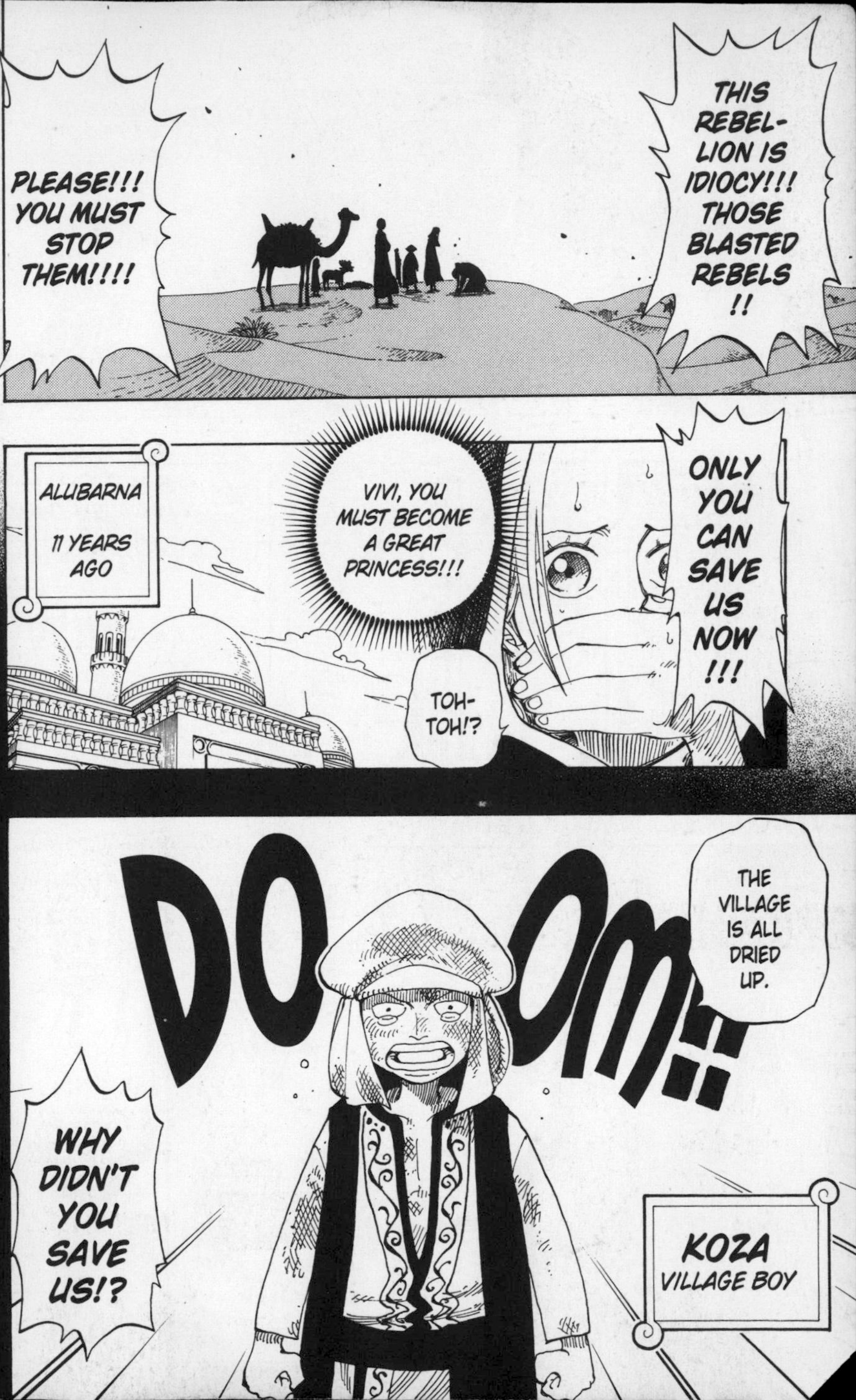
THIS REBEL-LION IS IDIOCY!!! THOSE BLASTED REBELS!!
PLEASE!!! YOU MUST STOP THEM!!!!
ONLY YOU CAN SAVE US NOW!!!
VIVI, YOU MUST BECOME A GREAT PRINCESS!!!
ALUBARNA 11 YEARS AGO
TOH-TOH!?
THE VILLAGE IS ALL DRIED UP.
DO OM!!
KOZA VILLAGE BOY
WHY DIDN'T YOU SAVE US!?

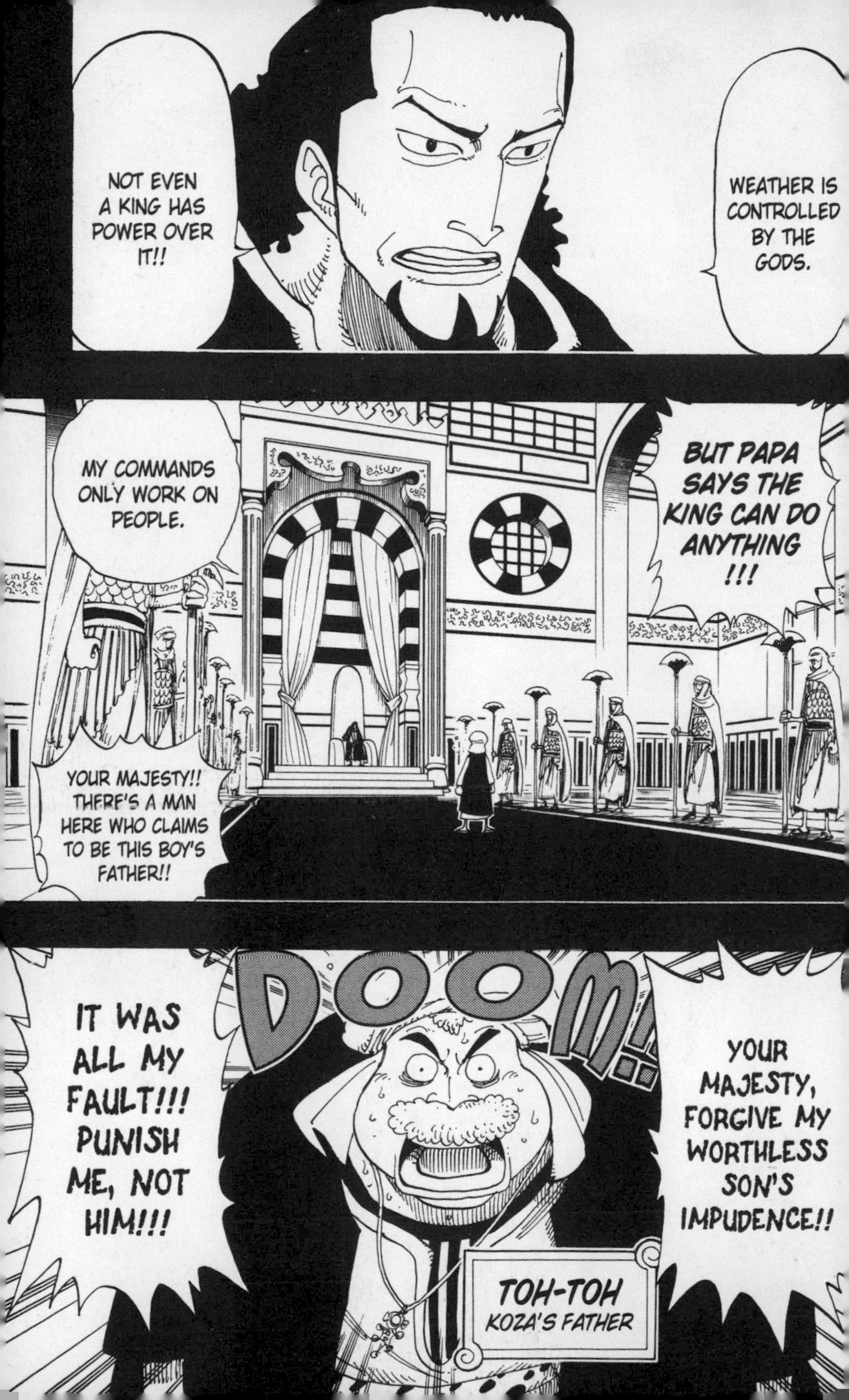
WEATHER IS CONTROLLED BY THE GODS.
NOT EVEN A KING HAS POWER OVER IT!!
BUT PAPA SAYS THE KING CAN DO ANYTHING !!!
MY COMMANDS ONLY WORK ON PEOPLE.
YOUR MAJESTY!! THERE'S A MAN HERE WHO CLAIMS TO BE THIS BOY'S FATHER!!
DOOM!!
YOUR MAJESTY, FORGIVE MY WORTHLESS SON'S IMPUDENCE!!
IT WAS ALL MY FAULT!!! PUNISH ME, NOT HIM!!!
TOH-TOH
KOZA'S FATHER

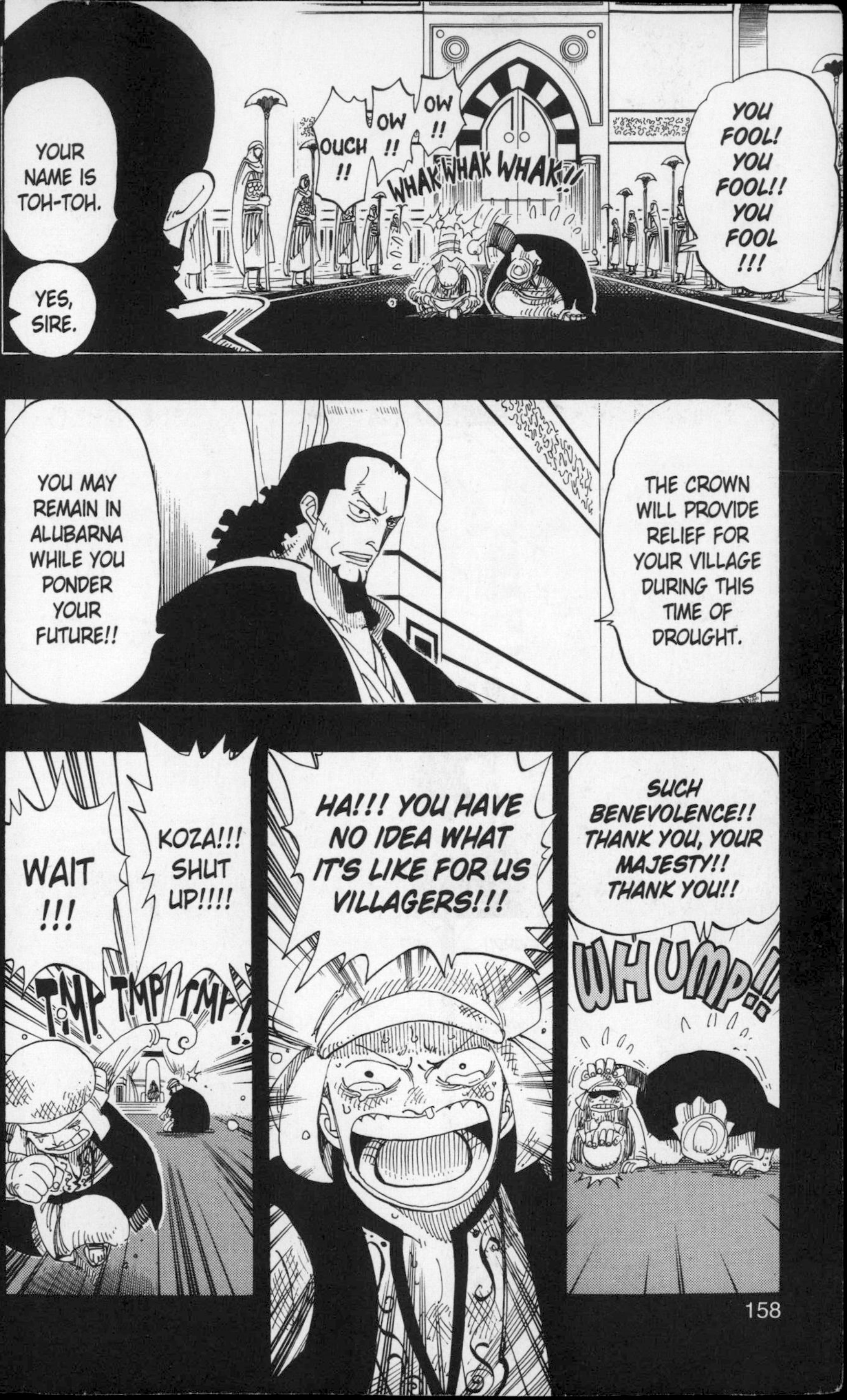
YOU FOOL! YOU FOOL!! YOU FOOL !!!
WHAK WHAK WHAK!!
OW !!
OW !!
OUCH !!
YOUR NAME IS TOH-TOH.
YES, SIRE.
THE CROWN WILL PROVIDE RELIEF FOR YOUR VILLAGE DURING THIS TIME OF DROUGHT.
YOU MAY REMAIN IN ALUBARNA WHILE YOU PONDER YOUR FUTURE!!
SUCH BENEVOLENCE!! THANK YOU, YOUR MAJESTY!! THANK YOU!!
WHUMP!!
HA!!! YOU HAVE NO IDEA WHAT IT'S LIKE FOR US VILLAGERS!!!
KOZA!!! SHUT UP!!!!
WAIT !!!
TMP TMP TMP!!

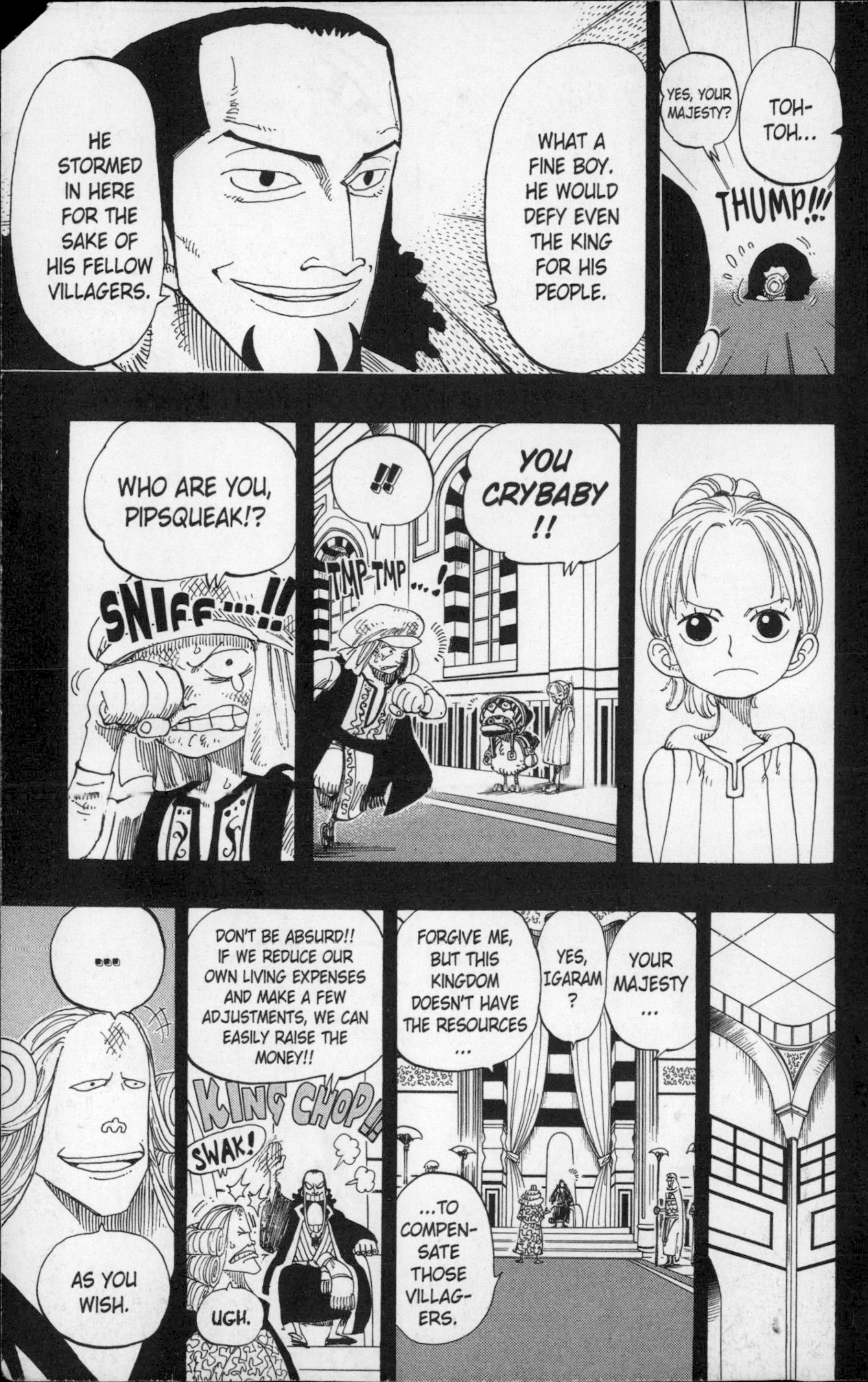
TOH-TOH...
YES, YOUR MAJESTY?
THUMP!!!
WHAT A FINE BOY. HE WOULD DEFY EVEN THE KING FOR HIS PEOPLE.
HE STORMED IN HERE FOR THE SAKE OF HIS FELLOW VILLAGERS.
YOU CRYBABY!!
!!
TMP TMP...!
WHO ARE YOU, PIPSQUEAK!?
SNIFF...!!
YOUR MAJESTY...
YES, IGARAM?
FORGIVE ME, BUT THIS KINGDOM DOESN'T HAVE THE RESOURCES...
...TO COMPENSATE THOSE VILLAGERS.
DON'T BE ABSURD!! IF WE REDUCE OUR OWN LIVING EXPENSES AND MAKE A FEW ADJUSTMENTS, WE CAN EASILY RAISE THE MONEY!!
KING CHOP!!
SWAK!
UGH.
...
AS YOU WISH.

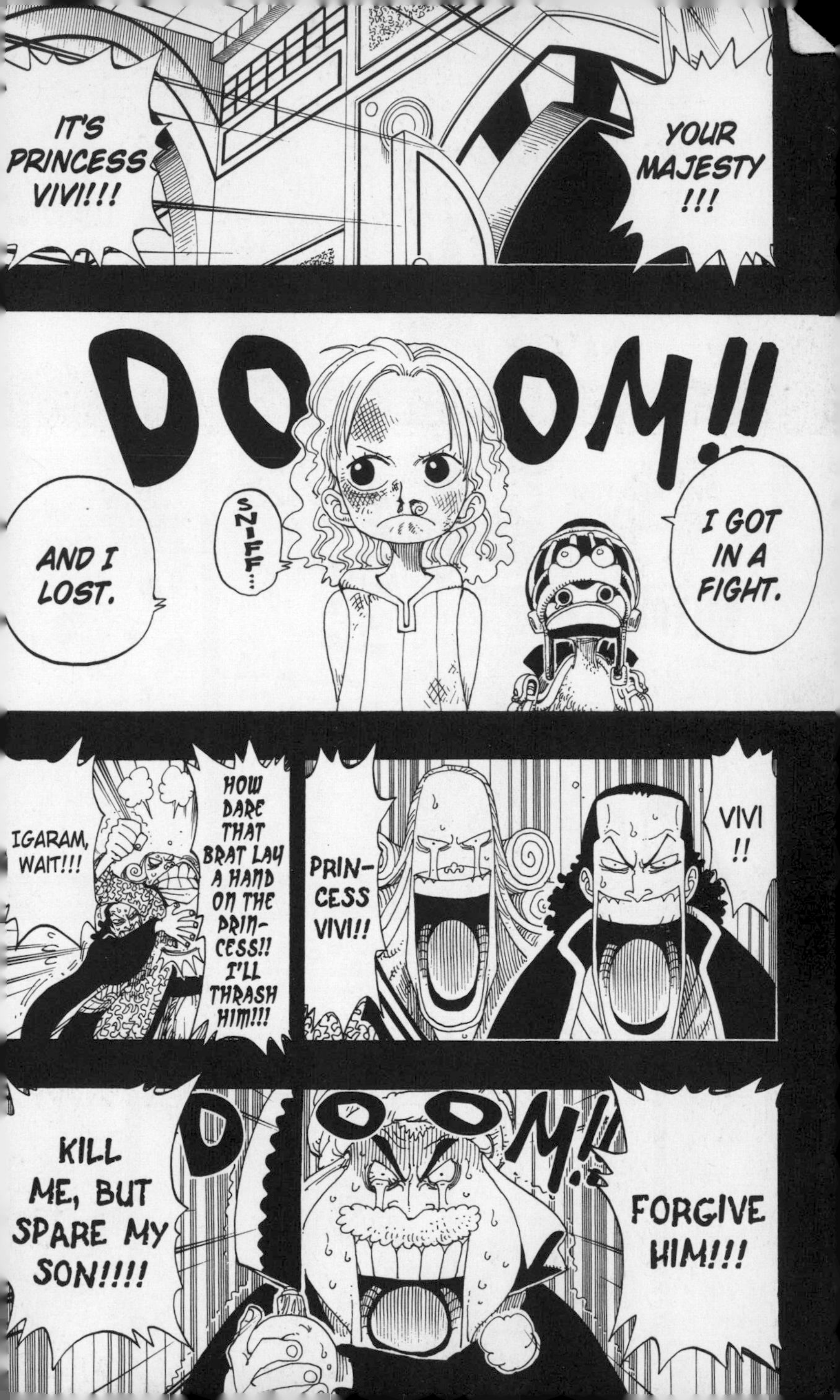
YOUR MAJESTY!!!
IT'S PRINCESS VIVI!!!
DOOM!!
I GOT IN A FIGHT.
SNIFF...
AND I LOST.
VIVI!!
PRIN-CESS VIVI!!
HOW DARE THAT BRAT LAY A HAND ON THE PRIN-CESS!! I'LL THRASH HIM!!!
IGARAM, WAIT!!!
FORGIVE HIM!!!
DOOM!!
KILL ME, BUT SPARE MY SON!!!!

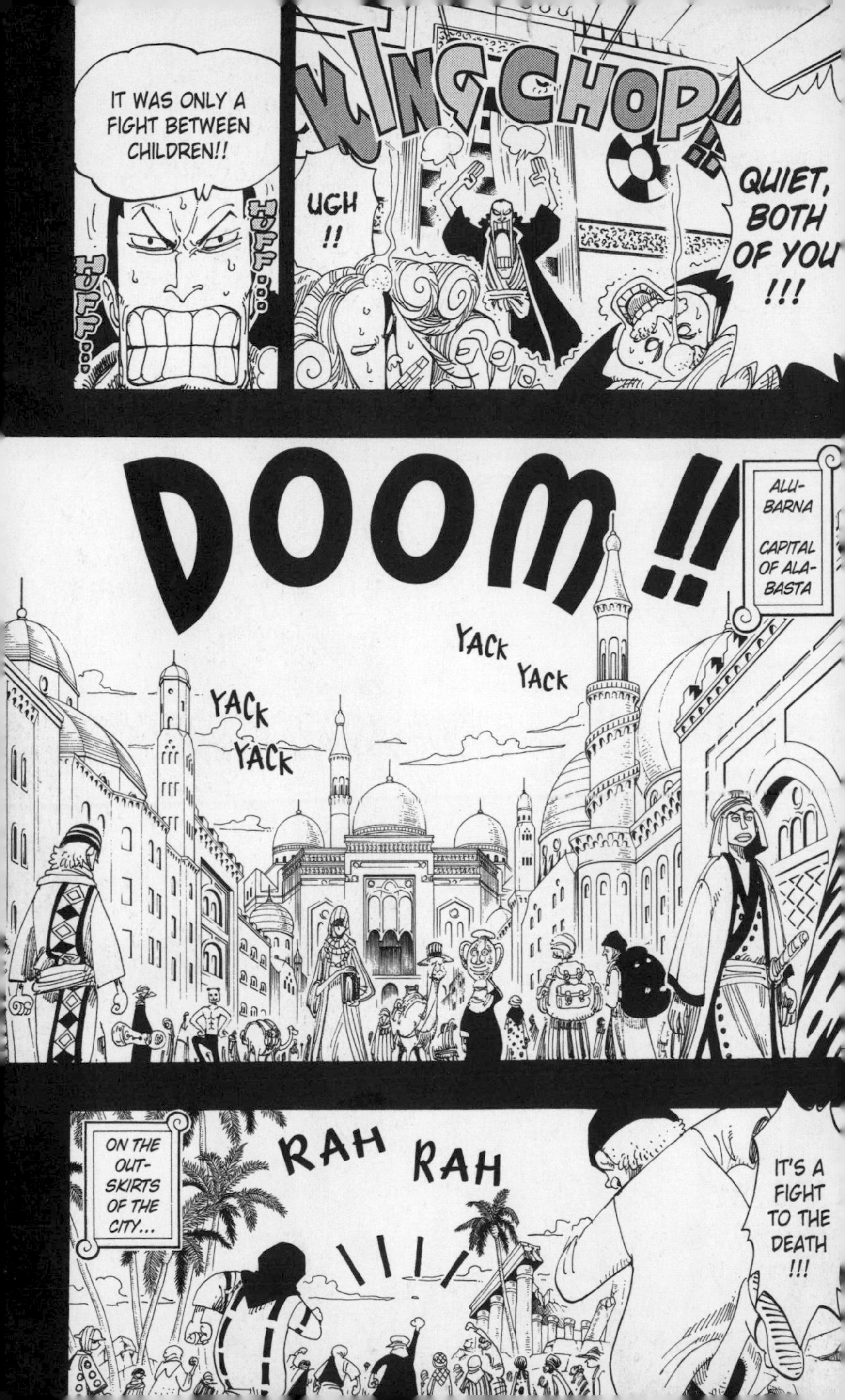
WING CHOP
QUIET, BOTH OF YOU!!!
UGH!!
IT WAS ONLY A FIGHT BETWEEN CHILDREN!!
HUFF HUFF...
HUFF...
ALUBARNA
CAPITAL OF ALABASTA
DOOM!!
YACK YACK
YACK YACK
ON THE OUTSKIRTS OF THE CITY...
RAH RAH
IT'S A FIGHT TO THE DEATH!!!

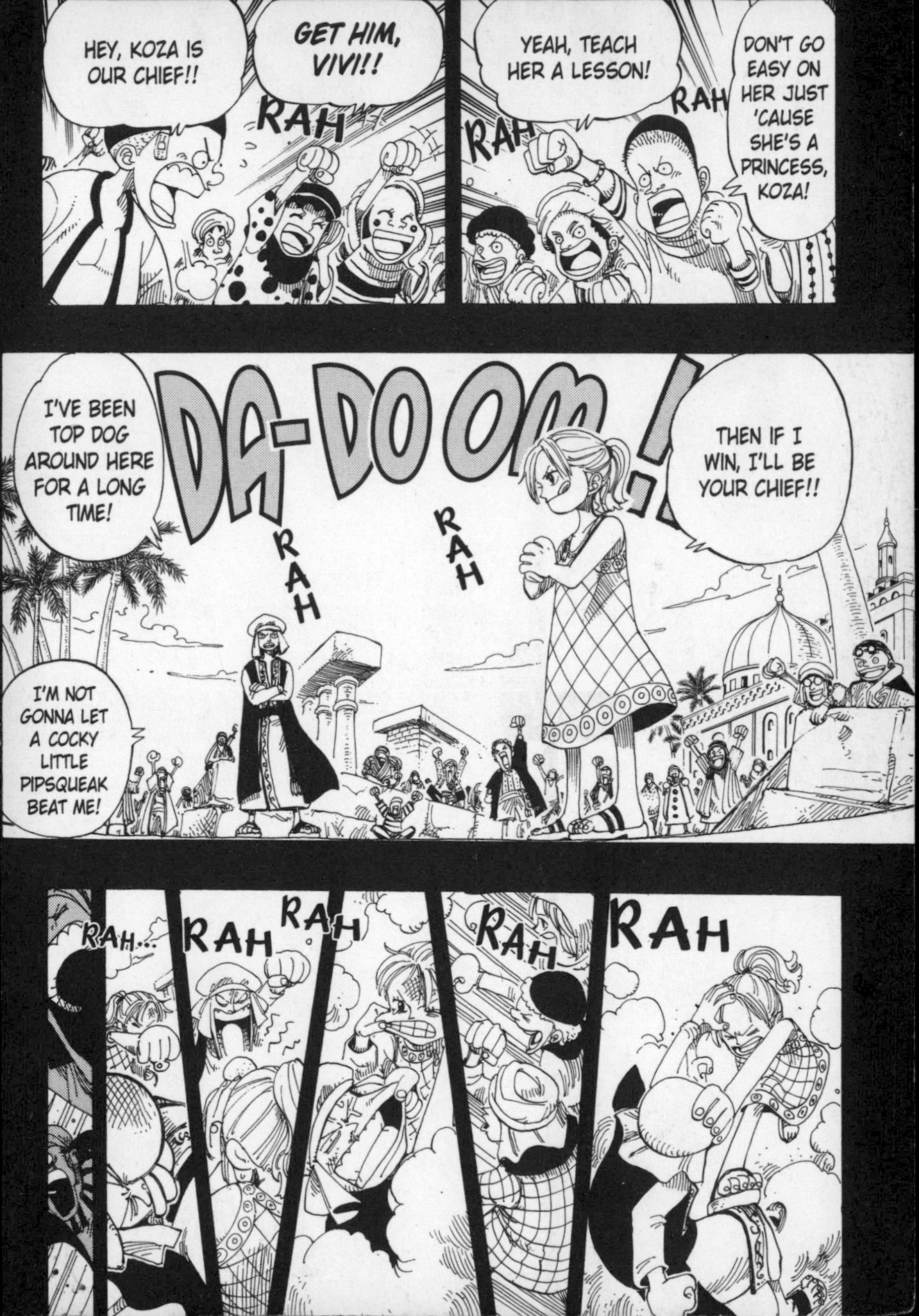
DON'T GO EASY ON HER JUST 'CAUSE SHE'S A PRINCESS, KOZA!
RAH
YEAH, TEACH HER A LESSON!
RAH
GET HIM, VIVI!!
HEY, KOZA IS OUR CHIEF!!
RAH
THEN IF I WIN, I'LL BE YOUR CHIEF!!
DA-DOOM!!
RAH
RAH
I'VE BEEN TOP DOG AROUND HERE FOR A LONG TIME!
I'M NOT GONNA LET A COCKY LITTLE PIPSQUEAK BEAT ME!
RAH
RAH
RAH
RAH
RAH...

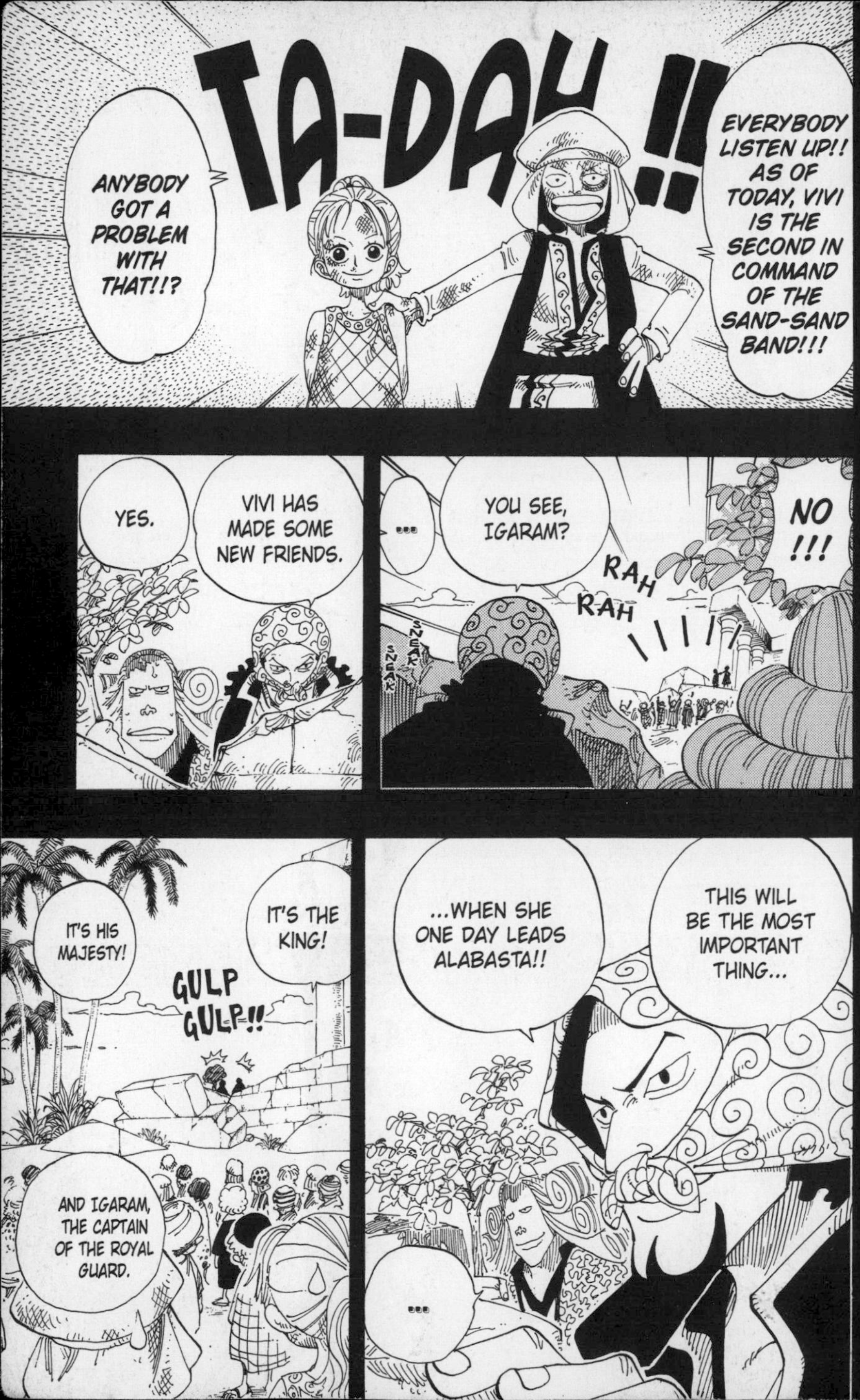
EVERYBODY LISTEN UP!! AS OF TODAY, VIVI IS THE SECOND IN COMMAND OF THE SAND-SAND BAND!!!
TA-DAH!!
ANYBODY GOT A PROBLEM WITH THAT!!?
NO !!!
RAH RAH
YOU SEE, IGARAM?
...
SNEAK SNEAK
VIVI HAS MADE SOME NEW FRIENDS.
YES.
THIS WILL BE THE MOST IMPORTANT THING...
...WHEN SHE ONE DAY LEADS ALABASTA!!
...
IT'S THE KING!
IT'S HIS MAJESTY!
GULP GULP!!
AND IGARAM, THE CAPTAIN OF THE ROYAL GUARD.

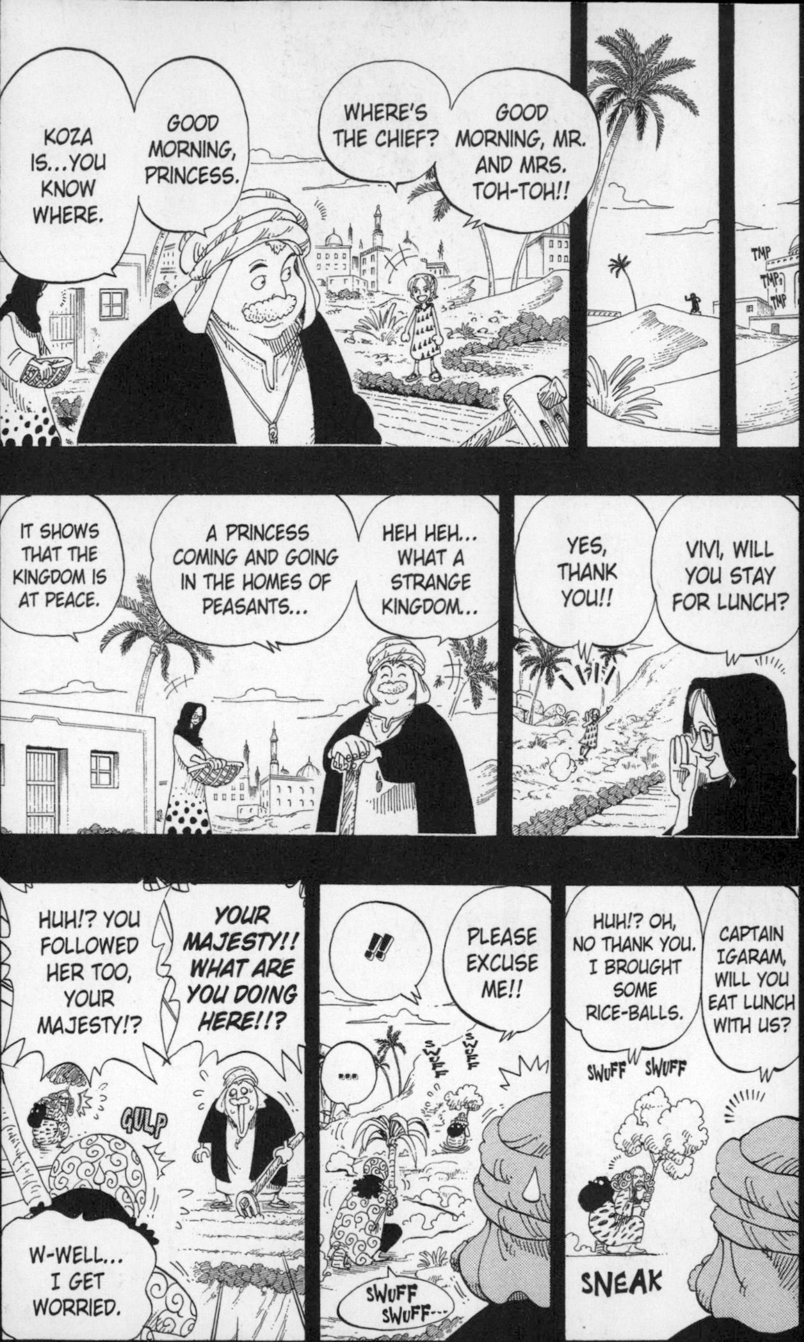
TMP
TMP
TMP
GOOD MORNING, MR. AND MRS. TOH-TOH!!
WHERE'S THE CHIEF?
GOOD MORNING, PRINCESS.
KOZA IS...YOU KNOW WHERE.
VIVI, WILL YOU STAY FOR LUNCH?
YES, THANK YOU!!
HEH HEH... WHAT A STRANGE KINGDOM...
A PRINCESS COMING AND GOING IN THE HOMES OF PEASANTS...
IT SHOWS THAT THE KINGDOM IS AT PEACE.
CAPTAIN IGARAM, WILL YOU EAT LUNCH WITH US?
HUH!? OH, NO THANK YOU. I BROUGHT SOME RICE-BALLS.
SWUFF SWUFF
SNEAK
PLEASE EXCUSE ME!!
!!
SWUFF SWUFF
...
SWUFF SWUFF...
YOUR MAJESTY!! WHAT ARE YOU DOING HERE!!?
HUH!? YOU FOLLOWED HER TOO, YOUR MAJESTY!?
GULP
W-WELL... I GET WORRIED.

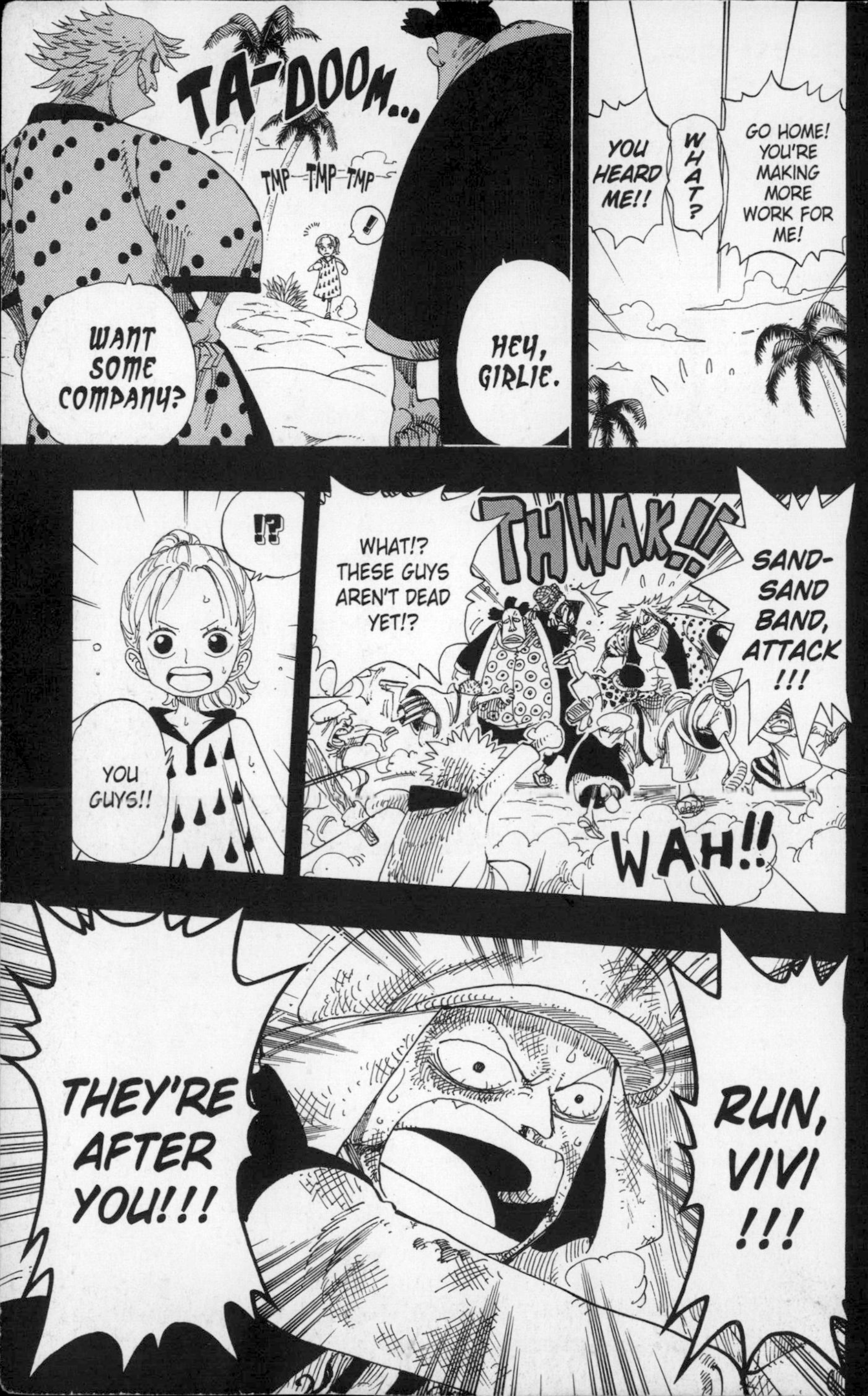
GO HOME! YOU'RE MAKING MORE WORK FOR ME!
WHAT?
YOU HEARD ME!!
TA-DOOM...
TMP TMP TMP
!
HEY, GIRLIE.
WANT SOME COMPANY?
SAND-SAND BAND, ATTACK!!!
THWAK!!
WHAT!? THESE GUYS AREN'T DEAD YET!?
WAH!!
!?
YOU GUYS!!
RUN, VIVI!!!
THEY'RE AFTER YOU!!!

Question Corner

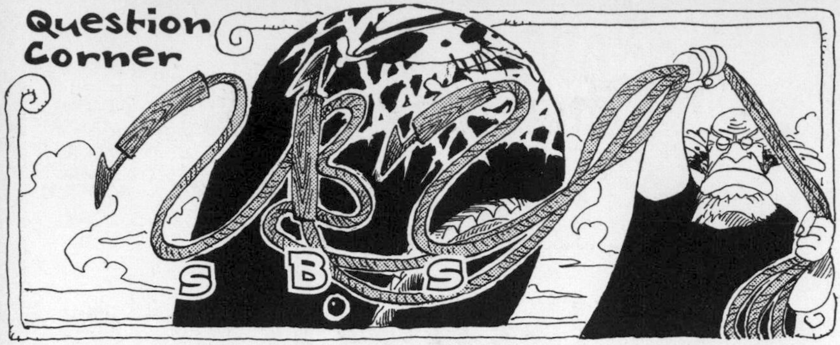
S.B.S.

Q: Hey, Oda Baby, just how bad is Zolo's sense of direction? Use Xs and Ys to explain!! By order of Zolo.

A: Er, let's see... X times y? Okay, next.

Q: We're a married couple and we're big fans of the Hiking Bear. ♡ How is one punished when one forgets to bow to him? (Mountain climbing etiquette.) This worries us so much that we can't make babies.

A: Can't make babies? That's a problem. But this is important, so please remember--the Hiking Bear loves mountains, and he never forgives bad-mannered climbers. The punishment is one hour of sitting, meditation style. This is harsh. After all, taking for granted the Bear's beloved mountains is a serious offense. (From *The Drum Animal Encyclopedia*)

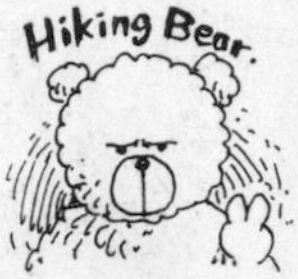
Hiking Bear.

Q: Hello, I have a question for you, Oda Sensei. "Krieg" is the German word for war. *One Piece* seems to have a lot of German in it. Is there a connection between pirates and Germany?

A: Hmm... I don't think so. I just selected words that had the meanings I wanted and a good "feeling" to them. The theme of the Krieg story was "war," so I chose a word that was easy to remember.

Q: Happy New Year!!
Hey, you!! Oda!! Can you beat up my gorilla?
This is the end of the Question Corner.

A: Hey, what's up!? Anyway, see you in the next volume. Huh? A gorilla? No way I can beat it up. Besides, it's got enormous spiritual power. But it likes bananas, right? Maybe I can use a banana to trap it.

Chapter 164:
I LOVE MY COUNTRY

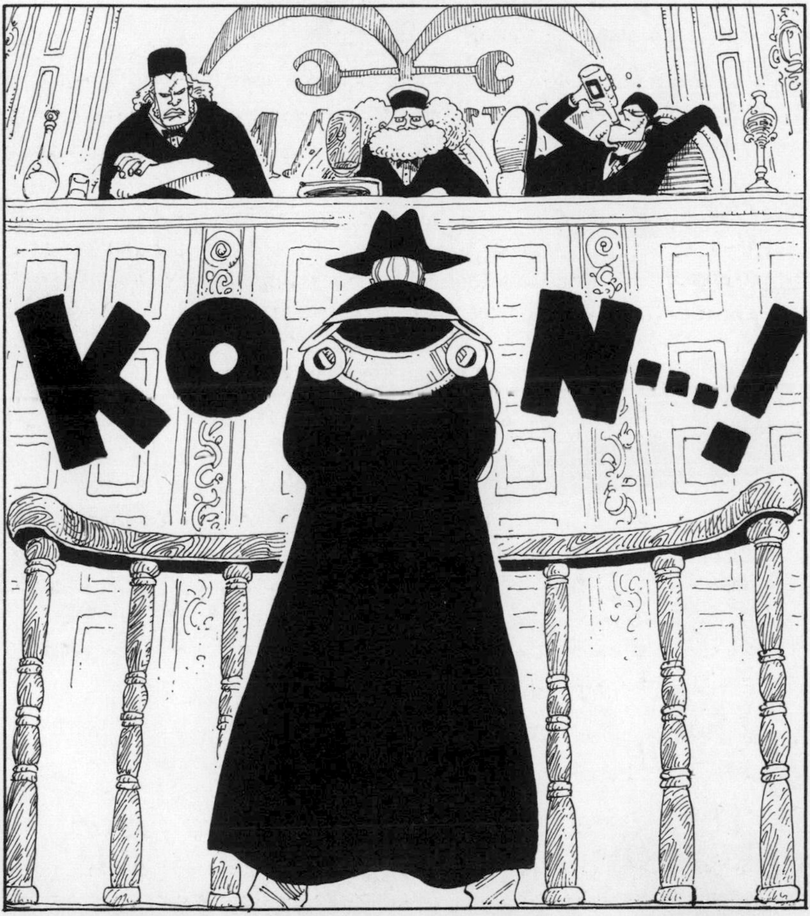
KO...N...!

DJANGO'S DANCE PARADISE, VOL. 30: "NAVAL HEADQUARTERS TRIAL VERDICT: DEATH BY HANGING"

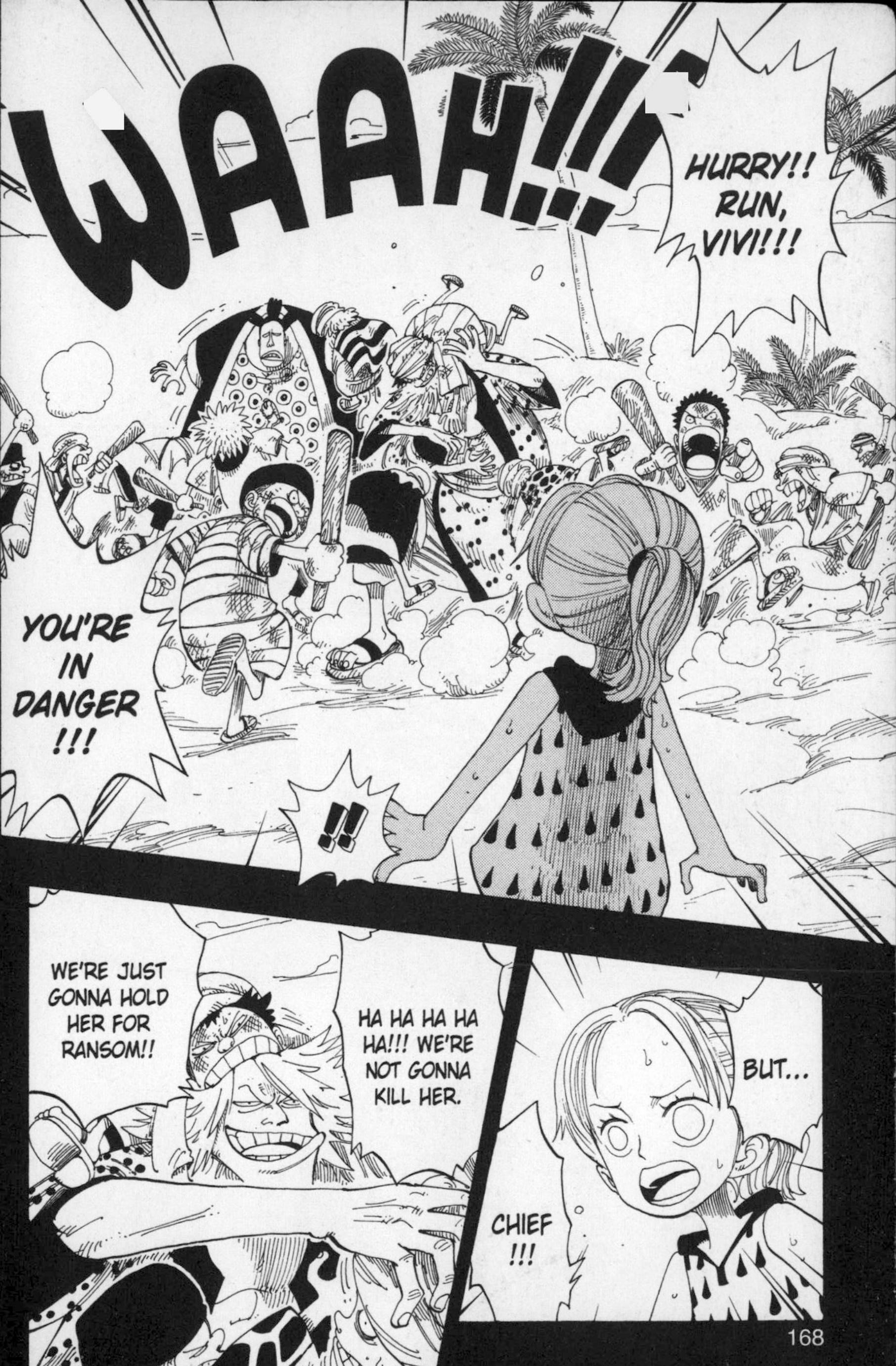
WAAAH!!!
HURRY!! RUN, VIVI!!!
YOU'RE IN DANGER!!!
!!
BUT...
CHIEF!!!
HA HA HA HA HA!!! WE'RE NOT GONNA KILL HER.
WE'RE JUST GONNA HOLD HER FOR RANSOM!!

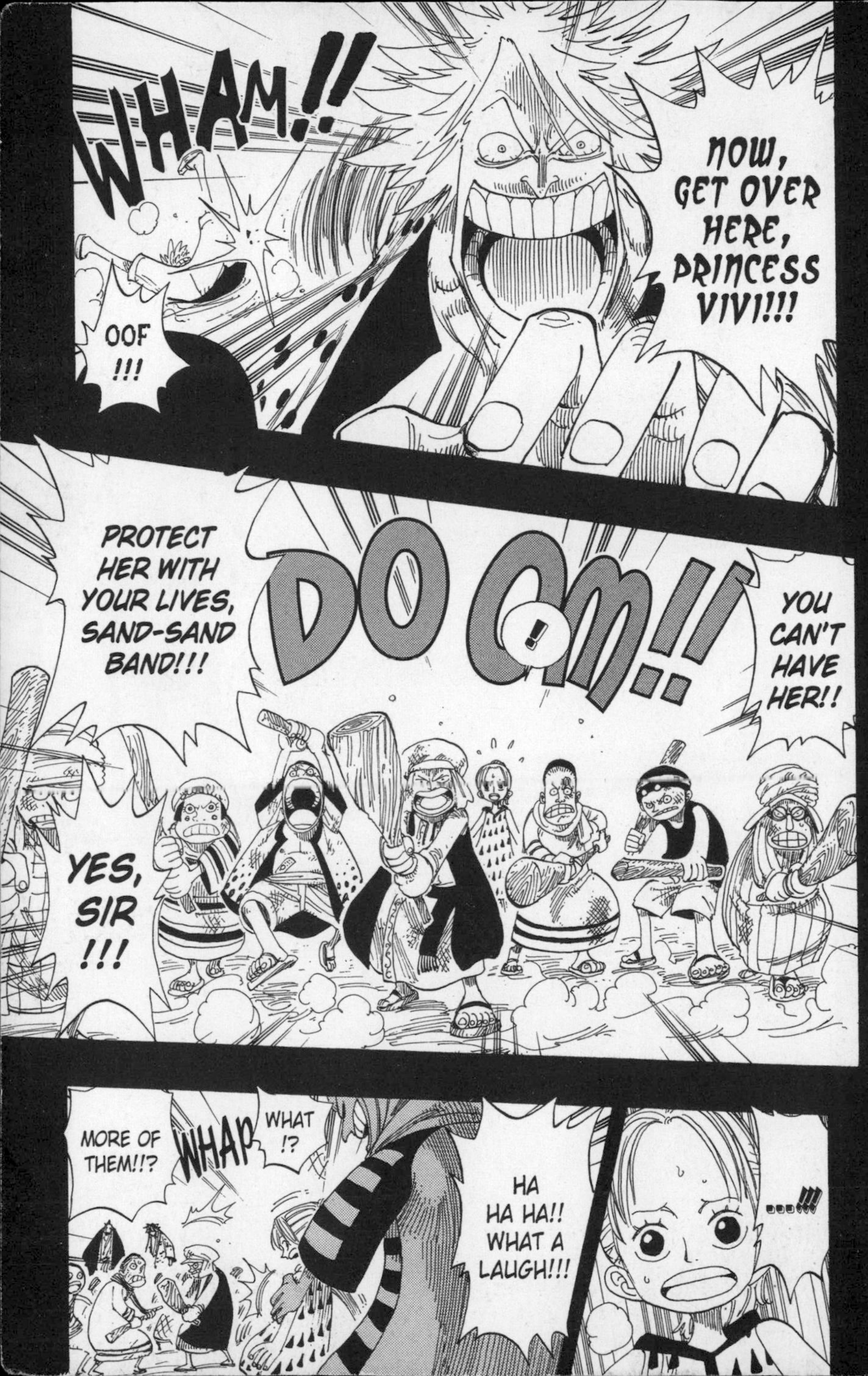
NOW, GET OVER HERE, PRINCESS VIVI!!!
WHAM!!
OOF !!!
YOU CAN'T HAVE HER!!
DOOM!!
PROTECT HER WITH YOUR LIVES, SAND-SAND BAND!!!
YES, SIR !!!
...!!!
HA HA HA!! WHAT A LAUGH!!!
WHAT !?
WHAP
MORE OF THEM!!?

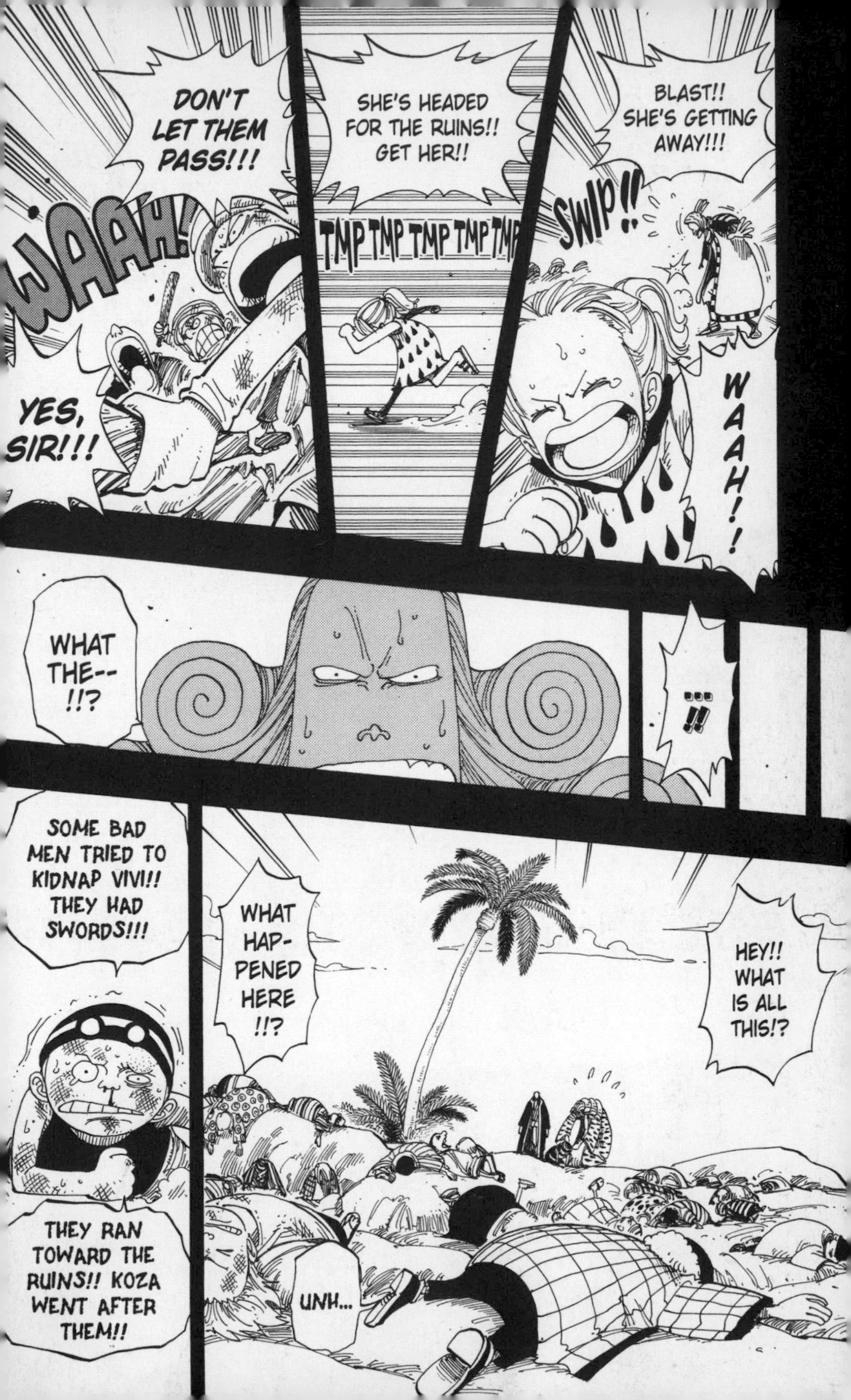
BLAST!! SHE'S GETTING AWAY!!!
SWIP!!
WAAH!!
SHE'S HEADED FOR THE RUINS!! GET HER!!
TMP TMP TMP TMP TMP
DON'T LET THEM PASS!!!
WAAH!
YES, SIR!!!
...!!
WHAT THE-- !!?
HEY!! WHAT IS ALL THIS!?
WHAT HAP-PENED HERE !!?
UNH...
SOME BAD MEN TRIED TO KIDNAP VIVI!! THEY HAD SWORDS!!!
THEY RAN TOWARD THE RUINS!! KOZA WENT AFTER THEM!!

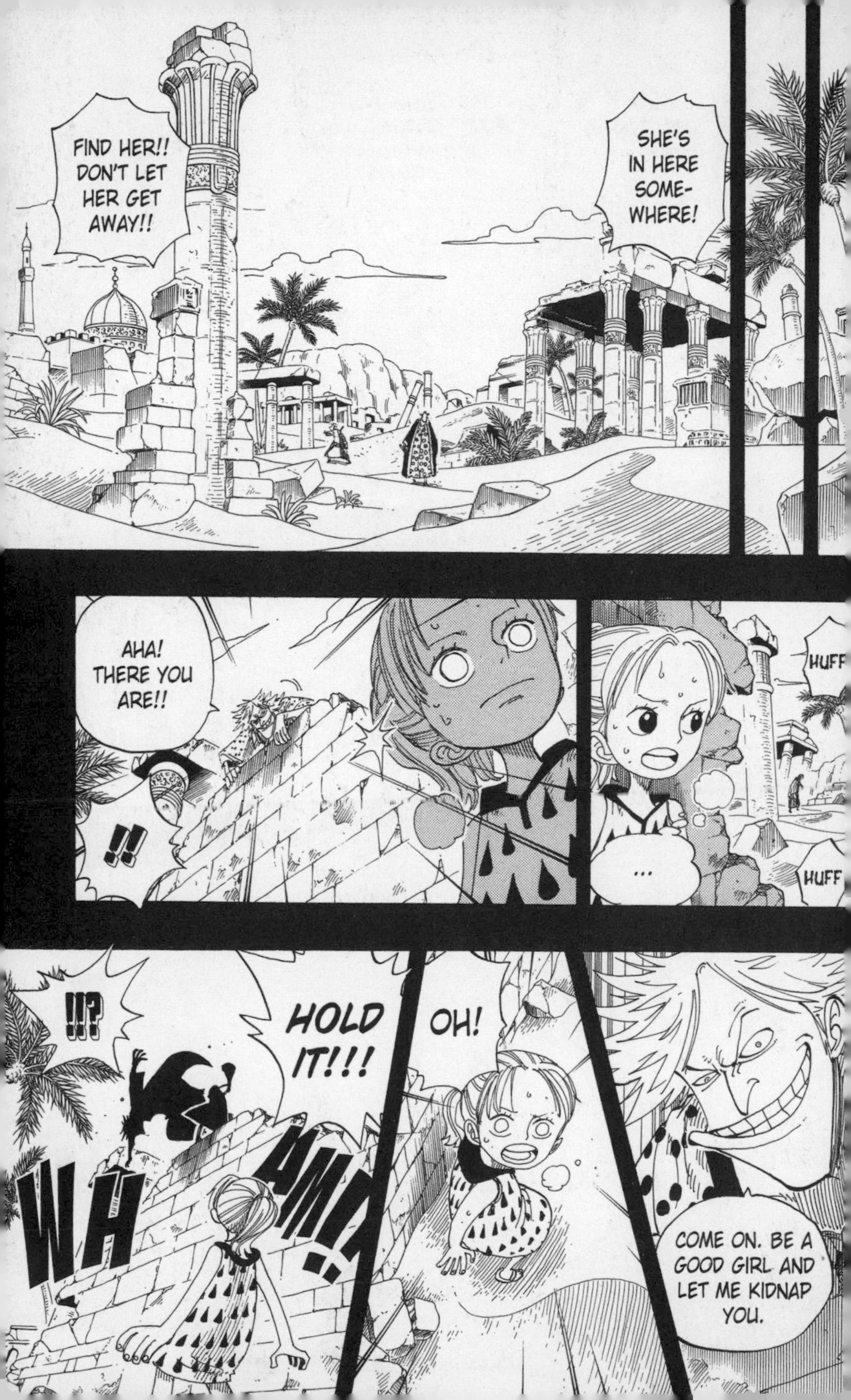
SHE'S IN HERE SOME-WHERE!
FIND HER!! DON'T LET HER GET AWAY!!
HUFF
...
HUFF
AHA! THERE YOU ARE!!
!!
COME ON. BE A GOOD GIRL AND LET ME KIDNAP YOU.
OH!
HOLD IT!!!
!!?
WHAM!!

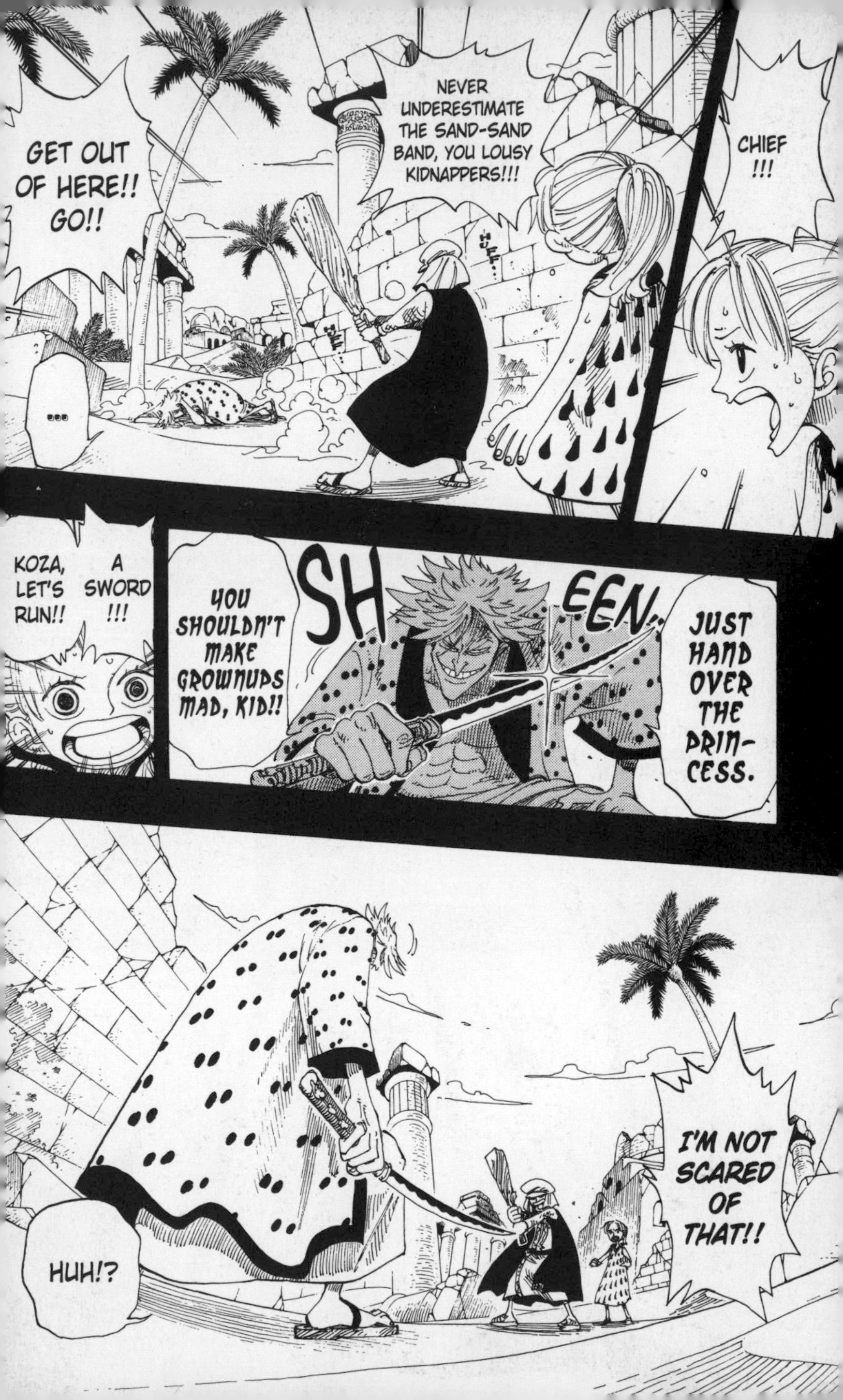
CHIEF!!!
NEVER UNDERESTIMATE THE SAND-SAND BAND, YOU LOUSY KIDNAPPERS!!!
HUFF...
GET OUT OF HERE!! GO!!
...
JUST HAND OVER THE PRIN-CESS.
SHEEN
YOU SHOULDN'T MAKE GROWNUPS MAD, KID!!
A SWORD!!!
KOZA, LET'S RUN!!
I'M NOT SCARED OF THAT!!
HUH!?

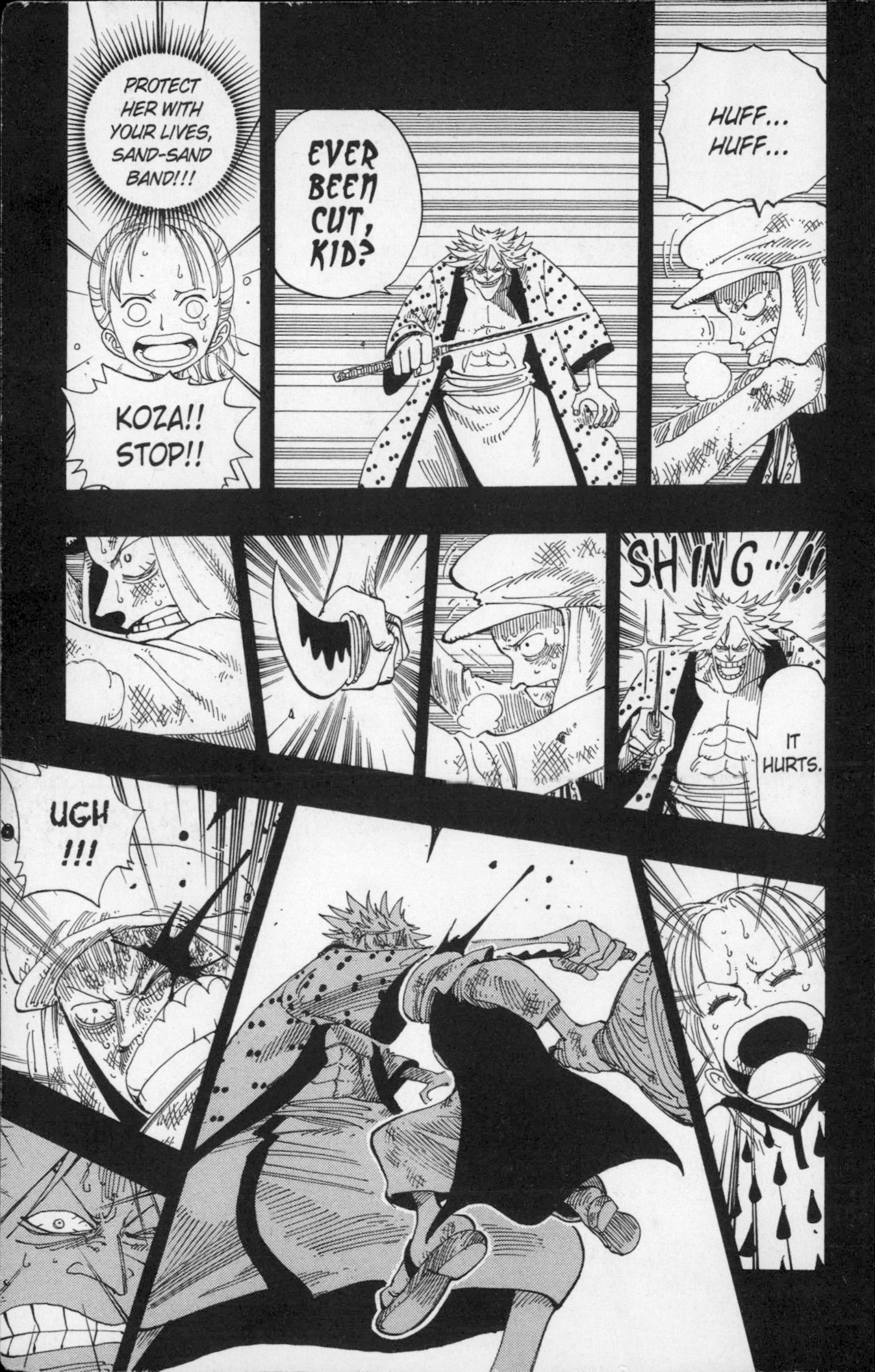
HUFF... HUFF...
EVER BEEN CUT, KID?
PROTECT HER WITH YOUR LIVES, SAND-SAND BAND!!!
KOZA!! STOP!!
SHING...!!
IT HURTS.
UGH !!!

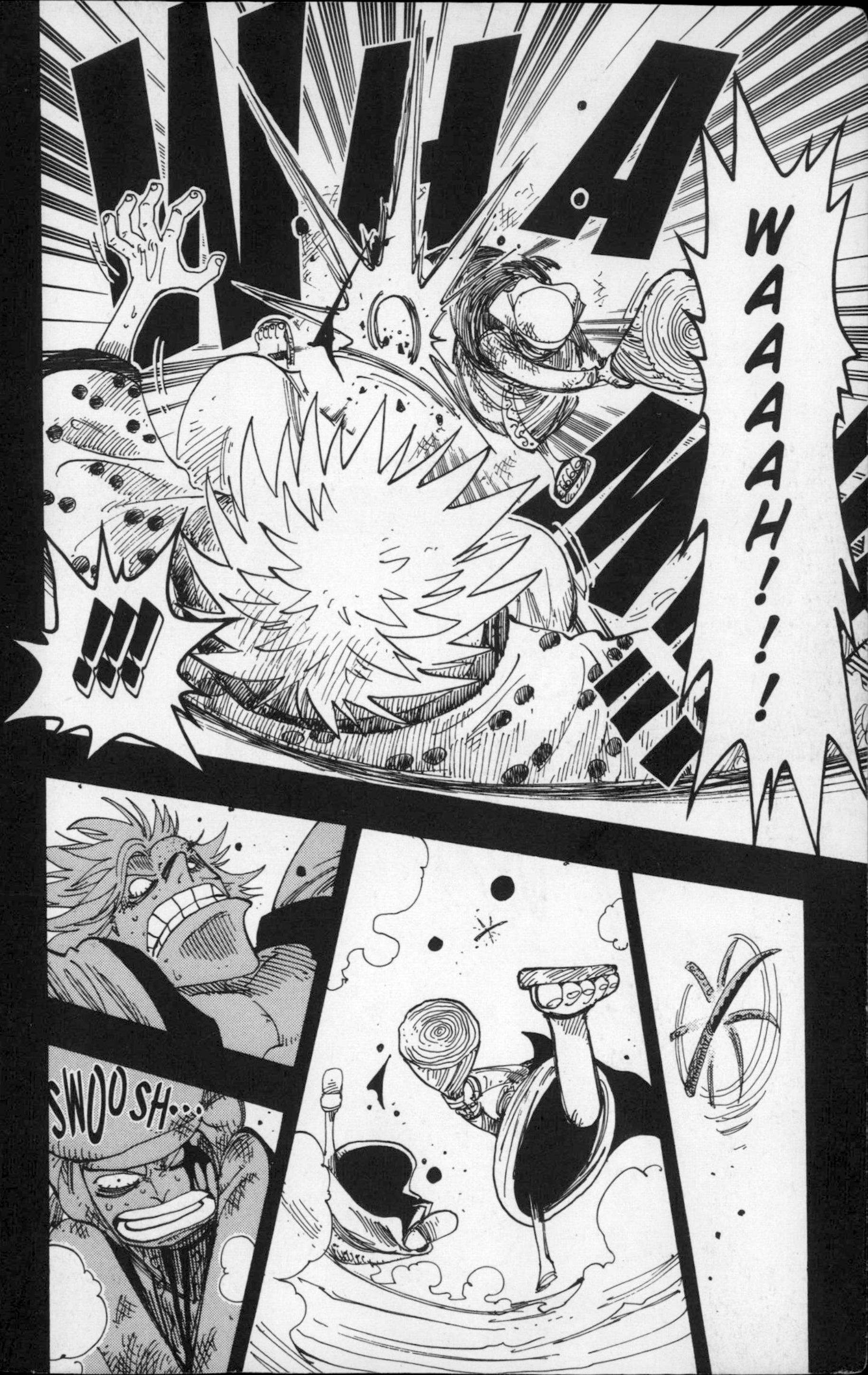
WAAAAH!!!
WHAM!!
!!!
SWOOSH...

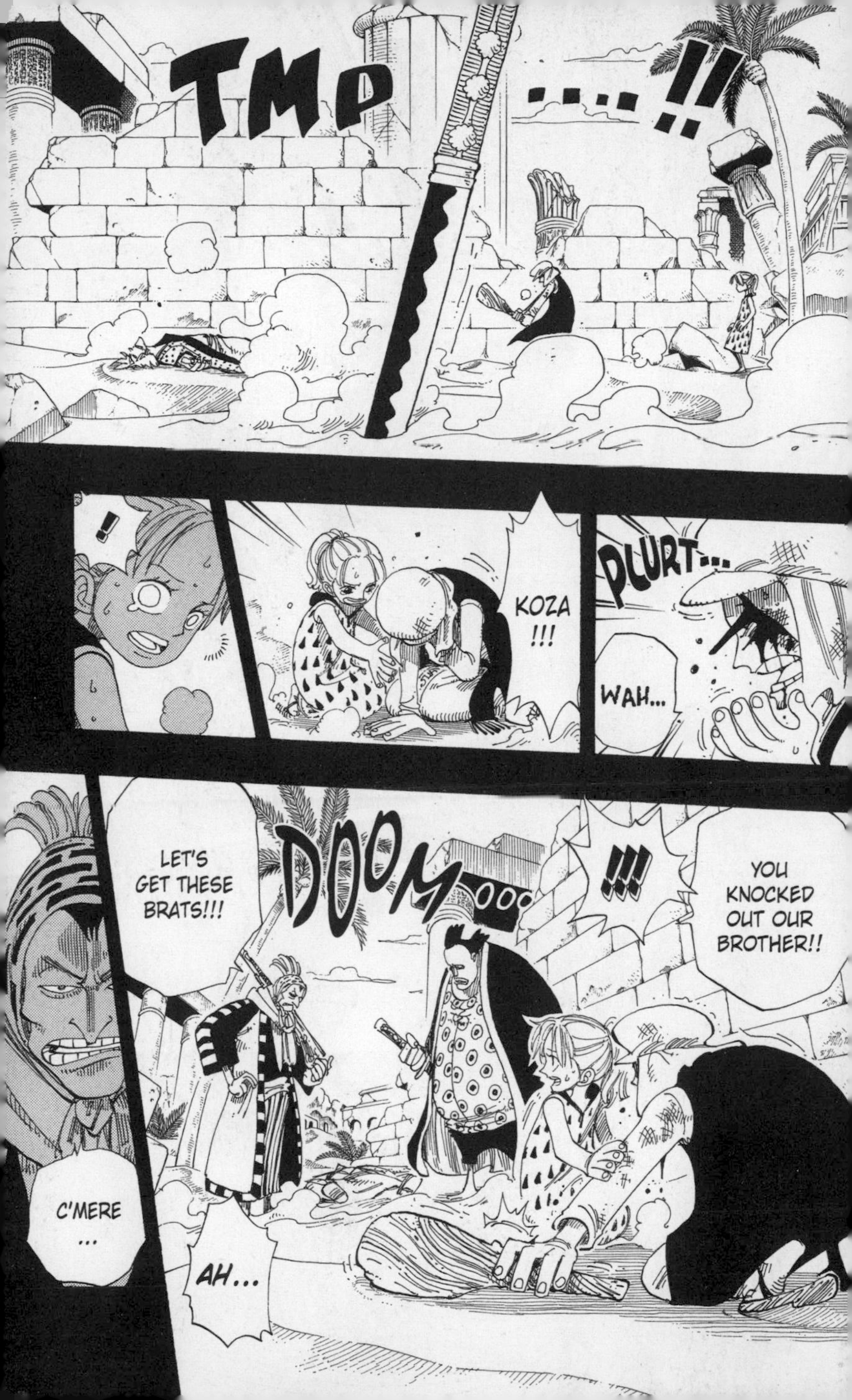

......!!
TMP
PLURT...
WAH...
KOZA !!!
!
YOU KNOCKED OUT OUR BROTHER!!
DOOM!!!
LET'S GET THESE BRATS!!!
AH...
C'MERE ...

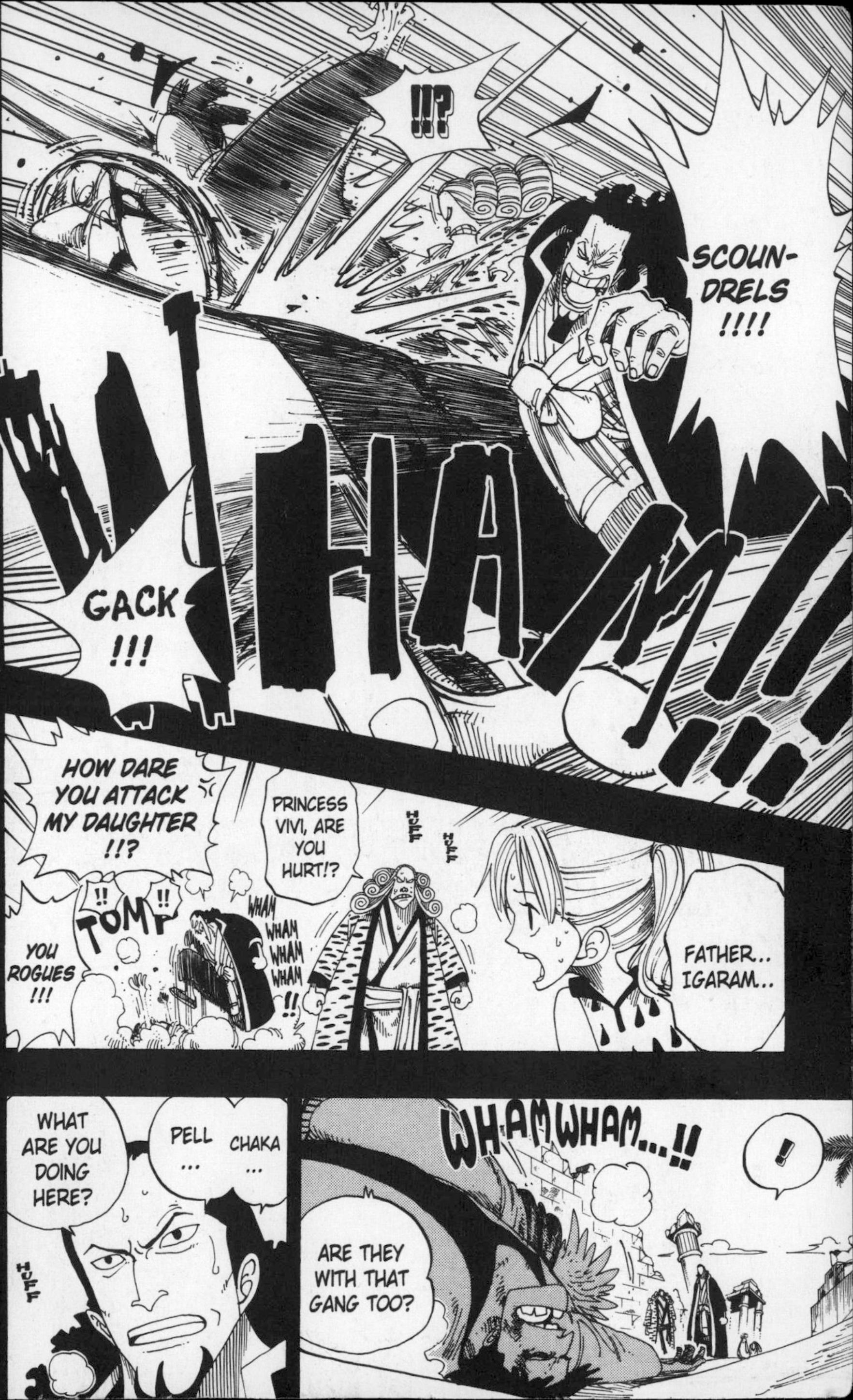
SCOUN-DRELS !!!!
!!?
WHAM!!...
GACK !!!
FATHER.. IGARAM..
PRINCESS VIVI, ARE YOU HURT!?
HUFF HUFF
HOW DARE YOU ATTACK MY DAUGHTER !!?
WHAM WHAM WHAM WHAM !!
!! TOMP !!
YOU ROGUES !!!
!
WHAM WHAM...!!
ARE THEY WITH THAT GANG TOO?
CHAKA ...
PELL ...
WHAT ARE YOU DOING HERE?
HUFF

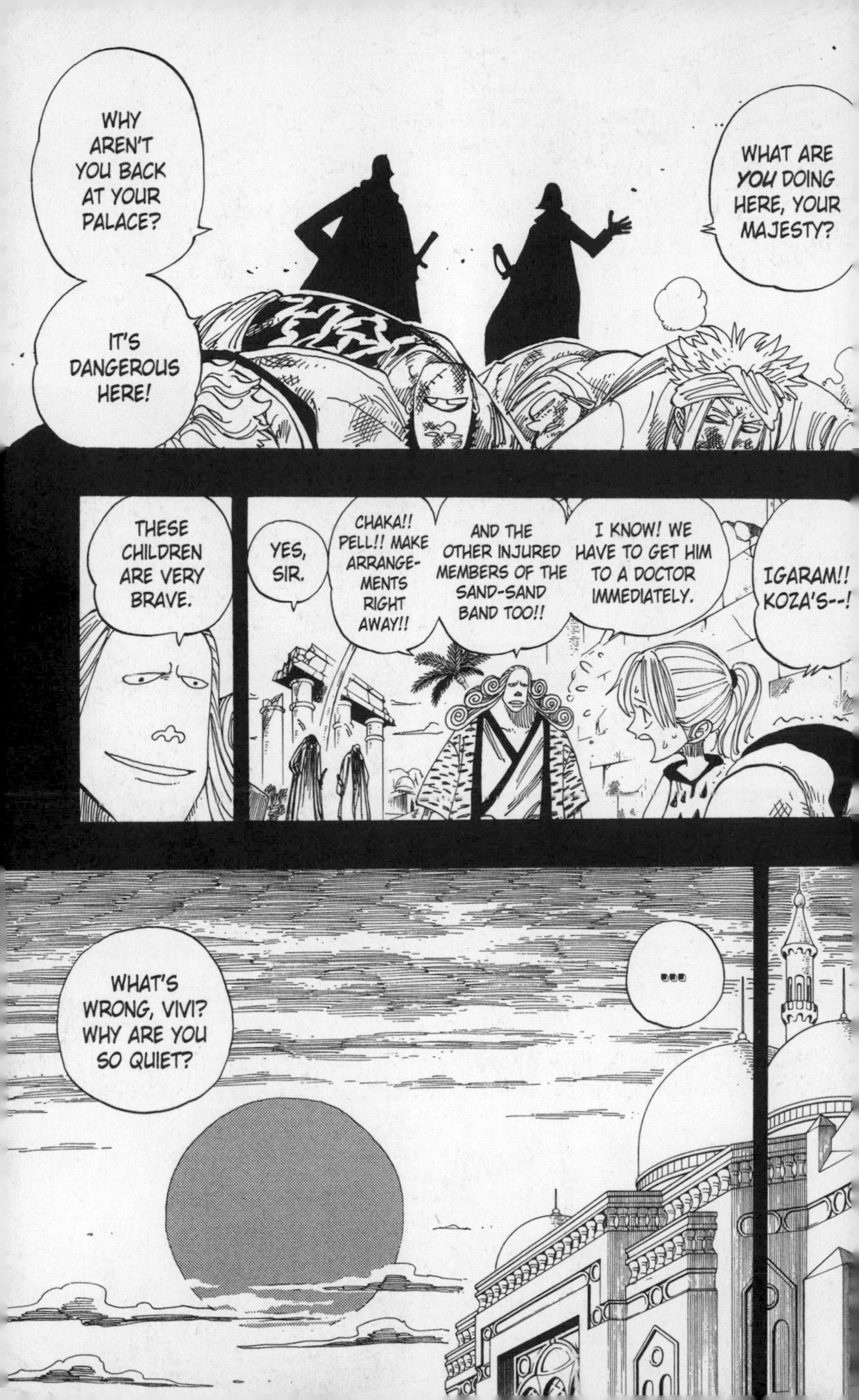
WHAT ARE YOU DOING HERE, YOUR MAJESTY?
WHY AREN'T YOU BACK AT YOUR PALACE?
IT'S DANGEROUS HERE!
IGARAM!! KOZA'S--!
I KNOW! WE HAVE TO GET HIM TO A DOCTOR IMMEDIATELY.
AND THE OTHER INJURED MEMBERS OF THE SAND-SAND BAND TOO!!
CHAKA!! PELL!! MAKE ARRANGE-MENTS RIGHT AWAY!!
YES, SIR.
THESE CHILDREN ARE VERY BRAVE.
WHAT'S WRONG, VIVI? WHY ARE YOU SO QUIET?
...

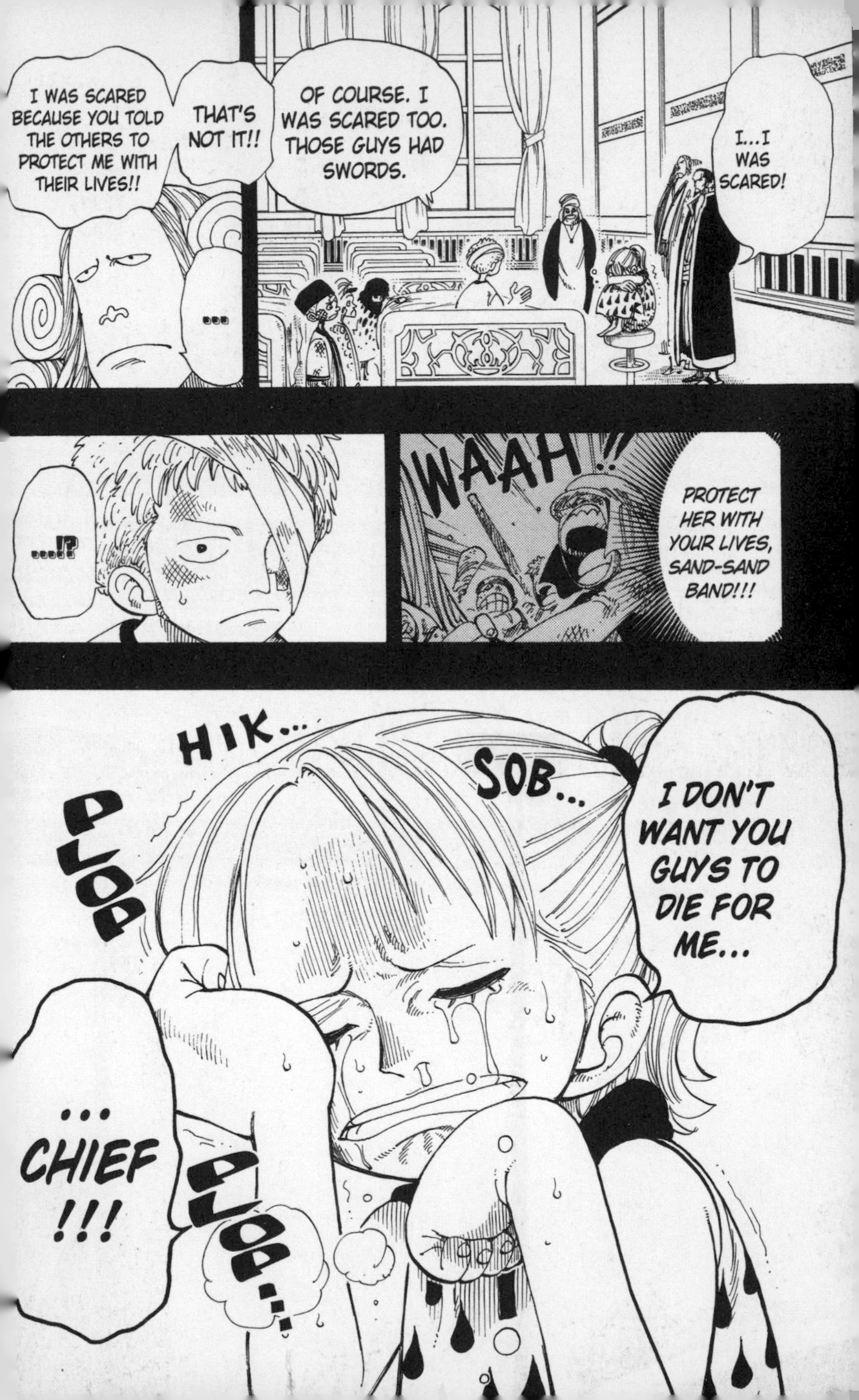
I...I WAS SCARED!
OF COURSE. I WAS SCARED TOO. THOSE GUYS HAD SWORDS.
THAT'S NOT IT!!
I WAS SCARED BECAUSE YOU TOLD THE OTHERS TO PROTECT ME WITH THEIR LIVES!!
...
WAAH!!
PROTECT HER WITH YOUR LIVES, SAND-SAND BAND!!!
...!?
I DON'T WANT YOU GUYS TO DIE FOR ME...
SOB...
HIK...
PLOP
...CHIEF!!!
PLOP...

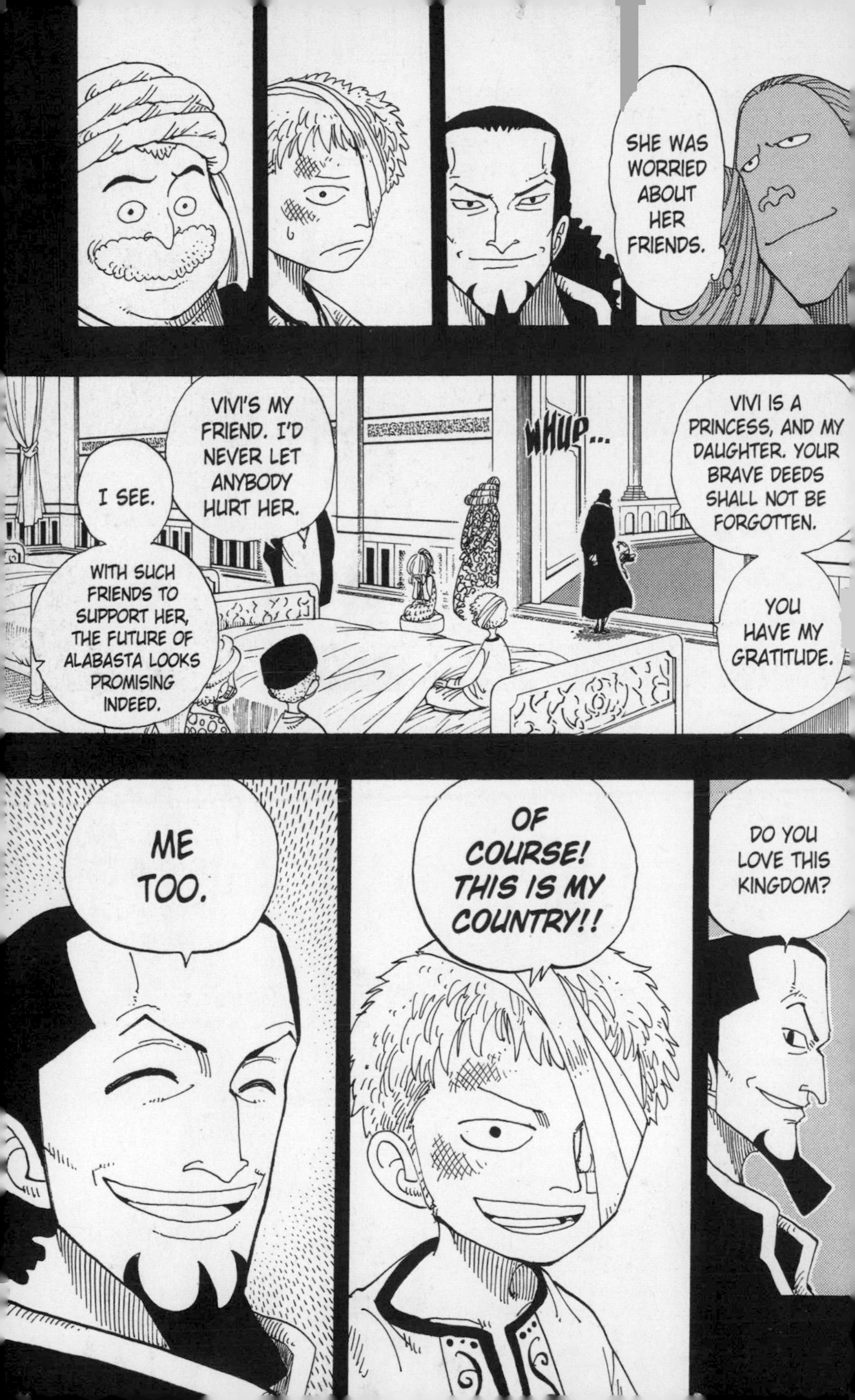
SHE WAS WORRIED ABOUT HER FRIENDS.
VIVI IS A PRINCESS, AND MY DAUGHTER. YOUR BRAVE DEEDS SHALL NOT BE FORGOTTEN.
YOU HAVE MY GRATITUDE.
WHUP...
VIVI'S MY FRIEND. I'D NEVER LET ANYBODY HURT HER.
I SEE.
WITH SUCH FRIENDS TO SUPPORT HER, THE FUTURE OF ALABASTA LOOKS PROMISING INDEED.
DO YOU LOVE THIS KINGDOM?
OF COURSE! THIS IS MY COUNTRY!!
ME TOO.

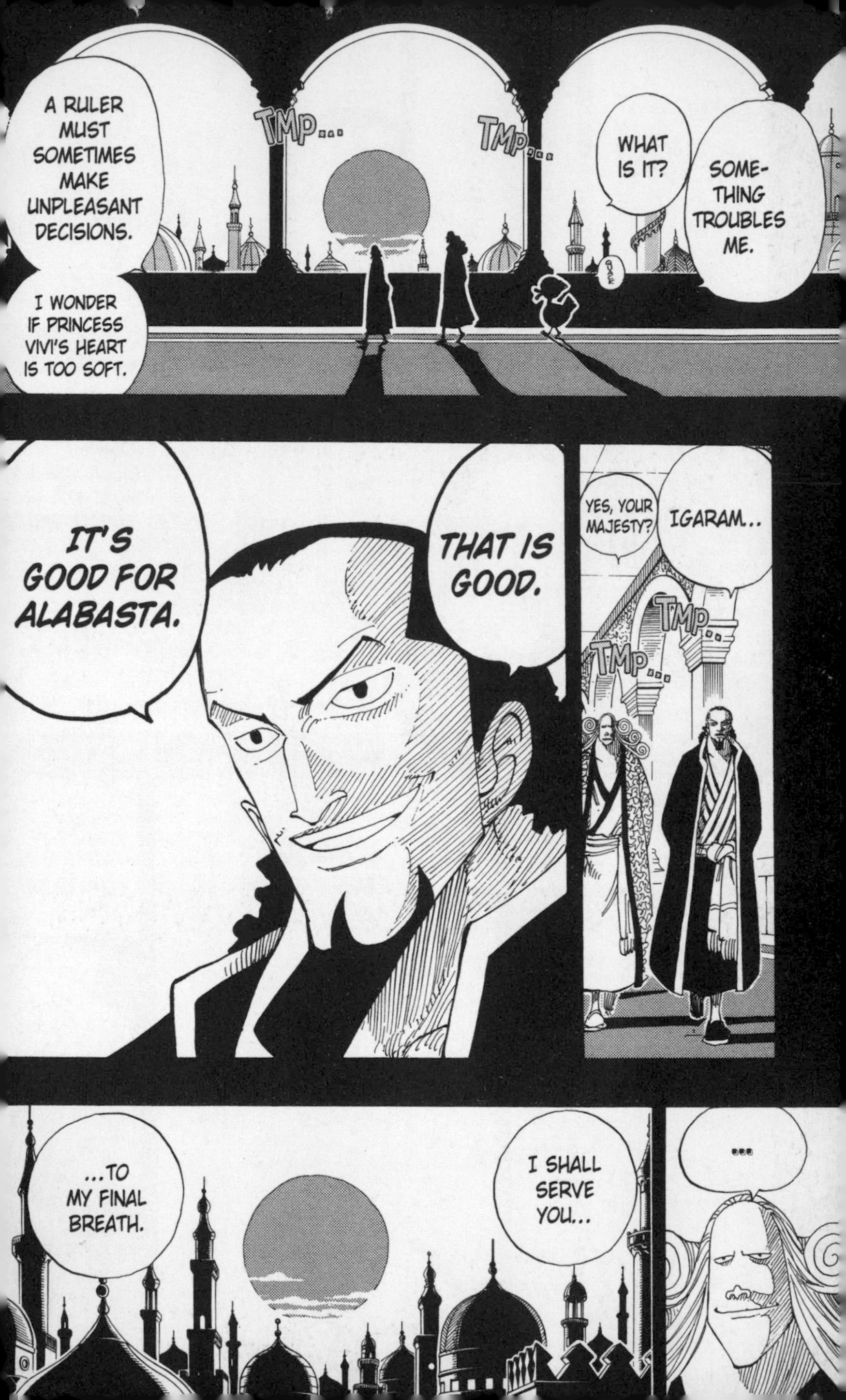
SOMETHING TROUBLES ME.
WHAT IS IT?
TMP...
TMP...
A RULER MUST SOMETIMES MAKE UNPLEASANT DECISIONS.
I WONDER IF PRINCESS VIVI'S HEART IS TOO SOFT.
IGARAM...
YES, YOUR MAJESTY?
TMP...
TMP...
THAT IS GOOD.
IT'S GOOD FOR ALABASTA.
...
I SHALL SERVE YOU...
...TO MY FINAL BREATH.

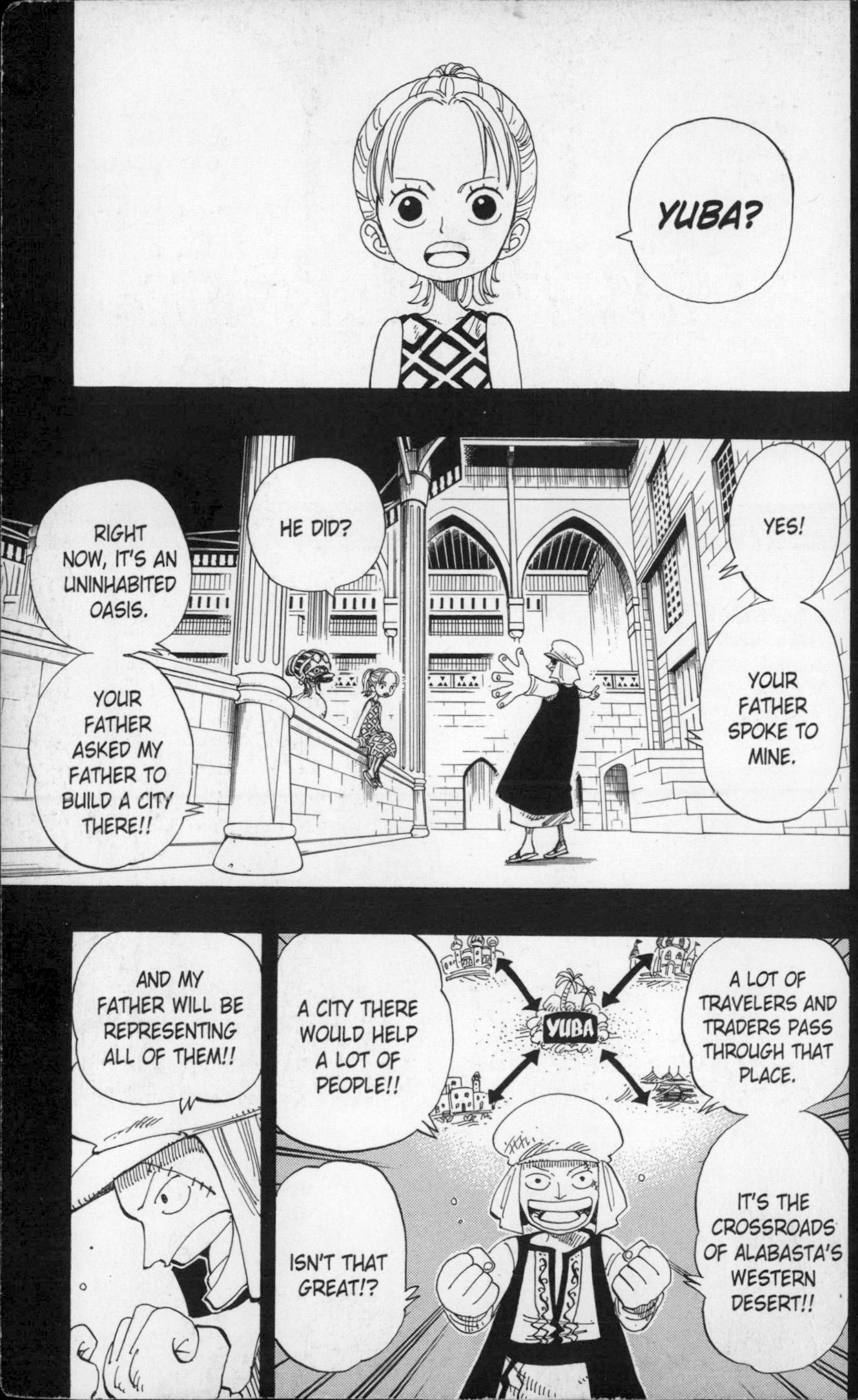
YUBA?
YES!
YOUR FATHER SPOKE TO MINE.
HE DID?
RIGHT NOW, IT'S AN UNINHABITED OASIS.
YOUR FATHER ASKED MY FATHER TO BUILD A CITY THERE!!
A LOT OF TRAVELERS AND TRADERS PASS THROUGH THAT PLACE.
YUBA
IT'S THE CROSSROADS OF ALABASTA'S WESTERN DESERT!!
A CITY THERE WOULD HELP A LOT OF PEOPLE!!
ISN'T THAT GREAT!?
AND MY FATHER WILL BE REPRESENTING ALL OF THEM!!

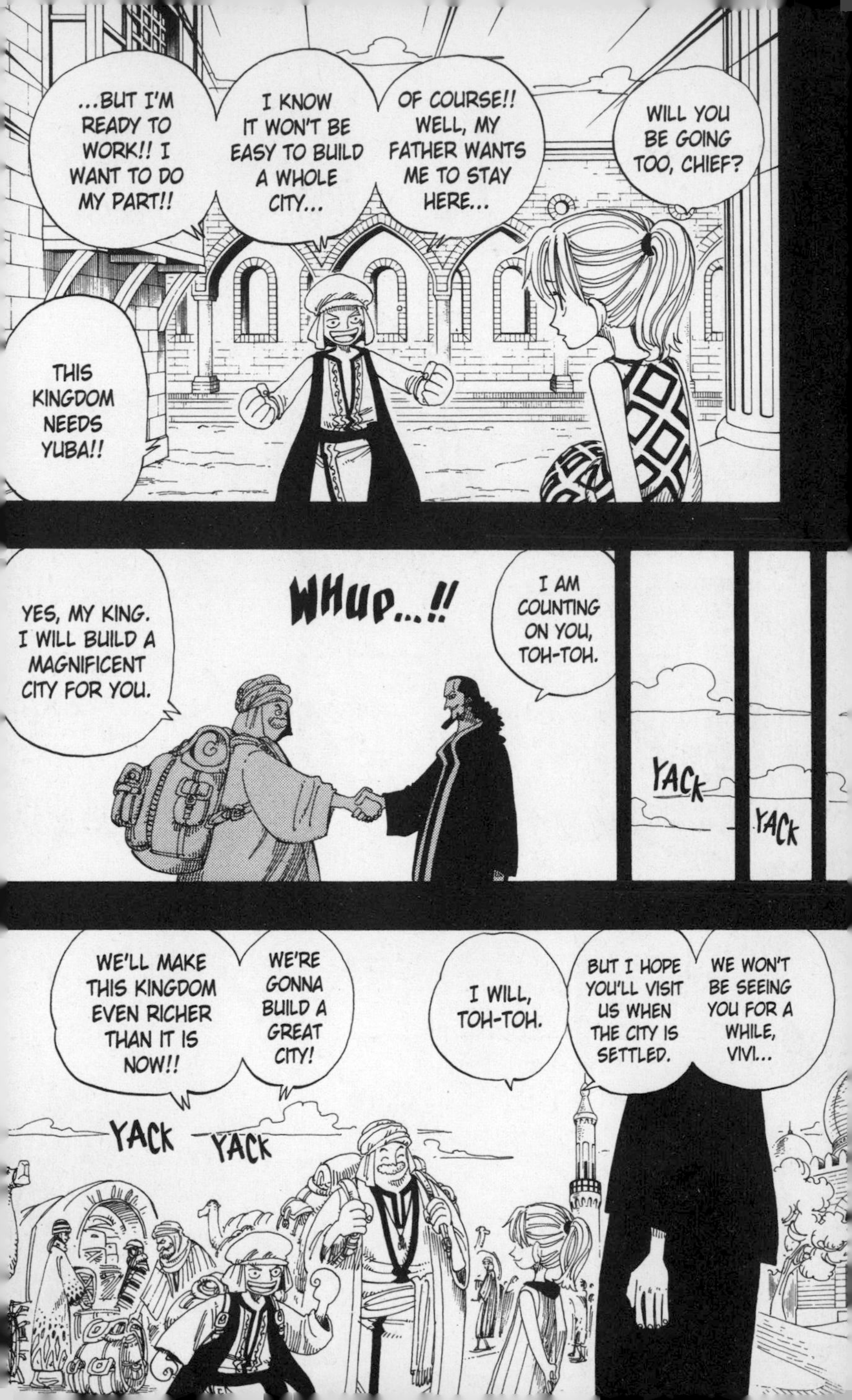
WILL YOU BE GOING TOO, CHIEF?
OF COURSE!! WELL, MY FATHER WANTS ME TO STAY HERE...
I KNOW IT WON'T BE EASY TO BUILD A WHOLE CITY...
...BUT I'M READY TO WORK!! I WANT TO DO MY PART!!
THIS KINGDOM NEEDS YUBA!!
YACK
YACK
I AM COUNTING ON YOU, TOH-TOH.
WHUP...!!
YES, MY KING. I WILL BUILD A MAGNIFICENT CITY FOR YOU.
WE WON'T BE SEEING YOU FOR A WHILE, VIVI...
BUT I HOPE YOU'LL VISIT US WHEN THE CITY IS SETTLED.
I WILL, TOH-TOH.
WE'RE GONNA BUILD A GREAT CITY!
WE'LL MAKE THIS KINGDOM EVEN RICHER THAN IT IS NOW!!
YACK
YACK

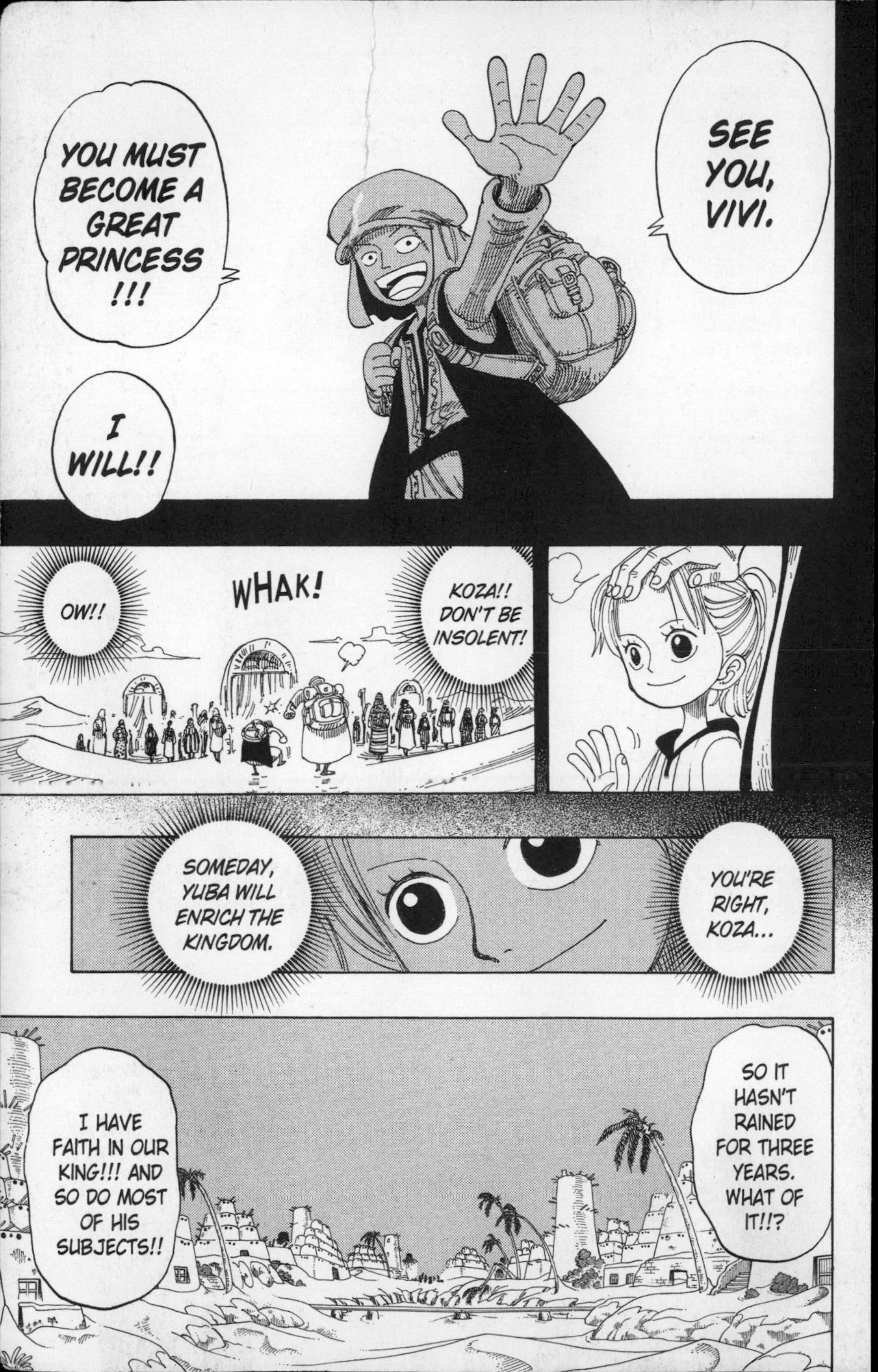
SEE YOU, VIVI.
YOU MUST BECOME A GREAT PRINCESS!!!
I WILL!!
KOZA!! DON'T BE INSOLENT!
WHAK!
OW!!
YOU'RE RIGHT, KOZA...
SOMEDAY, YUBA WILL ENRICH THE KINGDOM.
SO IT HASN'T RAINED FOR THREE YEARS. WHAT OF IT!!?
I HAVE FAITH IN OUR KING!!! AND SO DO MOST OF HIS SUBJECTS!!

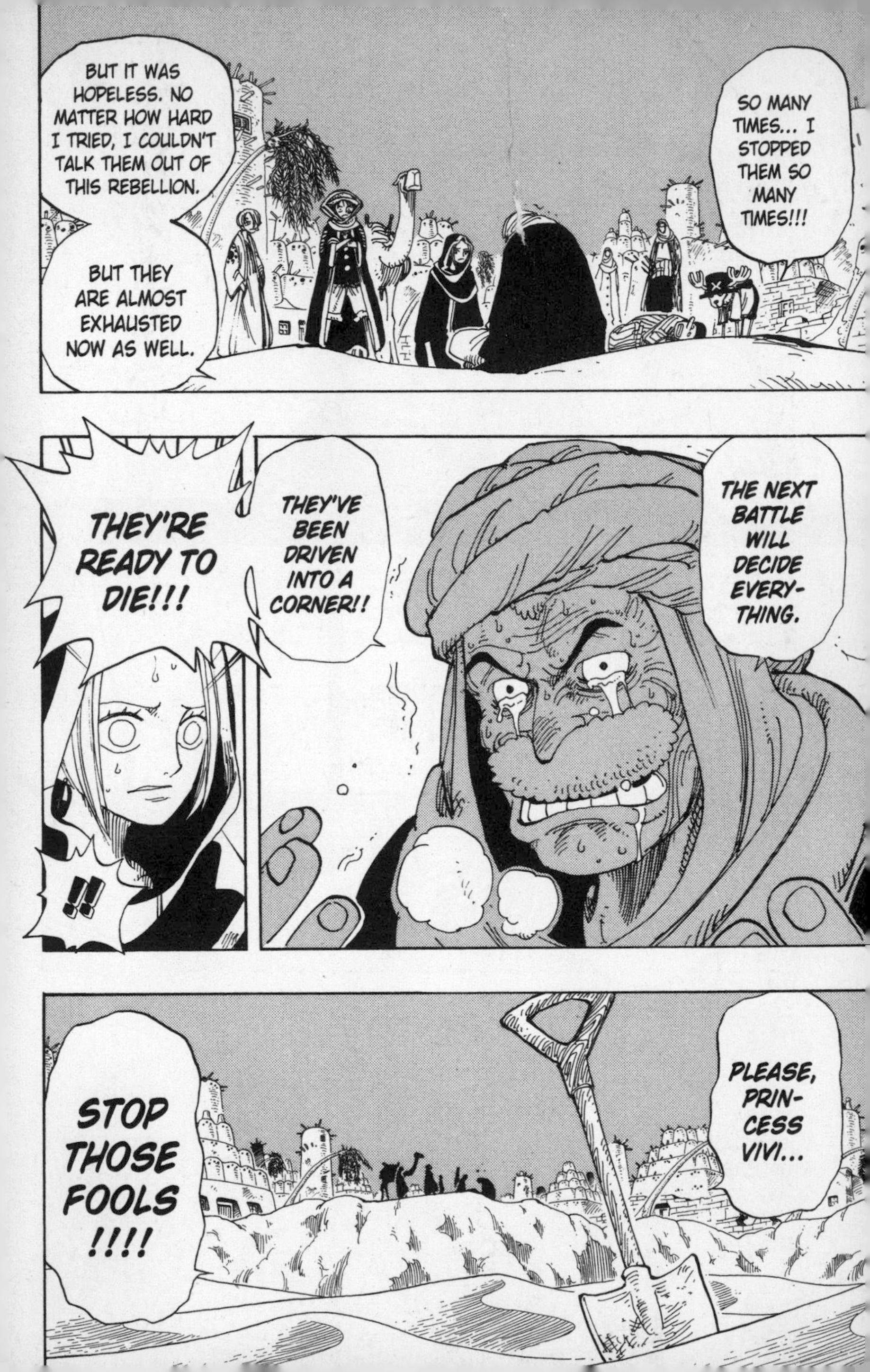
SO MANY TIMES... I STOPPED THEM SO MANY TIMES!!!
BUT IT WAS HOPELESS. NO MATTER HOW HARD I TRIED, I COULDN'T TALK THEM OUT OF THIS REBELLION.
BUT THEY ARE ALMOST EXHAUSTED NOW AS WELL.
THE NEXT BATTLE WILL DECIDE EVERY-THING.
THEY'VE BEEN DRIVEN INTO A CORNER!!
THEY'RE READY TO DIE!!!
!!
PLEASE, PRIN-CESS VIVI...
STOP THOSE FOOLS !!!!

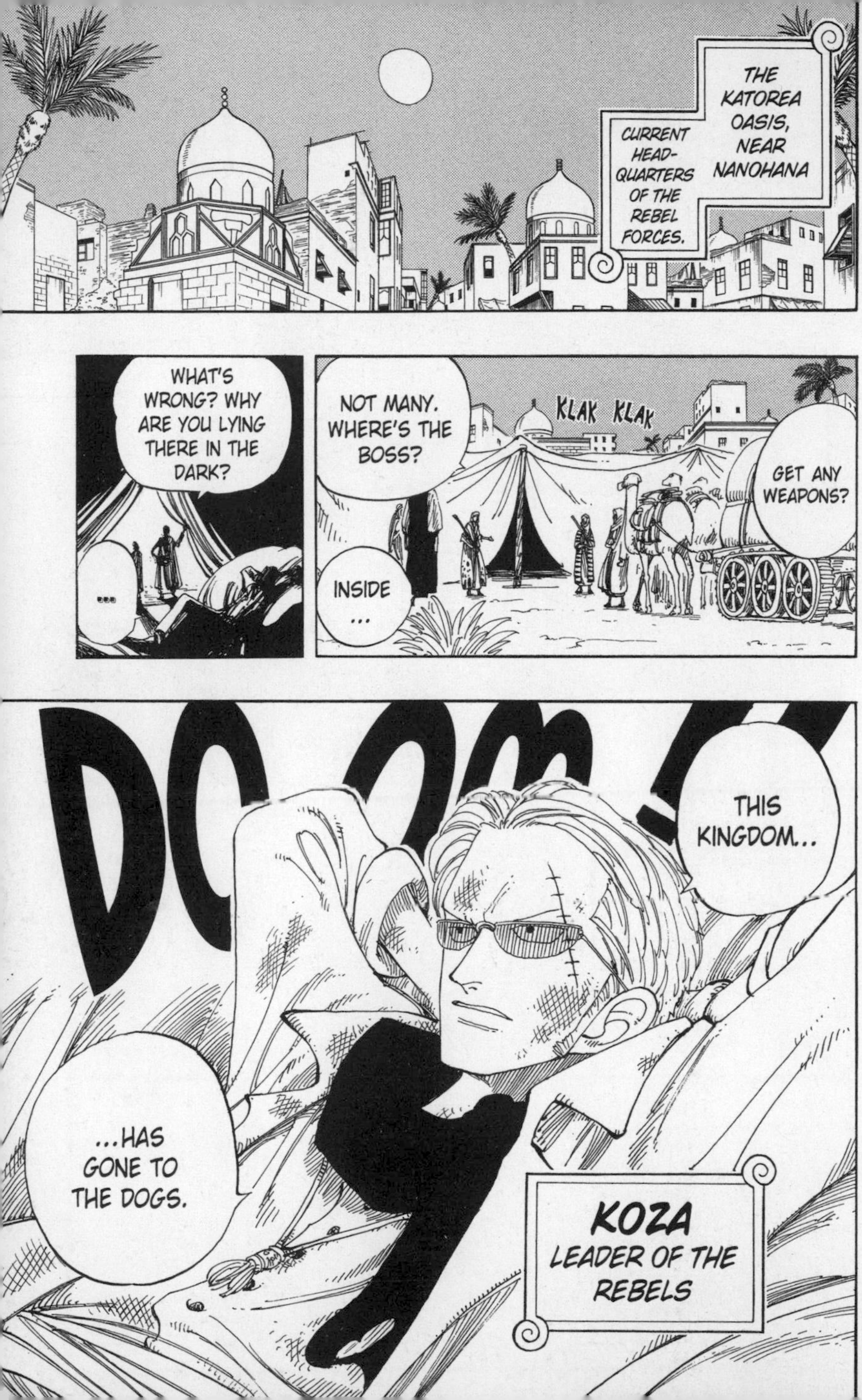
THE KATOREA OASIS, NEAR NANOHANA
CURRENT HEAD-QUARTERS OF THE REBEL FORCES.
KLAK KLAK
GET ANY WEAPONS?
NOT MANY. WHERE'S THE BOSS?
INSIDE ...
WHAT'S WRONG? WHY ARE YOU LYING THERE IN THE DARK?
...
DOOM!!
THIS KINGDOM...
...HAS GONE TO THE DOGS.
KOZA
LEADER OF THE REBELS

Chapter 165: OPERATION UTOPIA

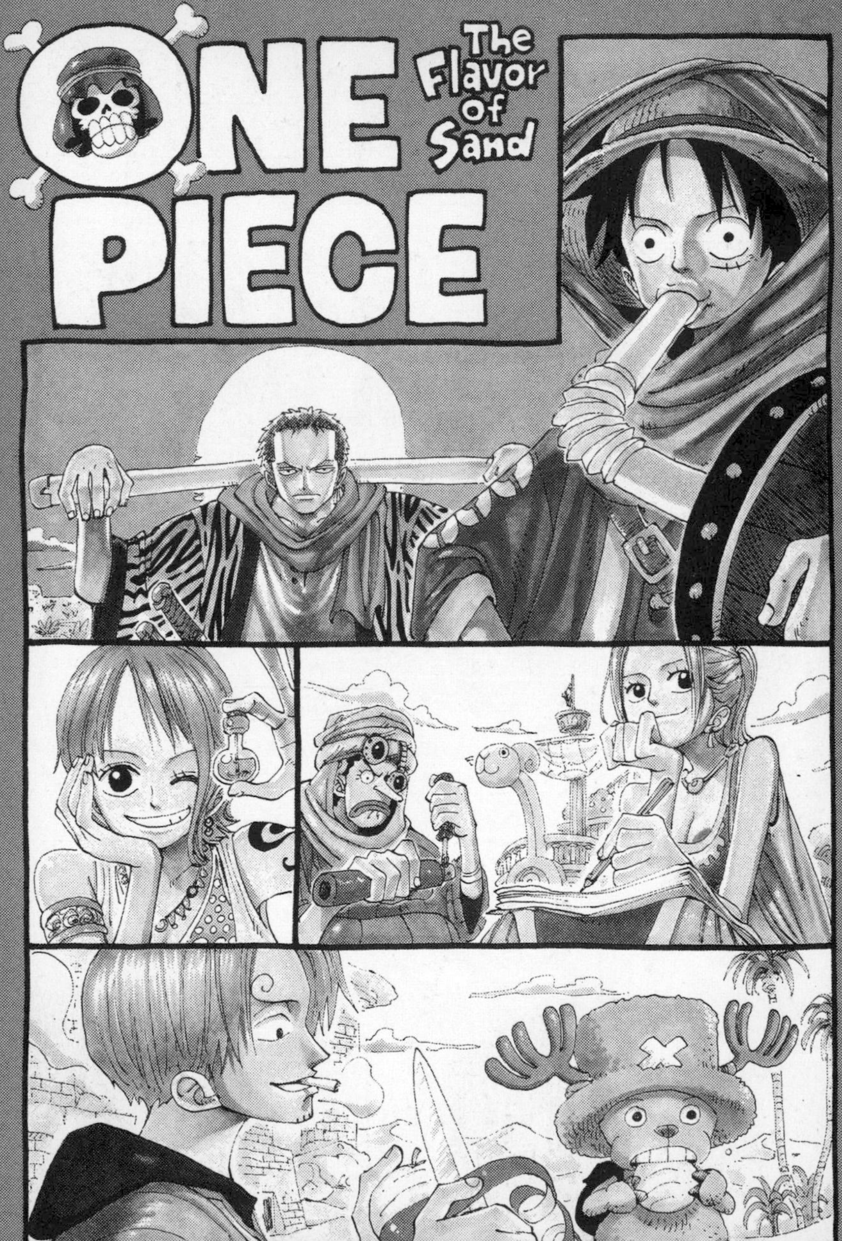
ONE PIECE
The Flavor of Sand

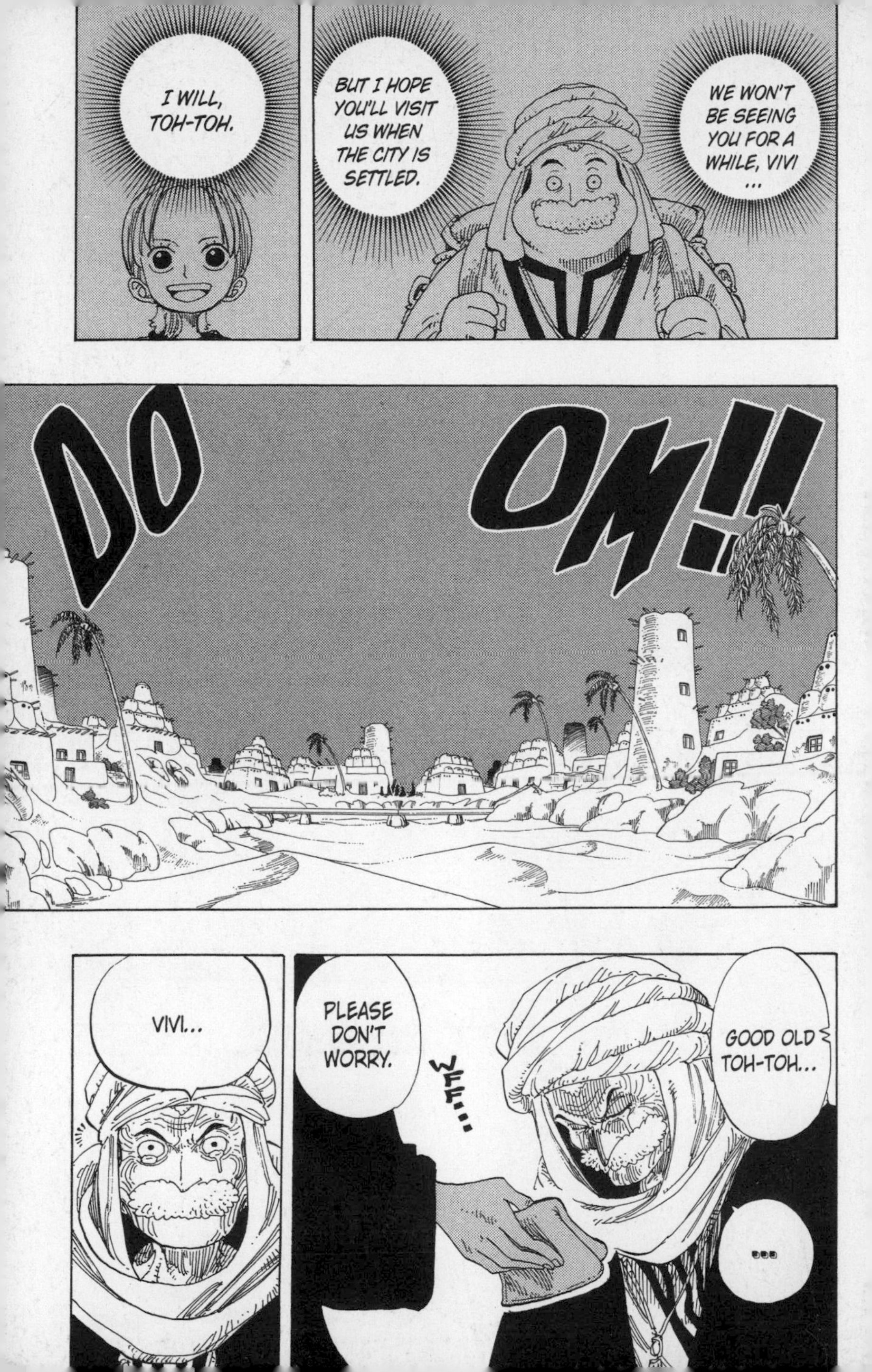

WE WON'T BE SEEING YOU FOR A WHILE, VIVI ...
BUT I HOPE YOU'LL VISIT US WHEN THE CITY IS SETTLED.
I WILL, TOH-TOH.
DO OM!!
GOOD OLD TOH-TOH...
PLEASE DON'T WORRY.
WFF...
...
VIVI...

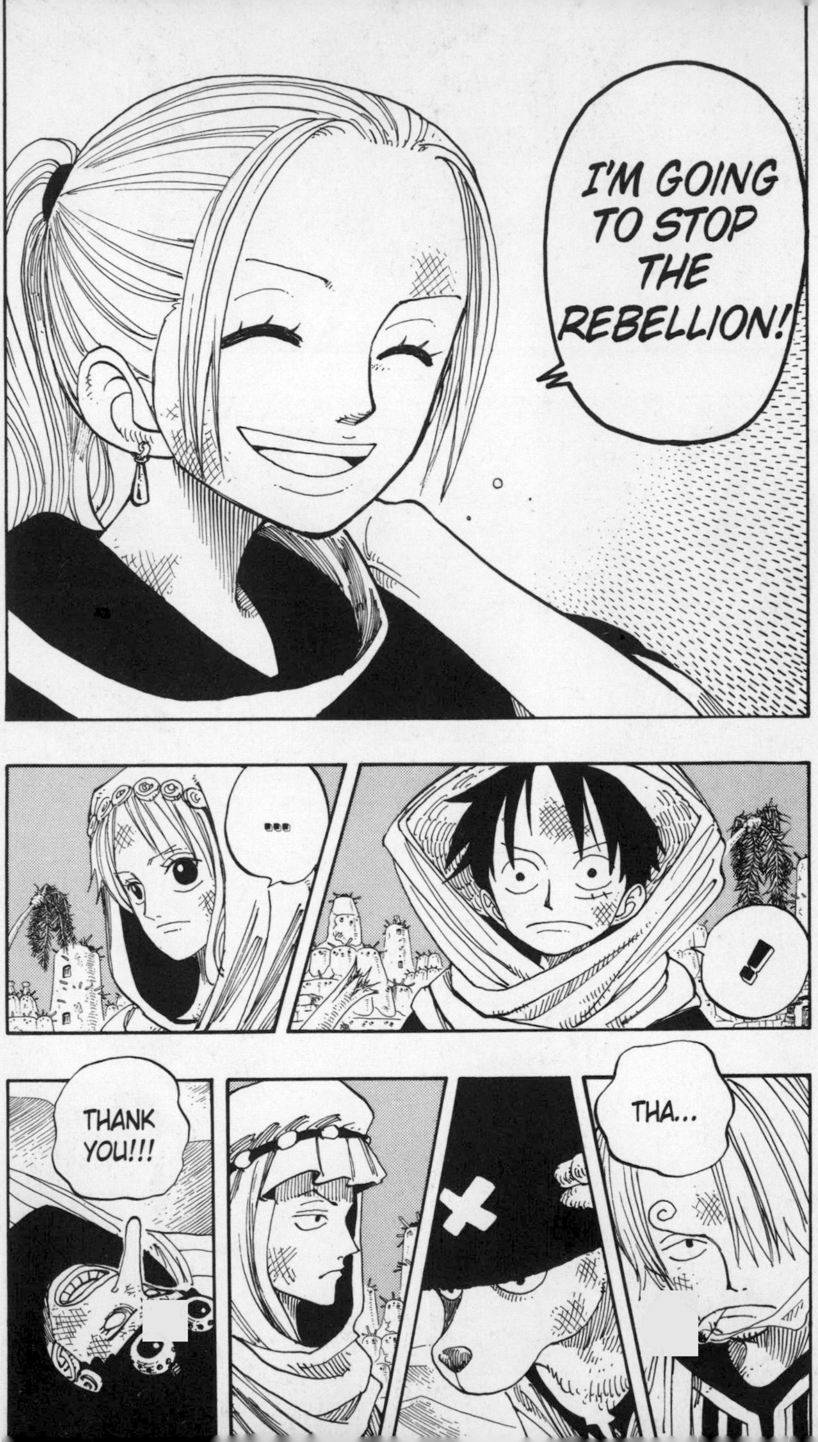
I'M GOING TO STOP THE REBELLION!
!
...
THA...
THANK YOU!!!

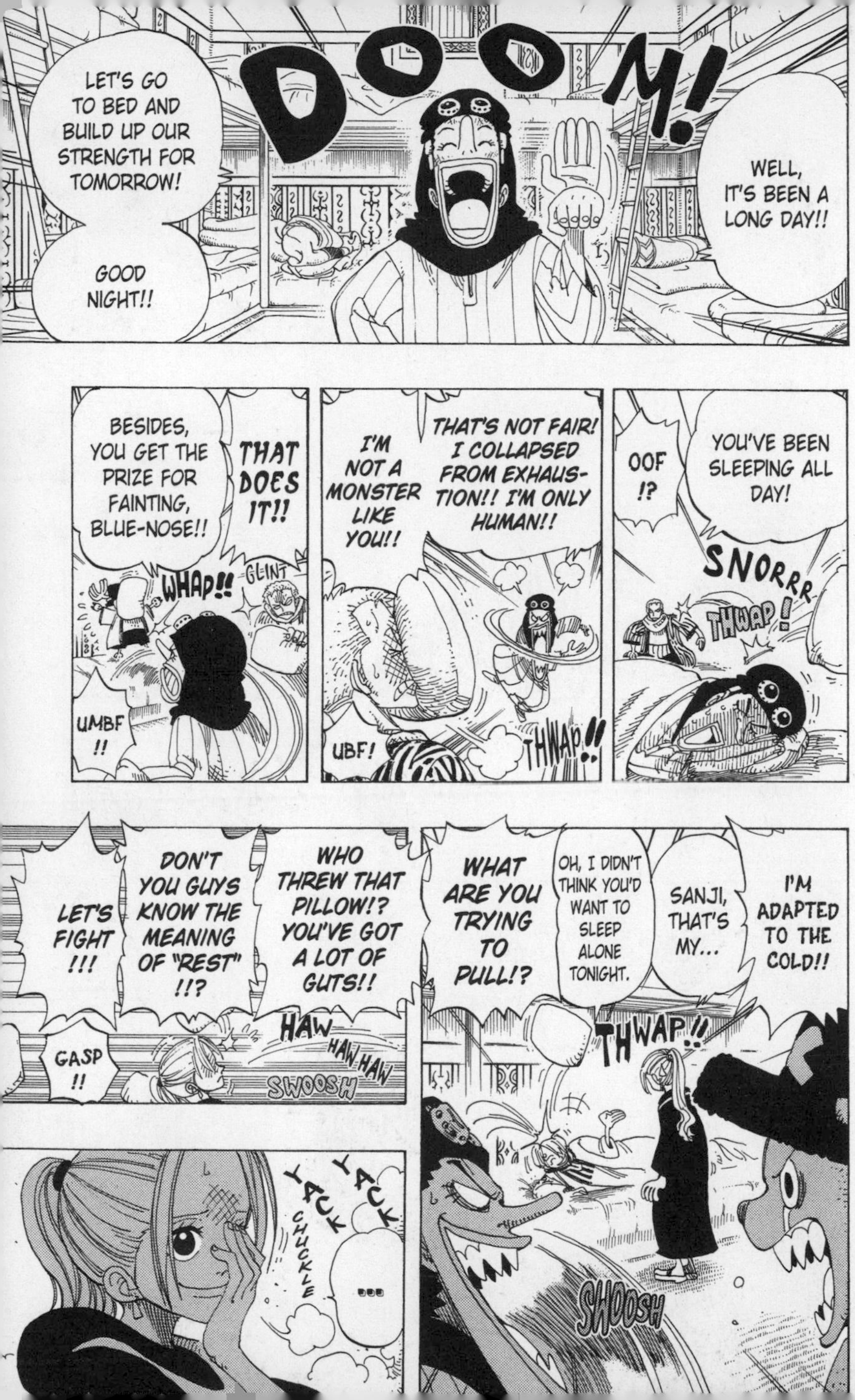
WELL, IT'S BEEN A LONG DAY!!
DOOM!
LET'S GO TO BED AND BUILD UP OUR STRENGTH FOR TOMORROW!
GOOD NIGHT!!
YOU'VE BEEN SLEEPING ALL DAY!
OOF !?
SNORRRR
THWAP!
THAT'S NOT FAIR! I COLLAPSED FROM EXHAUS- TION!! I'M ONLY HUMAN!!
I'M NOT A MONSTER LIKE YOU!!
THWAP!!
UBF!
THAT DOES IT!!
BESIDES, YOU GET THE PRIZE FOR FAINTING, BLUE-NOSE!!
GLINT
WHAP!!
UMBF !!
I'M ADAPTED TO THE COLD!!
SANJI, THAT'S MY...
OH, I DIDN'T THINK YOU'D WANT TO SLEEP ALONE TONIGHT.
WHAT ARE YOU TRYING TO PULL!?
THWAP!!
SWOOSH
WHO THREW THAT PILLOW!? YOU'VE GOT A LOT OF GUTS!!
DON'T YOU GUYS KNOW THE MEANING OF "REST" !!?
LET'S FIGHT !!!
HAW HAW HAW
SWOOSH
GASP !!
YACK YACK
CHUCKLE
...

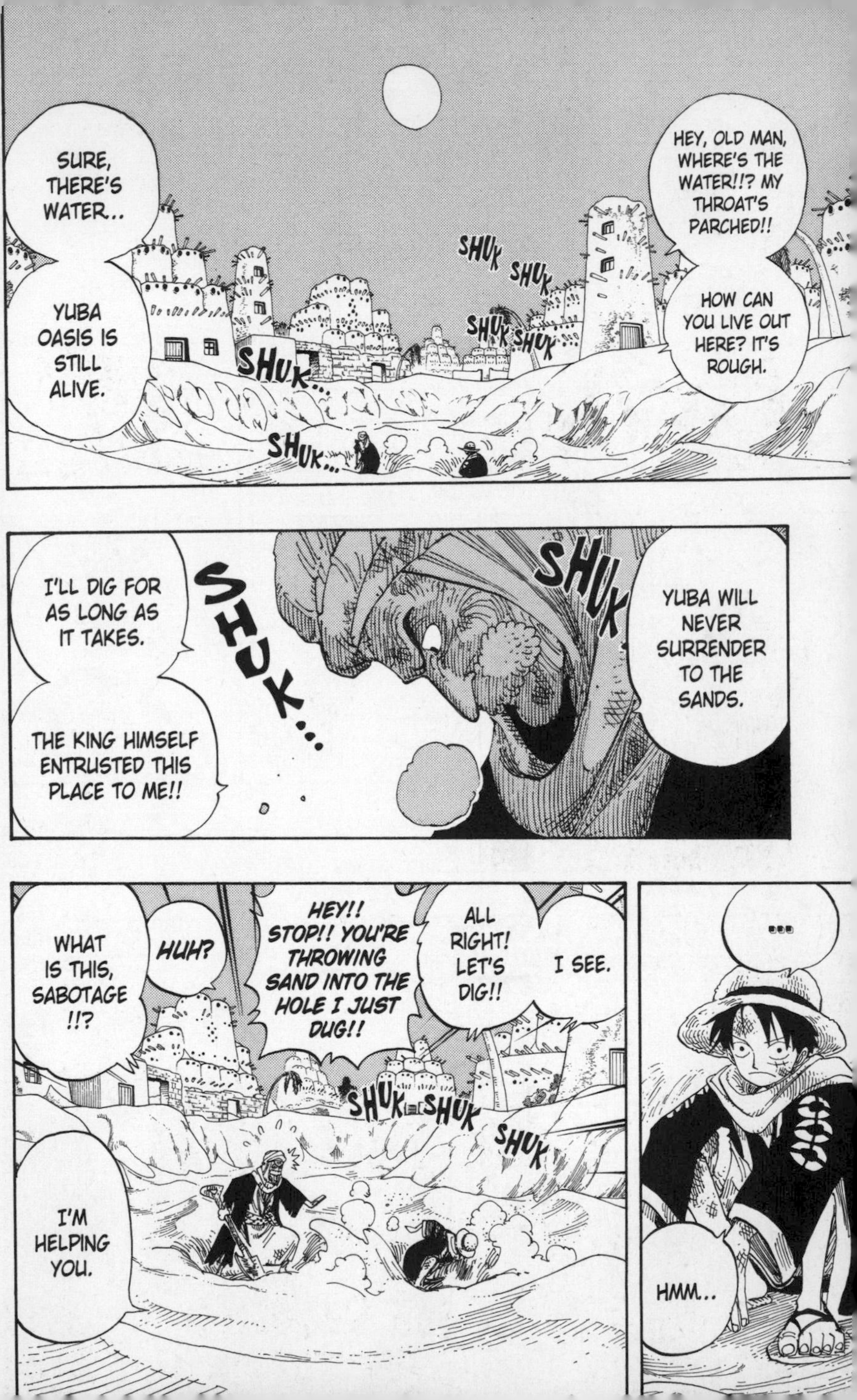
HEY, OLD MAN, WHERE'S THE WATER!!? MY THROAT'S PARCHED!!
HOW CAN YOU LIVE OUT HERE? IT'S ROUGH.
SHUK SHUK
SHUK SHUK
SHUK...
SHUK...
SURE, THERE'S WATER...
YUBA OASIS IS STILL ALIVE.
YUBA WILL NEVER SURRENDER TO THE SANDS.
SHUK
SHUK...
I'LL DIG FOR AS LONG AS IT TAKES.
THE KING HIMSELF ENTRUSTED THIS PLACE TO ME!!
...
HMM...
I SEE.
ALL RIGHT! LET'S DIG!!
SHUK SHUK SHUK
HEY!! STOP!! YOU'RE THROWING SAND INTO THE HOLE I JUST DUG!!
HUH?
WHAT IS THIS, SABOTAGE!!?
I'M HELPING YOU.

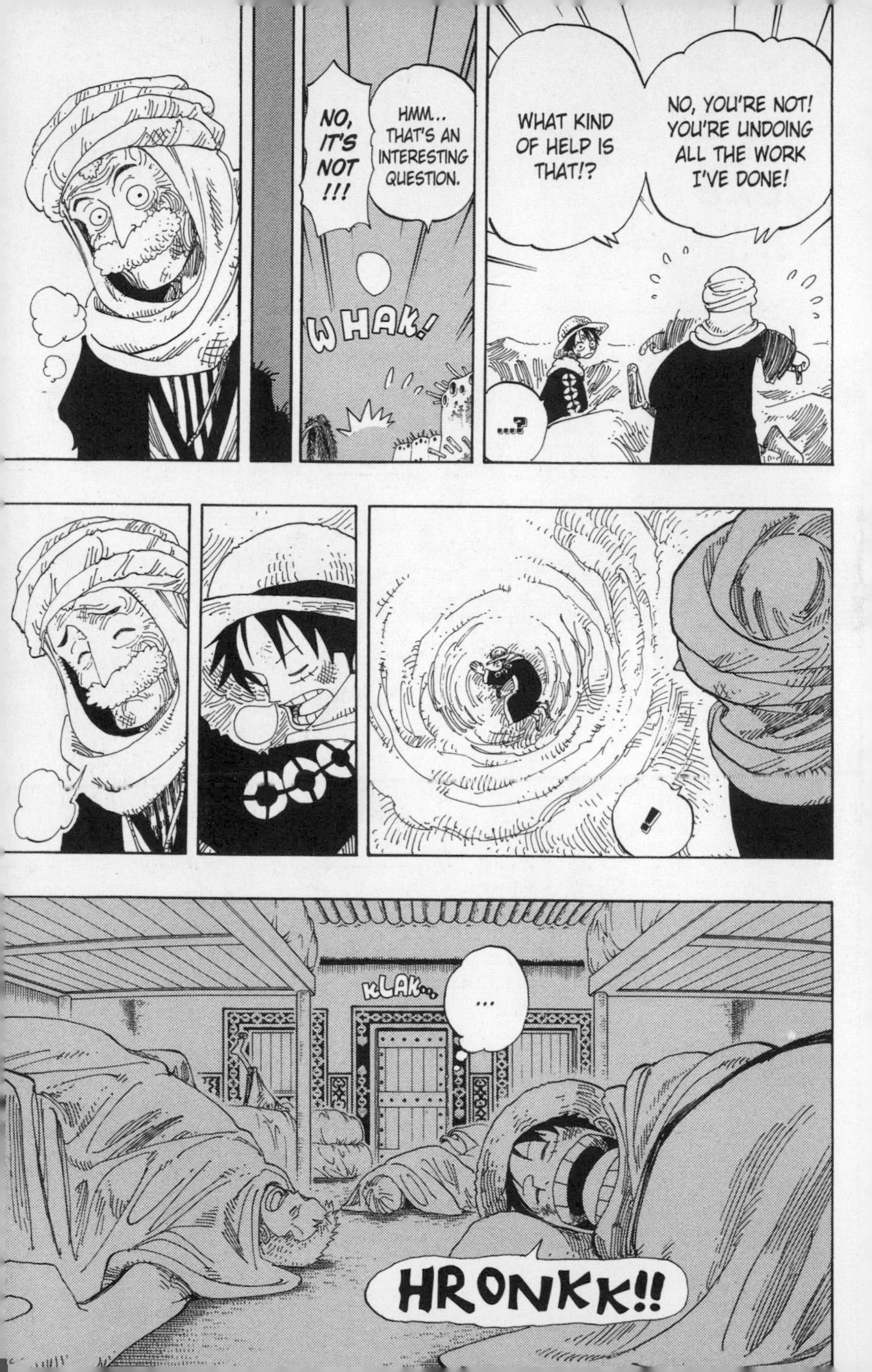
NO, YOU'RE NOT! YOU'RE UNDOING ALL THE WORK I'VE DONE!
WHAT KIND OF HELP IS THAT!?
...?
HMM.. THAT'S AN INTERESTING QUESTION.
NO, IT'S NOT !!!
WHAK!
!
KLAK...
...
HRONKK!!

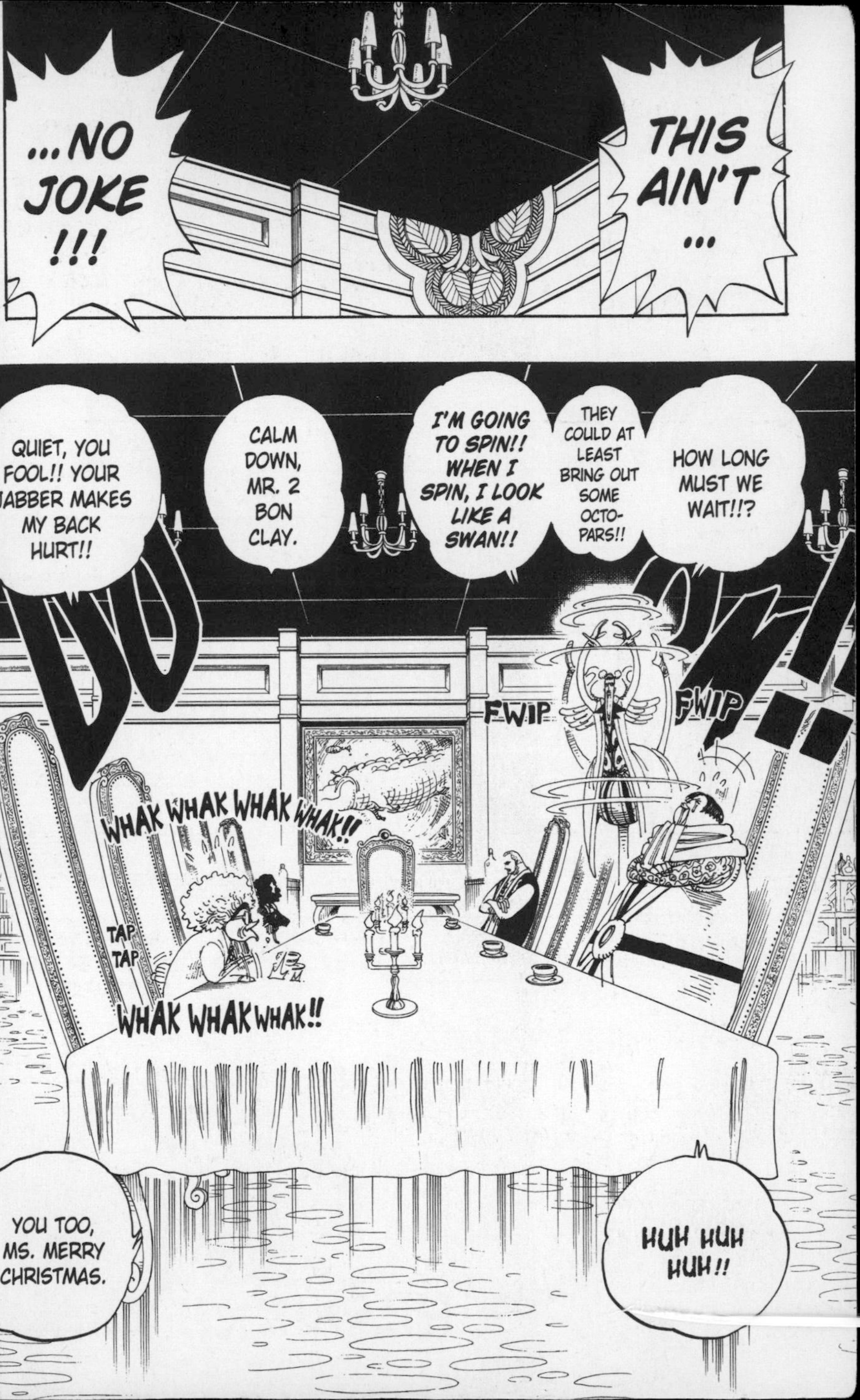
THIS AIN'T ...
...NO JOKE !!!
HOW LONG MUST WE WAIT!!?
THEY COULD AT LEAST BRING OUT SOME OCTO-PARS!!
I'M GOING TO SPIN!! WHEN I SPIN, I LOOK LIKE A SWAN!!
CALM DOWN, MR. 2 BON CLAY.
QUIET, YOU FOOL!! YOUR JABBER MAKES MY BACK HURT!!
FWIP
FWIP
WHAK WHAK WHAK WHAK!!
TAP TAP
WHAK WHAK WHAK!!
HUH HUH HUH!!
YOU TOO, MS. MERRY CHRISTMAS.

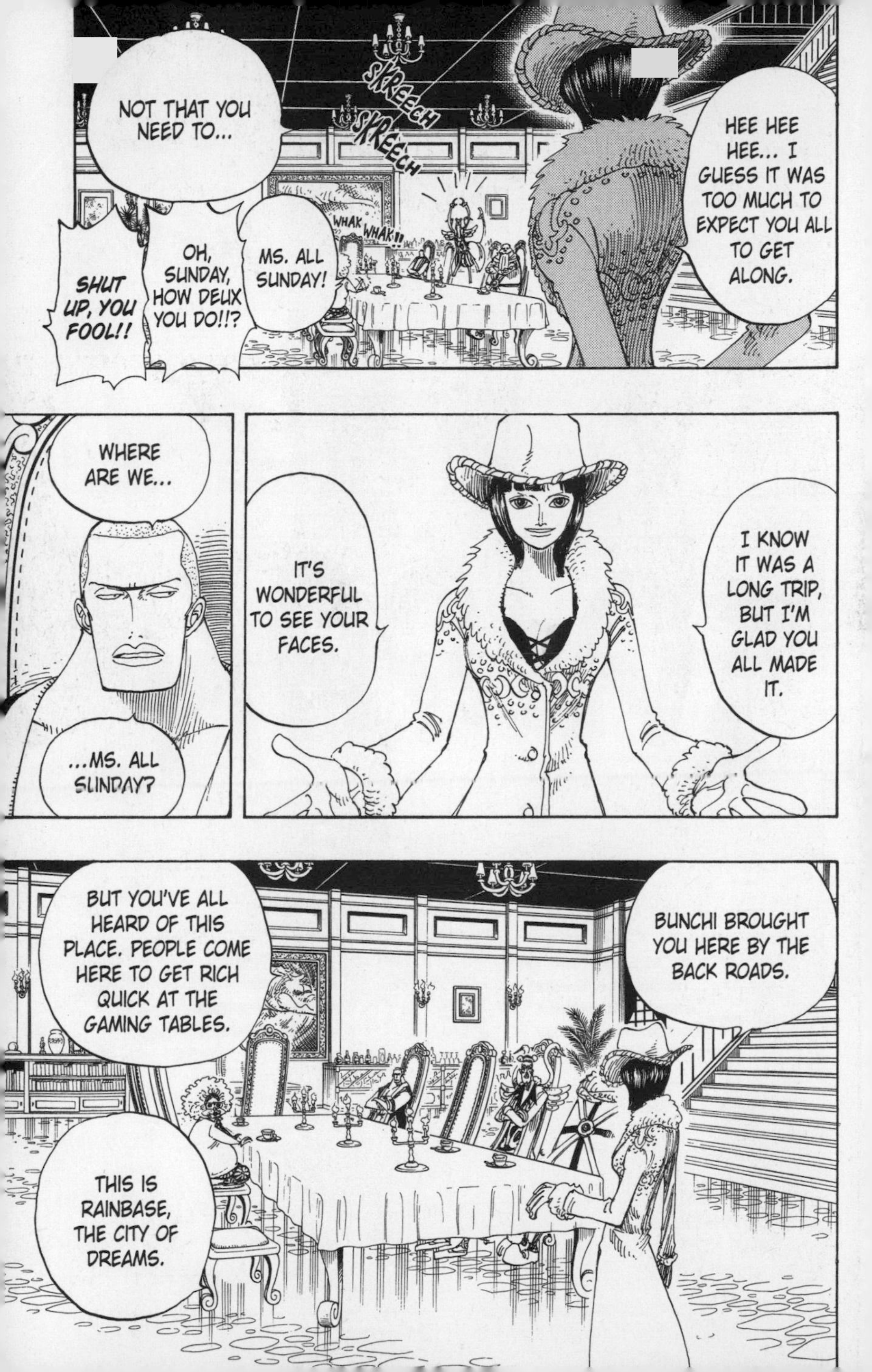
HEE HEE HEE... I GUESS IT WAS TOO MUCH TO EXPECT YOU ALL TO GET ALONG.
SKREECH
SKREECH
NOT THAT YOU NEED TO...
MS. ALL SUNDAY!
WHAK WHAK!!
OH, SUNDAY, HOW DEUX YOU DO!!?
SHUT UP, YOU FOOL!!
I KNOW IT WAS A LONG TRIP, BUT I'M GLAD YOU ALL MADE IT.
IT'S WONDERFUL TO SEE YOUR FACES.
WHERE ARE WE...
...MS. ALL SUNDAY?
BUNCHI BROUGHT YOU HERE BY THE BACK ROADS.
BUT YOU'VE ALL HEARD OF THIS PLACE. PEOPLE COME HERE TO GET RICH QUICK AT THE GAMING TABLES.
THIS IS RAINBASE, THE CITY OF DREAMS.

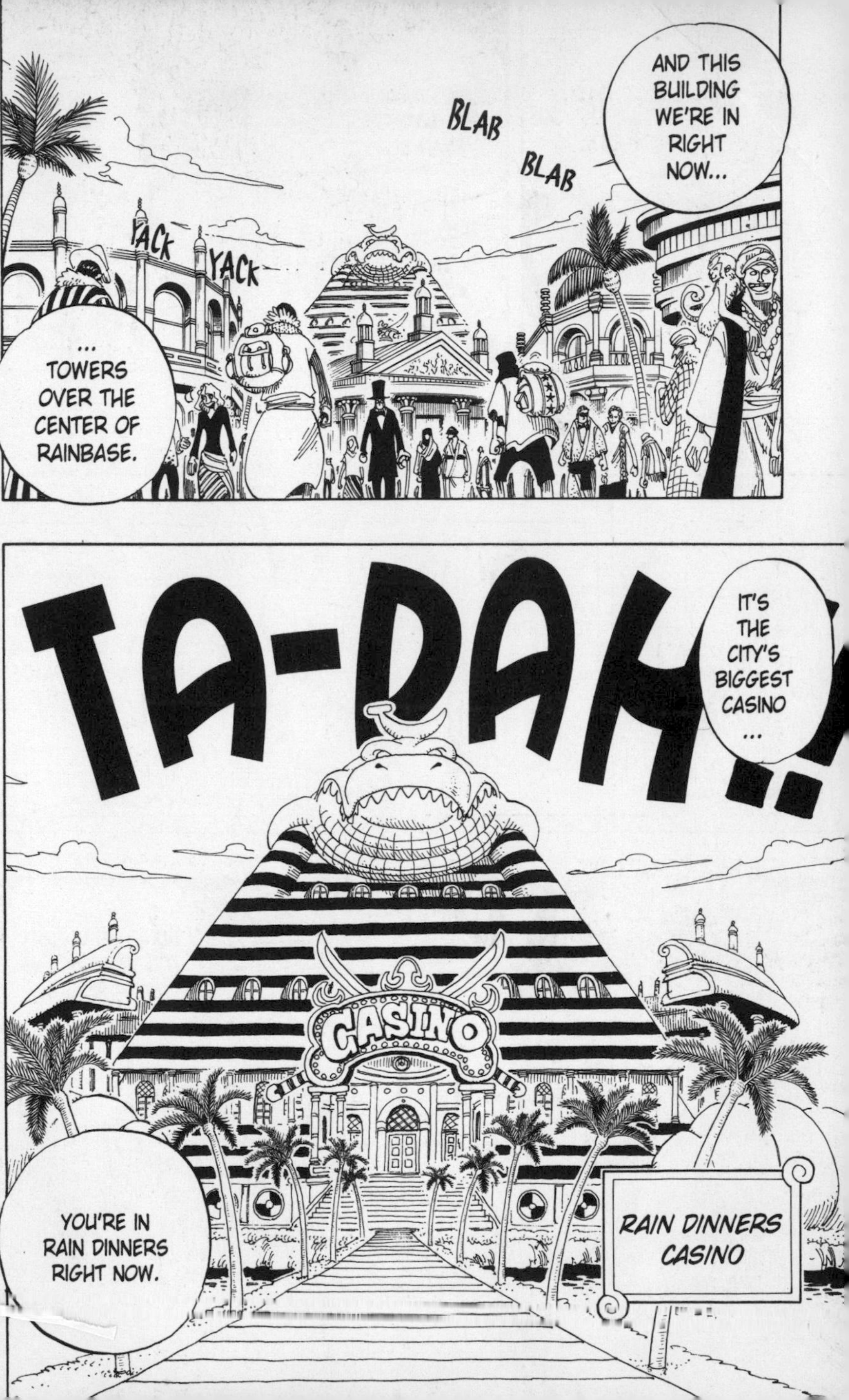
AND THIS BUILDING WE'RE IN RIGHT NOW...
BLAB
BLAB
YACK
YACK
... TOWERS OVER THE CENTER OF RAINBASE.
TA-DAH!!
IT'S THE CITY'S BIGGEST CASINO ...
RAIN DINNERS CASINO
CASINO
YOU'RE IN RAIN DINNERS RIGHT NOW.

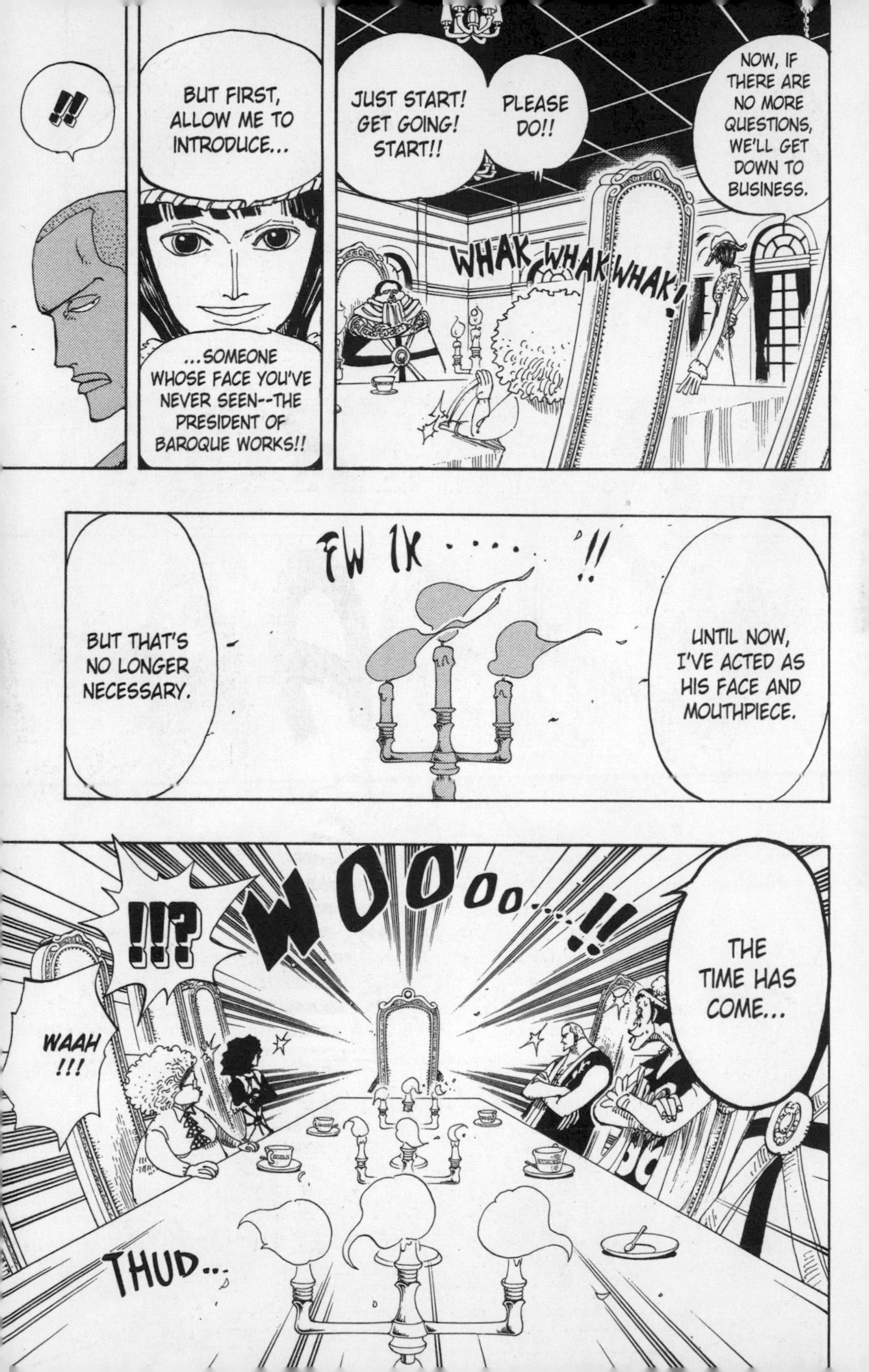
NOW, IF THERE ARE NO MORE QUESTIONS, WE'LL GET DOWN TO BUSINESS.
PLEASE DO!!
JUST START! GET GOING! START!!
WHAK WHAK WHAK!
BUT FIRST, ALLOW ME TO INTRODUCE...
...SOMEONE WHOSE FACE YOU'VE NEVER SEEN--THE PRESIDENT OF BAROQUE WORKS!!
!!
UNTIL NOW, I'VE ACTED AS HIS FACE AND MOUTHPIECE.
FWIK.....!!
BUT THAT'S NO LONGER NECESSARY.
THE TIME HAS COME...
WOOOo...!!
!!?
WAAH!!!
THUD...

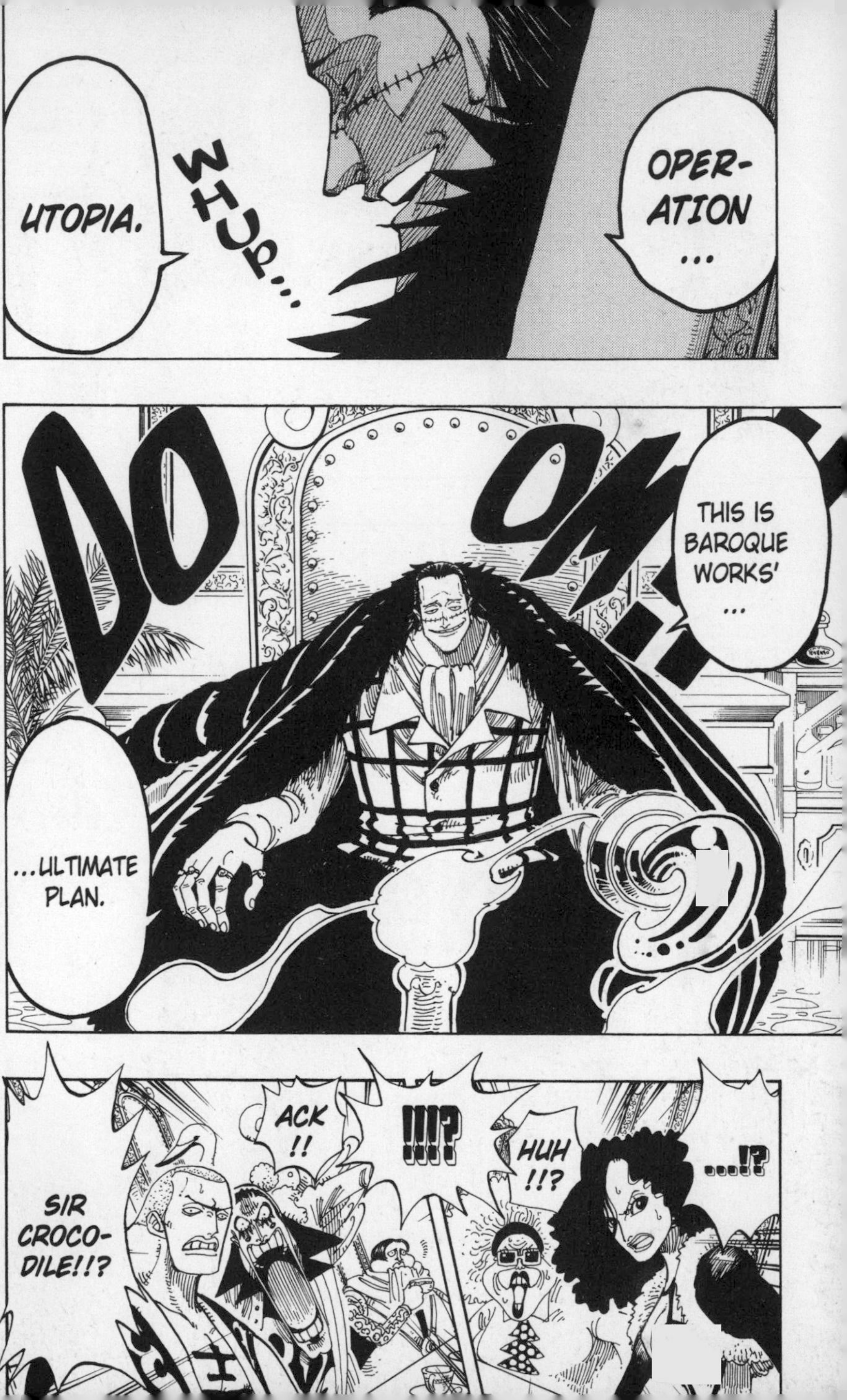
OPERATION ...
WHUP...
UTOPIA.
THIS IS BAROQUE WORKS' ...
DOOM
...ULTIMATE PLAN.
...!?
HUH !!?
!!!?
ACK !!
SIR CROCODILE!!?

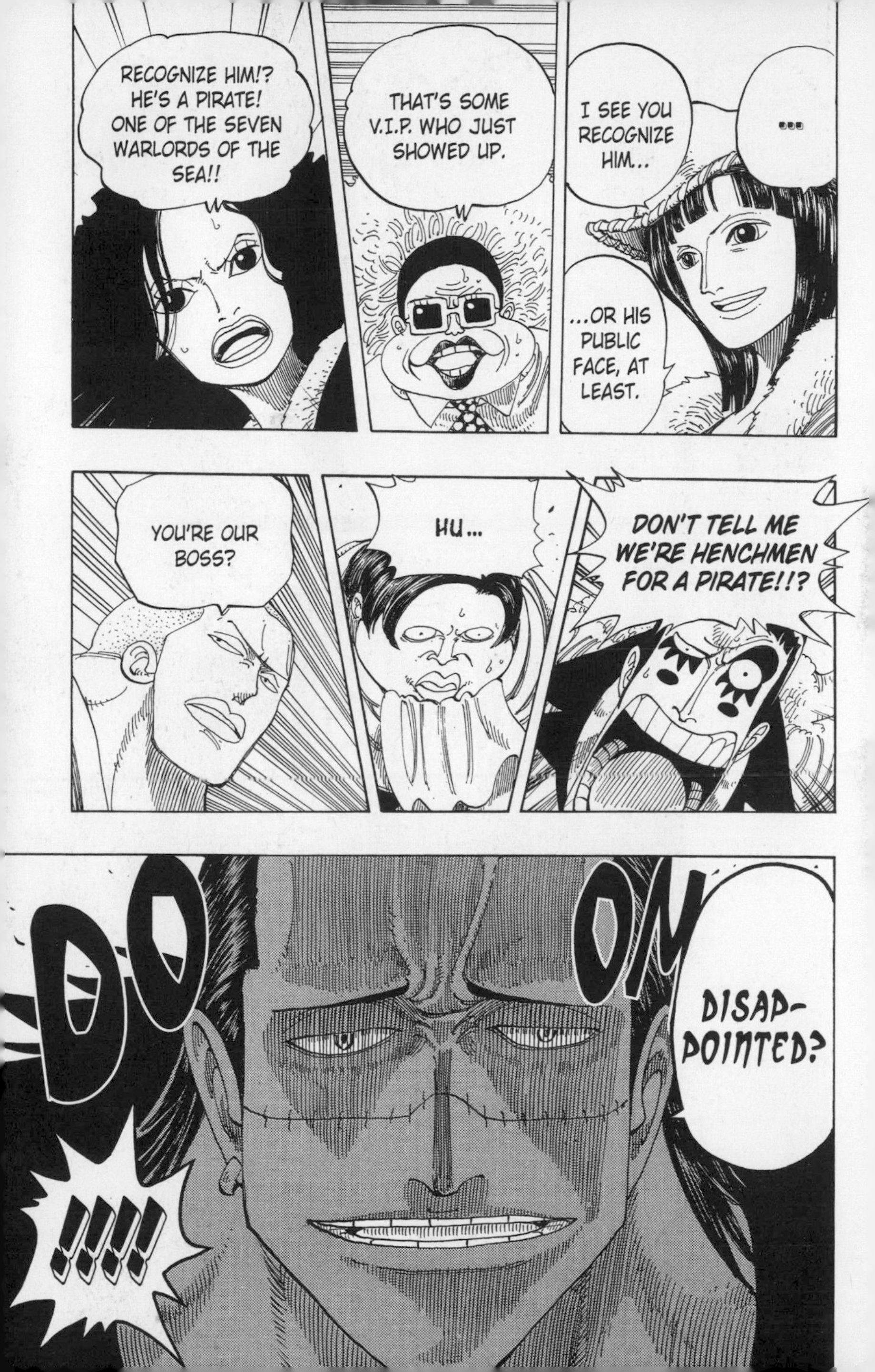
...
I SEE YOU RECOGNIZE HIM...
...OR HIS PUBLIC FACE, AT LEAST.
THAT'S SOME V.I.P. WHO JUST SHOWED UP.
RECOGNIZE HIM!? HE'S A PIRATE! ONE OF THE SEVEN WARLORDS OF THE SEA!!
DON'T TELL ME WE'RE HENCHMEN FOR A PIRATE!!?
HU...
YOU'RE OUR BOSS?
DISAP-POINTED?
DO-OM
!!!!!

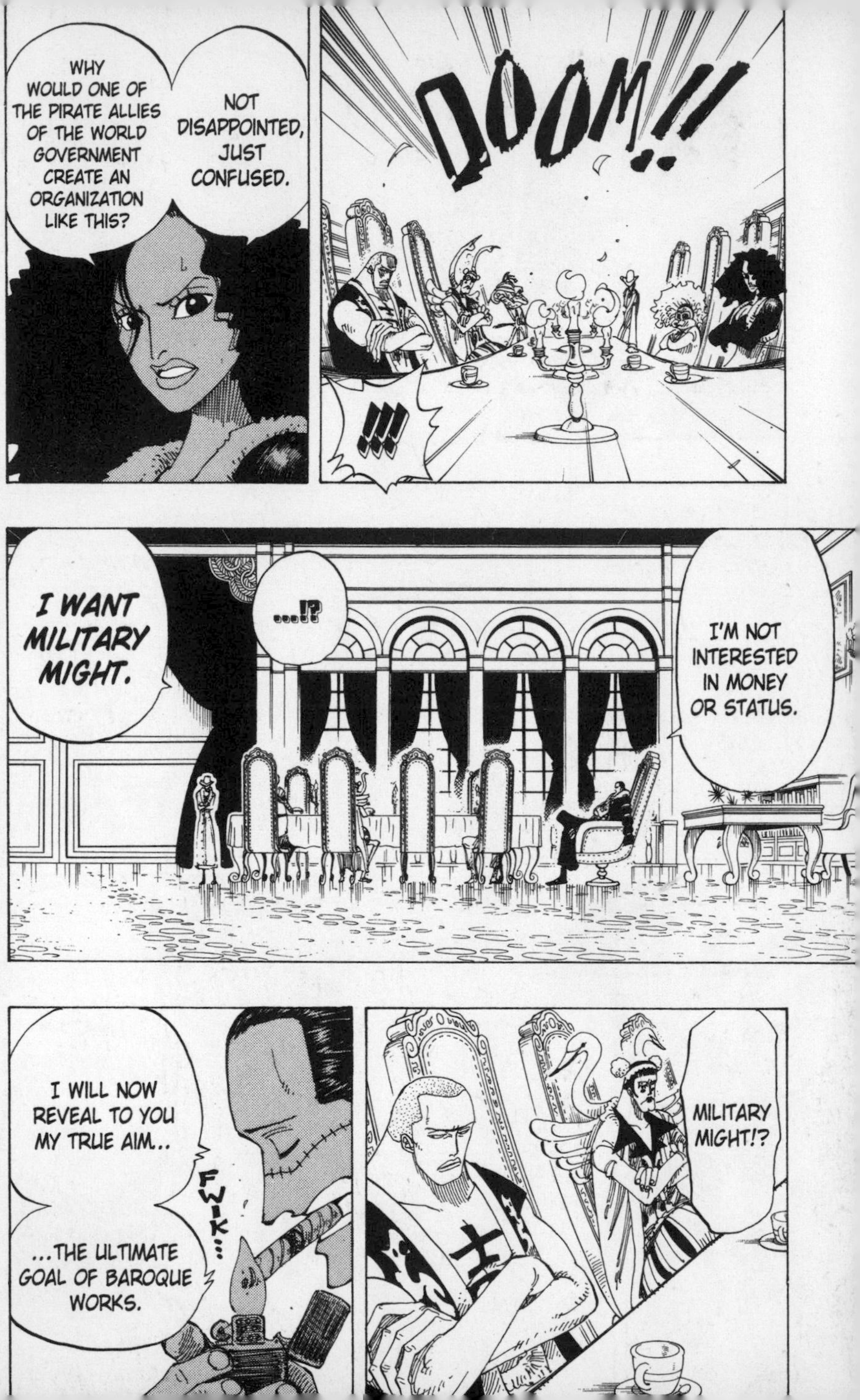
DOOM!!
!!!
NOT DISAPPOINTED, JUST CONFUSED.
WHY WOULD ONE OF THE PIRATE ALLIES OF THE WORLD GOVERNMENT CREATE AN ORGANIZATION LIKE THIS?
I'M NOT INTERESTED IN MONEY OR STATUS.
...!?
I WANT MILITARY MIGHT.
MILITARY MIGHT!?
I WILL NOW REVEAL TO YOU MY TRUE AIM...
FWIK...
...THE ULTIMATE GOAL OF BAROQUE WORKS.

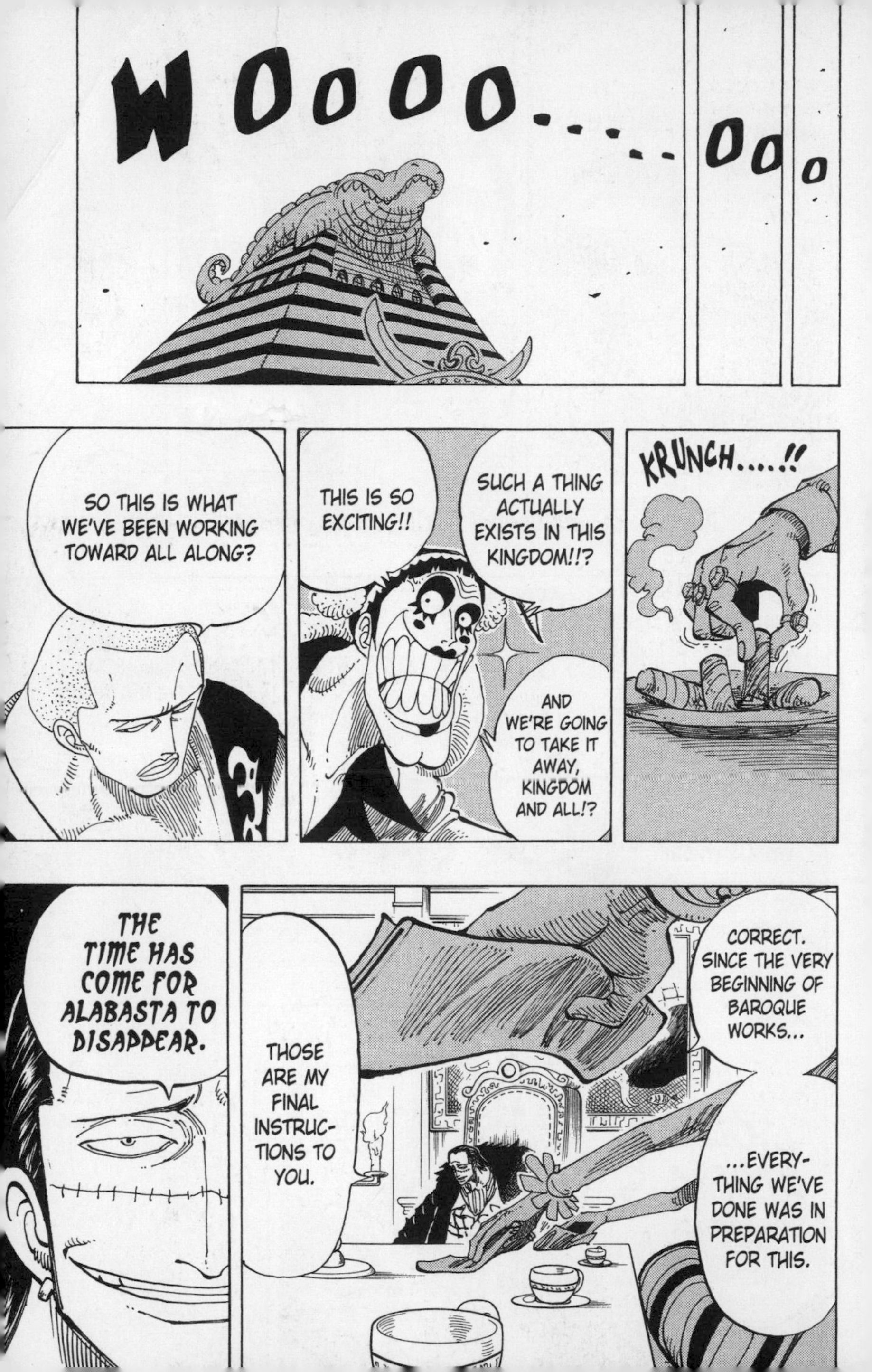
WOOOO.....OOo
KRUNCH.....!!
SUCH A THING ACTUALLY EXISTS IN THIS KINGDOM!!?
THIS IS SO EXCITING!!
AND WE'RE GOING TO TAKE IT AWAY, KINGDOM AND ALL!?
SO THIS IS WHAT WE'VE BEEN WORKING TOWARD ALL ALONG?
CORRECT. SINCE THE VERY BEGINNING OF BAROQUE WORKS...
...EVERY-THING WE'VE DONE WAS IN PREPARATION FOR THIS.
THOSE ARE MY FINAL INSTRUC-TIONS TO YOU.
THE TIME HAS COME FOR ALABASTA TO DISAPPEAR.

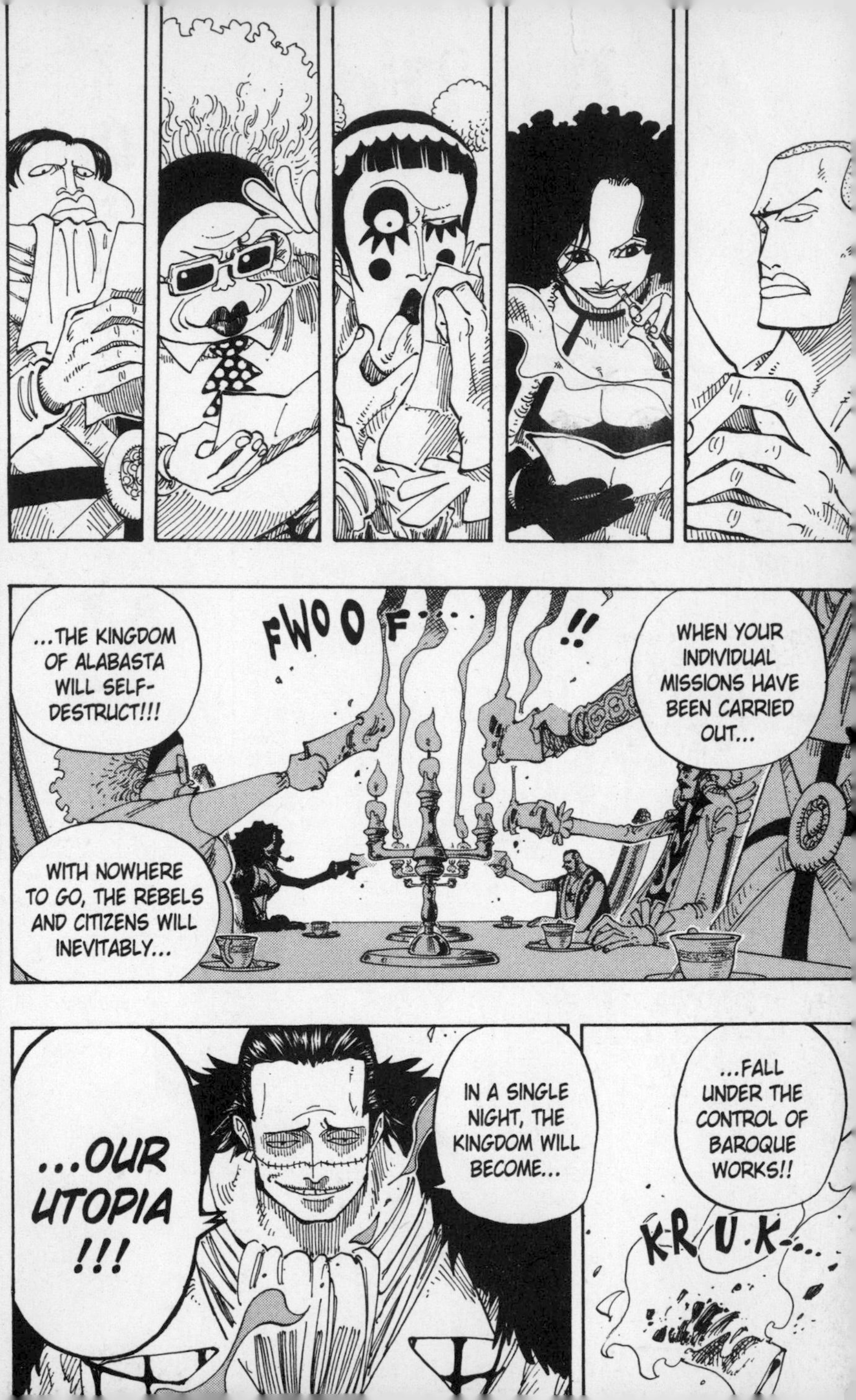
WHEN YOUR INDIVIDUAL MISSIONS HAVE BEEN CARRIED OUT...
!!
FWOOF...
...THE KINGDOM OF ALABASTA WILL SELF-DESTRUCT!!!
WITH NOWHERE TO GO, THE REBELS AND CITIZENS WILL INEVITABLY...
...FALL UNDER THE CONTROL OF BAROQUE WORKS!!
KRUK...
IN A SINGLE NIGHT, THE KINGDOM WILL BECOME...
...OUR UTOPIA!!!

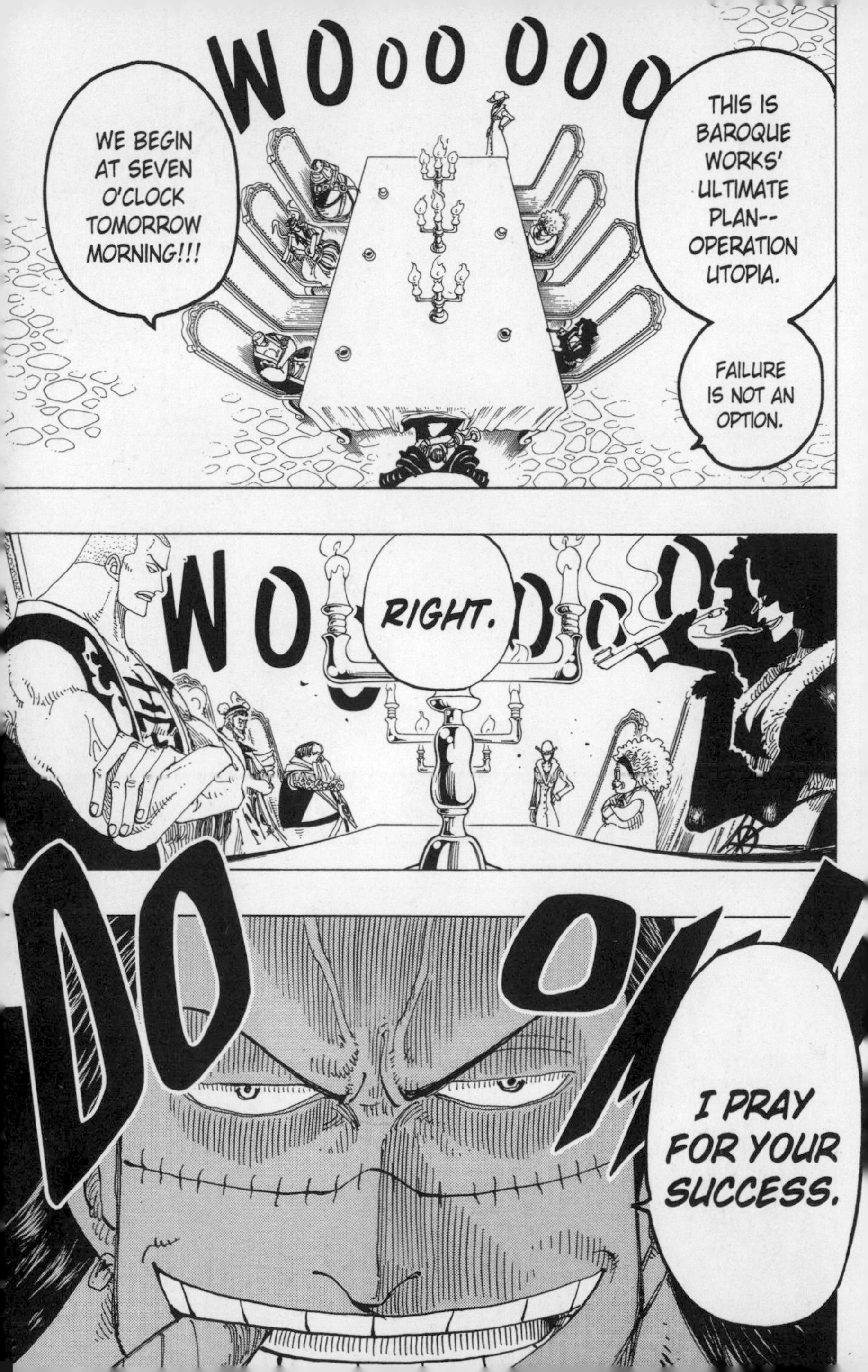
WOOOOOO
THIS IS BAROQUE WORKS' ULTIMATE PLAN-- OPERATION UTOPIA.
FAILURE IS NOT AN OPTION.
WE BEGIN AT SEVEN O'CLOCK TOMORROW MORNING!!!
RIGHT.
I PRAY FOR YOUR SUCCESS.

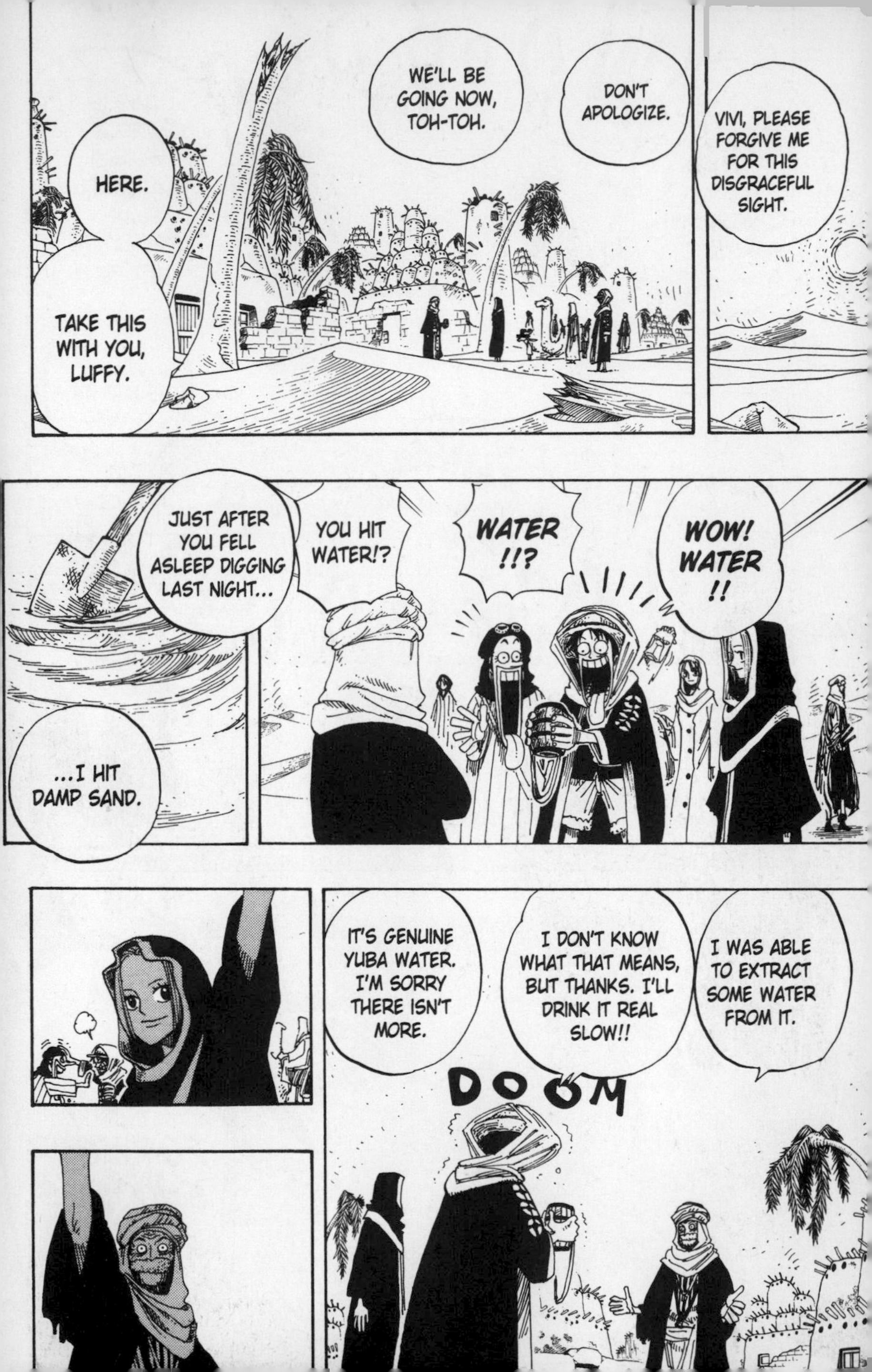
VIVI, PLEASE FORGIVE ME FOR THIS DISGRACEFUL SIGHT.
DON'T APOLOGIZE.
WE'LL BE GOING NOW, TOH-TOH.
HERE.
TAKE THIS WITH YOU, LUFFY.
WOW! WATER !!
WATER !!?
YOU HIT WATER!?
JUST AFTER YOU FELL ASLEEP DIGGING LAST NIGHT...
...I HIT DAMP SAND.
I WAS ABLE TO EXTRACT SOME WATER FROM IT.
I DON'T KNOW WHAT THAT MEANS, BUT THANKS. I'LL DRINK IT REAL SLOW!!
IT'S GENUINE YUBA WATER. I'M SORRY THERE ISN'T MORE.
DOOM

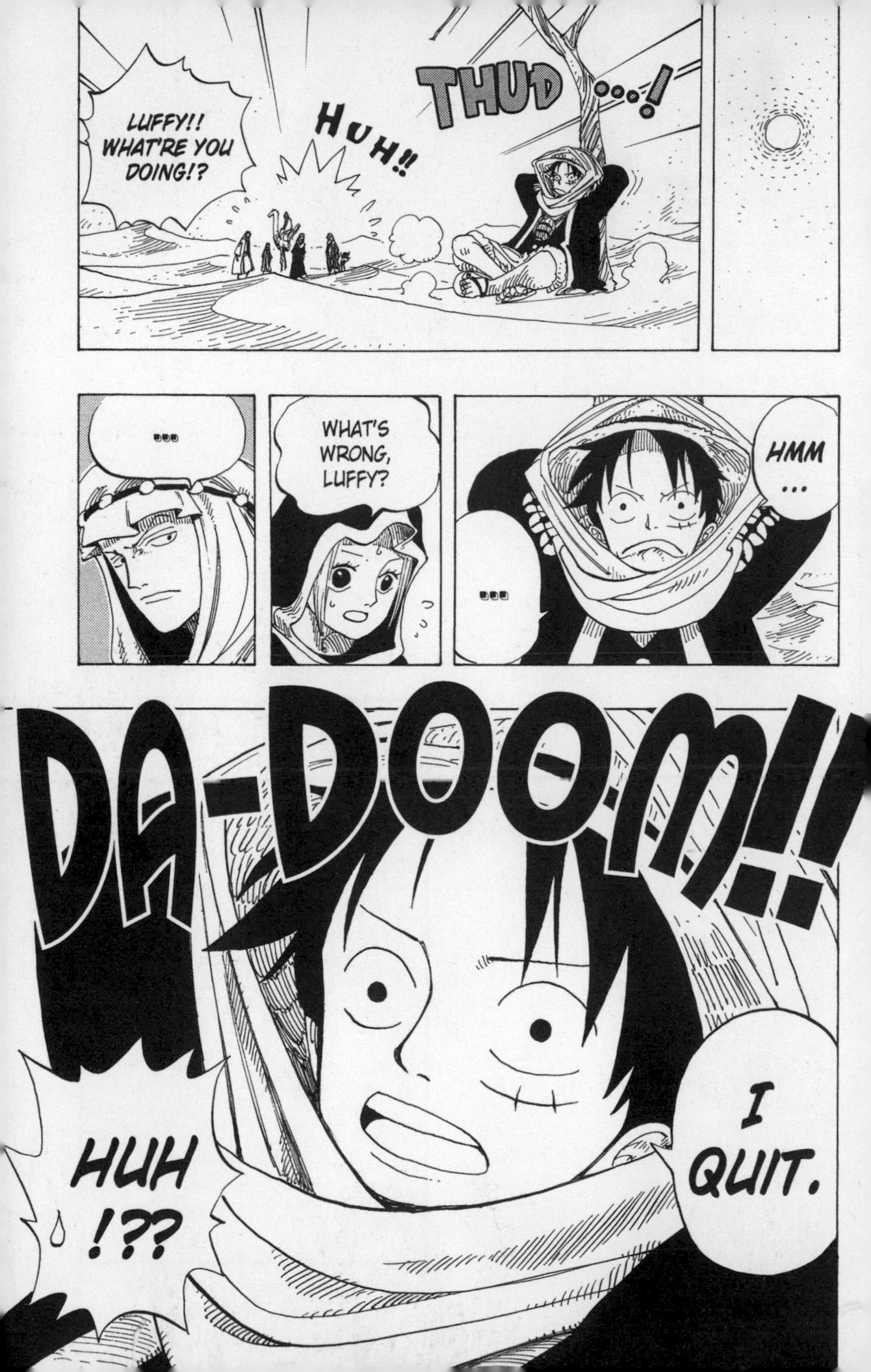

THUD...!
HUH!!
LUFFY!! WHAT'RE YOU DOING!?
HMM ...
...
WHAT'S WRONG, LUFFY?
...
DA-DOOM!!
I QUIT.
HUH !??

WIP WIP

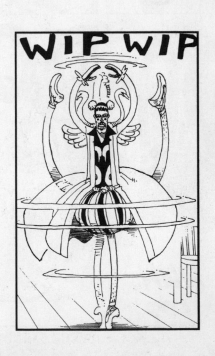

Chapter 166:
LUFFY VS. VIVI

TEXT ON FAN: OBJECTION

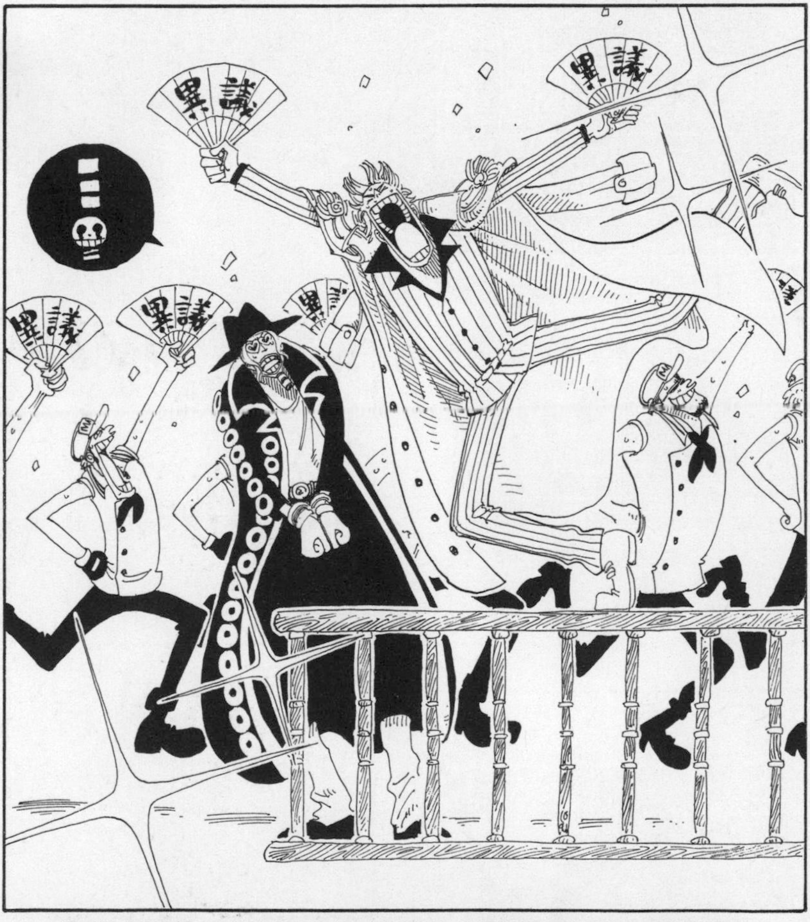
異議
異議
異議
異議

DJANGO'S DANCE PARADISE, VOL.31: "FULLBODY'S MANLY DANCE WITH TEARFUL PROTESTS!!"

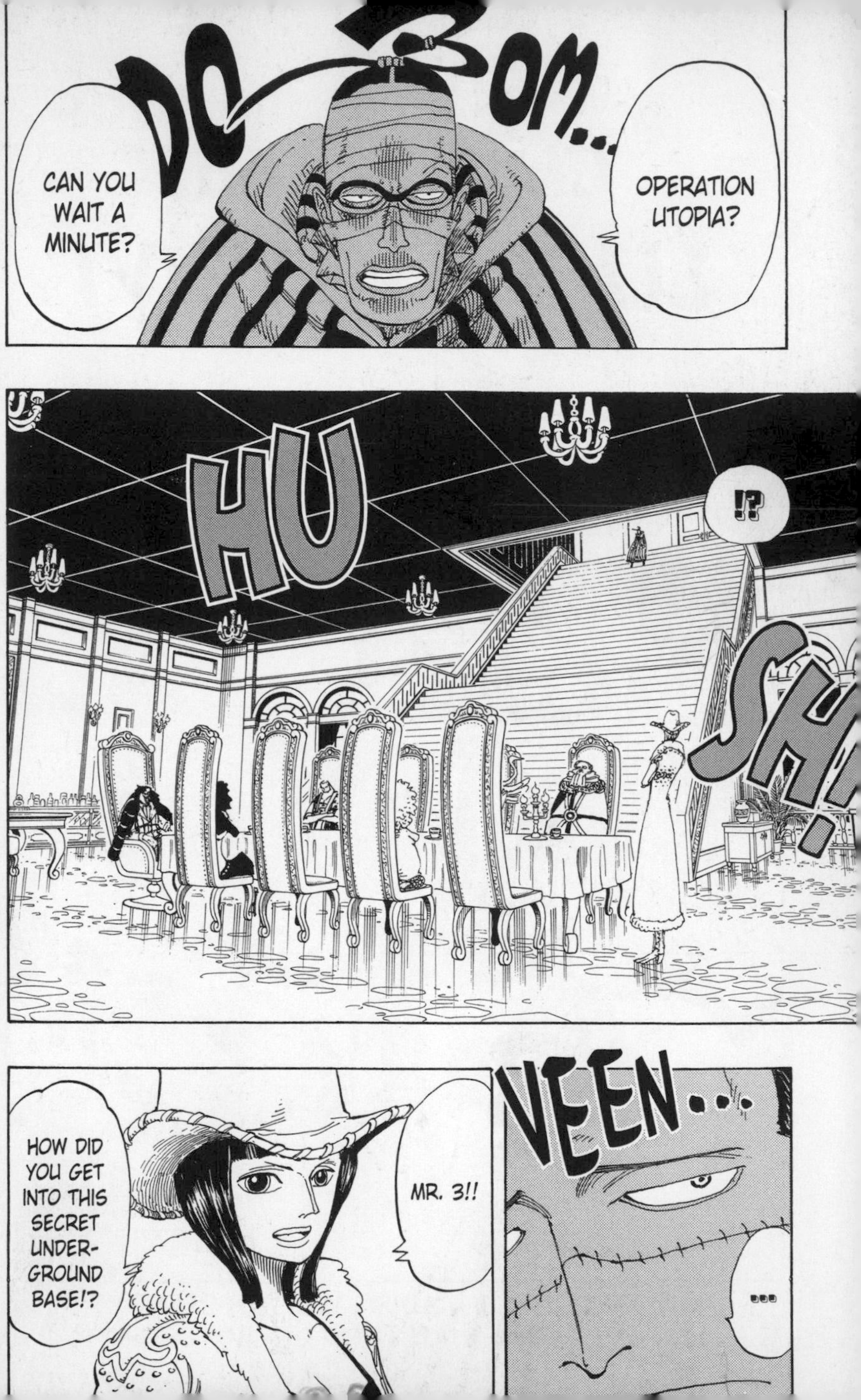
DOBOM...
OPERATION UTOPIA?
CAN YOU WAIT A MINUTE?
HU
SH
!?
VEEN...
...
MR. 3!!
HOW DID YOU GET INTO THIS SECRET UNDER-GROUND BASE!?

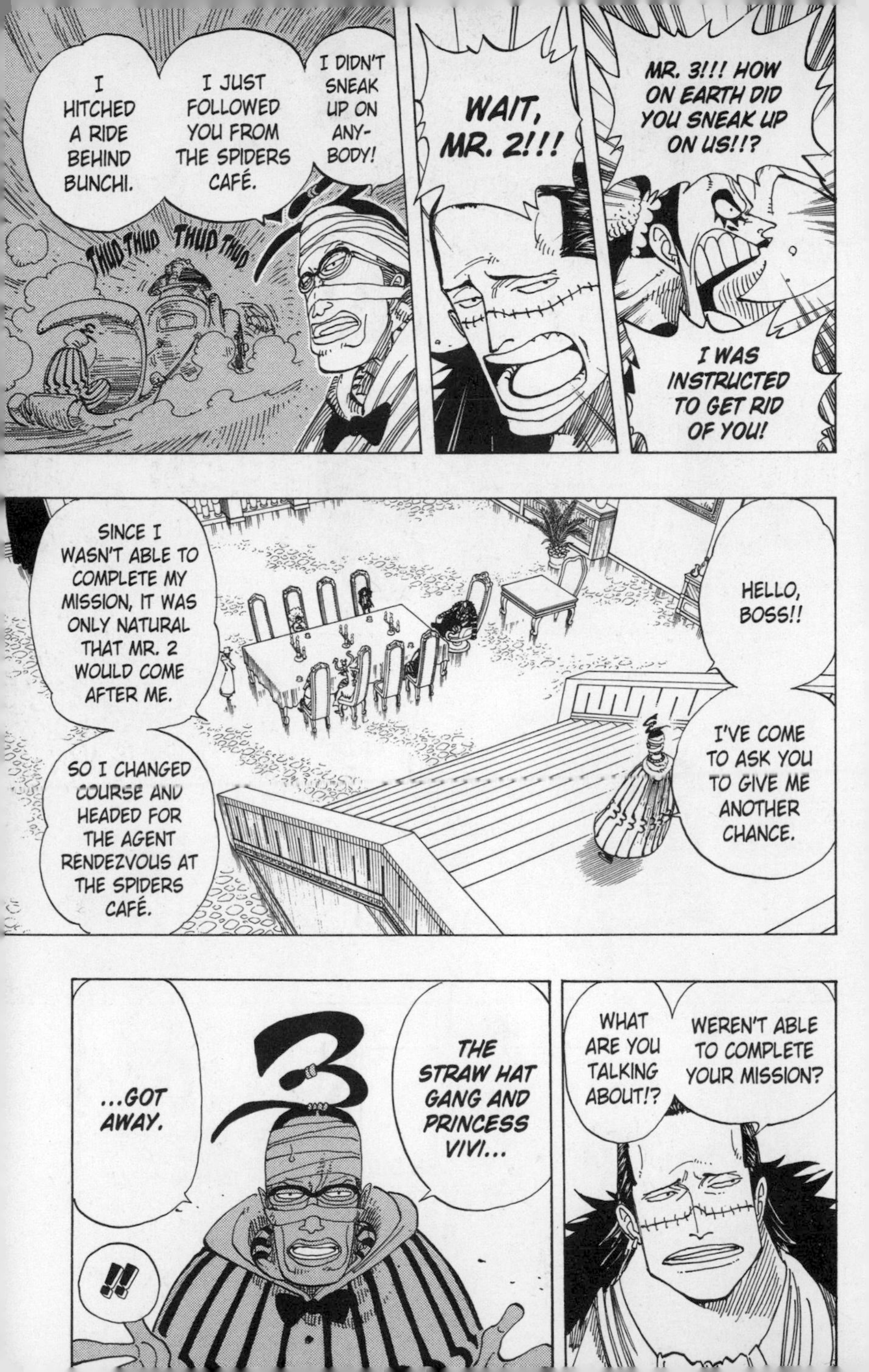
MR. 3!!! HOW ON EARTH DID YOU SNEAK UP ON US!!?
I WAS INSTRUCTED TO GET RID OF YOU!
WAIT, MR. 2!!!
I DIDN'T SNEAK UP ON ANYBODY!
I JUST FOLLOWED YOU FROM THE SPIDERS CAFÉ.
I HITCHED A RIDE BEHIND BUNCHI.
THUD THUD THUD THUD
HELLO, BOSS!!
I'VE COME TO ASK YOU TO GIVE ME ANOTHER CHANCE.
SINCE I WASN'T ABLE TO COMPLETE MY MISSION, IT WAS ONLY NATURAL THAT MR. 2 WOULD COME AFTER ME.
SO I CHANGED COURSE AND HEADED FOR THE AGENT RENDEZVOUS AT THE SPIDERS CAFÉ.
WEREN'T ABLE TO COMPLETE YOUR MISSION?
WHAT ARE YOU TALKING ABOUT!?
THE STRAW HAT GANG AND PRINCESS VIVI...
...GOT AWAY.
!!

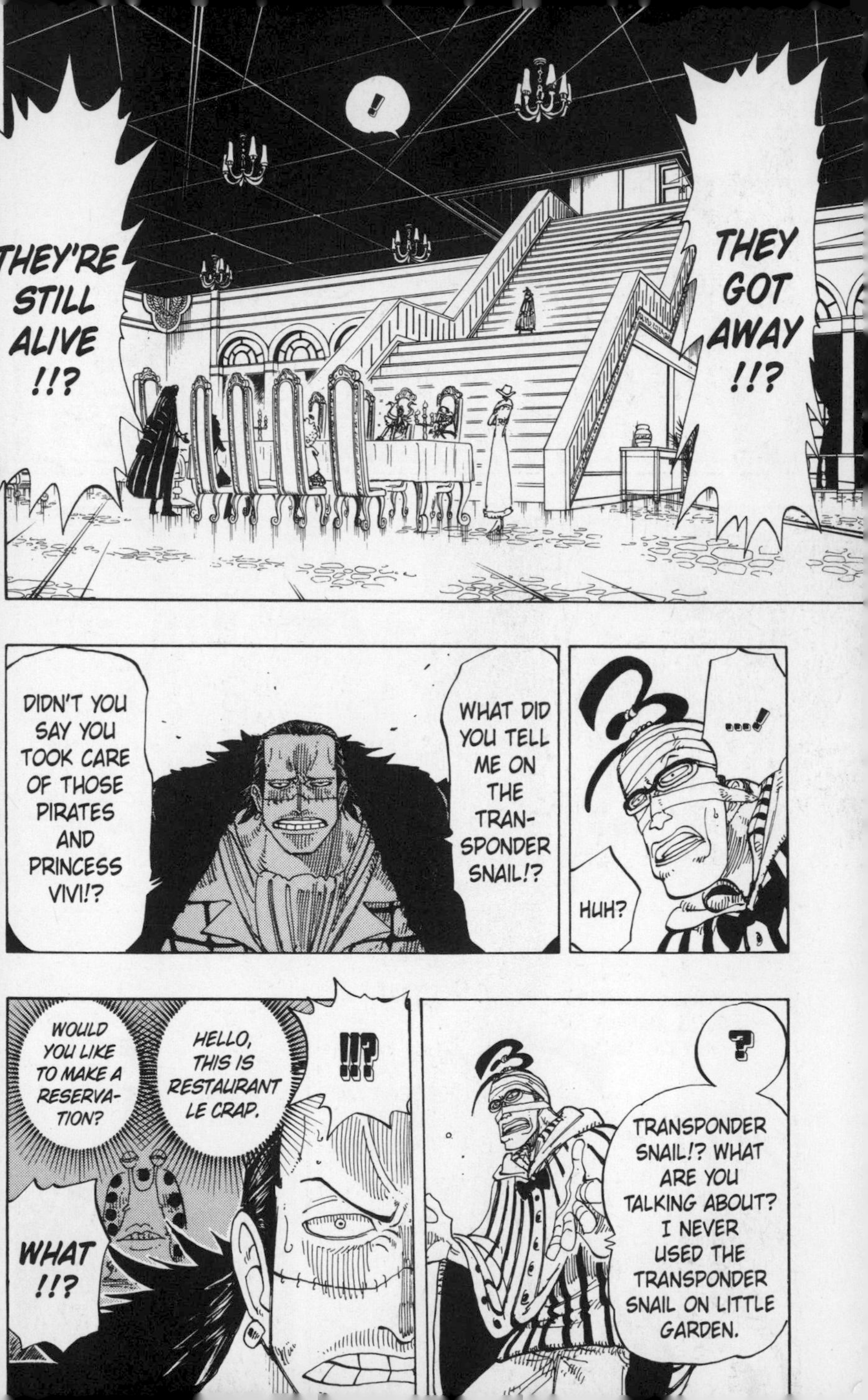
THEY GOT AWAY!!?
!
THEY'RE STILL ALIVE!!?
...!
HUH?
WHAT DID YOU TELL ME ON THE TRANSPONDER SNAIL!?
DIDN'T YOU SAY YOU TOOK CARE OF THOSE PIRATES AND PRINCESS VIVI!?
?
TRANSPONDER SNAIL!? WHAT ARE YOU TALKING ABOUT? I NEVER USED THE TRANSPONDER SNAIL ON LITTLE GARDEN.
!!?
HELLO, THIS IS RESTAURANT LE CRAP.
WOULD YOU LIKE TO MAKE A RESERVATION?
WHAT!!?

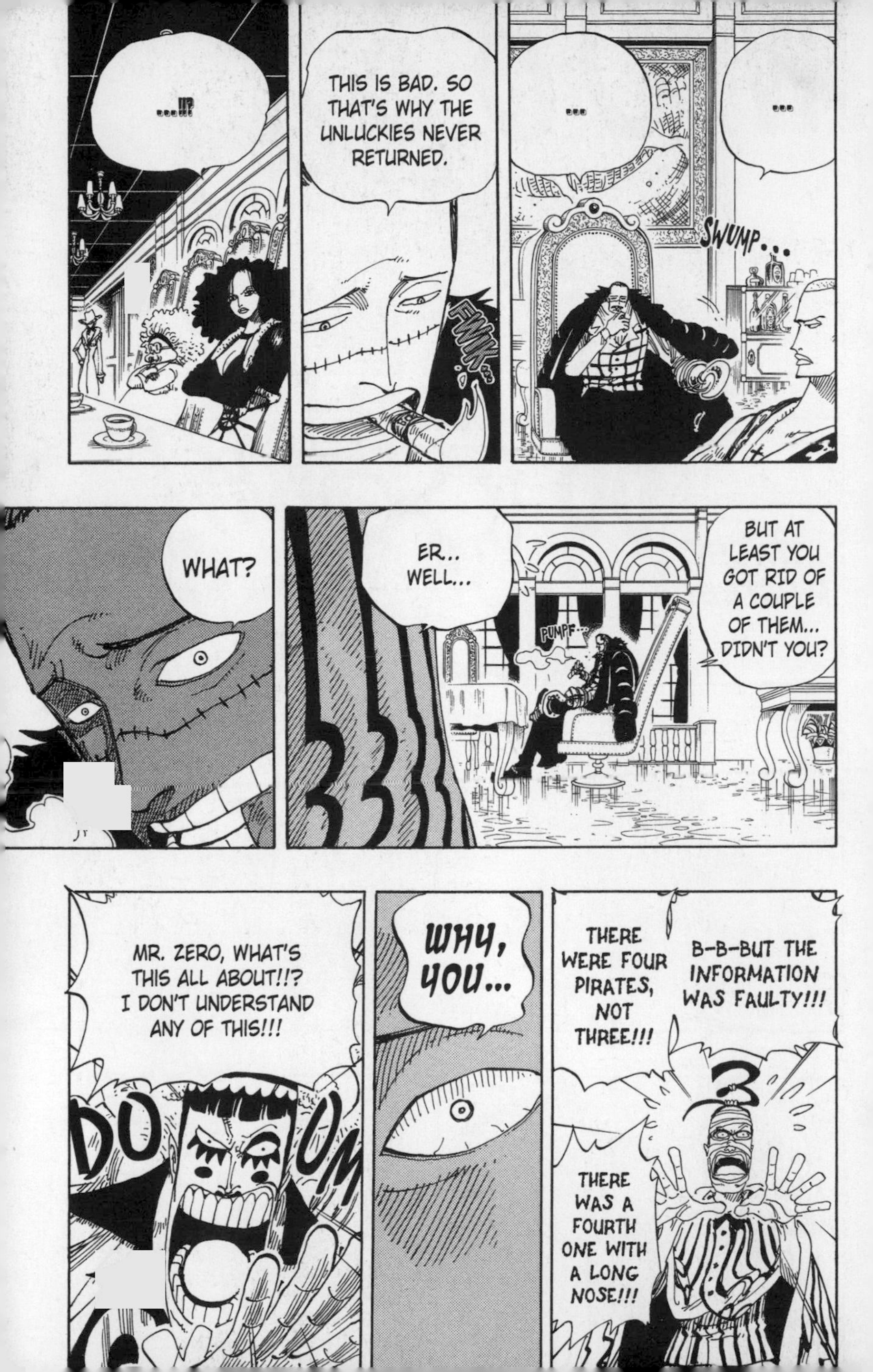
...
...
SWUMP...
THIS IS BAD. SO THAT'S WHY THE UNLUCKIES NEVER RETURNED.
FWIK...
...!?
BUT AT LEAST YOU GOT RID OF A COUPLE OF THEM... DIDN'T YOU?
PUMPF...
ER.. WELL...
WHAT?
B-B-BUT THE INFORMATION WAS FAULTY!!!
THERE WERE FOUR PIRATES, NOT THREE!!!
THERE WAS A FOURTH ONE WITH A LONG NOSE!!!
WHY, YOU...
MR. ZERO, WHAT'S THIS ALL ABOUT!!? I DON'T UNDERSTAND ANY OF THIS!!!
DOOM

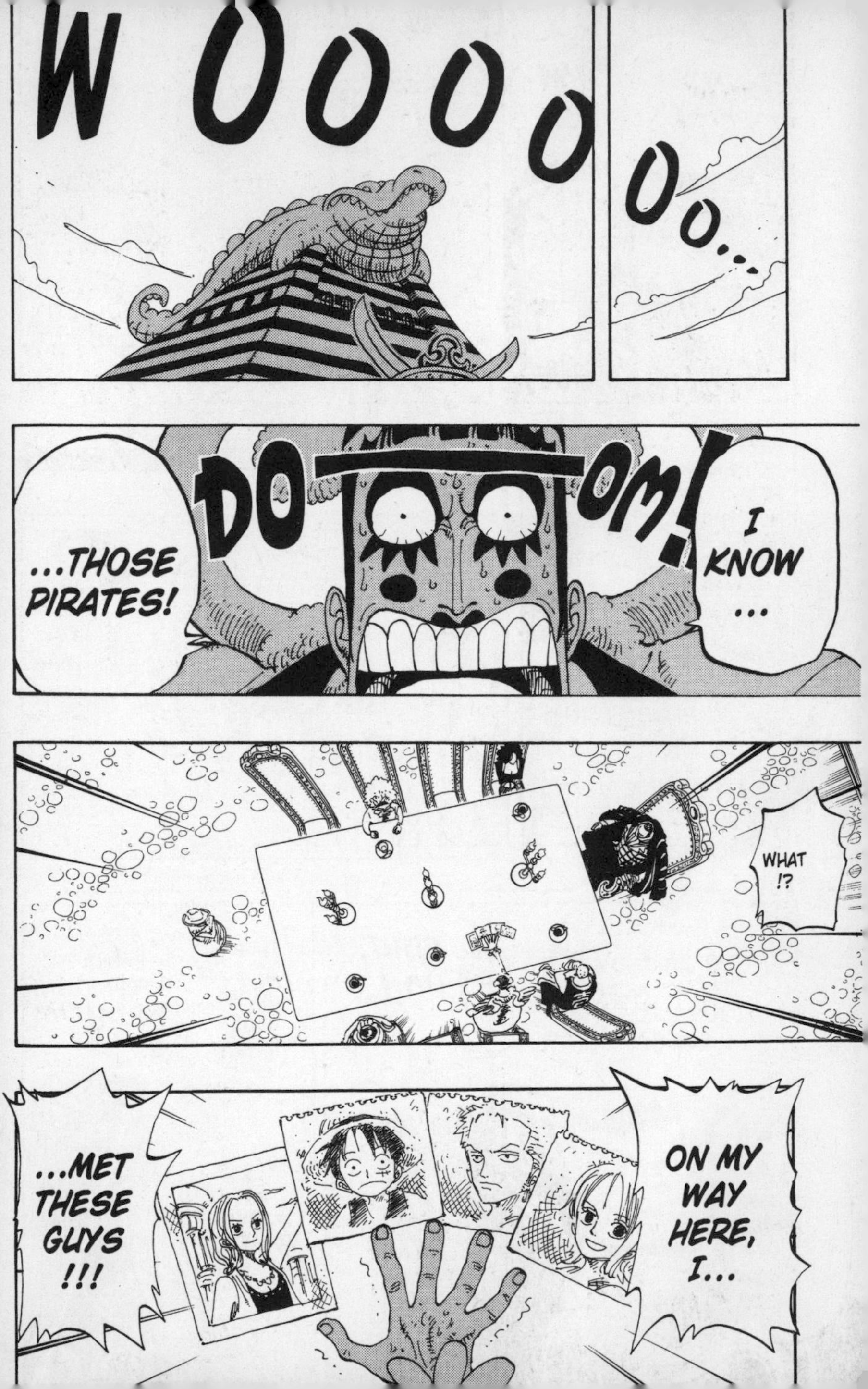
WOOOOOo...
I KNOW ...
DOOM!
...THOSE PIRATES!
WHAT !?
ON MY WAY HERE, I...
...MET THESE GUYS !!!

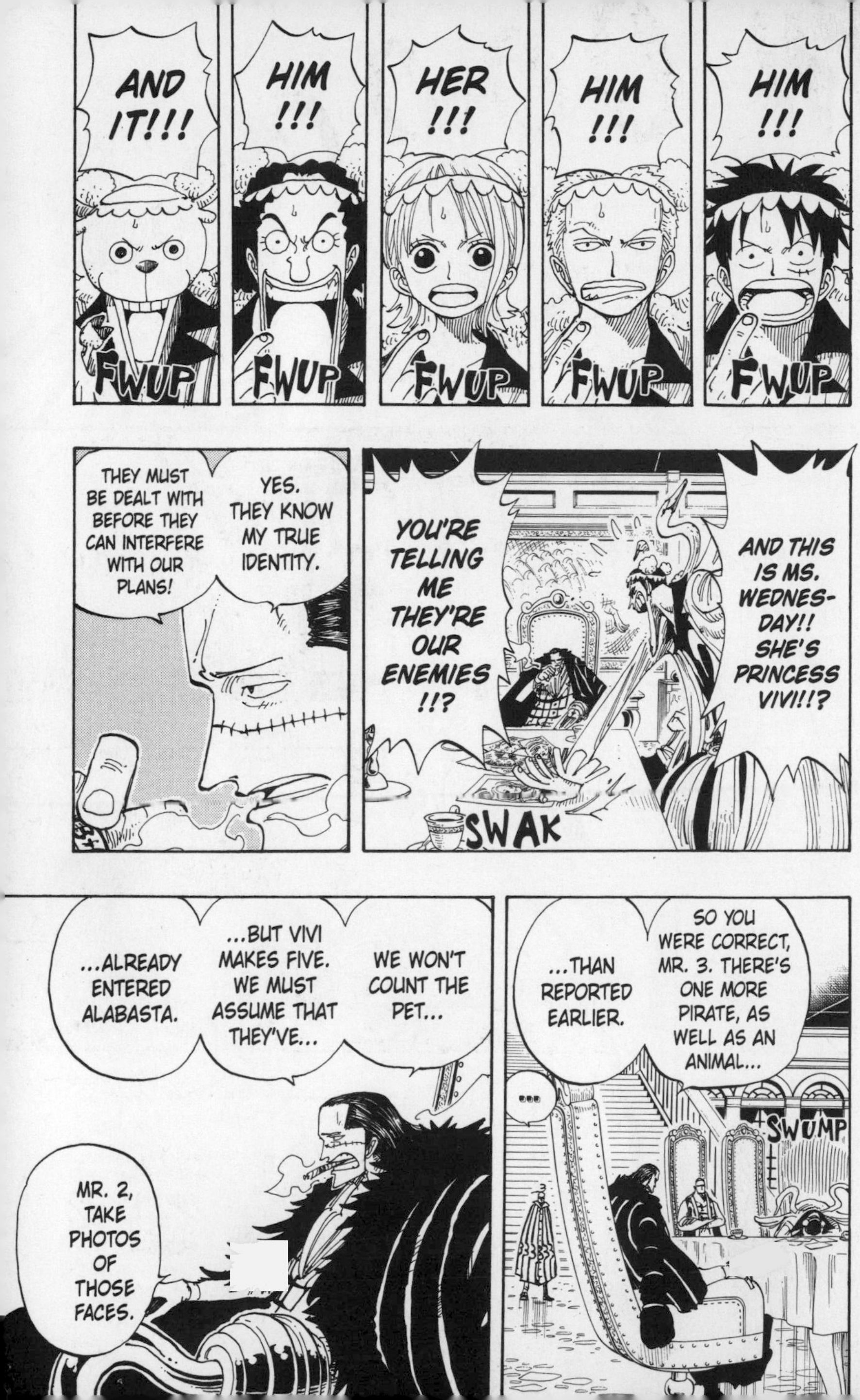
HIM!!!
FWUP
HIM!!!
FWUP
HER!!!
FWUP
HIM!!!
FWUP
AND IT!!!
FWUP
AND THIS IS MS. WEDNESDAY!! SHE'S PRINCESS VIVI!!?
YOU'RE TELLING ME THEY'RE OUR ENEMIES!!?
SWAK
YES. THEY KNOW MY TRUE IDENTITY.
THEY MUST BE DEALT WITH BEFORE THEY CAN INTERFERE WITH OUR PLANS!
SO YOU WERE CORRECT, MR. 3. THERE'S ONE MORE PIRATE, AS WELL AS AN ANIMAL...
...THAN REPORTED EARLIER.
...
SWUMP
WE WON'T COUNT THE PET...
...BUT VIVI MAKES FIVE. WE MUST ASSUME THAT THEY'VE...
...ALREADY ENTERED ALABASTA.
MR. 2, TAKE PHOTOS OF THOSE FACES.

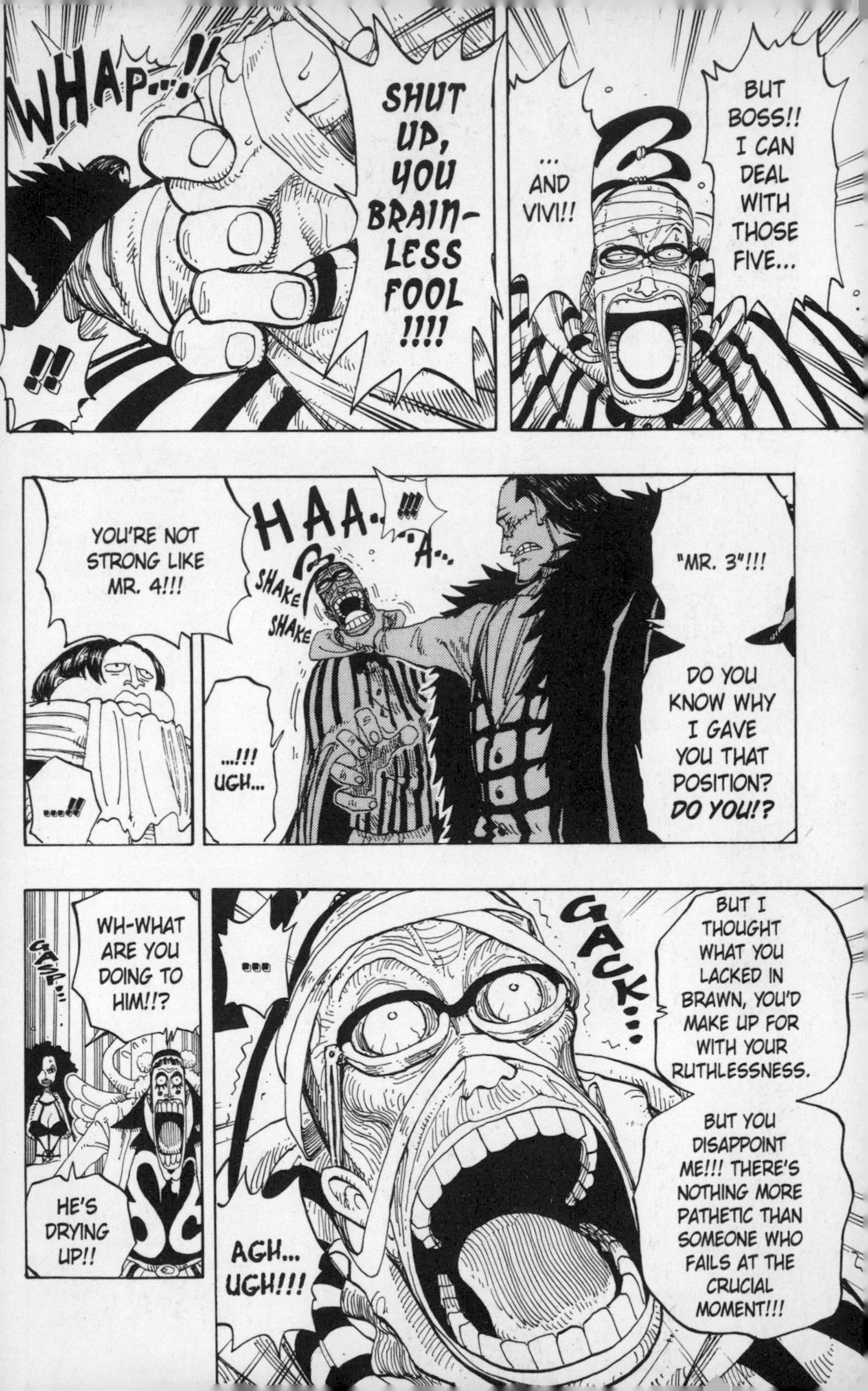
BUT BOSS!! I CAN DEAL WITH THOSE FIVE...
... AND VIVI!!
SHUT UP, YOU BRAIN-LESS FOOL !!!!
WHAP...!!
!!
"MR. 3"!!!
DO YOU KNOW WHY I GAVE YOU THAT POSITION? DO YOU!?
HAA...!!! ...A...
SHAKE
SHAKE
...!!! UGH...
YOU'RE NOT STRONG LIKE MR. 4!!!
...!!
BUT I THOUGHT WHAT YOU LACKED IN BRAWN, YOU'D MAKE UP FOR WITH YOUR RUTHLESSNESS.
BUT YOU DISAPPOINT ME!!! THERE'S NOTHING MORE PATHETIC THAN SOMEONE WHO FAILS AT THE CRUCIAL MOMENT!!!
GACK...
...
AGH... UGH!!!
WH-WHAT ARE YOU DOING TO HIM!!?
GASP...!!
HE'S DRYING UP!!

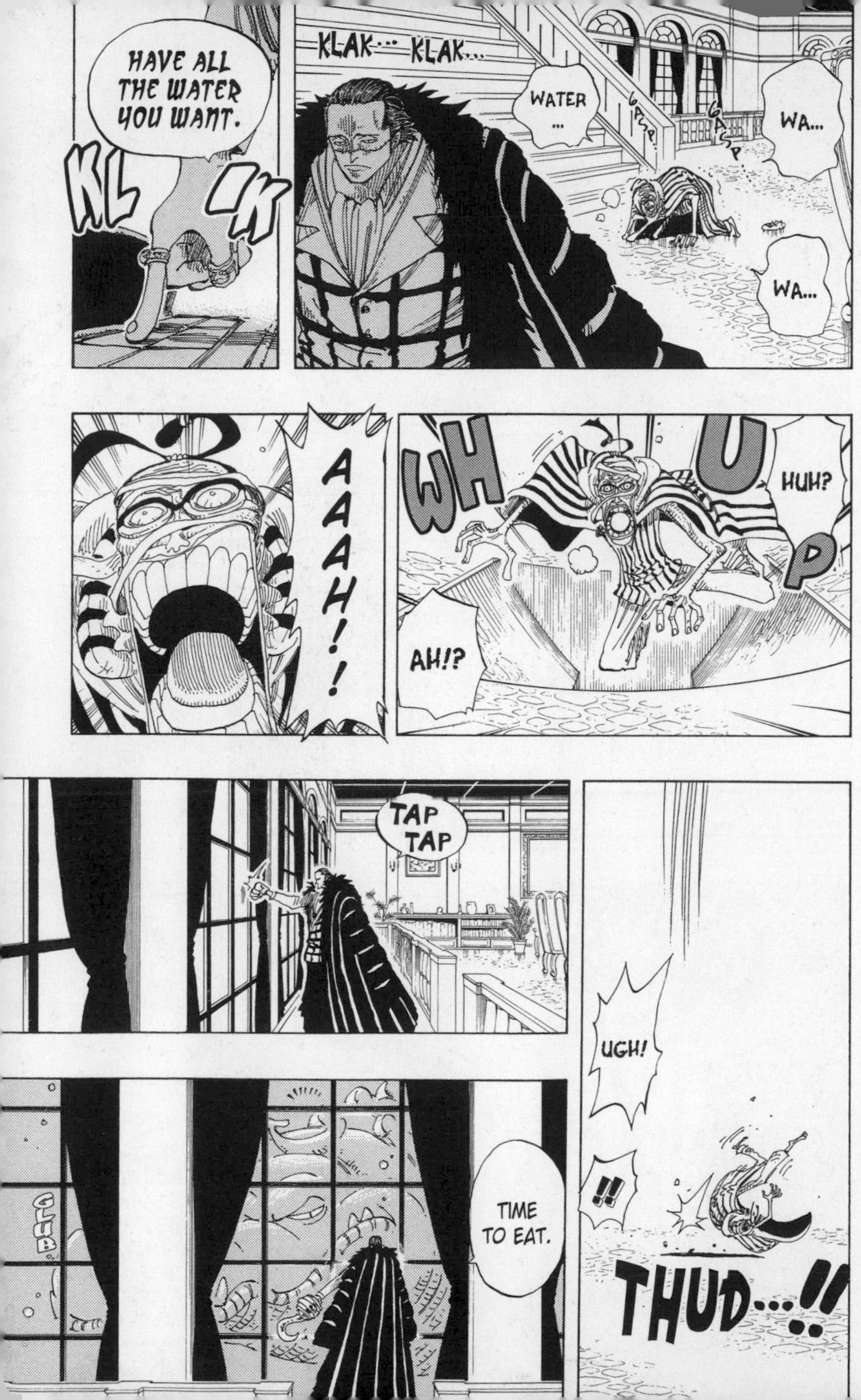
KLAK... KLAK...
WATER ...
GASP
GASP
WA...
WA...
HAVE ALL THE WATER YOU WANT.
KLIK
WHUP
HUH?
AH!?
AAAAH!!
UGH!
!!
THUD...!!
TAP TAP
TIME TO EAT.
GLUB

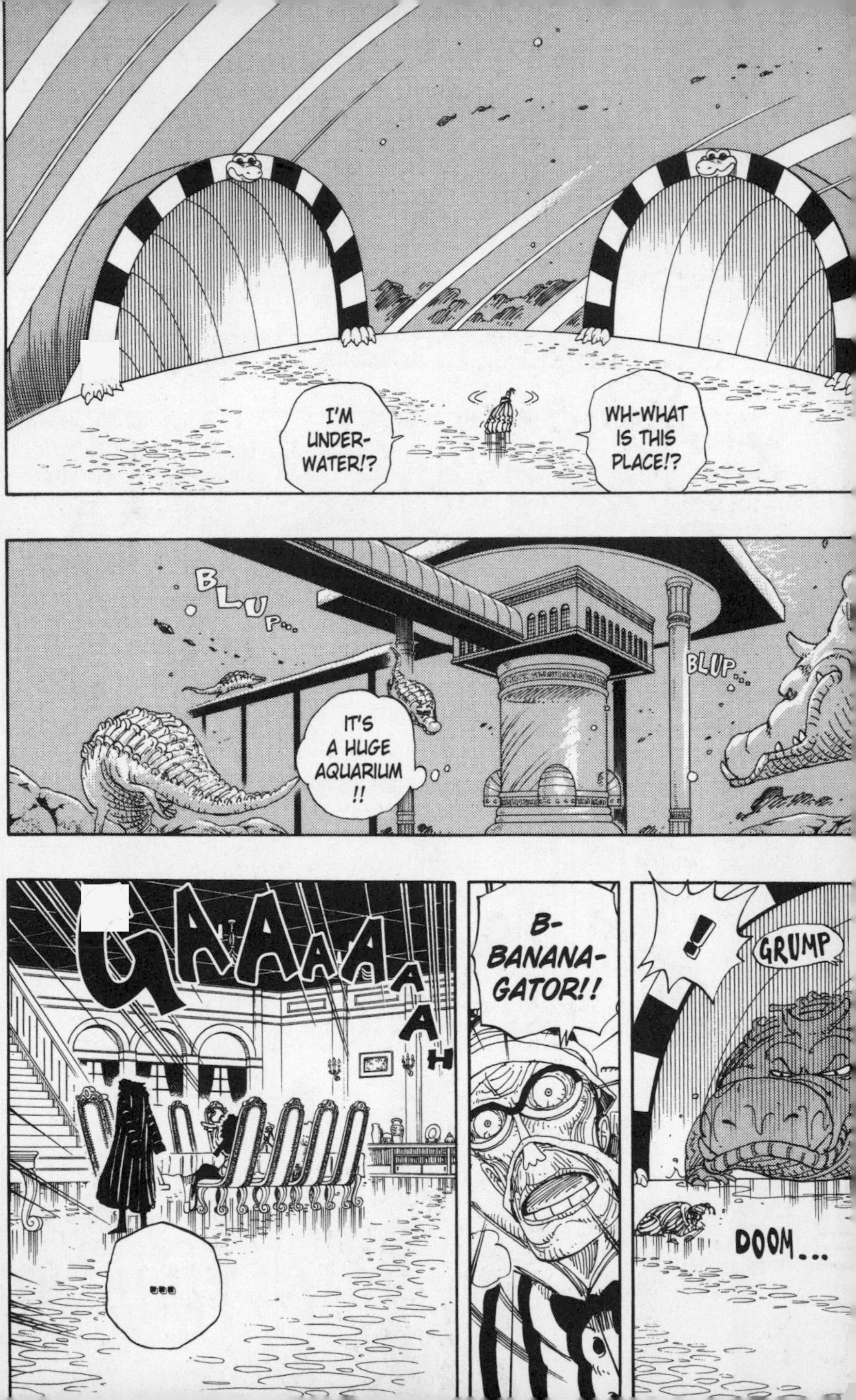
WH-WHAT IS THIS PLACE!?
I'M UNDER-WATER!?
BLUP...
BLUP...
IT'S A HUGE AQUARIUM !!
!
GRUMP
DOOM...
B-BANANA-GATOR!!
GAAAAAAAH
...

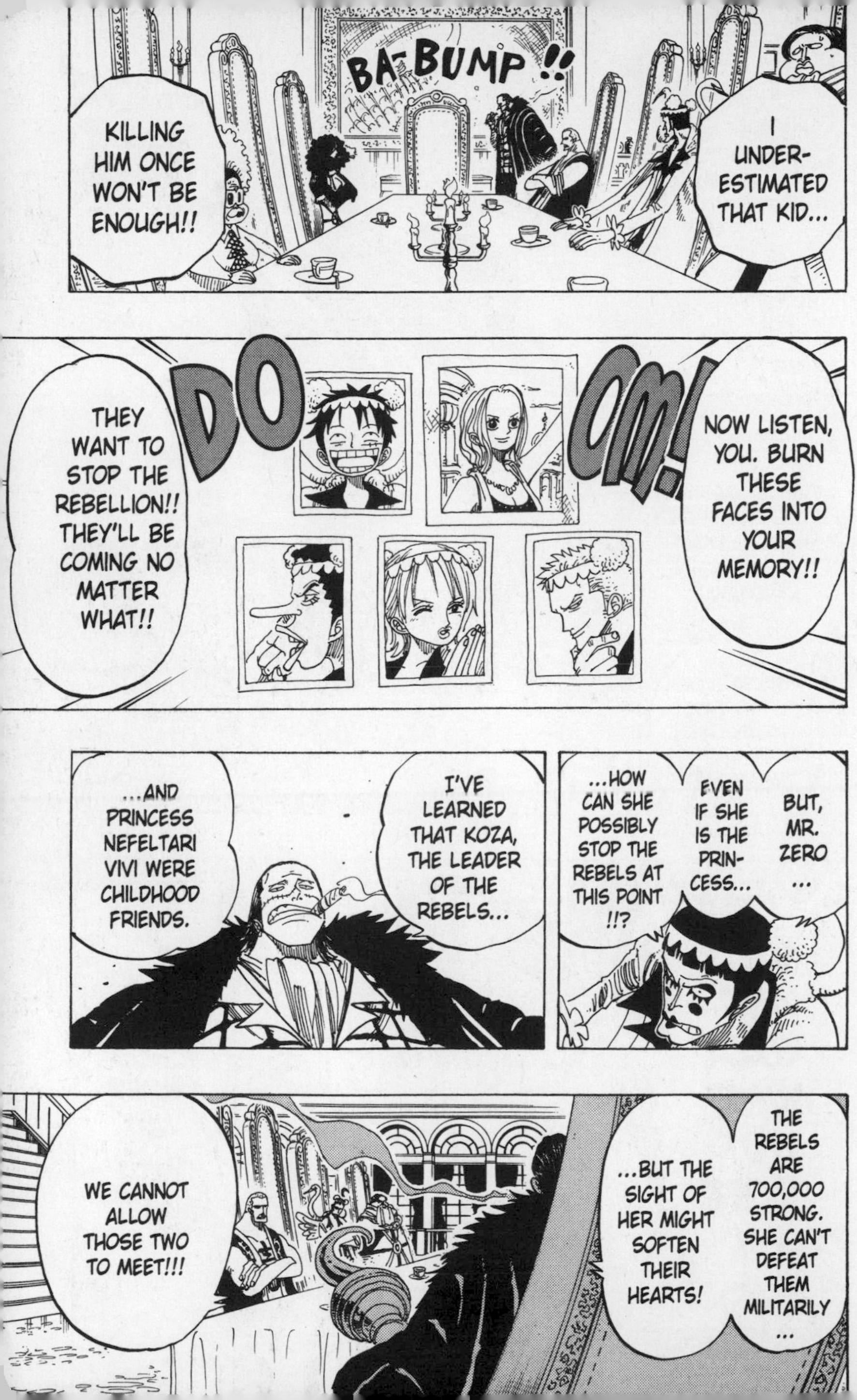
BA-BUMP!!
I UNDER-ESTIMATED THAT KID...
KILLING HIM ONCE WON'T BE ENOUGH!!
NOW LISTEN, YOU. BURN THESE FACES INTO YOUR MEMORY!!
DOOM!!
THEY WANT TO STOP THE REBELLION!! THEY'LL BE COMING NO MATTER WHAT!!
BUT, MR. ZERO...
EVEN IF SHE IS THE PRINCESS...
...HOW CAN SHE POSSIBLY STOP THE REBELS AT THIS POINT!!?
I'VE LEARNED THAT KOZA, THE LEADER OF THE REBELS...
...AND PRINCESS NEFELTARI VIVI WERE CHILDHOOD FRIENDS.
THE REBELS ARE 700,000 STRONG. SHE CAN'T DEFEAT THEM MILITARILY...
...BUT THE SIGHT OF HER MIGHT SOFTEN THEIR HEARTS!
WE CANNOT ALLOW THOSE TWO TO MEET!!!

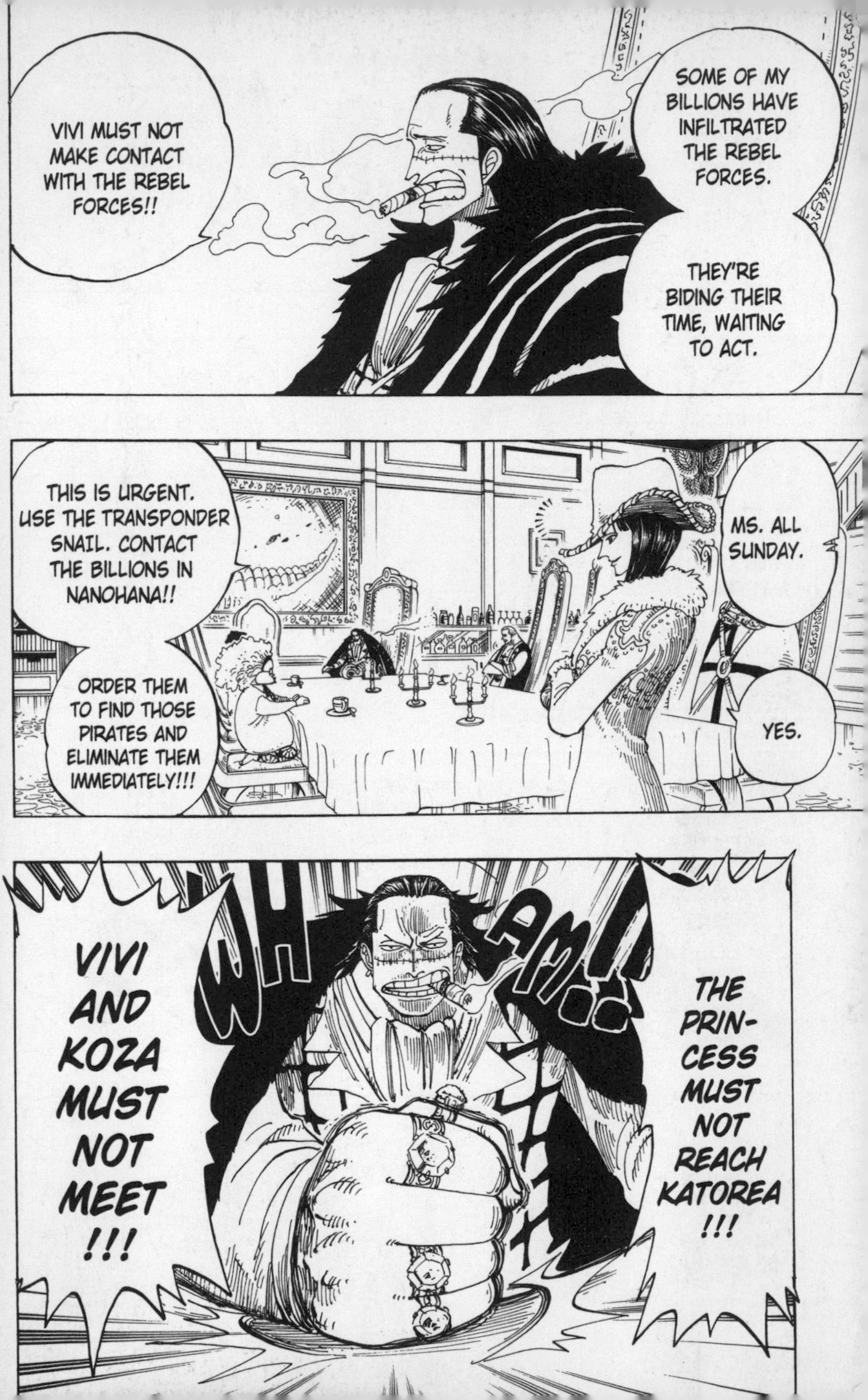
SOME OF MY BILLIONS HAVE INFILTRATED THE REBEL FORCES.
THEY'RE BIDING THEIR TIME, WAITING TO ACT.
VIVI MUST NOT MAKE CONTACT WITH THE REBEL FORCES!!
MS. ALL SUNDAY.
THIS IS URGENT. USE THE TRANSPONDER SNAIL. CONTACT THE BILLIONS IN NANOHANA!!
ORDER THEM TO FIND THOSE PIRATES AND ELIMINATE THEM IMMEDIATELY!!!
YES.
WHAM!!
THE PRIN-CESS MUST NOT REACH KATOREA!!!
VIVI AND KOZA MUST NOT MEET!!!

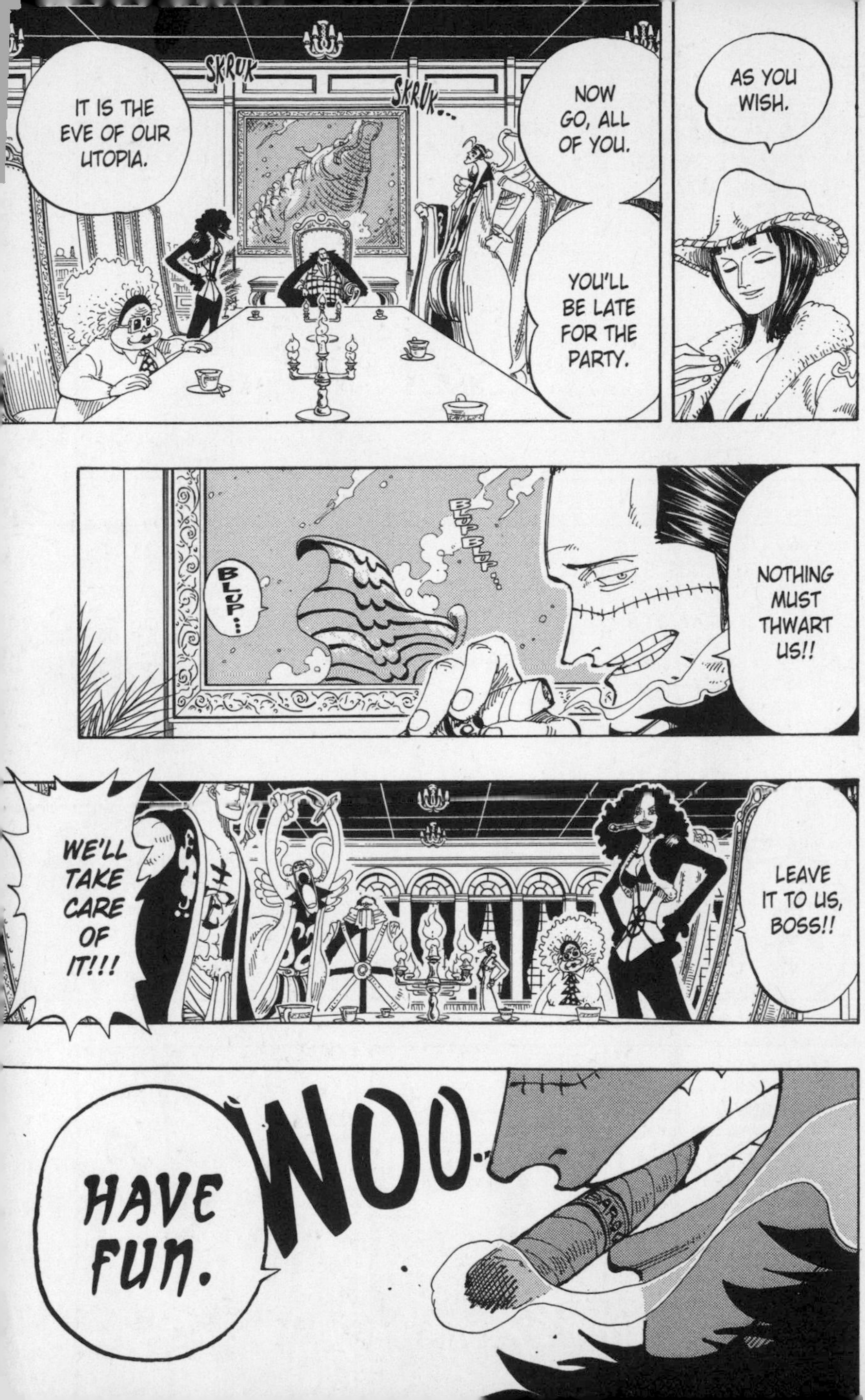
AS YOU WISH.
NOW GO, ALL OF YOU.
YOU'LL BE LATE FOR THE PARTY.
SKRUK...
SKRUK
IT IS THE EVE OF OUR UTOPIA.
NOTHING MUST THWART US!!
BLUP BLUP...
BLUP...
LEAVE IT TO US, BOSS!!
WE'LL TAKE CARE OF IT!!!
WOO..
HAVE FUN.

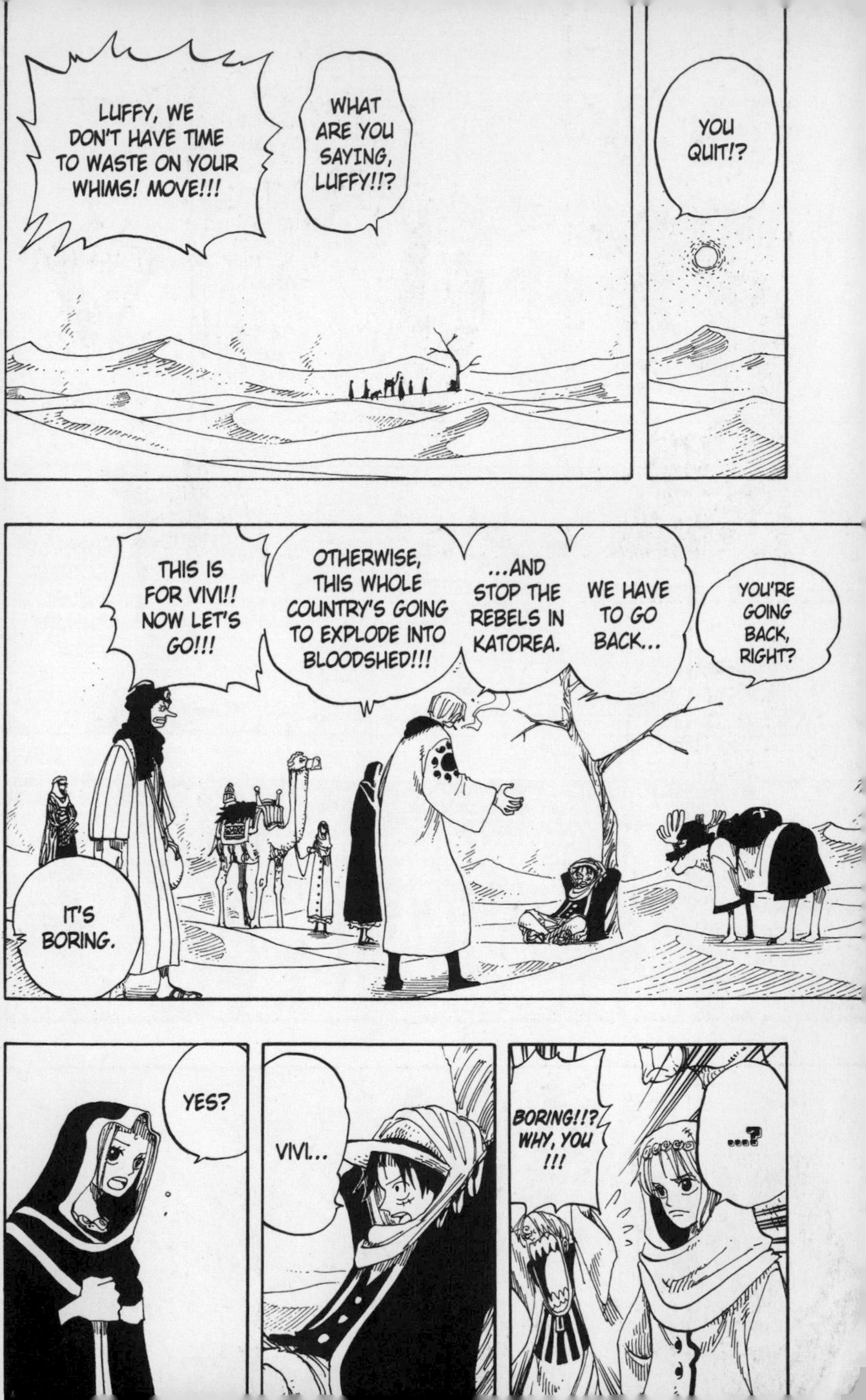
YOU QUIT!?
WHAT ARE YOU SAYING, LUFFY!!?
LUFFY, WE DON'T HAVE TIME TO WASTE ON YOUR WHIMS! MOVE!!!
YOU'RE GOING BACK, RIGHT?
WE HAVE TO GO BACK...
...AND STOP THE REBELS IN KATOREA.
OTHERWISE, THIS WHOLE COUNTRY'S GOING TO EXPLODE INTO BLOODSHED!!!
THIS IS FOR VIVI!! NOW LET'S GO!!!
IT'S BORING.
...?
BORING!!? WHY, YOU !!!
VIVI...
YES?

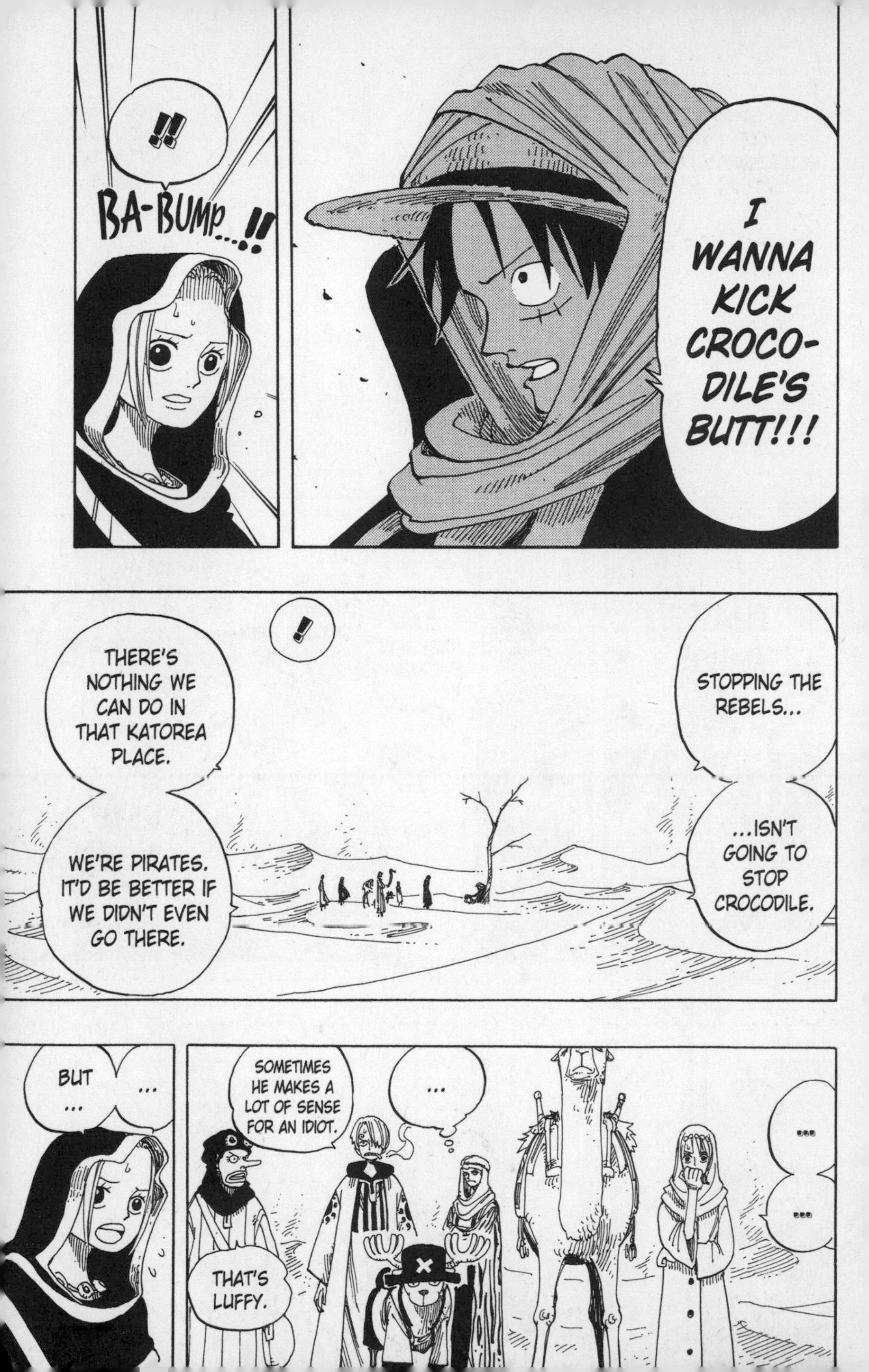
I WANNA KICK CROCODILE'S BUTT!!!
!!
BA-BUMP...!!
STOPPING THE REBELS...
...ISN'T GOING TO STOP CROCODILE.
!
THERE'S NOTHING WE CAN DO IN THAT KATOREA PLACE.
WE'RE PIRATES. IT'D BE BETTER IF WE DIDN'T EVEN GO THERE.
...
...
...
SOMETIMES HE MAKES A LOT OF SENSE FOR AN IDIOT.
THAT'S LUFFY.
...
BUT ...

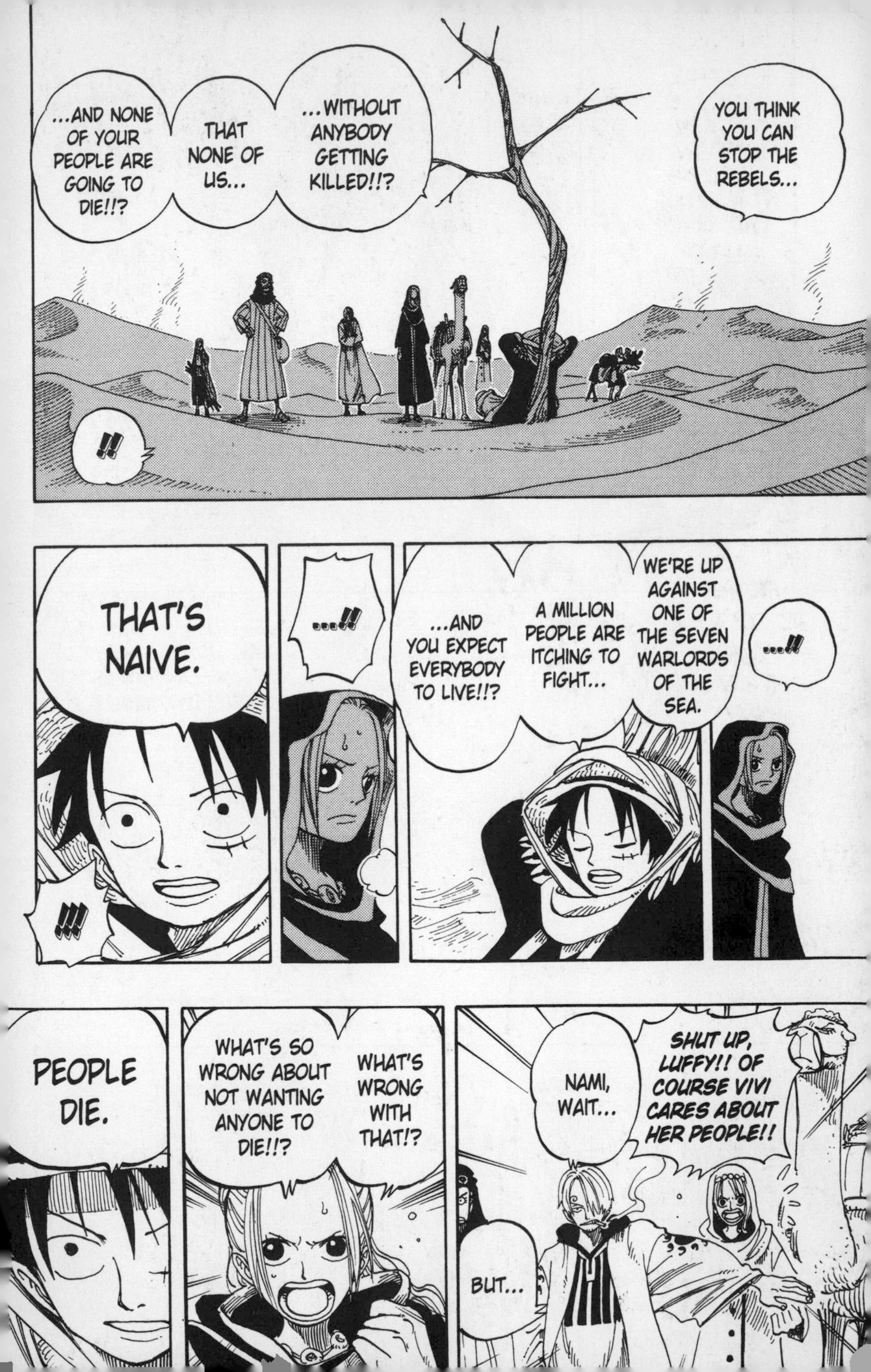
YOU THINK YOU CAN STOP THE REBELS...
...WITHOUT ANYBODY GETTING KILLED!!?
THAT NONE OF US...
...AND NONE OF YOUR PEOPLE ARE GOING TO DIE!!?
!!
...!!
WE'RE UP AGAINST ONE OF THE SEVEN WARLORDS OF THE SEA.
A MILLION PEOPLE ARE ITCHING TO FIGHT...
...AND YOU EXPECT EVERYBODY TO LIVE!!?
...!!
THAT'S NAIVE.
!!!
SHUT UP, LUFFY!! OF COURSE VIVI CARES ABOUT HER PEOPLE!!
NAMI, WAIT...
BUT...
WHAT'S WRONG WITH THAT!?
WHAT'S SO WRONG ABOUT NOT WANTING ANYONE TO DIE!!?
PEOPLE DIE.

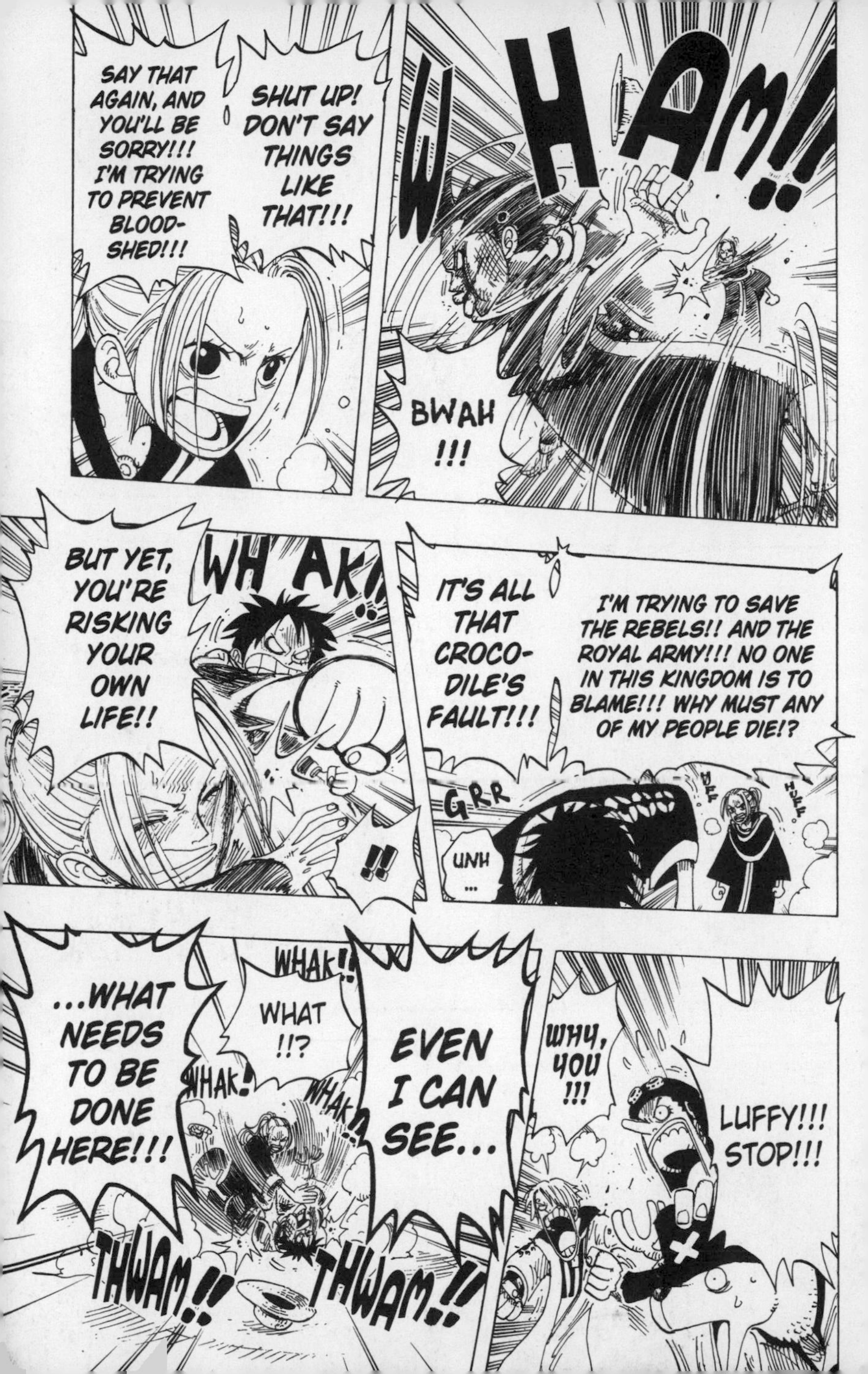
WHAM!!
BWAH !!!
SHUT UP! DON'T SAY THINGS LIKE THAT!!!
SAY THAT AGAIN, AND YOU'LL BE SORRY!!! I'M TRYING TO PREVENT BLOOD-SHED!!!
I'M TRYING TO SAVE THE REBELS!! AND THE ROYAL ARMY!!! NO ONE IN THIS KINGDOM IS TO BLAME!!! WHY MUST ANY OF MY PEOPLE DIE!?
HUFF
HUFF
IT'S ALL THAT CROCO-DILE'S FAULT!!!
GRR
UNH ...
WHAK!!
BUT YET, YOU'RE RISKING YOUR OWN LIFE!!
!!
LUFFY!!! STOP!!!
WHY, YOU!!!
EVEN I CAN SEE...
WHAK!!
WHAT !!?
WHAK!
WHAK!!
THWAM!!
THWAM!!
...WHAT NEEDS TO BE DONE HERE!!!

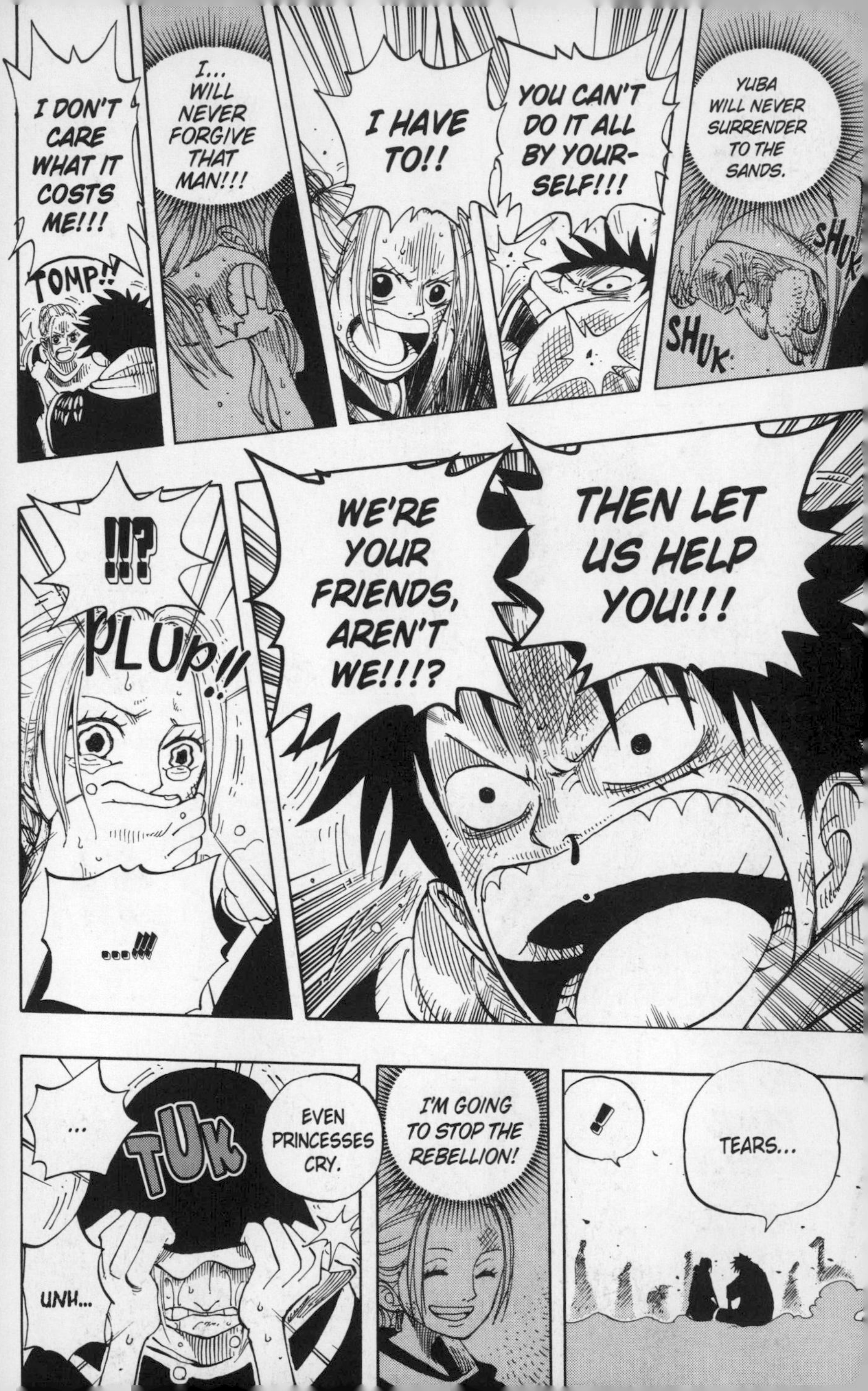
YUBA WILL NEVER SURRENDER TO THE SANDS.
SHUK
SHUK
YOU CAN'T DO IT ALL BY YOURSELF!!!
I HAVE TO!!
I... WILL NEVER FORGIVE THAT MAN!!!
I DON'T CARE WHAT IT COSTS ME!!!
TOMP!!
THEN LET US HELP YOU!!!
WE'RE YOUR FRIENDS, AREN'T WE!!!?
!!?
PLUP!!
...!!!
TEARS...
!
I'M GOING TO STOP THE REBELLION!
EVEN PRINCESSES CRY.
TUK
...
UNH...

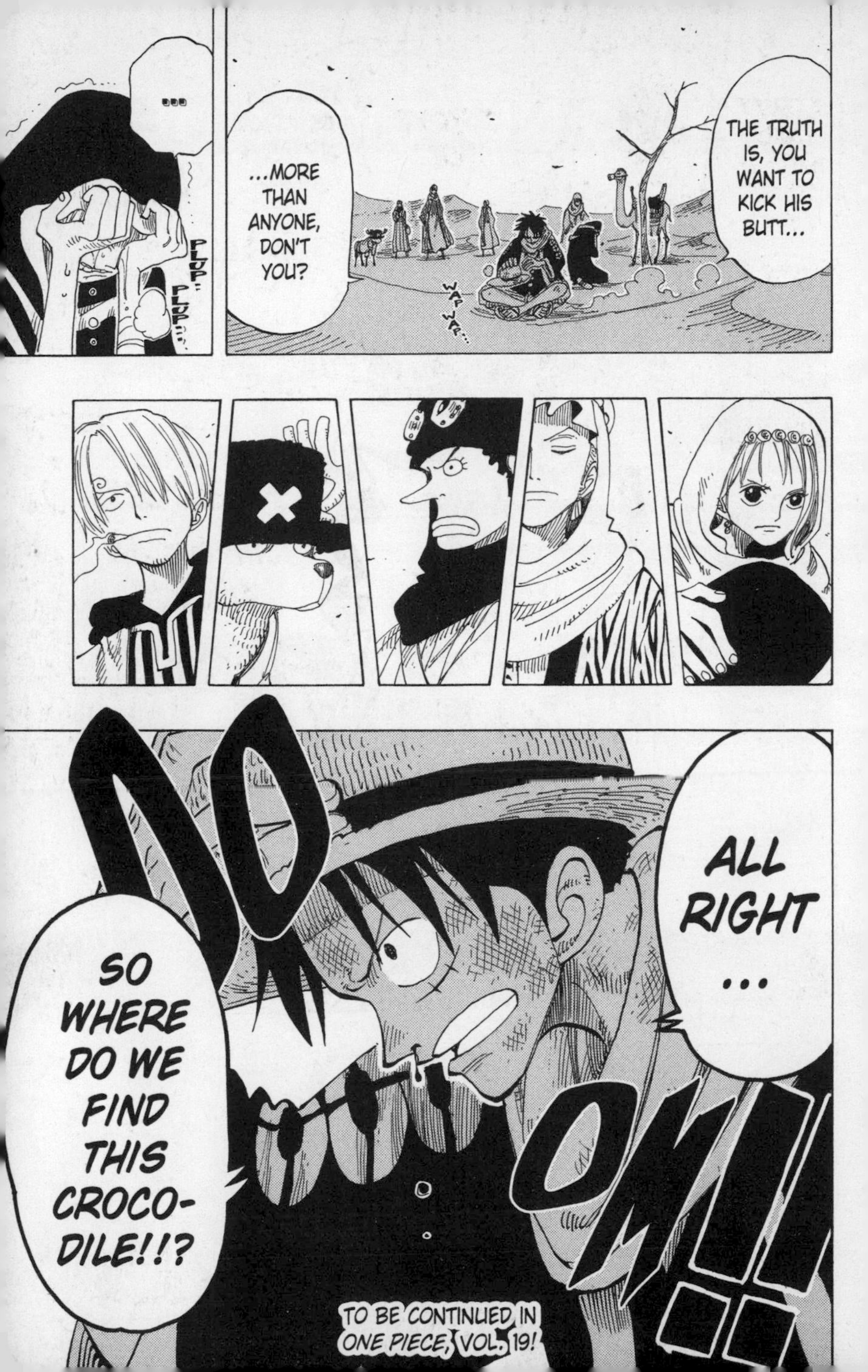
THE TRUTH IS, YOU WANT TO KICK HIS BUTT...
...MORE THAN ANYONE, DON'T YOU?
WAP WAP...
...
PLUP... PLUP...
ALL RIGHT...
DO
SO WHERE DO WE FIND THIS CROCO-DILE!!?
ON!!
TO BE CONTINUED IN ONE PIECE, VOL. 19!

COMING NEXT VOLUME:

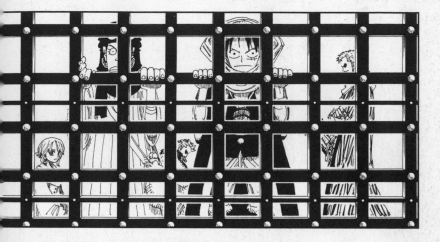

Heading to Rainbase to kick some Crocodile butt, Luffy and crew run into the persistent Captain Smoker. Fighting against Baroque Works and the Navy at the same time won't be easy, especially when they fall into a trap set by Mr. Zero!! The Baroque Works' "Operation Utopia" is about to start—with the destruction of the Kingdom of Alabasta its main objective. The Straw Hats are the only ones who can stop their evil plan, but first they'll have to escape their indestructible cage!!

ON SALE NOW!

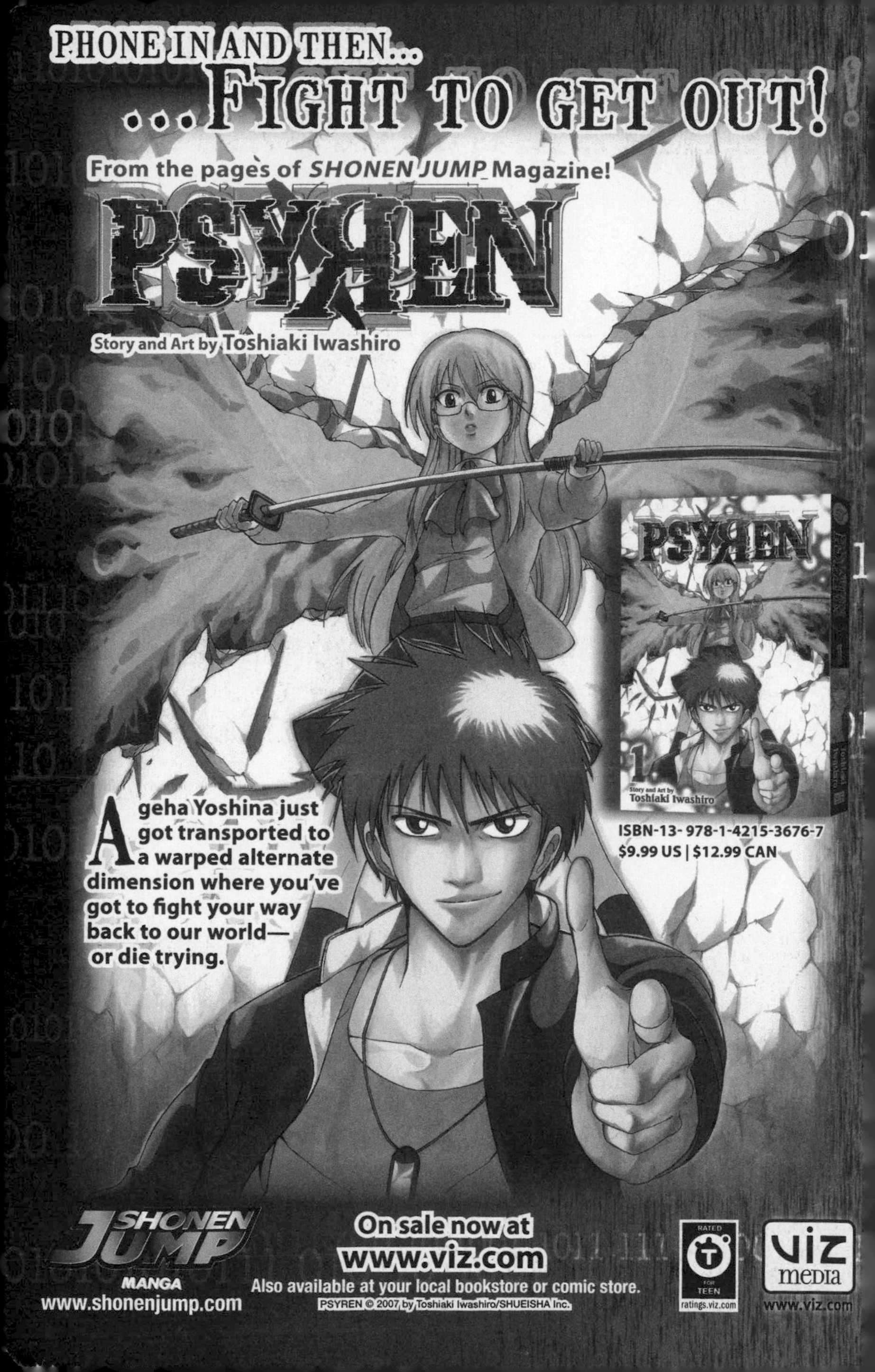
PHONE IN AND THEN...
...FIGHT TO GET OUT!
From the pages of SHONEN JUMP Magazine!
PSYREN
Story and Art by Toshiaki Iwashiro
PSYREN
1
Story and Art by
Toshiaki Iwashiro
ISBN-13- 978-1-4215-3676-7
$9.99 US | $12.99 CAN
Ageha Yoshina just got transported to a warped alternate dimension where you've got to fight your way back to our world—or die trying.
SHONEN JUMP
MANGA
www.shonenjump.com
On sale now at
www.viz.com
Also available at your local bookstore or comic store.
PSYREN © 2007 by Toshiaki Iwashiro/SHUEISHA Inc.
RATED
T
FOR
TEEN
ratings.viz.com
VIZ
media
www.viz.com

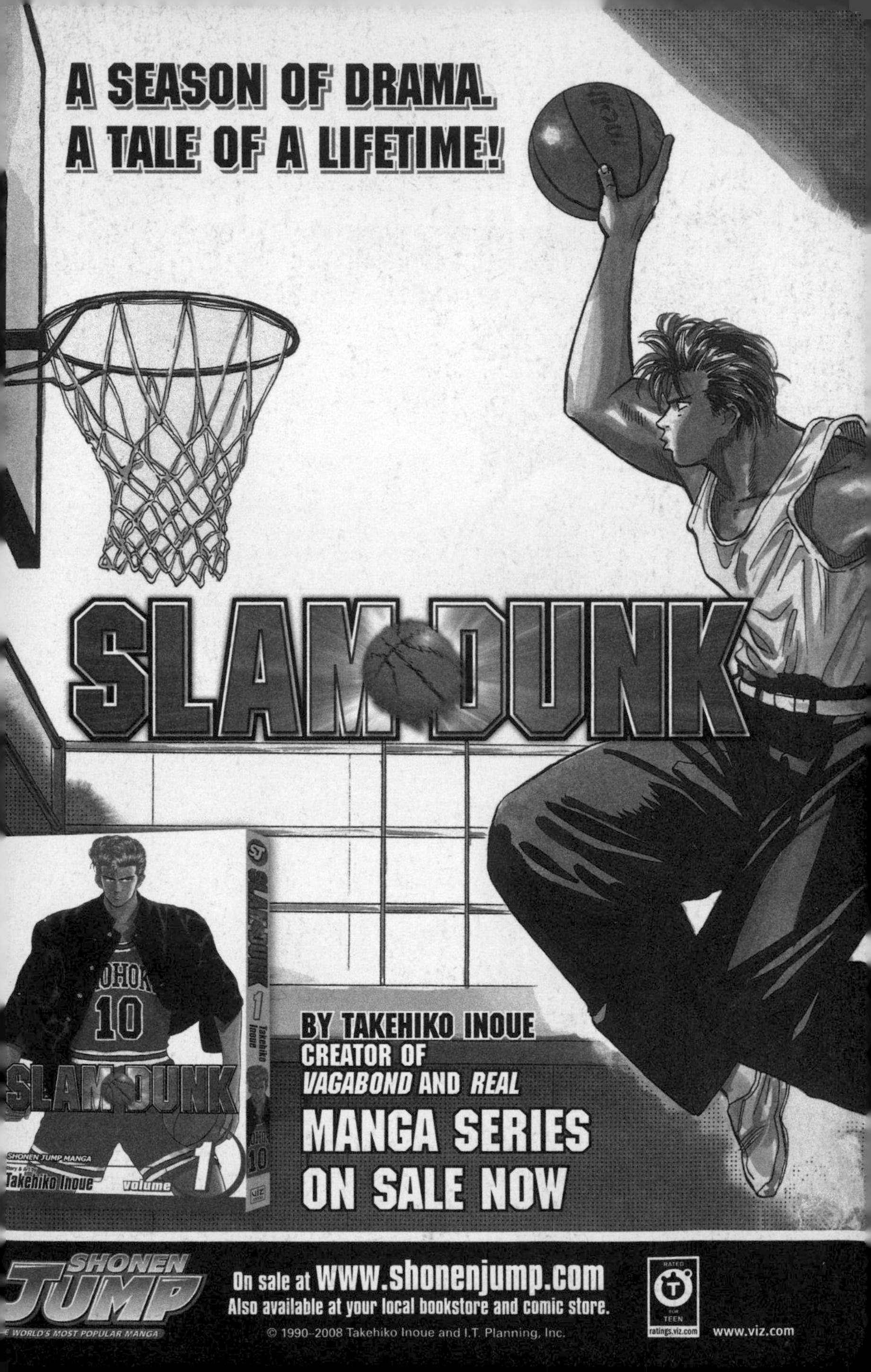
A SEASON OF DRAMA.
A TALE OF A LIFETIME!
SLAM DUNK
SLAM DUNK
SHONEN JUMP MANGA
Takehiko Inoue
volume 1
BY TAKEHIKO INOUE
CREATOR OF
VAGABOND AND REAL
MANGA SERIES
ON SALE NOW
SHONEN JUMP
E WORLD'S MOST POPULAR MANGA
On sale at www.shonenjump.com
Also available at your local bookstore and comic store.
© 1990–2008 Takehiko Inoue and I.T. Planning, Inc.
RATED T FOR TEEN
ratings.viz.com
www.viz.com

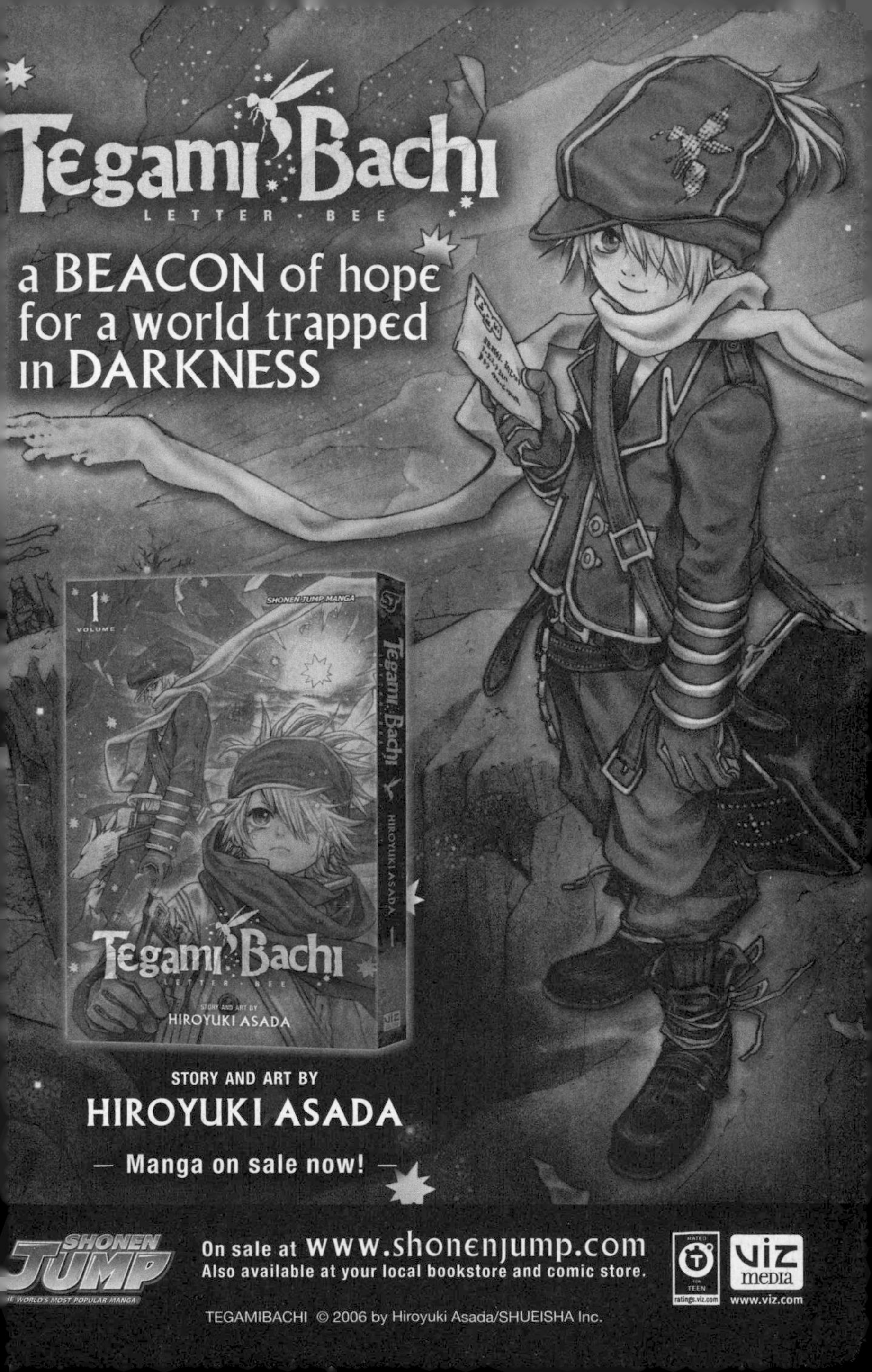
Tegami Bachi
LETTER • BEE
a BEACON of hope for a world trapped in DARKNESS
SHONEN JUMP MANGA
1 VOLUME
Tegami Bachi
LETTER BEE
STORY AND ART BY
HIROYUKI ASADA
STORY AND ART BY
HIROYUKI ASADA
— Manga on sale now! —
SHONEN JUMP
THE WORLD'S MOST POPULAR MANGA
On sale at www.shonenjump.com
Also available at your local bookstore and comic store.
RATED T FOR TEEN
ratings.viz.com
VIZ media
www.viz.com
TEGAMIBACHI © 2006 by Hiroyuki Asada/SHUEISHA Inc.

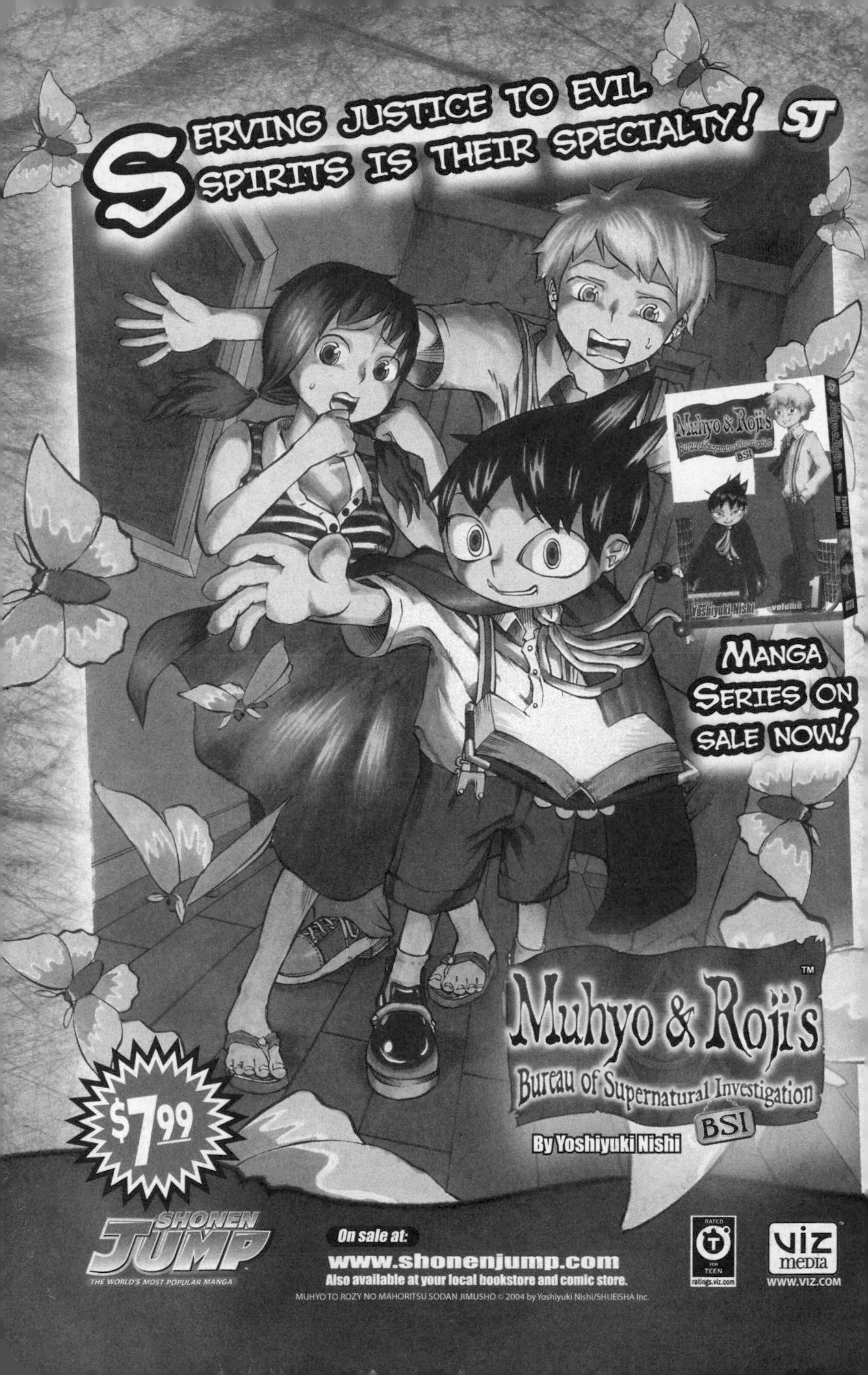
SERVING JUSTICE TO EVIL SPIRITS IS THEIR SPECIALTY!
SJ
MANGA SERIES ON SALE NOW!
Muhyo & Roji's™
Bureau of Supernatural Investigation
BSI
By Yoshiyuki Nishi
$7.99
SHONEN JUMP
THE WORLD'S MOST POPULAR MANGA
On sale at:
www.shonenjump.com
Also available at your local bookstore and comic store.
MUHYO TO ROZY NO MAHORITSU SODAN JIMUSHO © 2004 by Yoshiyuki Nishi/SHUEISHA Inc.
RATED T FOR TEEN
ratings.viz.com
viz media
WWW.VIZ.COM

The World's Greatest Manga
Now available on your iPad

Full of FREE previews and tons of
new manga for you to explore

From legendary manga like *Dragon Ball* to *Bakuman*, the newest series from the creators of *Death Note*, the best manga in the world is now available on the iPad through the official VIZ Manga app.

- **Free App**
- **New content weekly**
- **Free chapter 1 previews**

You're Reading in the Wrong Direction!!

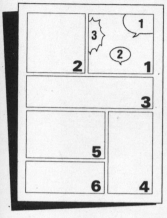

Whoops! Guess what? You're starting at the wrong end of the comic!

...It's true! In keeping with the original Japanese format, **One Piece** is meant to be read from right to left, starting in the upper-right corner.

Unlike English, which is read from left to right, Japanese is read from right to left, meaning that action, sound effects and word-balloon order are completely reversed...something which can make readers unfamiliar with Japanese feel pretty backwards themselves. For this reason, manga or Japanese comics published in the U.S. in English have sometimes been published "flopped"—that is, printed in exact reverse order, as though seen from the other side of a mirror.

By flopping pages, U.S. publishers can avoid confusing readers, but the compromise is not without its downside. For one thing, a character in a flopped manga series who once wore in the original Japanese version a T-shirt emblazoned with "M A Y" (as in "the merry month of") now wears one which reads "Y A M"! Additionally, many manga creators in Japan are themselves unhappy with the process, as some feel the mirror-imaging of their art skews their original intentions.

We are proud to bring you Eiichiro Oda's **One Piece** in the original unflopped format. For now, though, turn to the other side of the book and let the journey begin...!

—Editor